EDUCATING EDUCATORS WITH
SOCIAL MEDIA

CUTTING-EDGE TECHNOLOGIES IN HIGHER EDUCATION

Series Editor: Charles Wankel

Forthcoming Volumes:

CUTTING-EDGE TECHNOLOGIES IN HIGHER EDUCATION
VOLUME 1

EDUCATING EDUCATORS WITH SOCIAL MEDIA

EDITED BY

CHARLES WANKEL

St. John's University, New York, USA

IN COLLABORATION WITH

MATTHEW MAROVICH
KYLE MILLER
JURATE STANAITYTE

United Kingdom – North America – Japan
India – Malaysia – China

Emerald Group Publishing Limited
Howard House, Wagon Lane, Bingley BD16 1WA, UK

First edition 2011

Copyright © 2011 Emerald Group Publishing Limited

Reprints and permission service
Contact: booksandseries@emeraldinsight.com

British Library Cataloguing in Publication Data
A catalogue record for this book is available from the British Library

ISBN: 978-0-85724-649-3
ISSN: 2044-9968 (Series)

CONTENTS

LIST OF CONTRIBUTORS

Malik Aleem Ahmed	Delft University of Technology, Delft, The Netherlands
Mark Bailey	Pacific University, Forest Grove, OR, USA
Lisa Blaschke	University of Maryland, College Park, MD, USA
Lisa Chamberlin	University of Wisconsin-Stout, Menomonie, WI, USA
Joseph Rene Corbeil	University of Texas at Brownsville/Texas Southmost College Brownsville, TX, USA
Maria Elena Corbeil	The University of Texas at Brownsville/ Texas Southmost College Brownsville, TX, USA
Campbell Dalglish	City University of New York, New York City, NY, USA
Martina A. Doolan	University of Hertfordshire, Hatfield, England
Gloria Edwards	Georgian Court University, Lakewood, NJ, USA
Mark A. Gammon	Connect.Us Labs, Boulder, CO, USA
Oliver Grundmann	University of Florida, Gainesville, FL, USA
Hope J. Hartman	City University of New York, New York City, NY, USA
Nina Heinze	Knowledge Media Research Center, Tuebingen, Germany
Gila Kurtz	University of Maryland, University College, Adelphi, MD, USA

ix

David G. Lebow	HyLighter LLC, Tallahassee, FL, USA
Kay Lehmann	University of Wisconsin-Stout, Menomonie, WI, USA
Dale W. Lick	HyLighter LLC and Florida State University, Tallahassee, FL, USA
Beth Martin	North Carolina State University, Raleigh, NC, USA
Gail O. Mellow	LaGuardia Community College, Queens, NY, USA
Lina Morgado	Universidade Aberta, Lisbon, Portugal
Barbra F. Mosley	North Carolina Agricultural and Technical State University, Greensboro, NC, USA
Caroline Lego Muñoz	Fairleigh Dickinson University, Madison, NJ, USA
Larysa Nadolny	West Chester University of Pennsylvania, West Chester, PA, USA
Stella C. S. Porto	University of Maryland, University College, Adelphi, MD, USA
Wolfgang Reinhardt	University of Paderborn, North Rhine-Westphalia, Germany
Kyle F. Reinson	St. John Fisher College, Rochester, NY, USA
Steve Rhine	Willamette University, Salem, OR, USA
Jeremy Sarachan	St. John Fisher College, Rochester, NY, USA
Danielle M. Stern	Christopher Newport University, Newport News, VA, USA
Marlyn Tadros	New England Institute of Art, Brookline, MA, USA
Terri L. Towner	Oakland University, Rochester, MI, USA
Charles Wankel	St. John's University, Queens, NY, USA

Joanne White	University of Colorado, Boulder, CO, USA
Michael D. D. Willits	Hampton Roads Virtual Learning Center at WHRO, Norfolk, VA, USA
Diana D. Woolis	Knowledge in the Public Interests, Founding Partner, NY, USA

PART I
VARIETIES OF SOCIAL MEDIA: PLATFORM, TECHNOLOGY, SPATIAL

NEW DIRECTIONS IN TEACHING TECHNOLOGIES: INTRODUCTION TO EDUCATING EDUCATORS WITH SOCIAL MEDIA

Charles Wankel

This volume is aimed at instructors in schools of education and those who support them. It is meant to be a window by which the decisions, experiences, and evaluations of your colleagues' use of social media in teaching can be examined. Rather than a recipe book with specific steps, it is meant to be a sauna that gets your creative juices flowing. Social media are used by people of all ages in the second decade of the 21st century, so having your learners get involved in using Facebook events for service learning projects in your town can be applicable for when they move onto teaching learners at other levels.

Joseph Rene Corbeil and Maria Elena Corbeil in *The Birth of a Social Networking Phenomenon* start the discussion of how we often make first steps in engaging social media due to pure serendipity. The Corbeils provide an overview of how social networking tools like Twitter have established themselves as powerful communication and collaboration tools in social, political, and educational arenas. Hence, the logical implication for educators is to experiment with social media and to explore its potential for communication and collaboration both in and out of the classroom. The authors analyze the *Social Networking Cooperative Project* case study, which

Educating Educators with Social Media
Cutting-edge Technologies in Higher Education, Volume 1, 3–11
Copyright © 2011 by Emerald Group Publishing Limited
All rights of reproduction in any form reserved
ISSN: 2044-9968/doi:10.1108/S2044-9968(2011)0000001003

was specifically developed to explore the potential use of microblogging in higher education. In the project, graduate students in an online educational telecommunications course were assigned to cooperative groups to conduct research on a social networking tool and analyze its potential for teaching or training applications. The groups were instructed to select one social networking tool or platform, register or become a member, establish a virtual community, and use only that platform to collaborate on the project. The case study demonstrates the potential of microblogging tools for extending social, cognitive, and teacher presence in online and face-to-face courses.

In *Facebook and Education: A Classroom Connection?* Terri L. Towner and Caroline Lego Muñoz discuss Facebook's potential to support teaching and learning. How do college students and instructors use Facebook? How is Facebook being used for specific educational practices and education-related socialization? What can we say about the general attitudes toward Facebook among educators by now? Authors share survey data collected in the spring of 2009 from undergraduate and graduate students and instructors regarding their attitudes toward Facebook. The findings suggest that college students use Facebook primarily for informal learning purposes, such as student-to-student interactions about nonrequired course-related matters. Next, students also use Facebook for formal learning purposes, such as student-to-student interactions about required course components. However, students are less likely to use Facebook for informal teaching purposes, which include instructor–student communication about nonre-quired course-related matters, and formal teaching purposes, which is instructor–student communication about required course matters that may be formally assessed. Therefore, students perceive Facebook as more of an informal or formal learning tool and not as a formal teaching device. The survey also suggests that faculty are reluctant to adopt Facebook for educational practices. And yet those who already use Facebook in education acknowledge its educational merit. Interestingly, instructors feel that Facebook is an educational tool better used by students rather than by teachers. Consistent with students' views, instructors perceive Facebook as a formal learning tool rather than a formal teaching tool.

Drawing on the surveys and experiences using Facebook in multiple classroom settings, Towner and Muñoz pose specific suggestions on how instructors should use Facebook as an educational tool. The general recommendation for instructors is to create a professional Facebook profile that is conscious of privacy, professionalism, and instructor–student boundaries. Facebook course groups can serve to engage students: groups contain course material, such as the syllabus and lecture notes. Instructors are advised to not require course participation on Facebook.

Malik Aleem Ahmed, author of *Social Media for Higher Education in Developing Countries – An Intercultural Perspective*, observes a trajectory in which higher education institutions in developing countries are only slowly starting to tinker about with the use of social media like social networking sites, wikis, and blogs, despite the evidence from developed countries that social media are beneficial in the provision of quality education and production of valuable research. Ahmed proposes a holistic view on what changes we can expect to witness in the future: according to the *Information Technology Alteration – Design and Management Framework*, if intercultural variations of values exist between technology producing countries and technology consuming countries, then social media systems should be customized, redesigned, and altered in cross-cultural implementations. This chapter shows how the process of engaging social media can lead toward resolving quality issues in the higher education sector of developing countries.

A Social Media Approach to Higher Education, by Marlyn Tadros, is rich in examples of using social media in the classroom; it discusses the benefits of using social media for both students and teachers as well as some of the drawbacks and obstacles. Tadros strongly believes that digital natives will transform the landscape of higher education in the future, so long as the educators of today can begin to embrace the proper use of social media in their courses. Tadros concludes that resistance to change is unacceptable, and dogmatically using traditional methods is an unsustainable alternative: the implications of moving towards social media are vast and rewarding in many ways. Educators, therefore, need to seize the opportunity of this milestone and utilize it in the interest of students.

Stella Porto, Gila Kurtz, and Lisa Blaschke in *Creating an Ecosystem for Lifelong Learning through Social Media: A Graduate Experience* approach the topical issue of selecting the right social media tools for use in higher education. This chapter provides examples of how social media tools are being used within the Master of Distance Education and E-learning program at the University of Maryland University College to create and sustain an ecosystem of lifelong learning, student support, reflection, and practical research within the program.

The Networked Class in a Master Program: Personalization and Openness through Social Media, by Lina Morgado, looks at the ways in which social media in an online Master's degree program at Universidade Aberta, Portugal, have been used in an effort to move toward a networked class – a distributed, open and personalized environment that empowers learners on many levels. Tools and services used include Twitter, Facebook, Delicious, Diigo, blogs, wikis and Second Life, among many others that students have been using to perform their tasks and publish their work.

Nina Heinze and Wolfgang Reinhardt, authors of *Future Social Learning Networks at Universities: An Exploratory Seminar Setting* propose a student-centered approach to teaching and learning by integrating social media in real-life settings under a constructivist perspective. The outlined learning design is based on the seven pedagogical goals of constructivist learning environments design. It illustrates how these seven goals were applied to integrate the challenges of real-world environments like distributed teams or interdisciplinary research backgrounds and non-native language require-ments into a controlled university setting to create rich learning experiences and foster key competencies. Much emphasis is placed on the use of social media and its potential for collaboration and communication in geogra-phically distant teams to provide students with experience in the potentials and shortcomings of these tools.

The contribution outlines how the use of social media can be applied to alleviate the shortcomings of head-on education and provide students with the possibilities to actively engage in learning activities. In this seminar setting students from two geographically distant universities from either the computer sciences or educational sciences had to collaborate with each other in small teams using social media to solve scientific problems in the field of Technology Enhanced Learning, create artifacts like architectures, working prototypes and wikis, and organize their learning and scientific working activities. Topics covered included smart devices for learning, the potentials of m- and u-learning, primary and secondary learning experiences, game-based learning, the semantic web, and awareness in collaborative learning settings. The courses were held simultaneously at both universities with the broadcasting of one classroom to the other. Video and audio were shared in real-time, and students held presentations together with students from the other university. They researched and prepared using only social media, without having met in real life.

In addition, this chapter describes several methods that were used to monitor and evaluate the students' engagement and performance as well as the learning arrangement itself. The depicted combination of qualitative and quantitative measures to evaluate the students' dedication and progress as well as the design of the course provides insights that can be applied to constructivist course settings in short- and long-term evaluations to make a thorough investigation of the quality of learning environments that place emphasis on the use and application of social media in formal learning scenarios. This provides a base, which enables an improvement of such settings and can lead to the development of optimized learning scenarios.

In *Connecting Future Teachers with the Teachers of Today*, Larysa Nadolny dissects the aspects of programs aimed to train teachers: many of these programs are not successful in integrating classroom experiences beyond formal teaching requirements. This challenge is reinforced by the fact that teachers are not entering the profession with the skills and experiences necessary to effectively use technology in the classroom. In a case study from The Educational Technology course at West Chester University of Pennsylvania, Nadolny demonstrates how the project culminated not only in connecting teacher candidates with current classroom teachers, but also utilizing new learning technologies (such as wikis, YouTube, iMovie and screencasting) throughout the process. The program received enthusiastic positive feedback from its students.

In *Role of the Tutor in Enabling Student Learning through the Use of a Wiki*, Martina A. Doolan clarifies the role of the tutor in enabling student learning through the use of technologies like Wikis. Doolan has developed the CLAT (Collaborative Learning through Assessment and Technology) pedagogical model, which has been successfully used and evaluated across a number of academic disciplines over the course of five years in higher education. The model emerged as an outcome of studies in higher education focusing on the learner experiences of using social networking technologies such as Wikis. Doolan's analysis leads to a set of guiding principles on how the role of the tutor in establishing a Wiki learning environment can be enacted as this area of practice develops further.

Gloria Edwards and Barbra F. Mosley in *Technology Integration Can Be Delicious: Social Bookmarking as a Technology Integration Tool* present the merits of social bookmarking as a technology integration tool for pre- and in-service teachers. Delicious, a social bookmarking tool, is introduced as a strong Web 2.0 tool that contributes towards meaningful learning in and out of the classroom. The authors piloted Delicious in seven technology courses with specific instructions for collecting quality education websites with great learning potential. A total of 106 pre-service teachers located and standardized meaningful social bookmarks using four of the five formal elements in the Delicious environment. The culminating activity for the participants was the successful completion of an abbreviated lesson plan which detailed their rationale for integrating the technology into a classroom. Over 300 quality, user-friendly, interactive, content-specific, educational websites were located by students who would absolutely consider using them in their classrooms. The students benefited from the merits of collaboration and sharing through social bookmarking with Delicious and simultaneously experienced how ready-access to quality technology tools ultimately contributed toward meaningful learning. Authors observe that what once started as a single idea for facilitating the use of Web 2.0 tools in a technology integration course blossomed into a plethora of ideas for on-going learning experiences that validate the merits of collaboration and sharing through social bookmarking with Delicious.

In *Public Issues, Private Concerns: Social Media and Course Management Systems in Higher Education*, Jeremy Sarachan and Kyle Reinson contemplate what may be an inevitable shift away from closed and impersonal course management systems (CMS) toward more open access and user-friendly social media. Accounting for how digital technologies have changed the form in which content is universally exchanged, they suggest educators revise more traditional CMS systems and re-think methods of disseminating and collecting student assignments. As students collaborate with each other and potentially with contributors from outside a course, digital revisions to text and multimedia creations enhance online student portfolios and help build important skill sets based on collaboration. A course's online presence, therefore, should address an increasingly networked "information society" and afford students more opportunities for access to information while encouraging a more conversational pedagogical mindset. Authors also take the importance of "place" within online educational spaces into consideration, suggesting that the concept of the "Third Place" – a home away from home – is present within social media and may more effectively create a nurturing and supportive educational environment.

Beth Martin in *Web 2.0: Anxiety, Libraries, and Pedagogies* looks at innovative delivery of research methods courses. When developed by faculty members and librarians/instructional technologists, research methods courses can move beyond database navigation and PowerPoint presentations when incorporating social media. This chapter discusses case studies for two undergraduate research method courses, one for a junior seminar in the hard sciences and the second for a class on the history of African American mathematicians. The courses were developed at a private, four-year Historically Black College/University (HBCU) through a faculty/library collaboration. These classes used a variety of social media tools including Google Maps, Flickr, Delicious, Yahoo Pipes, Meebo, YouTube, iTunes U and the Moodle Learning Management System. Each case study defines and describes how each tool was used and the collaboration between faculty and librarians/technologists to implement social media. Martin discusses student and faculty assessment of the program as well as anecdotal evidence for each study, and provides implementation tips. These case studies describe ways to create an interactive, collaborative learning experience for students and faculty while alleviating library anxiety.

David G. Lebow, Dale W. Lick, Hope J. Hartman, Campbell Dalglish, and Oliver Grundmann discuss state-of-the-art tools of social annotation in *Social Annotation to Enhance Learning and Assessment in Higher Education*. Social annotation products make the thinking of learners "transparent" – visible and easily accessible for sharing with others, self-reflection, and feedback. This is accomplished by enabling almost any number of users to have threaded discussions linked to selected sections of a web page. This chapter reports experiences from three instructors who use a social annotation product, HyLighter, to enhance teaching, learning and assessment activities in three different areas of the college curriculum. Dalglish teaches screenplay writing. He describes how he used HyLighter to improve students' writing and critical review skills. Grundmann teaches online graduate-level courses in pharmaceutical and forensic sciences. He describes the application of HyLighter to help students learn about chemical structures and related analytical principles. Hartman is a professor of educational psychology. She discusses her use of HyLighter to implement an alternative multiple-choice assessment approach in educational and developmental psychology courses. The chapter concludes with thoughts on the potential of social annotation technology to shift the focus of learning systems from content to be learned to what is going on inside the minds of learners.

In *Our Head in the Cloud: Transforming Work on College Completion* Diana D. Woolis and Gail O. Mellow provide an in-depth overview and future implications gained from the Global Skills for College Completion (GSCC) project which targets to achieve a significant increase in the historically low pass rates of basic skills (reading, writing and math competencies that are seen as required in order to maintain a "C" or better grade in college level work) students in American community colleges. The initiative is funded by the Bill and Melinda Gates Foundation as part of an ambitious goal to double the number of young adults in the U.S. with a postsecondary credential by 2020. Part of the GSCC initiative is to help faculty to discover and design basic skills pedagogy via the use of a community of innovation – an online set of tools and processes embedded in faculty work. Woolis and Mellow, together with their team, designed what they have termed a managed digital environment, in which the community work is taking place. The authors describe the GSCC project, the managed digital environment, and the research they drew on to build it. Preliminary data and observations are included. The chapter concludes with an invitation to share the view of how social media can fundamentally change the shape of higher education innovation, research, and evaluation based upon emergent trajectories of the GSCC project.

In *Enhancing In-Class Participation in a Web 2.0 World*, Steve Rhine and Mark Bailey draw on existing knowledge that there are significant barriers to fostering student participation in class. These barriers include dynamics related to class size and available time, as well as personal dimensions such as gender, age, and learning preferences. Authors propose that the emergence of new forms of social media can help break down those barriers by enabling the collaborative construction of understanding. Their study raises a number questions: Does concurrent use of a shared learning document during class provide a means of enhancing participation and learning? Assuming the natural tendency of students' attention to wander over time, can providing a parallel learning and sharing space serve to "focus distraction" in productive ways? During graduate and undergraduate courses in two different universities, the authors used a single Google document, open to every class member. Rhine and Bailey analyzed these collaborative documents and their uses are described, along with student reports and videos. Data indicate that this approach indeed created the intended type of participatory space. Its use often broadened the numbers of students involved and increased the quality of spoken and virtual conversations as students negotiated meaning. Where attention began to drift, the shared document created new opportunities for students to stay focused and explore course content through its use as an alternative back-channel. This approach also facilitated self-differentiation, as students determined which mix of available media best met their needs.

Mark Gammon and Joanne White in *(Social) Media Literacy: New Challenges and New Opportunities for Educators* shed light on the paradox that while contemporary students are digital natives who use social media daily, these same young people are still in need of direction and core media literacy skills to be efficient as students. Educators and students need to recognize that both have significant roles to play in developing a rigorous approach to media literacy. In embracing all forms of media as well as roles that extend beyond passive consumption, both educators and students are able to discover newly empowering skills that will provide best-practice opportunities for better civic and educational engagement. This chapter highlights the rapidly expanding roles of social media in higher education and provides educators with information and direction that will help them to better understand how they can engage in this important dialogue not only with students, but also with their colleagues and within their own lives.

Danielle M. Stern and Michael D. D. Willits in *Social Media Killed the LMS: Re-imagining the Traditional Learning Management System in the Age of Blogs and Online Social Networks* theorize how faculty and students actually envision the changing role of learning technologies, particularly the learning management systems (LMS) and social media, in their everyday education. Grounded in critical pedagogy and building from a brief history of the learning management system and new social media learning technologies, the authors examine which features have been most beneficial to the shared learning experience between faculty and students. Stern and Willits create a working model of a re-imagined learning technology platform that integrates the best tools of the LMS with the more collaborative features of social media in common use among today's students and faculty. The authors envision a shift from that of a management system to a dynamic platform built from the ground-up to integrate traditional course technologies such as gradebooks and testing with the open nature of social media. Toward this end, the chapter includes examples of combining Wordpress, Buddypress and Twitter into a trifold approach that reaches beyond the physical classroom walls to build a community of learning where students are the educators via content creation and critical analysis of cultural institutions.

In *Twitter in Higher Education*, Kay Lehmann and Lisa Chamberlin provide insight into how short messages sent via Twitter can be a very powerful tool for teaching and learning. Although Twitter itself is relatively simple, the benefits of using this tool can be immense. Educators and their students can use Twitter to tap into an immediately available global network of experts, educators and fellow students interested in educational topics. Students, faculty, and other university personnel including librarians are using Twitter in a wide variety of ways to communicate both inside the classroom and beyond.

You can understand that this collection is actually presenting you with a community of talented creative adventuresome colleagues in a learning community that we wish you will join. That is, we hope you will connect with, collaborate with, innovate with, and learn with the chapter authors and the wider society of creative instructors. We realize these technologies are moving targets, and that different and better ones will soon appear. However, we hope you will join us in preparing for the future by moving toward it through the use of these social technologies.

THE BIRTH OF A SOCIAL NETWORKING PHENOMENON

Joseph Rene Corbeil and Maria Elena Corbeil

ABSTRACT

Social networking tools, like Twitter, are beginning to demonstrate their potential as powerful communication and collaboration tools in social, political, and educational arenas. As smart phones and mobile computing devices become less expensive and more powerful, they will also become more pervasive. As a matter of economics, institutions will need to adapt to learning experiences that can occur in a wide range of contexts and over multiple channels. Having more technologically adept learners will also compel educators to develop innovative ways to promote students' active learning and equitable participation in class discussions. Given the increased popularity and exponential growth of Twitter, educators have begun to experiment with it to determine its potential for communication and collaboration, both in and out of the classroom. Through a brief description and history of microblogging and the emergence of Twitter, examples of how instructors are integrating microblogs into their courses, and an overview of a social networking cooperative project case study, this chapter tells the story of how the authors' use of microblogs evolved from purely recreational to authentic instructional uses for their online classes.

Educating Educators with Social Media
Cutting-edge Technologies in Higher Education, Volume 1, 13–32
Copyright © 2011 by Emerald Group Publishing Limited
All rights of reproduction in any form reserved
ISSN: 2044-9968/doi:10.1108/S2044-9968(2011)0000001004

INTRODUCTION

Our first exposure to microblogging came on February 15, 2007, when our brother-in-law documented the birth of his son. He invited family and friends from around the country to subscribe to a little-known social networking service called Twitter. In the days leading up to the birth, he posted regular status reports. Moments after the baby was born, congratulations were communicated and pictures were posted online for all to see. This event was the first documented twittered birth.

Since then, we have followed the tweets of family and friends and the occasional celebrity. We never considered Twitter to be a viable tool for education, that is, until Summer 2009, when two events with worldwide implications brought microblogging into the mainstream: the Iranian presidential election and the death of Michael Jackson. In both cases, Twitter played a key role in spreading the news around the world, literally, as it was unfolding. Its impact on facilitating instantaneous communication and its ability to bring people together made us consider that it could serve a similar purpose for our online courses.

To explore the potential use of microblogging in education, a social networking cooperative project was developed. Graduate students in an online educational telecommunications course were assigned to cooperative groups to conduct research on a social networking tool and analyze its potential for teaching and training applications. The groups were instructed to select one social networking tool or platform, register or become a member, establish a virtual community, and use only that platform to collaborate on the project.

Through a brief description and history of microblogging and the emergence of Twitter, examples of how instructors are integrating microblogs into their courses, and an overview of a social networking cooperative project case study, this chapter tells the story of how two instructors' use of microblogs evolved from purely recreational to authentic instructional uses for their online classes.

BLOGS ANNOUNCE THE BIRTH OF MICROBLOGGING

When tracing the history of the seemingly recent explosion of social media (e.g., blogs, Twitter, Facebook, LinkedIn, and YouTube), Barnhardt (2009) recalled that in the early 1990s, forwarding emails "was the first opportunity that people had to engage their social networks" (para. 1), because it allowed them to easily share information. Boyd and Ellison (2007) added that in 1997, SixDegrees.com became the first social network site to combine the features, that up until then, other online services had only offered separately, such as creating profiles, receiving updates from specific groups and sharing and searching friend lists. Barnhardt attributed people's need to be connected to others as the foundation for the modern-day replacement for email forwards – the microblog.

Born from the blog, a microblog maintains many of the blog's features such as providing a forum in which contributors build an online community by regularly sharing information about their daily lives or topics of interest; privacy features for managing membership and participant access; and a variety of methods to post, including "text messaging, instant messaging, E-mail, or digital audio" (Wikipedia, 2010, para. 3). As its name implies, the major difference between a blog and a microblog is that a microblog requires that posts be made with a limited number of text characters as well as smaller audio and video files. In addition, because participation involves short messages that are easy to post through a variety of mobile technologies, microblogs facilitate much more frequent updates than a blog. "Compared to regular blogging, microblogging fulfills a need for an even faster mode of communication. By encouraging shorter posts, it lowers users' requirement of time and thought investment for content generation" (Java, Finin, Song, & Tseng, 2007, para. 2). For example, Java et al. (2007) noted, "on average, a prolific blogger may update her blog once every few days; on the other hand a microblogger may post several updates in a single day" (para. 2). This feature allowed microblogs, such as Twitter, to become the communication tool of choice when significant, worldwide events were unfolding, such as the elections in Iran and Michael Jackson's death in the summer of 2009.

THE EMERGENCE OF TWITTER

Tracing the history of Twitter reveals the impact that microblogging has had on communication worldwide. Founded on March 21, 2006, by Biz Stone, Evan Williams, and Jack Dorsey (Arrington, 2008), Twitter quickly became the "the service most commonly associated with microblogging" (Barnhardt, 2009). It is a free, online social networking and microblogging service that allows individuals to answer the question, "What are you doing?" by posting short messages of 140 characters or less, through the Twitter web site, Short Messaging Service (SMS), or smart phones and mobile devices. Among Twitter's features, registered users can post their own messages (tweets) as well as other user's messages (retweets) that they find interesting and want to share with their friends and followers; read their followers' tweets; post a direct, private message to any one of their followers; and use Twitter or a search engine to find tweets that have been grouped using hashtags (a word or phrase that represents the topic, preceded with a hash symbol [#], e.g., #socialpresence). Through these frequent, brief communications between members, who are categorized as either "friends" or "followers," depending on the level of access they are granted by each user, Twitter has created a worldwide online community, which has exploded in the past year.

Kevin Weil (2010) reported Twitter's exponential growth of tweets per day, from 5,000 in 2007 and 300,000 in 2008 to 35 million at the end of 2009. In February 2010, the number of tweets per day had exploded to 50 million, "an average of 600 tweets per second" (para. 2). According to McGiboney (2009), the use of mobile devices has helped increase Twitter usage, noting "unique visitors to Twitter increased 1,382 percent year-over-year, from 475,000 unique visitors in February 2008 to 7 million in February 2009" (para. 1). Despite the popular belief that primarily adolescents and young adults use social networking and microblogging sites such as Twitter, the average age of users is 31 (Fox, Zickuhr, & Smith, 2009, para. 4). With these statistics, it is likely that a large percentage of adult learners are engaging in microblogging. Costa, Beham, Reinhardt, and Sillaot (2008) observed,

> Although its main purpose apparently aims at answering "what are you doing?", its usage is far from being restricted to what at first may seem a rather trivial way of prompting communication. The number of Twitter users has increased massively in the last months. It has also made its way across different sectors, among which education and research are included. (p. 2)

As Twitter emerged on the scene as the leader in microblogging, its features and the birth of millions of new tweeters have significantly impacted the way people communicate in their personal, professional, and academic lives.

THE FORMATIVE YEARS – TWITTER EXPERIENCES GROWING PAINS

With more than 100 million registered users, and growing by approximately 300,000 new users per day, it is not surprising that after 4 years, Twitter is beginning to experience some growing pains (Vellante, 2010). Among its most pressing challenges is ensuring that its infrastructure is able to meet current and future demands. As Twitter's popularity increases, the more susceptible it becomes to service outages, some reportedly lasting for hours. In addition, the sheer volume of spam (unsolicited messages posted in rapid succession) is a persistent problem exacerbating Twitter's capacity, while flooding people's timelines with worthless or distracting information. Although new antispamming protocols have been implemented and the overall volume of spam is decreasing, it continues to be an ongoing challenge. Ethical issues are also a concern in Twitter. Although the *Terms of Service* has strong language prohibiting unethical or unlawful practices, including invasion of privacy, fraud, identity theft, cyber-bullying, impersonating people or organizations, and copyright infringement, users must be careful about what they post and who they choose to follow. With increased access comes increased risk.

In addition to these challenges, educators who use Twitter in their classes must also address a series of instructional and pedagogical challenges, including how to adapt to communication in 140 character increments, managing a constant stream of comments, most of which are peripheral to the topics being discussed in class, cheating and unethical behavior by students, dangers of outside influences, and the potential for distraction in the face-to-face classrooms. For example, Sugato Chakravarty, a professor of consumer sciences and retailing at Purdue University, who allows students in his lecture classes to post questions through Twitter, warned that the use of Twitter raises issues of classroom management and cheating (Young, 2009c). Chakravarty cautioned, "you are vulnerable" because "students really don't hold back. If you say something wrong or something that they don't agree with, then they'll let you know, and everybody else will see it" (para. 7). He also acknowledged that early in the semester, some students attempted to cheat by asking their classmates for answers to a quiz through Twitter. Yet, according to Chakravarty, the sense of anonymity afforded by Twitter leads to student questions that he has never heard before, justifying its continued use in his classes.

Young also cited examples of how Twitter can waste valuable classroom time and lead to class disruptions. Monica Rankin, a professor of history at the University of Texas at Dallas, who also uses Twitter in her classes, warned that although she has not yet experienced any, "there is certainly the potential for disaster" (Young, 2009c, Potential for Disaster section, para. 2). Her class meets face-to-face on 2 out of 3 days per week. On the 3rd day, her students participate through a back-channel discussion using

Twitter. In one instance, while discussing the issue of abortion, the dialog became so enflamed that she was forced to change the topic. In addition, of the 90 students enrolled in her course, only a handful of students were using or had any experience with Twitter, so at the beginning of the course, a lot of time was lost to assist students in setting up accounts and becoming familiar with the technology. Despite some challenges and setbacks, Ms. Rankin concluded that the experiment went "pretty well," but that the use of Twitter is not appropriate "for every professor, or every course" (Young, 2009c, Potential for Disaster section, para. 7). Despite the growing pains and setbacks experienced by some educators, professors like Chakravarty and Rankin believe that the benefits outweigh the risks.

TWITTER GOES TO COLLEGE

An extensive search for applications of Twitter in higher education revealed that microblogs are primarily used in four ways: (1) during face-to-face classes to encourage students' equitable participation; (2) outside of class to establish authentic communication and collaboration with professional clients and experts in the field; (3) beyond face-to-face and online class time to promote extended interaction with the course content, with other students, and with the instructor; and (4) as a professional resource for educators.

For example, in one application of Twitter in the classroom, Young (2009b) reported how in the spring of 2009, Cole W. Camplese asked his face-to-face graduate students at Pennsylvania State University to bring their laptops to class. Using Twitter, they were encouraged to share notes and questions with each other during the class lectures. The instructor noted that although it took some time for them to understand, it was okay to tweet during class, before long, students, especially the shy ones, were posting questions. When asked about the possibility of class disruptions, Camplese responded, "that his hope is that the second layer of conversation will disrupt the old classroom model and allow new kinds of teaching in which students play a greater role and information is pulled in from outside the classroom walls" (para. 5). Du, Carroll, and Rosson (2010) agreed, noting that microblogging provides opportunities for active learning that are not usually supported in traditional face-to-face and online courses. They described that opportunities for students to engage in active learning, such as questioning, debate, explaining, and discussion, are usually limited in traditional classes due to turn-taking (students need to take turns while talking, so some may not express themselves), time constraints (class time needed to cover content), and the power structure (the instructor is the expert who imparts knowledge). Microblogs, on the contrary, allow for communication to occur parallel to the course enabling students to initiate discussions. Ebner and Schiefner (2008) noted, "according to Dewey (1916), learning is a cognitive and social process that develops through conversation. Communication, therefore, is an essential part through all learning processes and microblogging can extend our possibilities" (p. 159).

To study the impact of social media on course communication and active learning in the classroom, in the spring of 2009, Du et al. (2010) integrated a microblog in an undergraduate engineering course with 45 seniors. With a large screen in the front of the classroom, students were able to view their questions and comments, which they could post anonymously throughout the class lecture. Both the instructor and the students had the option to reply verbally or through the microblog. The authors noted, "though simple in concept, this is a rather bold idea in that any student has the same right as others (including the teacher) to 'say' something" (p. 3). Students used the microblog during class to report problems with technology and clarify deadlines; greet others; network and participate in icebreakers; reflect upon course content; share external resources; raise questions; and poll other students. The authors added that as class sizes increase, the activities that microblogging facilitates can help build a community of learners, alleviating the feeling of isolation students in large classes oftentimes report.

In an example of the use of microblogging outside of the classroom, Michelle Everson (2009), an educational psychology professor, used Twitter to enhance statistical literacy in her graduate statistics courses. During the summer of 2009, she presented an extra credit opportunity to her graduate students, where they could earn one point for each tweet they posted on a statistics-related topic, for up to five extra credit points. The graduate students actively "tweeted about things they were finding in the news and online sources related to statistics (e.g., news reports that included statistical information, uses or misuses of statistics, interesting graphs, cartoons, data sets, websites that taught statistics, survey or poll results, YouTube videos, etc.)" (para. 1). Of the 20 students enrolled in her summer course, 15 signed up for a Twitter account and participated in the experiment. She was so excited at the level of student involvement that she plans to continue using Twitter in future classes.

Students in communication-related fields at Marquette University provide examples of the uses of Twitter to establish authentic communication and collaboration with clients and experts outside of the classroom. Using

Twitter to network with experts in the fields of advertising and public relations, they are learning how to incorporate social media in the marketing strategies that they are developing for actual clients (Perez, 2009). In one project, students included microblogging in a campaign for a nonprofit organization. The instructor reported that after the students created the client's Twitter account, they immediately received inquiries and within weeks had over 260 followers. Perez added, the professors "see it as their responsibility to teach students about Twitter because social media knowledge is becoming essential to their future fields-communications, advertising, public relations and marketing" (para. 16). Because Twitter has become a powerful, viral marketing tool, instructors are incorporating it into their curriculum to ensure that their students are highly prepared for the demands of the job.

Similarly, microblogs are also being used to train professionals in healthcare by helping the students engage with the content and each other outside of the boundaries of class. Betty C. Chung (2009) requires students in one of her online wellness classes to use Twitter to report their findings on research of wellness topics. She noted, "I am hoping that students will learn how to convey credible health information over the Net in a concise format and learn how exciting it is to share what they have learned" (para. 1). These applications of microblogging promote student interaction with the course content over extended periods, beyond the classroom meetings (Ebner & Maurer, 2008).

In addition to creating a community of learners in their courses, on a personal and professional level, educators are exploiting Twitter's features to promote their programs; network with colleagues; and keep up with the latest issues, news, and strategies in their fields. In *10 high fliers on Twitter*, Young (2009a) interviewed Jay Rosen, an associate professor of journalism, who noted the importance of his Twitter friends and followers: "The fact that they're watching the news for me, scouting the Web for me, and editing the Web in real time – that's the value of it" (para. 11). In the same article, Howard Rheingold, a lecturer at the University of California at Berkeley added, "As a relatively new teacher, Twitter is really my main connection to other educators who are using Web technologies in their teaching ... I use it to find suggestions of things to do, and to bounce things off people" (para. 13). Similarly, researchers at Graz University of Technology (Ebner, 2009; Ebner & Maurer, 2008) have been conducting research on the use of Twitter to enhance learner critical reflection and engagement in face-to-face lectures and conference presentations in higher education. In one study, Ebner (2009) described how during the keynote address at an international e-learn conference in Italy, participants posted questions, comments, and links to external resources through Twitter, which was being projected in the main conference room. The use of microblogging allowed conference participants as well as those who could not attend access to the discussion during the keynote address.

As educators find innovative and productive ways to integrate Twitter into their teaching and professional activities, it is not surprising that according to a Faculty Focus (2009) report, "higher education professionals are adopting Twitter at a faster rate than the average Internet user" (p. 9). The report added,

> In higher education, many of the first adopters were professionals involved in marketing, admissions and alumni relations. Today a growing number of professors use Twitter to connect with like-minded colleagues around the country (or world) as well as in the classroom to keep students engaged, communicate important deadlines, and encourage succinct dialogue. (p. 4)

It is no surprise then, that in recent years, increased attention in the research (Anderson, Rourke, Garrison, & Archer, 2001; Dunlap & Lowenthal, 2009; Garrison, Anderson, & Archer, 2000; Goldman, Cohen, & Sheahan, 2008; Kok, 2008; Lowenthal & Dunlap, 2010; Stodel, Thompson, & MacDonald, 2006; Whipp & Lorentz, 2009) has focused on the impact of social media on cognitive, social, and teacher presence on learning in higher education, and especially, in online environments.

In 2000, Garrison, Anderson, and Archer observed that in a learning environment, teachers and students are participants in a community of inquiry. The *Community of Inquiry* framework they developed included three components:

- *Cognitive presence*: "the extent to which the participants in any particular configuration of a community of inquiry are able to construct meaning through sustained communication" (Garrison et al., 2000, p. 89).
- *Social presence*: "the ability of participants in the Community of Inquiry to project their personal characteristics into the community, thereby presenting themselves to the other participants as 'real people' " (Garrison et al., 2000, p. 89).
- *Teacher presence*: provides the tools by which social and cognitive presence are established in a learning environment to promote educational outcome attainment (Garrison et al., 2000).

Effectively establishing a learning environment that is conducive to learning "necessitates sustained and authentic communication between and among teachers and students" (Anderson et al., 2001, p. 3). Teacher presence is therefore established through teaching; the design and administration of the learning environment, content, activities, and evaluation; and promoting communication (Anderson et al., 2001). In these aspects, Twitter and other social media platforms are ideal for facilitating and enhancing presence in face-to-face and online learning environments. To study the effect of microblogging on students' perceptions of "presence" in an online graduate program, the authors developed a social networking project for one of their online courses.

THE SOCIAL NETWORKING PROJECT CASE STUDY

Thirty-two students enrolled in two sections of a graduate-level educational telecommunications course were assigned to cooperative groups and instructed to conduct research on a social networking tool to analyze its potential for teaching and training applications. The majority of students enrolled in this course were educators, including K-12 teachers, college professors, tutors, and corporate trainers.

Working in groups of four or five, students were instructed to select one social networking tool or platform; create an account; establish a virtual community; and use only that platform to discuss, plan, and collaborate on the project. Both class sections chose Twitter as their social networking tool of choice. For 12 weeks, the teams explored, experienced and documented Twitter's capabilities and limitations. The project culminated with an online, synchronous class session, during which the teams reported their findings. Students' perceptions of microblogging through Twitter as an educational communication and collaboration platform were solicited through a survey in which the following question was asked: How does microblogging impact *cognitive presence* (the process of constructing meaning through collaboration), *social presence* (the feeling of being there), and *teacher presence* (the level of access to your instructor)?

Regarding cognitive presence, students noted,

> Cognitive presence in this course was certainly intact. This experience has taught me that things can get done even when all the members of a team are in remote locations.

> Microblogs make working on collaborative projects much easier and offer real time data and communication. They also provide effortless and almost instantaneous access to instructors and other learners.

Through the class discussions, I feel like there is a collaboration of ideas and opinions. Reading other students' comments makes me think about my own opinions.

I assigned a collaborative project for students in one of my own classes. I found the students feel completely comfortable with logging in their daily progress to inform their peers of what they have completed and what their friends should do to help. I feel we can all get things done with these networking tools.

Regarding social presence, students commented,

Microblogs impacts social presence by allowing discussions to occur organically, with responses, as would happen in a F2F conversation or discussion.

Microblogs are good tools to use when you need an immediate presence because you can get word out to so many so quickly.

While we don't see each other face to face, I feel like I am getting to know my classmates as the course progresses and we utilize these social networking tools.

Regarding teacher presence, students noted,

In a face-to-face course students tend to hold on to their questions until the class meets again. Through microblogging, my experience has been that the professor usually answers rather quickly to any such inquiries.

While I believe that teacher presence is less than in a traditional classroom, I feel it is still there. I can expect to receive a response to a question directed towards my instructors or classmates within a day, even with the 3-hour time difference.

Teacher presence through all the tools in our classes seems to be better than in a face-to-face class. My professors have been more available using our tools than a professor with limited office hours on a campus.

Overall, students overwhelmingly reported that microblogs were an effective communication tool for use in and out of the classroom, especially in higher education e-learning settings. Therefore, the preliminary results of the Social Networking Project Case Study support the findings in the literature regarding presence. Dunlap and Lowenthal (2009) noted, "because of Twitter's ability to enable persistent presence (Siemens, 2007), our social interactions occurred more naturally and immediately" (p. 4). Based on students' perceptions of the use of microblogs through the social networking project, the authors of this chapter believe that it has demonstrated potential for extending social, cognitive, and teacher presence in online and face-to-face courses.

A TWITTER COMPROMISE – THE EDMODO
EXPERIMENT

During the social networking project, several students expressed concerns and reservations about using microblogs, especially Twitter, in educational environments. Generally, students believed that Twitter worked well for personal communications. However, when used in educational contexts, some students were concerned of the possibility of mixing personal, trivial, or potentially inappropriate messages with class-related messages. As one student noted, "when you follow someone or someone follows you, everyone sees each other's tweets." This real and valid concern led the instructor to consider other microblogging alternatives.

After researching a variety of platforms (e.g., identi.ca, StatusNet, Jaiku, Posteros, and Tumblr), Edmodo, a free social networking and microblogging service designed specifically for education, was selected as a viable substitute to Twitter. By limiting access to educational endeavors, teachers and students can send notes, links, files, alerts, assignments, and events to each other in a secure environment, enabling its members to enjoy all the benefits of microblogging, without some of the more serious drawbacks. For example, to facilitate multiple, simultaneous discussions, teachers can create "groups" for each of their classes. Each group is assigned its own unique code, which is distributed by teachers to all the class members. The groups are self-contained, so no one without access may view the discussions, unless the instructor designates them as public. An added feature of Edmodo is that students can also create their own groups. Participants can opt to receive posts through their cell phones, email, Twitter, or through an RSS feed posted on the course home page (Fig. 1).

Over the past year, Edmodo was used in two, online graduate-level educational technology courses. In addition to setting up a discussion group for the class, each cooperative team also created its own group. The instructor posted course-related news, announcements, and discussions to the main group, whereas students used their cooperative groups for project-related planning and discussions. After nearly a year of use, students' perceptions toward Edmodo were generally positive. Table 1 represents a compilation of the key features, advantages, and disadvantages of the two microblogging platforms (Twitter and Edmodo) based on student observations.

After experimenting with Twitter and Edmodo, students and faculty who participated in the social networking project recognized that they both possess instructional and educational value. However, these tools do not

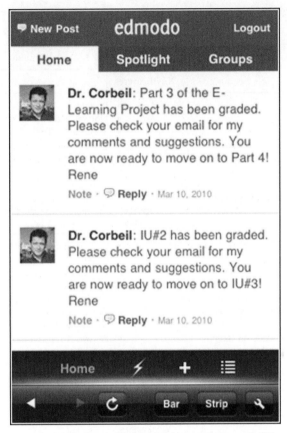

Fig. 1. A Screenshot of Edmodo Accessed through iPhone.

come without limitations. For example, although Twitter is easy to set up and use and has millions of users, it is a favorite tool for spammers and is subject to frequent outages. Furthermore, the potential for private and inappropriate messages being accidentally posted to academic discussions can create distractions and potentially embarrassing situations for instructors and students. The 140-character limit on messages also places limitations on how much information can be conveyed. Although Twitter may be appropriate for use by adult learners, it would not be a safe environment for younger learners and could create legal problems for teachers and school districts.

Table 1.   A Comparison of Twitter's and Edmodo's Key Features, Strengths, and Weaknesses.

Twitter	Edmodo
Key Features	
• Public	• Private
• Ubiquitous	• Not yet widely used/recognized
• Millions of users	• Thousands of users
• Requires an email account	• Does not require an email account
• 140-character limit on text messages	• No limit to message length
• Posts only text messages	• Upload and share files
• Enables searching messages by topic	• Conduct polls
• Enables grouping messages by topic	• Share calendar, etc.
Strengths	
• Easy to share files, pictures, videos, and links	• Easy to share files, pictures, videos, and links
• Follow breaking world news as it happens	• Upload documents to shared workspaces
• Share and receive timely information	• Send individual or group messages
• Network efficiently with large groups of people	• Create groups to separate discussions by class or topic
• Communicate while on the go	• Password protection keeps spammers and others out
• Participate in real world events and discussions	• Messages not limited to 140 characters
• Promote programs easily and inexpensively, reaching large audiences	• Safe environment for younger students
	• Messages are threaded for easier reading
Weaknesses	
• Concerns over student privacy	• Network connectivity problems can cause site to run slowly
• Network connectivity issues during high traffic	• Students have limited access to the outside world
• Access blocked through firewalls in some work and educational settings	• Sometimes posts may take several minutes to appear
• Sometimes difficult to filter out spammers	• Still in beta stage – still has bugs
• Weak search engine for finding people	
• May not be appropriate for younger students	

In contrast, Edmodo, which was specifically designed for education, provides a more controlled environment. Class members can easily share files, pictures, videos, and links in a closed environment that is free from spammers and Internet predators. Yet, because Edmodo is new and still under development, it is subject to frequent outages and crashes. However, the service continues to improve with each major software update. In addition, the greatest benefit of Edmodo is also its biggest limitation. Although the closed system keeps undesirables out, it also segregates its users from the worldwide microblogging community.

As educators weigh the advantages and disadvantages of Twitter versus Edmodo, the decision regarding which platform to adopt will center around two main considerations: (1) who are your learners? and (2) what do you want them to do? If your learners are adults and you want them to network with and gather information from a worldwide audience, then Twitter is the most effective tool. On the contrary, if your learners are young or you want to exclude outsiders and minimize nonacademic conversations, then Edmodo is the more appropriate choice (Fig. 2).

Because the social networking project was conducted in a graduate-level educational telecommunications course, a combination of the two platforms was used. Edmodo was incorporated seamlessly into the courseware management system's announcement page to facilitate communication with class members, work on cooperative projects, and disseminate class-specific news and announcements. An added benefit was that students could select to have the Edmodo messages forwarded to their Twitter accounts, thereby giving them access to the course communications from their mobile devices and smart phones. Twitter was also integrated into the course to encourage students to network with the larger educational technology community and follow news and research trends from around the world. Given the success of the project, future research will be conducted to determine how these communication tools impact teaching and learning as well as students' perceptions of cognitive presence, social presence, and teacher presence.

SUMMARY

As Twitter celebrates its 4th birthday, it is quickly gaining momentum as one of the technological innovations that will revolutionize communication and collaboration in education. A Google Scholar search for "Twitter in education," resulted in approximately 75,500 articles dedicated to the topic. An additional 36,000 articles also addressed "social networking in

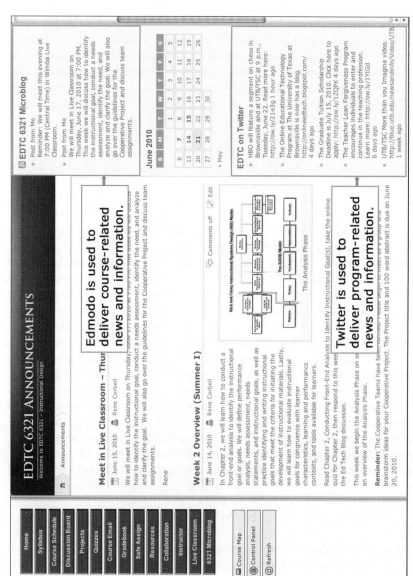

Fig. 2.   A Screenshot of the Course Home Page with Embedded Edmodo and Twitter Feeds.

education," with a significant number of recent studies focusing on educational applications of microblogging in higher education. It is clear that social networking and microblogging are hot topics currently being addressed in the educational research literature.

Although predicting the future is not easy, as early as 2008, in a report titled, *The future of higher education: How technology will shape learning*, Glenn predicted that "technological innovation may now be changing the very way that universities teach and students learn" (p. 4). According the report,

> No generation is more at ease with online, collaborative technologies than today's young people – "digital natives", who have grown up in an immersive computing environment. Where a notebook and pen may have formed the tool kit of prior generations, today's students come to class armed with smart phones, laptops and iPods. (p. 5)

According to Ebner (2009), "a driving force in digital learning will be mobility" (p. 92), and mobile computing devices, which are commonplace on today's college campuses, are already influencing the daily behavior of learners and instructors (Motiwalla, 2007). With the number of mobile technologies with Internet access predicted to reach 1 billion worldwide by 2013 (Gonsalves, 2009), distance and mobile learning are quickly making the transition from alternative to mainstream methods of instructional delivery.

Whereas experts are not predicting that the traditional university will become obsolete any time soon, educators are exploring the potential of these technologies. As a matter of economics, institutions will need to adapt to learning experiences that can occur in a range of contexts and over multiple channels, both in and out of the classroom. As an agent of change, social media tools, such as microblogs, can also help mitigate some of the infrastructure costs educational institutions must incur while providing simple, yet effective tools for communication, collaboration, and research in traditional and nontraditional learning environments. Likewise, the traditional classroom model of the instructor transferring information to the learner will need to give way to a more collegial approach that emphasizes an exchange of information between and among peers.

In an article titled, *Collaborate or die: The future of education*, Chris Yeh (2008), Vice President of enterprise marketing for PBworks, an open-source online collaboration tool, suggested that we are entering the "age of collaboration" (para. 1). With an entire generation of students for whom social networks are an important source of information and communication, Yeh believes that the greatest challenge facing today's educators is adapting an educational system "whose foundations were laid out in the 19th century to serve a 21st century world" (para. 3). In addition, although educators have a generally positive view of the changes that technology has ushered in higher education, Glenn (2008) observed, "many institutions struggle with the twin challenges of rising information technology (IT) costs and the need to avoid technological obsolescence" (p. 5). Yeh added, currently microblogs are used primarily for personal, rather than academic purposes. However, because of the ability of social media to increase productivity, as well as the "number of pioneers who are helping usher in the new age of collaboration" (para. 12), Yeh is optimistic about its future in education.

The first twittered baby is now 3 years old. As he grows, the applications of social media in education will also continue to grow and improve. One sign that Twitter is beginning to mature was revealed with the Library of Congress's announcement on April 14, 2010, that it would begin to maintain a digital archive of every tweet that was ever broadcast on Twitter since its inception (Raymond, 2010). Although the vast majority of tweets will range from the superficial and mundane, a significant number of tweets, like President-elect Barack Obama's announcement of his win of the 2008 presidential election, will have vast cultural and historical significance for future generations of readers and researchers.

Social networking tools, like Twitter and its younger sibling, Edmodo, have demonstrated their potential as powerful communication and collaboration tools in social, political, and educational arenas. As mobile communication and computing technologies become less expensive and more powerful, they will also become more pervasive. Having more techno-logically adept learners will compel institutions to offer more educational experiences through mobile learning, enabling students and instructors to remain in continuous communication, both in and out of the classroom.

REFERENCES

Anderson, T., Rourke, L., Garrison, D. R., & Archer, W. (2001). Assessing teaching presence in a computer conferencing context. *Journal of Asynchronous Learning Networks*, 5(2), 1–17.
Arrington, M. (2008). Scoble interviews Twitter founders Evan Williams and Biz Stone, May 30. *TechCrunch*. Available at http://techcrunch.com/2008/05/30/scoble-interviews-twitter-founders-evan-willams-and-biz-stone/
Barnhardt, D. (2009). The evolution of social media: From email forwards to microblogging. *The Practitioner*, Available at http://wunderkindpr.com/blog/?p=106

Boyd, D. M., & Ellison, N. B. (2007). Social network sites: Definition, history, and scholarship. *Journal of Computer-Mediated Communication, 13*(1), 210–230. Available at http://jcmc.indiana.edu/vol13/issue1/boyd.ellison.html

Chung, B. C. (2009). Professors are not sold on Twitter's usefulness, August 26. [Web log comment], *The Chronicle of Higher Education.* Available at http://chronicle.com/blogPost/Professors-Are-Not-Sold-on/7821/

Costa, C., Beham, G., Reinhardt, R., & Sillaot, M. (2008). Microblogging in technology enhanced learning: A use-case inspection of PPE Summer School 2008, September. Workshop at the European Conference on Technology Enhanced Learning (ECTEL), Maastricht, Netherlands, pp. 1–9. Available at https://togather.eu/bitstream/123456789/365/4/ectel_2008_sirtel_twitter_final.pdf

Du, H., Carroll, J., & Rosson, M. B. (2010). Public micro-blogging in classrooms: Towards an active learning environment, April. Paper presented at the CHI 2010 Conference, Atlanta, GA. Available at http://cs.unc.edu/~julia/accepted-papers/Public-Micro-blogging.pdf

Dunlap, J. C., & Lowenthal, P. R. (2009). Tweeting the night away: Using Twitter to enhance social presence. *Journal of Information Systems Education, 20*(2), 129–136.

Ebner, M. (2009). Introducing live microblogging: How single presentations can be enhanced by the mass. *Journal of Research in Innovative Teaching, 2*(1), 91–100. Available at http://www.nu.edu/assets/resources/pageResources/7638_JournalofResearch09.pdf#page=96

Ebner, M., & Maurer, H. (2008). Can microblogs and weblogs change traditional scientific writing? *Annual Proceedings of the 2008 E-Learn Conference,* Las Vegas, NV (pp. 768–776). Available at http://lamp.tu-graz.ac.at/~i203/ebner/publication/08_elearn01.pdf

Ebner, M., & Schiefner, M. (2008). Microblogging: More than fun? In: I. A. Sanchez & P. Isais (Eds), *Annual Proceedings of the IADIS Mobile Learning Conference,* Algarve, Portugal (pp. 155–159). Available at http://lamp.tu-graz.ac.at/~i203/ebner/publication/08_mobillearn.pdf

Everson, M. (2009). [Listserv] Re: [DEOS-L] Twitter in education: Any advice? The Distance Education Online Symposium Listserv [DEOS-L], August 18. Available at DEOS-L@lists.psu.edu. Retrieved on August 18, 2009.

Faculty Focus.com (2009). Twitter in higher education: Usage habits and trends of today's college faculty, 1–19. Available at http://www.facultyfocus.com/free-report/twitter-in-higher-education-usage-habits-and-trends-of-todays-college-faculty/

Fox, S., Zickuhr, K., & Smith, A. (2009). Twitter and status updating. *Pew Research Center.* Available at http://www.pewinternet.org/Experts/~/link.aspx?_id=6C747837133C4A-54A4D0351E2683478B&_z=z

Garrison, D. R., Anderson, T., & Archer, W. (2000). Critical inquiry in a text-based environment: Computer conferencing in higher education. *The Internet and Higher Education, 2*(2–3), 87–105.

Glenn, M. (2008). The future of higher education: How technology will shape learning. *Economist Intelligence Unit, New Media Consortium.* Available at http://www.nmc.org/pdf/Future-of-Higher-Ed-(NMC).pdf

Goldman, R. H., Cohen, A. P., & Sheahan, F. (2008). Using seminar blogs to enhance student participation and learning in public health school classes. *American Journal of Public Health, 98*(9), 1658–1663. Available at http://www.web20erc.eu/node/55

Gonsalves, A. (2009). One billion mobile Internet devices seen by 2013. *Information Week*, December 9. Available at http://www.informationweek.com/news/internet/webdev/show Article.jhtml?articleID = 222001329

Java, A., Finin, T., Song, X., & Tseng, B. (2007). Why we Twitter: Understanding microblogging usage and communities. *Annual proceedings of the 9th WebKDD and 1st SNA-KDD 2007 workshop on web mining and social network analysis*, San Jose, CA (pp. 56–65). Available at http://ebiquity.umbc.edu/_file_directory_/papers/369.pdf

Kok, A. (2008). Metamorphosis of the mind of online communities via e-learning. *International Journal of Instructional Technology and Distance Learning*, 5(10), 25–32. Available at http://itdl.org/Journal/Oct_08/Oct_08.pdf#page = 29

Lowenthal, P. R., & Dunlap, J. C. (2010). Investigating Twitter's ability to enhance social presence, April. Paper presented at the annual meeting of the American Education Research Association, Denver, CO. Available at http://www.slideshare.net/plowenthal/aera2010-investigating-social-presence-and-twitter

McGiboney, M. (2009). Twitter's sweet smell of success. *Nielsen Wire*, March 18. Available at http://blog.nielsen.com/nielsenwire/online_mobile/twitters-tweet-smell-of-success/

Motiwalla, L. F. (2007). Mobile learning: A framework and evaluation. *Computers & Education*, 49, 581–596. Available at http://www.qou.edu/english/scientificResearch/distanceLearning/mobileLearning.pdf

Perez, E. (2009). Professors experiment with twitter as teaching tool. *Journal Sentinel Online*, April 26. Available at http://www.jsonline.com/news/education/43747152.html

Raymond, M. (2010). How tweet it is! Library acquires entire Twitter archive, April 14. Available at http://blogs.loc.gov/loc/2010/04/how-tweet-it-is-library-acquires-entire-twitter-archive/

Stodel, E. J., Thompson, T. L., & MacDonald, C. (2006). Learners' perspectives on what is missing from online learning: Interpretations through the Community of Inquiry framework. *The International Review of Research in Open and Distance Learning*, 7(3). Available at http://www.irrodl.org/index.php/irrodl/article/view/325/743

Vellante, D. (2010). Twitter: Growing pains, promises, potential pitfalls, April 19. Available at http://www.internetevolution.com/author.asp?section_id = 654&doc_id = 190618

Weil, K. (2010). Measuring Tweets. *Twitter Blog*. Available at http://blog.twitter.com/2010/02/measuring-tweets.html

Whipp, J. L., & Lorentz, R. A. (2009). Cognitive and social help giving in online teaching: An exploratory study. *Education Technology Research Development*, 57, 169–192.

Wikipedia. (2010). Microblogging. Available at http://en.wikipedia.org/wiki/Microblogging

Yeh, C. (2008). Collaborate or die: The future of education. *University Business*, November. Available at http://www.universitybusiness.com/viewarticle.aspx?articleid = 1168

Young, J. (2009a). 10 high fliers on Twitter. *The Chronicle of Higher Education*, Available at http://chronicle.com/article/10-High-Fliers-on-Twitter/16488

Young, J. (2009b). Professor encourages students to pass notes during class via Twitter. *The Chronicle of Higher Education*. Available at http://chronicle.com/blogPost/Professor-Encourages-Students/4619/

Young, J. (2009c). Teaching with Twitter: Not for the faint of heart. *The Chronicle of Higher Education*. Available at http://chronicle.com/article/Teaching-With-Twitter-Not-for/49230/

FACEBOOK AND EDUCATION: A CLASSROOM CONNECTION?

Terri L. Towner and Caroline Lego Muñoz

ABSTRACT

Facebook has become an essential part of student life for most college students; it serves not only as a primary tool of communication but also electronic socialization (Golder, Wilkinson, & Huberman, 2007). Indeed, the vast majority of college students have a Facebook account and are spending a considerable amount of time logged in (Salaway, Caruso, & Nelson, 2008). Yet, can this predominately social space also become a place for learning? To date, the reactions of using social network sites for educational purposes are mixed and empirical research is limited. Issues relating to privacy and safety and an erosion of professional boundaries are the primary reasons cited to not employ social network sites in a classroom. However, other researchers have supported the notion of using social network sites in education (Greenhow & Robelia, 2009a, 2009b; Tynes, B. M. (2007). Internet safety gone wild?: Sacrificing the Educational and Psychosocial benefits of online social environments. Journal of Adolescent Research, 22(6), 575–584. *Available at http:// jar.sagepub.com/cgi/content/abstract/22/6/575. Retrieved on March 25, 2010; Muñoz, C. L., & Towner, T. (2010). Social networks: Facebook's role in the advertising classroom.* Journal of Advertising Education, 14(1), 20–27. *This chapter serves to further this discussion by sharing the findings from surveys of instructors and students regarding their*

Educating Educators with Social Media
Cutting-edge Technologies in Higher Education, Volume 1, 33–57
Copyright © 2011 by Emerald Group Publishing Limited
All rights of reproduction in any form reserved
ISSN: 2044-9968/doi:10.1108/S2044-9968(2011)0000001005

attitudes toward Facebook. Specifically, we report how each use Facebook both socially and professionally. Most important, we discuss instructors and students' perceptions of Facebook as an informal and formal teaching tool, particularly its effectiveness as an instructional or course tool, communication device, and in assisting students in their education and learning. Drawing on the survey and experiences using Facebook in multiple classroom settings, we pose specific suggestions on how instructors should use Facebook. In conclusion, the chapter supports the thesis that Facebook and education can indeed be connected.

INTRODUCTION

Social network sites have revolutionized the way individuals connect, interact, and share information. Yet, can social network sites also transform educational practices? At present, there is little empirical research that has explored the role of social network sites (SNS) in education. SNS and education research have concentrated on student attitudes toward instructor profiles (Mazer, Murphy, & Simonds, 2007, 2009), issues related to privacy (Acquisti & Gross, 2006; Dwyer, Hiltz, & Passerini, 2007; Ellison, Steinfield, & Lampe, 2007; Gross & Acquisti, 2005; Lampe, Ellison, & Steinfield, 2006; Stutzman, 2009; Stutzman & Kramer-Duffield, 2008; Thelwall, 2008; Tufekci, 2008), and SNS usage patterns that relate to education (Chu & Meulemans, 2008; Li & Pitts, 2009; Madge, Meek, Wellens, & Hooley, 2009; Mendez et al., 2009; Roblyer, McDaniel, Web, Herman, & Witty, 2010). Digital literacy and learning through SNS has only started to be addressed in the literature (Greenhow & Robelia, 2009a, 2009b). Whereas some researchers have explored student acceptance of faculty on Facebook (Hewitt & Forte, 2006; Ophus & Abbitt, 2009; Roblyer et al., 2010), very few have delved into the methodology of how Facebook should be employed in education (for notable exception, see Ophus & Abbitt, 2009). Instructors' attitudes and usage of social networks in education have received even less attention (for notable exception, see Roblyer et al., 2010). This chapter's purpose is to explore how college students and instructors use Facebook, understand how Facebook is being used for specific educational practices and education-related socialization, and general attitudes toward Facebook in education. This research is an initial step in educating faculty on whether and how the specific social network sites, Facebook, should be used in higher education. Ultimately, it should help further our understanding of the role that social network technology plays in education.

FACEBOOK OVERVIEW

Since its inception in 2004, Facebook has become immensely popular. To date (October 2010), Facebook reports over 500 million active users. Beyond posting status updates, users are sharing a tremendous amount of information – "more than 5 billion pieces of content (web links, news stories, blog posts, notes, photo albums, etc.) [are] shared each week." According to Facebook, the average user has 130 friends, is on Facebook more than 55 minutes per day, and is a member of 13 groups (Facebook Press Room: Statistics, 2010). As Facebook was initially developed for Harvard University students, 30% of Facebook users are college students (Facebook Press Room: Statistics, 2009) and their adoption rates are reported to be between 85 and 96% (Lampe et al., 2006; Salaway, Caruso, & Nelson, 2008; Stutzman, 2009; Tufekci, 2008). Usage rates are also quite high among undergraduate college students: 66.2% access it daily (Smith, Salaway, Caruso, & Katz, 2009) for approximately 51 minutes a day (Stutzman, 2009).

Although students are drawn to Facebook's downloadable gaming applications (e.g., Farmville and Marfia Wars), the primary reason why they use Facebook is to connect with friends (Joinson, 2008; Lampe et al., 2006; Luckin et al., 2009; Raacke & Bonds-Raacke, 2008; Salaway et al., 2008). Students are largely using Facebook to maintain their offline relationships rather than to make new friends (boyd & Ellison, 2008; Ellison et al., 2007; Lampe et al., 2006; Selwyn, 2007) and socialize into a new academic environment (Madge et al., 2009). Part of this Facebook socialization is actively occurring with their classmates. Eighty-five percent of students surveyed acknowledged using Facebook to communicate with students in their courses (Ophus & Abbitt, 2009). Students' level of personal involvement and time spent within Facebook coupled with Facebook's ability to foster community development are some of the reasons that educators have begun to integrate Facebook in their academic lives. Yet, can and should this predominately social space also become a place for learning?

FACEBOOK AND HIGHER EDUCATION

This chapter poses the question whether and how SNS and education should be connected. Yet, empirical evidence suggests that educational practices are already intersecting within these virtual spaces (e.g., Chu & Meulemans, 2008; Jones, Millermaier, Goya-Martinez, & Schuler, 2008b; Madge et al.,

2009; Mendez, et al., 2009; Ophus & Abbitt, 2009; Salaway et al., 2008). Currently, much of this research focuses on how students use SNS. To illustrate, Salaway et al. (2008) find that almost 49.7% of students report using SNS to discuss education, whereas Chu and Meulemans' (2008) study notes that educational topics are discussed by 67% of students surveyed. More recently, Madge et al.'s (2009) study of first-year undergraduate students shows that 46% of students use Facebook to discuss education. Communication with professors happens much less frequently. For instance, the 2008 Educause survey notes that only 5.5% of students communicated with their professors using SNS (Salaway et al., 2008).

As Facebook has increased in popularity, it is common to find students *and* faculty in the same social space. Thus, it is important to examine the implications for the educational process, as SNS can facilitate the frequency of more personalized faculty-to-student and student-to-student interactions. Mendez et al. (2009) find that 30% of undergraduate and graduate students surveyed had "friended" a faculty member. Sturgeon and Walker (2009) report that over 40% of faculty have students as friends and over 60% of students have faculty as friends. As students and faculty connect, what are the educational potentials? Mazer et al. (2007, 2009) find that teacher Facebook profiles rich in self-disclosure increases anticipated student motivation, affective learning, and teacher credibility. Students are more willing to communicate with their instructors if they already knew them on Facebook, as the SNS gives students another opportunity to connect with faculty (Sturgeon & Walker, 2009). In particular, students like having another means by which to interact with faculty and appreciate the chance to get to know them better (Hewitt & Forte, 2006). In addition, students who are offered virtual office hours through Facebook IM chat are more satisfied with their office hour experience than students who only have face-to-face office hours (Li & Pitts, 2009).

Facebook also allows students to communicate with other students about coursework. Students are already using SNS to assist them in completing their coursework (Chu & Meulemans, 2008; Greenhow & Robelia, 2009a, 2009b; Jones, Johnson-Yale, Millermaier, & Perez, 2008a; Madge et al., 2009; NSBA, 2007; Salaway et al., 2008). The latter empirical findings primarily address informal, nonrequired, education-related conversations between students. For example, Madge et al. (2009) find that 46% of first-year undergraduate students use Facebook to informally discuss academic work with other students on a daily or weekly basis. In contrast, only 7% use Facebook for formal learning, such as communicating with professors and asking other students about required course content. Roblyer et al. (2010) note that 6.5% of faculty and 4.2% of students "communicate on class projects" using Facebook. Research demonstrates that frequent student-to-student interaction in an online environment increases class satisfaction, a sense of community and class performance (Beaudoin, 2002; Dawson, 2006; Driver, 2002; Fulford & Zhang, 1993).

More recently, scholars have sought to find a relationship between college students' Facebook use and their academic achievement. However, the findings are fairly mixed. Karpinksi and Duberstein (2009) find that Facebook users have lower grade point averages (GPA) and spend less time studying than nonusers, suggesting that chatting, writing on walls, and poking distracts students from valuable study time. Yet, Pasek, more, and Hargittai (2009) find no negative relationship between Facebook use and students' grades when controlling for demographic variables. In fact, they find some evidence suggesting that Facebook use among students boosts grades (see also Kolek & Saunders, 2008). Some scholars suggest that teacher–student interaction on Facebook breeds familiarity and comfort among students, which creates a better learning environment (see Sturgeon & Walker, 2009). In addition, Mendez et al. (2009) conclude that students who have professors as Facebook friends have higher self-reported grade point averages than those who do not befriend faculty.

Despite Facebook's potential benefits in education, such as enhanced communication and learning, many instructors are not Facebook users and have elected not to use it for student-related academic purposes. Ajjan and Hartshorne (2008) find that only 8% of faculty report using social networking, and 74% of faculty do not currently use and have no plans to use social network sites. Whereas, Roblyer et al. (2010) find 73% of faculty at one university had Facebook accounts. Certainly, an increasing number of faculty are on Facebook; however, an accurate assessment of the adoption rate based on a random sample of faculty and instructors is thus far unavailable.

Furthermore, there is mixed acceptance for faculty on Facebook. Hewitt and Forte (2006) discover that a majority (66%) of students consider faculty on Facebook as acceptable, and Ophus and Abbitt's (2009) study find overall support from students on using Facebook in education. In contrast, Roblyer et al. (2010) report that only 26.6% of students surveyed "would welcome the opportunity to connect with faculty on Facebook" and 22.5% felt "Facebook is personal/social – not for education!" Faculty appear to be more tentative than students about creating an educational presence on Facebook, with 53% of faculty surveyed felt that is should not be used for education, because it is personal or social (Roblyer et al., 2010).

Further studies of social networking tools in education have focused on privacy and safety. Individuals input a tremendous amount of personal information on their Facebook profile page (Acquisti & Gross, 2006; Dwyer et al., 2007; Ellison et al., 2007; Gross & Acquisti, 2005; Lampe et al., 2006; Stutzman, 2009; Stutzman & Kramer-Duffield, 2008; Thelwall, 2008; Tufekci, 2008). Not surprisingly, students are genuinely concerned about how their personal information is going to be used. The ECAR undergraduate survey revealed that 54.4% of undergraduates were "at least moderately concerned" about their personal information being "misused." Students have increased their efforts to maintain privacy on Facebook. However, there are still some students who have not utilized the ample privacy protections that Facebook employs. A recent study reports that 87% of undergraduates surveyed put in place privacy profile restrictions (Salaway et al., 2008). In addition, Facebook's continual changes in their privacy policies have the potential to further impede students' privacy protection.

Another primary concern to both instructors and students is the erosion of professional boundaries. Within the SNS environment, it is easy to share too much information to unintended individuals. This can have implications for both students and instructors. Instructors can learn "too much" about a student, which can impact their student–teacher relationship. Furthermore, instructors have also faced sanctions because they have posted negative comments about their students, schools, and colleagues on SNS (Young, 2009). An additional issue that instructors must address is whether to "friend" a student. Facebook utilizes the term "friends" to indicate a social connection between two people. The word "friend" and the obvious connotations that it traditionally evokes are not appropriate for most student–teacher relationships. However, "friending" someone on Facebook is not the equivalent of establishing a real-life friendship (boyd, 2006; Dwyer et al., 2007; Golder, Wilkinson, & Huberman, 2007; Jones et al., 2008b). In conclusion, we simply do not know much about the effectiveness of using Facebook in an educational setting, nor how to effectively implement SNS, such as Facebook, in our courses. This dearth of educational research and instructor inexperience using Facebook for education, ultimately, may be the biggest hindrances blocking Facebook's educational application.

THE STUDY

To examine attitudes toward Facebook's role as an academic tool, an online survey of undergraduate and graduate students and college instructors was conducted. Specifically, this study sought to explore the following items:

- Student and instructor general usage rates of Facebook.
- Student Facebook usage related to socializing with their classmates.
- Student and instructor Facebook usage patterns related to education.
- Student and instructors attitudes toward using Facebook for educational purposes.

STUDENT SURVEY DATA

Data for this study were collected in the spring of 2009 (February 24–March 13, 2009), from undergraduate and graduate students at a private university on the East coast of the United States. The study and the online survey were advertised on the homepage of the university's courseware. The advertisement contained a project description and the survey link. When students clicked on the survey link, they were taken to the online survey. The survey was available for a period of 2 weeks. This recruitment method elicited 283 completed responses, a response rate of 3% of the total student population.[1] The respondents in this study are relatively representative of the typical university student. Seventy-two percent of the students classified themselves as undergraduates, with mostly junior (22%) and senior (25%) respondents. The average age of respondents is 24.19 years (SD = 7.76). Sixty-nine percent are women, and 68% identified themselves as Caucasian. The sample population's disciplinary background represents a broad range of majors: psychology (15%), education (13%), business (18%), communications (6%), and various other fields. When comparing the sample's demographics to information about the university's student population, this sample is representative with a few exceptions. Female, undergraduates, and younger students were slightly overrepresented.[2]

RESULTS

General Facebook Usage and Socializing with Classmates

Our study confirms that Facebook is a popular and frequently used site among university students. As Table 1 summarizes, 22% of students surveyed spent about 10–30 minutes on Facebook each day and 18%

Table 1. Facebook Student and Faculty Usage and Friends.

	Students (%)	Faculty (%)
In the past week, on average, approximately how many minutes per day did you use the social network sites Facebook?		
Less than 10 minutes	19	14
10–30 minutes	22	21
31–60 minutes	18	25
1–2 hours	16	20
2–3 hours	10	13
More than 3 hours	15	7
About how many total Facebook friends do you have?		
10 or less friends	6	6
11–50 friends	11	15
51–100 friends	12	17
101–150 friends	12	19
151–200 friends	11	17
201–250 friends	8	6
251–300 friends	7	7
301–400 friends	9	5
More than 400 friends	24	8
	$n = 283$	$n = 176$

spent 31–60 minutes. This is fairly consistent with Stutzman's (2009) findings and Facebook's usage statistics, reporting that undergraduate students spent 51 minutes a day on Facebook. Next, we asked students to indicate which of several features they have used on Facebook. Not surprisingly, 89% of respondents report that they have filled out their profile information such as contact information, education, interests, activities, and personal and work information. In addition, many have added photos (82%), social applications (42%), and videos (29%) to their profile.

Table 1 also illustrates that a majority of the sample (24%) report having more than 400 total friends on Facebook. Further analysis of our data reveal that students primarily use Facebook to maintain offline relationships, such as connecting with old friends (90%), a classmate (68%), or family (64%), than using Facebook to make new friends (35%). Freshman and sophomores are using Facebook more frequently to make new friends, compared to juniors and seniors. Overall, our results show that students report greater use of Facebook for maintaining offline relationships across all 4 years of school and at the graduate level.

The results also indicate that many of the students' Facebook relationships involve their classmates. Seventy-five percent of students report that they added a student(s) in their class as a "friend" and viewed profiles of student(s) in their classes. Similarly, 63% had written a note on the "wall" of a student(s) in their class, 59% sent a message through Facebook to student(s) in their class, 38% created and invited student(s) in their class to an "event," and 31% published notes and tagged student(s) in their class. These findings illustrate that Facebook is an important part of a student's social life, allowing them to connect with others through technology. This includes maintaining contact with peers and getting to know classmates better.

Educational Usage

The Internet's increasing popularity has led many social science scholars to examine the link between technology and teaching. Therefore, following Madge et al. (2009), we ask students how they use Facebook as an informal and formal learning tool. Most important, we assess students' perceptions of Facebook as an informal and formal teaching tool, particularly its effectiveness as an instructional or course tool, communication device, and in assisting students in their education and learning. In general, our study shows that students use Facebook primarily for *informal learning* purposes such as for student-to-student interactions about nonrequired course-related matters (e.g., this is usually self-motivated). Specifically, informal learning is unstructured learning that takes place outside of the classroom and does not lead directly to course certification, points, or credit. For example, learning that occurs during a student-to-student conservation in the university hallway about a current course topic. Next, students also use Facebook for *formal learning* purposes such as student-to-student interactions about required course components. That is, formal learning involves student exchanges that lead to official credit or certification, such as learning that occurs in a student study group for a graded exam. In contrast, students are less likely to use Facebook for *informal and formal teaching* purposes. Informal teaching includes instructor–student communication about nonrequired course-related matters, which is often unplanned and spontaneous. For example, learning that takes place in an instructor–student conservation, which occurs beyond the classroom, about course-related current events. Formal teaching is instructor–student communication about required course matters that may be formally assessed, such as an instructor contacting a student about their exam performance or students participating in an instructor-led discussion group.

Informal and Formal Learning: How Students Use Facebook for Learning

We find that students' Facebook usage extends beyond its social functions to educational uses. As Table 2 summarizes, we find that students are communicating with other students about their courses rather than just social events and experiences. On average, about 30% of students surveyed report using Facebook for these informal learning purposes about 1–5 times a semester. More than half of our respondents therefore use Facebook for some sort of informal academic purpose (52% on average).

Whereas Facebook is used primarily for informal learning purposes, we find that 46% of the respondents use Facebook for formal learning purposes such as communication and activities derived from a course's required components (e.g., assignments and exams). Table 3 shows that about 58% report that they use Facebook to ask other students questions about class

Table 2. How Students Use Facebook for Informal Learning.

Find other students in your course(s)	66%
Get contact information (email, phone number, etc.) of classmates	63%
Leave a message on a student's wall about a class	56%
Find out what you missed in a course from another student	51%
Setting up a meeting with other students	47%
Use Facebook chat to discuss something related to class	43%
Talk about a class lecture	38%
Obtain class notes from another student	36%
	$n = 283$

Table 3. How Students Use Facebook for Formal Learning.

Ask students questions about a class assignment/project	58%
Give help to other students about a class assignment/project	53%
Collaborate with other students on a course project using Facebook	45%
Ask students questions about an examination	45%
Give help to other student about an examination	41%
Help from study groups	33%
	$n = 283$

assignments or projects and 45% ask about exams. Of these students, 34% ask their classmates questions about required material about 1–5 times a semester. Interestingly, students also seem inclined to help their classmates. These findings suggest that Facebook is an ideal forum for formal learning, supporting interactions and conversations between peers about required course material. Facebook is more than just a social network for university students. For many, it also functions as both an informal and a formal learning network.

Informal and Formal Teaching: Student Perceptions of Using Facebook for Teaching

Consistent with prior research (Hewitt & Forte, 2006; Madge et al., 2009), we find that Facebook is largely used by students for communicating with other students, not with university faculty or staff. Unlike connecting with friends and classmates, only 12% of our respondents use Facebook to connect with faculty and staff. Recently, however, more and more instructors are entering the Facebook universe. Our survey respondents report that 39% of professors and 17% of teaching assistants had a Facebook profile. Of those students who had a professor or teaching assistant with a profile, more than half (53%) visited an instructor's profile on Facebook.

This seems to be the limit of student-to-instructor interaction, however, as few students are "friends" with their instructors. Of those students who had an instructor with a Facebook profile, we find that only 40% added their instructor as a "friend." Beyond this, few students interact and communicate with faculty on Facebook. This may reflect the fact that 57% of students are somewhat or very concerned with online privacy related to Facebook. Only 23% left a message on their instructor's Facebook "wall" and 13% sent a message to their instructor's Facebook inbox. Despite this, 41% agree or strongly agree that they would feel comfortable if an instructor requested them as a Facebook "friend," whereas 29% felt uncomfortable. In fact, students largely support instructors having a presence on Facebook (69%).

When respondents were asked if instructors should use Facebook for formal teaching, such as course or instructional purposes, 43% responded positively (albeit the minority). Of these students, a majority indicate that they would like instructors to use Facebook to contact students (83%) and to post announcements (85%), the class schedule or events (79%),

Table 4. Student Perspectives and Faculty Usage of Facebook for
Instructional Purposes.

	Students (%)	Faculty (%)
To post announcements	85	43
To contact students	83	48
To post class schedule or events	79	35
To post assignments	76	30
To post website links	71	30
To post handouts	70	.04
To post course syllabus	68	.08
To initiate in-class discussion or debates	60	30
To initiate outside class discussion or debates	60	43
To ask students to post items or material	55	26
To post photos	54	26
To post videos	48	.08
	$n = 121$	$n = 23$

Note: Student survey: "If an instructor used Facebook to help run/instruct a class how would you like them to use Facebook?" Faculty survey: "In general, how do you use Facebook as an instructional or course tool?"

assignments (76%), website links (71%), handouts (70%), and syllabus (68%) (Table 4). This is consistent with recent research, as Ophus and Abbitt's (2009) found that many students are willing to participate in instructor-related online discussions, join a Facebook group, and use Facebook for course-related quizzes and games.

A majority of the survey sample (57%) said instructors should not use Facebook for course or instructional purposes. Of these respondents, we asked students to write the primary reason why an instructor should not use Facebook for instructional reasons. We provide some examples of these responses in the following:

We do not need teachers using Facebook. Websites like webcampus [Blackboard] are much more useful and uninvasive. (Male, Computer graphics, age 19)

Facebook is one of many ways to communicate with people. Although it is not wrong for an instructor to have a Facebook profile, communication or assignment based needs should be left to in-person meetings during office hours, email, or in an emergency, over the phone. Facebook is a recreational website. It should not be used for things that could have influence over a course grade or other course related matter. (Male, Visual and performing arts, age 19)

Facebook encourages many frivolous activities, with however many applications and other friends might distract students. Also, Facebook is not a school controlled domain, and if it were unreachable the school could not intervene and fix the process. Ultimately, Facebook is distancing a professor and student, because while it provides a means for sending messages, it discourages a student from interacting with the professor in person. Ultimately, there is no advantage Facebook offers that is not available through webcampus, and Facebook is a utility for peers, friends, and family, not a learning facility. (Male, English, age 21)

There is no benefit to using Facebook over any other online application, and I wouldn't feel comfortable with professors viewing information about my personal life. (Female, Psychology, age 26)

FACULTY SURVEY DATA

Similar to the student survey, another online survey was conducted to explore faculty attitudes toward Facebook's role in the classroom. We recruited instructors with a mixed method approach using Facebook.[3] First, we placed an advertisement on Facebook, asking instructors to complete a survey about SNS and education. Next, we targeted instructors from relevant Facebook virtual groups such as "Classroom 2.0," "Educational Technologists," and "E-learning professionals."[4] To recruit faculty from these groups, we started a new topic on each discussion board, advertising the study and online survey link. Third, we created a Facebook group ("Facebook and Education Group: College Instructors") that described the study and linked participants to the online survey. The group page information also encouraged respondents to invite their Facebook friends to complete the survey. Last, we contacted the administrators of Facebook groups listed aforementioned, asking them to message their members about our survey project. Several administrators complied, sending a message containing the study description and survey link. In each recruitment method, respondents clicked on the survey link and answered survey questions about their attitudes toward Facebook and its role in class participation, learning, educational usage, and instructional usage. They also responded to survey questions about their general Facebook usage, web courseware usage, and demographics.

During the data collection period (September 29, 2008–February 1, 2009), 372 people clicked the link to begin the survey. Once the noncompletions were removed, 176 respondents remained for analysis. Of the respondents, 55% are women, and 86% identified themselves as Caucasian. The average age of respondents is 40.23 years (SD $= 9.30$). The sample includes full professors (6%), assistant professors (35%), associate professors (18%), instructors (17%), lecturers (9%), and teaching assistants (9%). Most of the instructors surveyed teach introductory courses (74%), are tenured or on the tenure track (58%), teach at a public university (46%), and have an average of 8 years of teaching experience. Eighty-six percent of the respondents teach in the United States. Last, the instructors' disciplinary background represents a broad range: English (15%), education (13%), business (4%), communications (8%), visual and performing arts (8%), and various other fields.

RESULTS

Faculty Facebook Usage

Indeed, Facebook is popular among students and faculty. Similar to students, Table 1 reports that 21% of instructors spend 10–30 minutes on Facebook each day and 25% of instructors spend about 31–60 minutes on Facebook. Consistent with Roblyer et al. (2010), there is no significant difference between faculty and students in the number of times they accessed Facebook. This suggests that Facebook has increased in popularity among adults, as SNS have become embedded in our social culture. Unlike students, few instructors (8%) have more than 400 Facebook friends. Table 1 reports that most instructors (19%) have about 101–150 Facebook friends. Similar to university students, instructors primarily use Facebook to connect with old friends (88%) and family (68%), rarely using the site to make new friends (18%). This is consistent with Sturgeon and Walker's (2009) study, finding that faculty began to use Facebook to communicate with their children and grandchildren. It is clear, therefore, that Facebook plays an important role in instructors' lives, particularly in maintaining offline relationships with current friends and family. Instructors also use Facebook to connect with faculty and staff (66%) and students at large (41%). As we expected, full and associate professors are less likely to use Facebook than assistant professors. Surprisingly, however, we find that assistant professors use Facebook more than lecturers and teaching assistants. That is, the younger, more inexperienced instructors, at least in the case of teaching assistants, were less likely to access Facebook. Although we are unable to offer a definitive explanation of this phenomenon, we postulate that teaching assistants have less leeway in the way that they can teach and administer their classes and are not rewarded for integrating innovative teaching tools. Also, using Facebook in education may be perceived as somewhat controversial and professionally risky, thereby reducing the likelihood that lecturers and teaching assistants adopt it. This last explanation, however, could also be relevant for nontenured assistant professors who are wary of jeopardizing their tenure chances.

We also find evidence that some instructors are incorporating Facebook into their professional lives as they connect with colleagues and students. In total, about half (46%) of our respondents report that they use Facebook both socially and as a faculty member. Therefore, for some instructors, Facebook is extending their personal identity into their professional ones. As these identities coexist, do instructors leverage Facebook to academically engage their students?

Educational Usage

To answer the aforementioned question, we ask instructors if they use Facebook as an instructional tool and assess their perceptions of its effectiveness as a course tool, communication device, and in assisting students in their education and learning. As we expected, faculty do use Facebook as a course tool. However, this is a minority: only 13% of respondents employed Facebook as an instructional tool. Of these instructors, most have used Facebook for introductory courses (59%) for two semesters on average. In general, Table 4 reports that these respondents largely utilize Facebook as a communication tool, particularly to contact students (48%), to post announcements (43%), and to post schedules and events (35%). About 60% of faculty perceived the latter communication devices as effective or very effective in assisting in education and learning. Indeed, when presented with the statement "Facebook increases the frequency of contact with my students in my courses," 90% agreed or strongly agreed. Table 4 further illustrates that some instructors also use Facebook as an online platform for posting class content. Twenty-six percent ask students to post items or material on Facebook. In addition, Facebook was used to initiate both outside (43%) and inside (30%) class discussion or debates among students. Sixty-seven percent agree or strongly agree that "Facebook encourages my students to participate more in outside discussion or debates." Less than half (38%) feel that Facebook aids in-class discussion and few use it to post handouts, syllabi, and videos. Of those using Facebook, we asked instructors to write the primary reason why

Facebook should be used as an instructional or course tool. We provide some examples of these responses below:

> To increase my accessibility to my students, especially in large freshmen lecture courses. (Male, Assistant Professor of Fine Arts, age 43).

> I use Facebook in order to help give myself a more "human" persona and become involved in my students' lives. Facebook is always a non-official part of the class, and I make all official announcements and distributions at class meetings or through email. (Male, Assistant Professor of Visual and Performing Arts, age 33)

> Because students are using it. Go where they are. (Male, Assistant Professor of Communications, age 34)

> To build a sense of community among my students. (Female, Teaching Assistant, English, age 29)

> Students live there. (Female, Assistant Professor of English, age 41)

Of the instructors using Facebook as a course tool, we find that attitudes toward Facebook's effectiveness as an instructional tool and assisting students' education and learning are fairly mixed. A majority of instructors (76%) said their students like that they use Facebook in their course. Sixty-two percent agree or strongly agree that they can post up-to-date material, as Facebook allows links to websites, online videos, newspapers articles, and more. However, only 24% report that they can easily post documents (e.g., Word files, pdf files, or powerpoint slides), create assignments (15%), and create tests and quizzes (10%) on Facebook. This reflects the fact that Facebook does not offer a feature or tab for pdf files, Word documents, Excel files, and powerpoint presentations. Instructors must link students to these files by using Google Docs or by downloading a file-sharing application. Many instructors are skeptical that Facebook aids student learning. Indeed, only 38% of our respondents agree or strongly agree that "Facebook increases their students' academic performance in their courses," whereas 14% disagree. Some said that Facebook was a distraction for students rather than a help (48%). Despite this, 67% agree or strongly agree that "Facebook allows students to learn from each other."

DISCUSSION

Students and faculty have *both* firmly integrated Facebook into their social lives. Usage rates for faculty and students were for the most part quite similar. As we expected (Ellison et al., 2007; Lampe et al., 2006;

Selwyn, 2007), students are simply transferring offline relationships to an online mode. There is little evidence here that students are moving online relationships offline (McMillan & Morrison, 2006). This suggests that Facebook is used largely to maintain already existing offline relationships rather than meeting new people (see boyd & Ellison, 2008). However, there was a slight tendency for freshmen and sophomores to use Facebook more to make new friends than for juniors and seniors. As Madge et al. (2009) suggest, new students use Facebook as a transition tool, helping them integrate socially into the university environment. The resulting communication can have far-reaching implications as students incorporate new classmates into existing social structures. For example, Facebook helps students settle into university life and can create a community of students (Madge et al., 2009). This can serve to benefit community formation within the classroom.

Our findings, consistent with previous work (Chu & Meulemans, 2008; Jones et al., 2008b; Madge et al., 2009; Mendez et al., 2009; Ophus & Abbit, 2009; Salaway et al., 2008), also suggest Facebook and educational practices are already connected. Informally, students are forming a community with their classmates, discussing their classes, requesting lecture notes, finding out what they missed in class, and creating meeting times with other students – all facilitated through Facebook. In addition to these informal learning practices, students are also participating in formal learning through Facebook through communicating about assignments and exams and offering and receiving help on required coursework. Our findings are not entirely surprising, given that Facebook is a virtual extension of a college student's life – a life that revolves around college.

Students, however, are less accepting of using Facebook for informal and formal teaching practices. Participation rates in informal teaching practices are much lower. For example, students do not commonly connect to faculty and staff through Facebook, view their profile, add them as a "friend," e-mail, or Instant Message them. This suggests that most students are not open to personal communication with their instructor through Facebook. Thus, instructors should foster instructor-to-student relationships on Facebook with caution, as some students are wary of a social relationship with an instructor (see also Mazer et al., 2007). However, the majority of students do seem to accept a faculty presence on Facebook and 41% would feel comfortable if an instructor requested them as a Facebook "friend." It seems that students will allow instructors into their social network, but prefer that instructors not be socially engaged with them. Yet, to what extent can we attribute this lower participation to the probable fact that most faculty at this

East Coast university do not have Facebook profile or have not made it available to their students? Therefore, students have not had an *opportunity* to connect with them over Facebook. Interestingly, students are more inclined to view Facebook as a platform for instructional materials and administrative uses that are used to support the learning process rather than using Facebook for learning that is formally assessed. This confirms Madge et al. (2009) whereby students felt Facebook should be used more for "departmental or module-related administrative arrangements." Overall, these student survey results suggest that Facebook plays an important role in students' informal discussion, communication, and learning beyond the classroom. Facebook is therefore perceived more as an informal or formal learning tool and is not viewed as a formal teaching device.

Our findings have demonstrated that students are using Facebook for educational practices – yet, do students fully *realize* that Facebook has assisted them in education or view Facebook as anything but a recreational tool? Have students had *enough opportunities* to experience informal or formal teaching on Facebook to allow them to evaluate its educational worth? Although our research does not specifically address these questions, student comments and the mixed support of teachers using Facebook for instruction suggest that students primarily view Facebook's function as recreational and have a hard time seeing it as an educational tool.

Similar to our student findings, our data suggest that faculty are also reluctant to adopt Facebook for educational practices: only 13% of instructor respondents report using it as a course tool. This number is especially low in light of the fact that we recruited from Facebook to an audience that was primarily supportive of using Facebook or social media in education. Yet, faculty that do use Facebook in education acknowledge its educational merit. Specifically, a majority of faculty respondents view Facebook as a strong communication and participation tool and feel that students liked that they use it in their courses. In general, faculty's usage of Facebook is somewhat consistent with the student data on how they would like to see Facebook used. Faculty are skeptical of how much Facebook would contribute to classroom learning; however, a strong majority feel like it would facilitate students learning from one another. This suggests that instructors believe that Facebook is an educational tool better used by students, rather than instructors. That is, consistent with student views, instructors perceive Facebook as a formal learning tool rather than a formal teaching tool.

Although our data strongly support that Facebook is being used for informal educational purposes and does posses educational merit, the extent to which it should be formally integrated into a course curriculum remains questionable. The authors contend, however, that this skepticism and doubt is attributed more to the lack of knowledge and experience using Facebook in this manner, than the true educational potential that Facebook holds. Ultimately, attitudes toward Facebook in the classroom must change before student and faculty overwhelming support social network sites' potential role in education. Facebook is evolving to include connections and information dissemination that extend beyond recreation. Students need to be shown that social network sites, like Facebook, can be effectively used to help facilitate all types of learning practices and students can acquire academic skills from their use. This change can only happen if instructors not only implement Facebook in their course but also adopt policies that do not cross professional boundaries or violate students' right to privacy in their Facebook space.

STRATEGIES TO CONNECT FACEBOOK TO EDUCATION

Facebook and education can be effectively connected; however, instructors need to think carefully about the ways they intend to introduce and administer Facebook in their courses. Based on the survey results aforementioned and our own classroom experiences, we offer suggestions on how instructors should use Facebook. First, instructors should create a professional Facebook presence. To protect personal privacy, we advocate actually creating a separate profile for professional use only (if an instructor already has a personal profile). The personal profile should have privacy protections to prohibit student access, whereas the professional profile should be opened to the university community. An instructor needs to maintain professionalism on their Facebook profile. For example, a professional head shot picture should be used for their image, status updates need to relate to campus life or course announcements, and personal information posted should be no different from what you would typically reveal in class about yourself. In addition, an instructor should not discuss a student, work colleague, or teaching incident (even in generalities) on their status update. Instructors should also post their contact information, office location, e-mail, and class schedule on their profile, given that some students use Facebook as an information directory. If an instructor has a professional Facebook profile, they should make their students aware of it by not only announcing it in class but also posting it along with their other contact information on their office door and syllabus. Creating a profile allows a student to e-mail you (even if you are not their "friend") and learn information about you. The latter may help facilitate their course selection and teacher–student relationship.

Whereas many instructors may end their Facebook educational involvement with a professional profile, another option is to create a group page for each of their classes. A group page has its own profile page, discussion board, membership list, a "wall," and a section for posting videos, photos, and events. Students do not have to be an instructor's "friend" to join the group. On the group page, an instructor can post their syllabus, lectures, and other class documents. However, documents must be converted to a weblink (through a website like Google Docs) or a third-party, file-sharing application. To be consistent with educational regulations, such as the U.S. federal law, FERPA (Family Education Rights and Privacy Act), instructors need to create a private course group. Therefore, only students enrolled in the class will have access to the course page.

Beyond setting up an infrastructure to use Facebook in education, instructors need to educate their students on how Facebook can be used in education. On the first day of class, an instructor needs to introduce and show their students their Facebook profile and group page. In addition, they need to teach their students that SNS have professional and educational merit. This part of the discussion can conclude with demonstrating Facebook's privacy settings. This ensures that students are aware of the privacy options and allows instructors an opportunity to strongly encourage students to use them. Furthermore, instructors should ask students whether they have used Facebook informally for education (e.g., received notes, asked questions, and located a classmate) to reinforce that most of them are already using Facebook for educational purposes. Instructors also need to state some of the benefits of using Facebook in education, such as community with your classmates, increased contact with fellow classmates and instructors, more convenient access to class materials, and an increased ability to share information. Lastly, to acclimate students to using Facebook in education, instructors could employ an icebreaker activity such as posting a course relevant article or video on the group page.

The authors strongly recommend that instructors respect students' privacy on Facebook and that some students are unwilling to accept, for now, Facebook's potential role in education. Therefore, an instructor should not require participation on Facebook. Participation should be optional; students should not be required to join a course Facebook group page or friend instructors. Instructors should also not request friendship from students. They may accept it – only when asked – but also remind students that they can see their status updates. Additionally, some instructors may decide not to view or post on students' profile pages and encourage students to "block" their access to their profiles (through privacy protection) if it makes their educational experience more comfortable. If an instructor decides to adopt these policies, they need to make their students aware of them.

The authors believe that most faculty could benefit from creating a professional profile to help facilitate student communication and teacher–student relationships. However, we are not advocating that Facebook can, nor should, be universally adopted by all faculty for implementation in their courses. Specific subject areas (e.g., communications, computer sciences, education, marketing, political science, psychology, and sociology) lend themselves more to using Facebook, given the overlap of course content and application. Courses that are strained to create a community, such as online distance classes, hybrid classes, and larger course sections, will potentially derive more benefits from using Facebook, compared to smaller, in-person courses.

CONCLUSION

Facebook is not an educational panacea; yet, it does offer instructors and students educational benefits. At present, it appears that its greatest strength is to facilitate education-related communications between students, offering new opportunities to collaborate and learn outside of the classroom. However, as more instructors adopt Facebook, its educational potential will become more apparent. Before students are willing to accept faculty on Facebook, faculty must first be present in the social network. Moreover, faculty need to model positive online behaviors and respect that Facebook is still a predominately social space. This, ultimately, warrants an understanding of what is deemed to be both acceptable and appropriate education-related behavior on Facebook and a willingness, by both students and faculty, to view Facebook as something beyond a recreational utility. It may also require creative responses to privacy and safety on Facebook to motivate faculty to use SNS and other technologies to enhance students' classroom environment. Overall, students, faculty, as well as administrators must be adept to change, as traditional tools, such as office hours and campus courseware, become outdated in today's classroom.

In our analyses, student and faculty respondents were drawn from a convenience sample and thus cannot be generalized to other student or faculty groups. The link for the online survey was also publicly posted; therefore, the identity of student and teacher cannot be guaranteed. In addition, there was a small sample size for both faculty using Facebook and students who had experienced Facebook in their courses. Given these limitations, we suggest that more empirical studies need to be conducted on integrating SNS into education. Specifically, our study suggests several directions for future research. First, using national surveys and experimental studies, scholars should continue to evaluate the effectiveness of integrating Facebook into the class setting, particularly to explore how Facebook contributes to the formation and quality of a class community, course satisfaction, and learning. Second, as instructors increasingly use Facebook in the classroom, it is important to examine the appropriate uses of Facebook and how to integrate them effectively into educational settings. In examining the latter, scholars should articulate what Facebook uses align with certain teaching and learning goals, how much time Facebook will take for instructors, how to provide students with guidelines for using Facebook, and how to facilitate student and instructor buy-in to using Facebook for education. Third, as SNS and other Web 2.0 technologies invade the classroom, there is a need to compare the effects of nontraditional tools such as Facebook, Instant Messaging, and virtual office hours alongside traditional, educational tools, such as courseware and face-to-face meetings. In sum, our research provides further evidence that Facebook and education are connected; however, the strength, longevity, and dimensions of this union remains to be seen.

NOTES

1. Four hundred and sixty-six people clicked on the survey link. We removed 183 surveys for non-completion.

2. Differences were as follows: 56% of the student population is female versus 69% of our respondents; 61% of the student population are undergraduates versus 72% of our respondents; the average age of the student population is 27.91 versus 24.19 for our respondents. The results of this study cannot be said to be generalizable to all schools and students in the United States.

3. Brickman-Bhutta (2009) argues that Facebook is well suited for survey research. The author finds that a survey conducted using Facebook was comparable to samples gathered by Gallup and the General Social Survey.

4. Other groups included "Using Wikis in Education," "E-learning in Developing Countries," "Second Life for Educators," "Teaching and Learning with Facebook," "Faculty Ethics on Facebook," and "Faculty and Staff Who Enjoy using Facebook to Help Students."

REFERENCES

Acquisti, A., & Gross, R. (2006). Imagined communities: Awareness, information sharing, and privacy on the Facebook. In: *The proceedings of privacy enhancing technology.* Available at http://petworkshop.org/2006/preproc/preproc_03.pdf. Retrieved on April 29, 2010.

Ajjan, H., & Hartshorne, R. (2008). Investigating faculty decisions to adopt Web 2.0 technologies: Theory and empirical tests. *The Internet and Higher Education, 11*(2), 71–80.

Beaudoin, M. (2002). Learning or lurking? Tracking the 'invisible' online student. *The Internet and Higher Education, 5*(2), 147–155.

boyd, d. m. (2006). Friends, friendsters, and top 8: Writing community into being on social network sites. *First Monday, 11*(12). Available at http://firstmonday.org/htbin/cgiwrap/bin/ojs/index.php/fm/article/view/1418/1336. Retrieved on April 11, 2009.

boyd, d. m., & Ellison, N. B. (2008). Social network sites: Definition, history, and scholarship. *Journal of Computer-Mediated Communication, 13*(1), 210–230.

Brickman-Bhutta, C. (2009). Not by the book: Facebook as sampling frame. Available at http://www.thearda.com/workingpapers/download/Not%20by%20the%20Book%20-%20Bhutta.doc. Retrieved on March 25, 2010.

Chu, M., & Meulemans, Y. N. (2008). The problems and potential of MySpace and Facebook usage in academic libraries. *Internet Reference Services Quarterly, 13*(1), 69–85.

Dawson, S. (2006). A study of the relationship between student communication interaction and sense of community. *The Internet and Higher Education, 9*(3), 153–162.

Driver, M. (2002). Exploring student perceptions of group interaction and class satisfaction in the web-enhanced classroom. *The Internet and Higher Education, 5*(1), 35–45.

Dwyer, C., Hiltz, S. R., & Passerini, K. (2007). Trust and privacy concern within social networking sites: A comparison of Facebook and MySpace. *Proceedings of AMCIS 2007,* Keystone, CO. Available at http://csis.pace.edu/~dwyer/research/DwyerAMCIS2007.pdf. Retrieved on March 23, 2009.

Ellison, N., Steinfield, C., & Lampe, C. (2007). The benefits of Facebook "friends:" Social capital and college students' use of online social network sites. *Journal of Computer-Mediated Communication, 12*(4), 1143–1168.

Facebook Press Room: Statistics. (2009). Statistics. Available at http://www.facebook.com/press/info.php?factsheet#!/press/info.php?statistics. Retrieved on November 1, 2009.

Facebook Press Room: Statistics. (2010). Statistics. Available at http://www.facebook.com/facebook?v=app_7146470109&ref=pf#!/press/info.php?statistics. Retrieved on April 1, 2010.

Fulford, C. P., & Zhang, S. (1993). The critical predictor in distance education. *The American Journal of Distance Education, 7*(3), 8–21.

Golder, S., Wilkinson, D., & Huberman, B. A. (2007). Rhythms of social interaction: Messaging within a massive online network. *Conference on communities and technologies.* Available at http://www.hpl.hp.com/research/idl/papers/facebook/facebook.pdf. Retrieved on March 25, 2010.

Greenhow, C., & Robelia, E. (2009a). Informal learning and identity formation in online social networks. *Learning, Media and Technology, 34*(2), 119–140.

Greenhow, C., & Robelia, E. (2009b). Old communication, new literacies: Social network sites as social learning resources. *Journal of Computer-Mediated Communication, 14*(4), 1130–1161.

Gross, R., & Acquisti, A. (2005). Information revelation and privacy in online social networks. *ACM Workshop on Privacy in the Electronic Society,* pp. 71–80.

Hewitt, A., & Forte, A. (2006). Crossing boundaries: Identity management and student/faculty relationships on the Facebook. Presented at the Computer Supported Cooperative Work Conference, Banff, Alberta, Canada.

Joinson, A. (2008). 'Looking at', 'looking up' or 'keeping up with' people? Motives and uses of Facebook. *Proceedings of the SIGCHI* (pp. 1027–1036).

Jones, S., Johnson-Yale, C., Millermaier, S., & Perez, F. S. (2008a). Academic work, the Internet and U.S. college students. *The Internet and Higher Education, 11*(3–4), 165–177.

Jones, S., Millermaier, S., Goya-Martinez, M., & Schuler, J. (2008b). Whose space is Myspace? A content analysis of Myspace profiles. *First Monday, 13*(9–1). Available at http://firstmonday.org/htbin/cgiwrap/bin/ojs/index.php/fm/article/view/2202/2024. Retrieved on May 14, 2009.

Karpinksi, A. C., & Duberstein, A. (2009). A description of Facebook use and academic performance among undergraduate and graduate students. Presented at the American Educational Research Association Annual Meeting, San Diego, California.

Kolek, E. A., & Saunders, D. (2008). Online disclosure: An empirical examination of undergraduate Facebook profiles. *NASPA Journal, 45*(1), 1–25.

Lampe, C., Ellison, N., & Steinfield, C. (2006). A Face(book) in the crowd: Social searching vs. social browsing. In: *Proceedings of ACM Special Interest Group on Computer-Supported Cooperative Work* (pp. 167–170). ACM Press. Available at http://portal.acm.org/citation.cfm?id=1180901. Retrieved on March 25, 2010.

Li, L., & Pitts, J. P. (2009). Does it really matter? Using virtual office hours to enhance student-faculty interaction. *Journal of Information Systems Education, 20*(2), 175–185.

Luckin, R., Clark, W., Graber, R., Logan, K., Mee, A., & Oliver, M. (2009). Do Web 2.0 tools really open the door to learning? Practices, perceptions and profiles of 11–16-year-old-students. *Learning, Media and Technology, 34*(2), 87–104.

Madge, C., Meek, J., Wellens, J., & Hooley, T. (2009). Facebook, social integration and informal learning at university: 'It is more for socialising and talking to friends about work than for actually doing work.' *Learning, Media and Technology, 34*(2), 141–155.

Mazer, J. P., Murphy, R. E., & Simonds, C. J. (2007). I'll see you on "Facebook": The effects of computer-mediated teacher self-disclosure on student motivation, affective learning, and classroom climate. *Communication Education, 56*(1), 1–17.

Mazer, J. P., Murphy, R. E., & Simonds, C. J. (2009). The effects of teacher self-disclosure via *Facebook* on teacher credibility. *Learning, Media and Technology, 34*(2), 175–183.

McMillan, S. J., & Morrison, M. (2006). Coming of age in the e-generation: A qualitative exploration of how the Internet has become an integral part of young people's lives. *New Media & Society, 8*, 73–95.

Mendez, J. P., Curry, J., Mwavita, M., Kennedy, K., Weinland, K., & Bainbridge, K. (2009). To friend or not to friend: Academic interaction on Facebook. *International Journal of Instructional Technology & Distance Learning, 6*(9), 33–47.

National School Board Association. (2007). Creating and connecting: Research and guidelines on social – and educational – networking. Available at http://www.nsba.org/SecondaryMenu/TLN/CreatingandConnecting.aspx. Retrieved on October 25, 2008.

Ophus, J. D., & Abbitt, J. T. (2009). Exploring the potential perceptions of social networking systems in university courses. *Journal of Online Learning and Teaching, 5*(4). Available at http://jolt.merlot.org/vol5no4/ophus_1209.htm. Retrieved on March 11, 2010.

Pasek, J., more, e., & Hargittai, E. (2009). Facebook and academic performance: Reconciling a media sensation with data. *First Monday, 14*(5). Available at http://www.uic.edu/htbin/cgiwrap/bin/ojs/index.php/fm/article/view/2498/2181. Retrieved on April 20, 2010.

Raacke, J., & Bonds-Raacke, J. (2008). MySpace and Facebook: Applying the uses and gratifications theory to exploring friend-networking sites. *Cyberpsychology & Behavior*, *11*(2), 169–174.

Roblyer, M. D., McDaniel, M., Webb, M., Herman, J., & Witty, J. V. (2010). Findings on Facebook in higher Education: A comparison of college faculty and student uses and perceptions of social networking sites. *The Internet and Higher Education*, *13*(3), 134–140.

Salaway, G., Caruso, J. B., & Nelson, M. R. (2008). *The ECAR Study of Undergraduate Students and Information Technology, Research Study* (Vol. 8). Boulder, CO: EDUCAUSE Center for Applied Research.

Selwyn, N. (2007). "Screw blackboard ... do it on Facebook!": An investigation of students' educational use of Facebook. Presented at the "Poke 1.0 – Facebook Social Research Symposium," University of London.

Smith, S., Salaway, G., & Caruso, J. B. with an Introduction by Richard N. Katz. (2009). The ECAR study of undergraduate students and information technology. *Research Study* (Vol. 6). Boulder, CO: EDUCAUSE Center for Applied Research. Available at http://www.educause.edu/ecar

Sturgeon, C. M., & Walker, C. (2009). Faculty on Facebook: Confirm or deny? Presented at the 14th Annual Instructional Technology Conference, Murfreesboro, Tennessee.

Stutzman, F. (2009). The state of things talking points. Available at http://fstutzman.com/wp-content/uploads/2009/05/talking_points.pdf. Retrieved on April 1, 2010.

Stutzman, F., & Kramer-Duffield, J. (2008). Experience and privacy: Exploring the disclosure behaviors of established Facebook users. *ASIST Annual Meeting. Conference Poster*.

Thelwall, M. (2008). Social networks, gender, and friending: An analysis of MySpace member profiles. *Journal of the American Society for Information Science and Technology*, *59*(8), 1321–1330.

Tufekci, Z. (2008). Can you see me now? Audience and disclosure regulation in online social network sites. *Bulletin of Science, Technology & Society*, *28*(1), 20–36.

Young, J. R. (2009). How not to lose face on Facebook, for professors. *The Chronicle of Higher Education*, *55*(22), A1, February 6, Available at http://firstmonday.org/htbin/cgiwrap/bin/ojs/index.php/fm/issue/view/206

SOCIAL MEDIA FOR HIGHER EDUCATION IN DEVELOPING COUNTRIES – AN INTERCULTURAL PERSPECTIVE ☆

Malik Aleem Ahmed

ABSTRACT

Higher education institutions (HEIs) in developed countries have started using social media for the provision of quality education and the production of valuable research; however, the picture is not very bright in case of many developing countries. Web 2.0 services and applications like social and professional networking systems, wikis, and blogs can facilitate in fostering discussion, improving online interaction, and enhancing collaboration among stakeholders of HEIs in developing countries. This process can lead toward resolving quality issues in the higher education sector of developing countries. Information Technology Alteration – Design and Management – Framework proposes that if intercultural variations of values exist between the technology producing country and technology consuming country then, Information and communication

☆ An earlier version of this chapter was presented under the title of "Web 2.0 as a tool for resolving issues related to quality in higher education in developing countries and technology alteration (design and management) framework" in INTED 2009 in Valencia (Spain).

Educating Educators with Social Media
Cutting-edge Technologies in Higher Education, Volume 1, 59–80
ISSN: 2044-9968/doi:10.1108/S2044-9968(2011)0000001006

technology systems – for example, Web 2.0 systems-should be customized, redesigned, and altered in cross-cultural implementations.

Higher education institutions (HEIs) in developed countries have started using social media for providing quality education and for producing valuable research; however, the picture is not very bright in case of many developing countries. I discuss that Web 2.0 applications can be useful in improving the situation in higher education sectors of developing countries. In the second section of the chapter, I explore some of the Web 2.0 services and applications like social and professional networking systems, wikis, and blogs. I discuss that Web 2.0 services and applications like social and professional networking systems, wikis, and blogs can be used to enhance the information capabilities of stakeholders and thus assist in peer-to-peer interaction and collaboration in the HEIs of the developing countries. This process can lead toward resolving quality issues in the higher education sector of developing countries. However, intercultural perspective on cross-cultural implementation of Web 2.0 applications, as presented in third and fourth sections, indicates that a gap might exist between the values supported by Web 2.0 applications and the values held in the HEIs of the specific developing country. This gap is discussed in the fourth section, in which information technology alteration framework (ITAF) is presented. Information Technology Alteration – Design and Management – Framework proposes that if intercultural variations of values exist between the technology producing country and technology consuming country then information and communication technology (ICT) systems – for example, Web 2.0 systems – should be customized, redesigned, and altered in cross-cultural implementations. For an illustration, I discuss the implementation of Web 2.0 services and applications in higher education sector of a developing country and demonstrate how the suggestions and propositions of ITAF are useful in this scenario.

WEB 2.0 IN HIGHER EDUCATION INSTITUTIONS

HEIs in developed countries have been using ICTs, tools, and systems for improving the quality of higher education and research (Ahmed, 2008b; Anderson, 2007; Oldervoll, Boge, & Stre, 2009). Learning management systems, collaborative learning tools, decision support systems, information systems, computer-aided ranking systems, and electronic blackboards are some of the tools and systems in use for past three decades. As in other areas, digital divide exists between the HEIs of developed and developing countries (Adam, 2003; UNESCO, n.d.). Several HEIs, especially the universities, in many developing countries possess basic ICT infrastructure, such as local area networks, Internet, computers, video, audio, storage equipment, and mobile technology facilities (Sife, Lwoga, & Sanga, 2007); however, they have not been able to utilize the ICTs for providing quality education, producing valuable research, and offering featured learning opportunities (Adam, 2003).

Some HEIs in developed countries have been using another technology – that is, computer-mediated communication (CMC) – since 1970s, which contributed toward the development of the Internet. One of the services of the Internet, which quickly evolved and became widely acceptable in 1990s, is the World Wide Web. In the past 20 years, the Web has become the most popular service of the Internet. For the last five years, the term Web 2.0 has been becoming common. Web 2.0 is the popular name of a new generation of Web applications, sites, and companies that emphasis openness, community, and interaction (David & Martin, 2006). Web 2.0 includes blogs, wikis, trackback, podcasting, video blogs, and different social networking tools (Alexander, 2006). Web 2.0 has also been referred as social web or social media because of its emphasis on the community, social interaction and user generated content.

Some researchers (Anderson, 2007; Franklin & Harmelen, 2007) have suggested that Web 2.0 is a technology with profound potential for inducing change in the HE sector. In developed countries, HEIs are using Web 2.0 for learning and teaching, scholarly research, academic publishing, and libraries (Anderson, 2007). Web 2.0 tools and applications are proving to be useful for fostering discussion and empowering the teachers, researchers, students, and other stakeholders. Web 2.0 technologies, tools, and services are also becoming integral for web-based CMC. Universities appear to be making provision for the social web by including the tools in virtual learning environments, portals or as standalone tools (McLoughlin, 2008). HEIs have started using wikis and blogs for learning and teaching. They are testing Folksonomies and blogs, including collective blogs, for scholarly research. They are experimenting with Web 2.0 for pre-publication papers and finding it to be helpful for academic publishing. Tagging, blog trackbacking, blog-rolling, and Rich Site Summary (RSS) syndication feeds concepts are similar to different concepts of library and knowledge management, which can be helpful in libraries, repositories, and for archiving (Anderson, 2007). This is truer for the HE sector in developed countries.

Many HEIs and universities in developing countries have the web presence. However, most of the web initiatives focus on one-way information flow. A quick online browsing survey of public and private sector HEIs of Pakistan showed that many of those HEIs focus on producing and disseminating information to the stakeholders, but they do not focus on acquiring the information from the stakeholders. They are missing the opportunities that could be explored by the social interactive nature of Web 2.0 applications and tools. One of those opportunities is the facilitation power of social media for generating ideas, improving interaction, and enhancing collaboration among the stakeholders.

WEB 2.0 IN HE FOR FOSTERING DISCUSSION AND COLLABORATION TO RESOLVE QUALITY ISSUES

Much of the literature of using Web 2.0 in higher educational settings focus on students and students–educators interaction but not on the interaction efforts for educators. There is a little literature available on utilizing Web 2.0 for stimulating discussion and improving collaboration to resolve quality issues in HE of developing countries. The following section explores this area.

Web 2.0 can assist in resolving many quality issues in HE sector of developing countries by providing collateral communication means and participatory content generation. To defend this claim, I use a proposition of indirect capabilities approach.

Capability approach (Sen, 1999) reminds us that instead of focusing on proving the resources we should focus on creating the circumstances for improving the capabilities of the stakeholders. Indirect capabilities approach (Ahmed, 2010a), based on capabilities approach (Nussbaum, 2000; Sen, 1999) and enabling technologies theories, holds that capabilities set and the functioning of the stakeholders can be improved indirectly by strengthening the institutions through different initiatives including ICT-related initiatives. In an ideal situation, improving the capabilities set and functioning of the stakeholders could then result in better performing institutions. It is a two way process.

On the basis of indirect capabilities approach, we can argue that Web 2.0 technologies and services can assist in improving the communication infrastructure and establishing participatory culture in HEIs. However, Web 2.0-related projects should not be focused on providing the resources to the institutions only but also enhance the capability set of the stakeholders.

Web 2.0 technologies and services can enhance the information capabilities (Ahmed, 2010c) – that is, capabilities to (1) access information and (2) produce information of the stakeholders. The user centeredness nature of Web 2.0 technologies complements the information production capabilities of the stakeholders. Web 2.0 applications and services can be used for the institutions-to-stakeholders, stakeholders-to-institutions, and stakeholders-to-stakeholders content generation, communication, interaction, and group work. The enhanced information capabilities can contribute toward the knowledge production, exchange of ideas, discussion, and interaction in different areas of educational setting including learning, teaching, research, libraries, support, public relations, students' recruitment, and administration. Social web can also be helpful in areas other than the main stream HE institutional activities. For example, Web 2.0 can provide means for the teachers, administrators, policy makers, researchers, learners, and other stakeholders, including industries, commerce, service sector, government bodies, and non-governmental organizations, to create new forms of community and interact online, discuss, review, give opinions, post best practices, and collaborate to think out the ways to resolve different challenges including quality related issues. In short, due to the interactive and collaborative assistive power, social media can contribute to the creation of a platform for educators and administrators to discuss and brainstorm. Some of the areas in which quality issues arise and discussions can be done are accessibility, syllabus, accountability, grading, certifications, inspection, distance education, formal learning, further education, empowerment, human resources, and research.

In the following subsections, I look at some of the applications and services of Web 2.0. I present some examples of the application or service usage in the HEIs of developed countries. Then I explore how that application or service can be used for participatory behavior, peer-to-peer interaction, and collaboration between educators in HE in developing countries. I also discuss some challenges and give some suggestions for using these Web 2.0 tools and applications in HE settings.

Social and Professional Networking

Social networking web systems are those sites in which users can socialize and interact with each other by using different tools, services, and applications. Some of the well-known examples of public social networking websites are facebook.com, myspace.com, and orkut.com. Specialized versions of social networking websites for professionals are known as professional networking websites. Professional networking websites aim at interaction, information generation, and participation of professionals with common interests. Professional networking websites provide many services of participatory nature including, but not limited to, becoming associates, forming online groups and communities, interacting, developing polls, discussions, recommendations, jobs posting, and applications. Linkedin.com is an example of professional networking website.

HEIs in the developed countries have realized the potential of social and professional networking websites. The enthusiasts in HEIs in developed countries have been experimenting and using the social and professional networking tools and systems. Eduspaces and Elgg are two of the popular tools for creating internal networking systems. Eduspaces is an example of general-purpose social networking site dedicated to education and educational technology. Elgg is anopen source social network software for education. Graz University of Technology, Austria, has been using Learnland as a social and learning tool, based on Elgg, since October 2006 (Ebner, Holzinger, & Maurer, 2007). Another example is from the University of Brighton. University of Brighton was one of the first universities of United Kingdom, which adopted Elgg as a social networking tool for its Community@Brighton at the university level.

Implementing stakeholders in the HEIs of developing countries could aim at forming the virtual networks of interested stakeholders with social and professional networking tools – for example, a networking website for educators in higher education. This initiative would assist them in interaction and informal communication. It would provide them a platform to share experiences, discuss new ideas, and brainstorm. These types of websites can also provide opportunities for relationship building and providing support in academic context. HE institutions in developing countries can use the external hosting social networking software like Ning for ease of maintenance.

Recently, initiators and enthusiasts in some HEIs of developed countries are following another trend. They have observed that stakeholders find it difficult to maintain accounts for different networking sites and do not regularly use educational social networking websites. As some public social networking websites have become very popular, especially with the students, therefore universities, institutions, and other entities have started making groups and pages on these sites. For example, a social networking site, PHD-Community for PhD candidates, was launched in early 2009 at Delft University of Technology in the Netherlands. After one year of operations, the creators realized that it would be better to stop the separate website and make a group on Linkedin because many PhD candidates had accounts on Linkedin. The chances of logging on and seeing the relevant information are better.

HEIs in developing countries could follow the similar strategy. As they usually possess limited financial and technical resources, which pose challenges in initiating, hosting, and sustaining the new systems, using the services and tools of publicly available social and professional networking websites seems a good alternative. Creating groups and maintaining them on these websites do not require much investment in terms of finances and technical knowledge. The external networking websites are relatively cheaper to setup and simpler to maintain. They provide easy ways to build communities and involve stakeholders in dialogue and engagement. Groups on the popular social and professional networking websites are easier and cheaper to maintain. At the same time, HEIs should be aware of different issues with public social and professional networking websites. These are the issues related to autonomy, identity, control, stability, and privacy.

Wikis

Wiki is a collaborative web space where anyone can add content and anyone can edit content that has already been published (Richardson, 2006). Wikis provide the opportunities of group-generated contents and collective knowledge production. Wikipedia (wikipedia.org) is a popular example of wikis, which is a publicly editable wiki system with an open philosophy.

In educational institutions of developed countries, teachers and students have begun using password-protected wikis to create their own textbooks and resource sites (Richardson, 2006). Wiki has been experimented since 2004 at Delft University of Technology in the Netherlands. The official wiki site (wiki.tudelft.nl) was launched in March 2009. The major objective of this wiki site is to provide, free and open, collaborating platform for the academic community of the Delft University of Technology.

HEIs in developing countries can tap the collaborative and content production facilitation powers of wikis for collaborative working, sharing knowledge, generating new ideas, responding to ideas, and for acquiring information on different issues. They can maintain knowledge bases about different topics. They can infuse a new sense of community in the geographically dispersed educators. HEIs can initiate the wikis at different levels – for example, large-scale sector-wide wiki, institutional-wide wiki, or departmental-wide wiki. For trustworthiness and reliability, HEIs in developing countries can implement editorial controlled wikis – for example, closed-up wikis like Citizendium or Google's Knol – in which a professional or a group of professionals from the academic background serves for the expert oversight. The stakeholders can also be educated that open wikis can be reliable in HE settings in a sense that peers can read the entry, review it, make changes, or add new contents.

In HE sector of developing countries, Wikis can be used in combination of collaborative editing tools for creating shared workspaces. A collaborative editing tool allows users in different locations to edit the same document at the same time. Examples are Google Docs and Spreadsheets26 (for text documents and spreadsheets), and Gliffy27 (for diagrams) (Franklin & Harmelen, 2007). Similarly, Wiki entries can be complemented with social bookmarking of related disciplinary subjects.

Blogs

A Weblog is a diary or journal-based Web site. It uses a straightforward content management tool, allowing users to easily create and update news pages and entries, without the need to worry about design or architectural issues. Content can be filtered according to attributes, including category and author, and there is usually a system that allows visitors to comment on individual blog entries (Gordon, 2006).

Blogs facilitate the users in generating contents. Blogs can be used for harnessing collective intelligence, sharing information, and for coining new ideas. They can be helpful in getting quick comments, suggestions, and feedback from others. Blogs foster regular and timely personal communication and dialogue for a defined team, community, or an interest group (Ward, 2006). The availability of bandwidth has made it easier to add multimedia contents in blogs. Audio blogs, also called podcasts, and video blogs, also called vlogs are becoming popular. Youtube (Youtube.com) hosts many vlogs.

Different universities in United Kingdom including University of Warwick and University of Leeds are using educational blogs (Franklin & Harmelen, 2007). Edublogs (Edublogs.org) is an example of a general-purpose educational blog.

In HE sector of developing countries, blogs can be used for sharing information and experiences, peer mentoring, reflecting and giving feedback. Blogs can function as a mechanism for reflective writing allowing bloggers to gain insights into their thoughts at a particular moment for a deeper reflection of an experience (Pulman, 2008). Concepts can be presented, attacked, sliced, diced, added to and subtracted from, mangled, massaged and molded (Penenberg, 2005). Blogs can also be proved helpful in collaborative content production. Blogs can also be used for getting the voices heard, starting discussion on different topics, and getting input. Teaching needs and issues can be conveyed, commented, discussed, criticized, and refined. Blogs can provide the worldwide audience, interaction, and feedback on different ideas. Facilities of podcasts and vlogs can help the education bloggers to convey their ideas in multimedia. Wordpress.com, Blogger.com, or some other developer-hosted platform can be used as a starting point. On a different scale, blogosphere for different stakeholder groups could be created. To nurture online discussion for resolving quality issues in HE of a group of stakeholder organizations in a developing country, a higher education quality blogosphere can be conceived and implemented. Members from the stakeholder organizations can create their blogs or participate in collaborative blogs. They can post ideas or give suggestions and comments on the posted blogs.

INTERCULTURAL PERSPECTIVE ON WEB 2.0 IMPLEMENTATION FOR HIGHER EDUCATION IN DEVELOPING COUNTRIES

ICTs can assist in bringing the change in HE sector of developing countries. Cultural-specific factors should be considered during the cross-cultural implementation of ICTs – including Web 2.0 technologies and applications in the HEIs of developing countries.

Above discussion points out some of the possibilities related to Web 2.0 that can be explored by HEIs in developing countries. However, possibilities and potential of the technologies are not enough to start and/or sustain the projects. Researchers have discussed that soft factors (Heeks, 2003) like policies, administration, leadership, politics, culture, economy, and skills along with infrastructure play role in initiating, implementing, and sustaining the ICT related project. An overlooked soft factor is the inter-relationship of technology and society. Researchers (Ess, 2008) have argued that the compatibility of technology with culture and values can play a vital role in the acceptance and usage of that technology. In this part of the chapter, I present ITAF and indicate the role of intercultural variations of values for implementing Web 2.0 technologies in cross-cultural scenarios. By cross-cultural scenarios, I mean the transferring and implementation of

ICT systems in a society that has cultural variations of values as compared to the society in which the system was developed.

INFORMATION TECHNOLOGY ALTERATION FRAMEWORK

Information Technology Alteration – Design and Management – Framework (ITAF) (Ahmed, 2008c) is a theoretical framework, which stresses the need of considering and accounting for intercultural variations of values for introducing and implementing the systems in cross-cultural scenarios. ITAF takes an intercultural perspective for cross-cultural implementation of ICT systems and tools. ITAF uses the propositions of capability approach, soft technological determinism, cultural pluralism, structuration theory in IT, value sensitive design, technology enactment framework, and different studies in science and technology filed. ITAF also make use of the empirical works and argumentations of (Hofstede, 1991) work on cultural dimensions and survey data from different waves of (WVS, n.d.). Because of the space limitation only the main propositions of ITAF are presented. Interested readers can refer to (Ahmed, 2008c, 2010b) for the discussion on background theories and justifications of propositions of ITAF.

The main argument of Information Technology Alteration – Design and Management – Framework (ITAF) is that ICTs including CMC systems can be used to unable technologies in strengthening the processes and procedures of public sector institutions of developing countries. If intercultural variations of values exist between the donor country, in which CMCs were developed, and the host country, then stakeholders have to take into account and plan for the variations while transferring and implementing systems. One of the factors in accounting and planning for the variations is to customize, modify, and if needed, alter the system. For achieving the right equilibrium, the system should not be altered to the extent that it reinforces existing institutional structures and values. System should support those values, which are considered more legitimate and necessary to bring the positive change (Ahmed, 2010b).

ITAF and Implementation of Web 2.0 Tools in HE in Developing Countries

Web 2.0 tools and services can be considered as a part of web-based CMC. In the following subsections, ITAF propositions are presented and then a discussion is made for implementing Web 2.0 tools and services in HE sector of developing countries.

Interinfluence of Technology and Society
The first and second propositions of ITAF are related to interinfluence of technology and society. As Fig. 1 shows:

Proposition 1. ITAF holds that values and structures can influence the shaping of ICTs. This proposition is based on soft technological determinism.

Proposition 2. However, at the same time, ICTs have the potential to influence on values and structures. This proposition is based on social shaping of technology.

Many of the technology producing countries – for example, United States, Germany, United Kingdom, and the Netherlands – value individualism, low power distance, low uncertainty avoidance (Hofstede, 1991), and more transparencies. These values can facilitate in building the social and organizational structures with more equality among societal levels, cooperative interaction across power levels, openness between different entities, greater level of trust on others and freedom of expression. The reflection and assumptions of these values can also be seen in Web 2.0 services and applications – for example, most of the Web 2.0 services and applications are based on openness, community, and interaction (David & Martin, 2006). These services and applications are based on idea generation and knowledge sharing, with tolerance for variety of ideas and thoughts. Web 2.0 services and applications have the potential to empower the values and structures of the aforementioned countries in a way that these applications encourage discussion, interaction, idea sharing, and collaboration among different users at different power levels. However, at the same time, Web 2.0 has the potential to encourage the societies with high individualism to value collectivism, group work, and community – for example, in the form of electronic community building.

Above discussion indicates that existing values of the society can influence in shaping ICTs including Web 2.0; however, at the same time, ICTs can also affect the values resulting in variations in the values at different times and spaces.

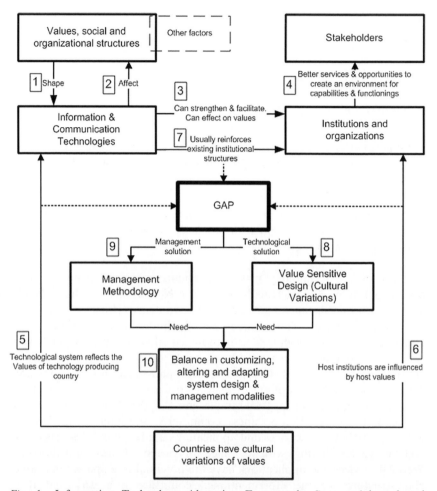

Fig. 1. Information Technology Alteration Framework. *Source:* Adapted and modified from Ahmed (2008c).

ICTs for Capabilities and Functioning
The third and fourth propositions of ITAF, which were indirectly mentioned in the second section, are related to the instrumental powers of ICTs for facilitating human capabilities and functioning. As Fig. 1 shows:

Proposition 3. ICTs can be used to alter the negative values and structures. ICTs can strengthen the institutions, which enables the institutions to provide better services and opportunities to the stake-holders. This proposition is based on enabling technologies argument and indirect capability approach.

Proposition 4. Thus, ICTs can help creating an environment for the stakeholders to use their capabilities and to function. This proposition is based on indirect capability approach.

HEIs in the developing countries can use social and professional networking systems, wikis, and blogs, to create an environment for the stakeholders to form social and professional networks, build communities, interact, post blogs, contribute and share ideas. Web 2.0 can be helpful in altering the negative values and structures like bureaucracy, insufficient communication, top-down information flow and less collaboration. Web 2.0 services and applications can be used to facilitate the stakeholders in using their communication, discussion, content generation, and idea sharing capabilities. Web 2.0 provides the means to stakeholders for getting their voices heard. Proper communication functioning can result in collaboration among different stakeholder groups, and improved collaborative capability can be helpful in resolving quality issues in higher education. Improved discussions and idea sharing can help in better policymaking and plans to provide an overall environment of improved capabilities and functioning, which in turn could result in resolving quality issues related to HE in developing countries.

Intercultural Variations of Values
The fifth proposition of ITAF is related to cultural diversity and the role of values in shaping of ICTs. As Fig. 1 shows:

Proposition 5. Cultural variations of values, social and organizational structures of the technology producing country affects in shaping the ICTs. Intercultural variations of values and structures exist between different countries.

As already discussed, Web 2.0 services and applications incorporate the assumptions of values and structures of the technology producing country. Moreover, implementation, management, and sustainability practices of Web 2.0 systems in HE in developed countries are based on values and structures of those specific countries.

The sixth proposition of ITAF is related to role of values in influencing the norms in institutions. As Fig. 1 shows:

Proposition 6. In the host country, institutions and organizations follow the norms, practices, and management styles influenced by values and structures (Ahmed, 2008c). Different management and implementation styles for technology implementation and sustainability are followed in the host country based on cultural variations of values, norms, and structures (Ahmed, 2010b; Ahmed & Hoven, 2008).

Work of Hofstede (2010) and different waves of World Values Survey (WVS, n.d.) shows intercultural variations of values, norms and structures exist between a developing country – for example, Pakistan – and many developed countries. On the basis of Hofstede (1991) work, Table 1 shows the indices for four cultural dimensions and their implications for the society and institutions in Pakistan.

Table 1 indicates that the society and institutions in Pakistan tend to be highly rule oriented; power inequalities are allowed to grow and people at the top try to strengthen their position. These values contribute toward strict adherence to hierarchy, centralization, corruption, nepotism, and gender differentiation in administrative roles (Islam, 2004). Some of these values are in sharp contrast to the values of openness and user-centeredness as supported by Web 2.0 tools and applications. Comparison of the empirical data of 4th wave of World Values Survey also shows that intercultural variations of different values with moral import – trust, respect, responsibility, equality and power distance – exist between the Netherlands and Pakistan (Ahmed & Hoven, 2008).

According to the data, as most of the people in Pakistan accept and expect the power to be distributed unequally (because of moderate to high power distance), most of the decisions including the technology-related decisions are made at the top. Many times, the decision makers at the top do not know about technology. They seldom consider the advice of technology

Table 1. Cultural Dimensions and Index of Pakistan.

Cultural Dimension	Index	Implications
Masculinity	50	• Highly rule orientation to reduce the amount of uncertainty
Individualism	14	• Inequalities of power and wealth have been allowed to grow within the society
Power distance	55	
Uncertainty avoidance	70	• Caste system does not allow significant upward mobility of citizens
		• Creates a situation where leaders have virtually ultimate power and authority, and the rules, laws, and regulations developed by those in power reinforce their own leadership and control

Source: Data and implications taken from Hofstede.

people and sometimes take decisions on intuitions. Technical managers and lower staff do not take the responsibilities. Moderate to high "collectivism" leads to the favours among the groups. Most of the people at all levels in the institutions of these countries may oppose any ICT initiative including Web 2.0 for different reasons. Some of them think that ICT automates the processes and automated systems offer less chances of corruption. Yet others oppose because they are not well versed with ICTs; most of the ICTs including Web 2.0 applications require some basic skills and they lack them. Fredland (2000) indicated that technology transfer from West in developing countries means transfer of culture and values associated with that technology. That may be seen as demeaning and may be destructive to indigenous practices. Moderate to high "masculinity" leads to the competition among people. Moderate to high "uncertainty avoidance" leads to the negative attitudes toward change. People are afraid of change and they tend to develop thinking that their way of doing things is the better way. ICT brings change so they turn against any new technology that threatens to change their way of working. A low to moderate "long term orientation" or in other words "short term orientation" leads to short sightedness. People in countries with low "long term orientation" do not tend to consider the future as more important. Moreover, ICT initiatives require financial and technical support in future to be sustainable; but because of "short term orientation" these issues are not taken into account and once the project finishes, most of institutions face difficulties in sustaining the ICTs implementations.

Technology Enactment and Using ICTs for Politics
The seventh proposition of ITAF is related to challenges posed by technology enactment. As Fig. 1 shows:

Proposition 7. Information and communication technologies are usually implemented to reinforce existing institutional structures because of technology enactment. This proposition is based on technology enactment framework.

Perceptions about Web 2.0 applications by the stakeholders can lead to an attempt to shape the design, implementation, and use of the system. The user-centeredness, openness, and bottom-up content communication approach might mean loss of control and loss of power for the bureaucrats and proponents of top-down approach of communication. In a HE sector of a developing country – for example, Pakistan – leadership at the top might favor to redesign and implement those systems that reinforce their own leadership and control. Similarly, if stakeholders including users have wrong perceptions about a Web 2.0 application – for example, information on wikis is not reliable – then they would not be using it as a reliable source to acquire information.

The Gap

A gap exists in the ICT system and the institutional structures, practices, and work for which the ICT system is intended. This is because of the difference in assumptions regarding the values on which ICTs are built on the basis of values and structures of technology producing country (Proposition 5) and practices, and norms in the institutions of technology consuming country on the basis of its cultural variations of values and structures (Proposition 6).

As already mentioned, Web 2.0 services and applications are based on idea generation and knowledge sharing with tolerance for various ideas and thoughts by different groups at different levels. Whereas in a society and institutions of a developing country – for example, Pakistan – power inequalities are allowed to grow with little tolerance to new ideas and thoughts. This shows that a gap exists between the cultural variations of values and structures of Pakistan and values supported by Web 2.0 services and applications.

ICT Systems Alteration

The eighth proposition of ITAF stresses on systems alteration for cross-cultural implementation. As Fig. 1 shows:

> **Proposition 8.** ICT systems should be customized, adapted, and altered according to the local values and structures. This proposition is based on the idea of broadening up the scope of value sensitive design for considering intercultural variations of values during the implementation of imported ICT systems.

Detailed study and analysis needs to be done to propose the customizations and alterations in the design and working modalities of Web 2.0 systems, services, and applications for each implementation in HE of a developing country. Here a simple Web 2.0-related example is given.

Public editable wiki is based on an open philosophy. This means that anyone can join, create new wiki page, and edit the existing wiki page. Open wikis might not be very successful on as-is-basis in the higher education sector in a developing country. There might be a need to customize or change the design of wikis to be more successful in HE – that is, care should be taken that wikis are implemented in such a way that there is a proper oversight mechanism for the related topics because of the tendency for high rule-orientation to reduce the amount of uncertainty. These types of considerations could help in reducing the resistance to accept wikis in HE sector work environment and in sustaining the wiki system in the longer run.

Management Methodology
The ninth proposition of ITAF is related to the alteration in management and implementation modalities. As Fig. 1 shows:

Proposition 9. Different management and implementation styles for technology implementation and sustainability should be used in different cultures and societies.

As discussed by Ahmed (2008d) for parliamentary Web portal development projects, there can be different administrative, operational, and management issues, challenges, and problems during the project conception and implementation of Web 2.0 related systems in HE in developing countries. These include:

1. Unawareness about Web 2.0 usage and potentials
2. Unwillingness of some stakeholders to introduce new systems
3. Slow and bureaucratic working styles in the institutions
4. Resistance by the staff
5. Favoritism and corruption during different phases
6. Decisions regarding development and hosting platforms
7. Over optimism
8. Technocratic approaches
9. Poor interpersonal relationships
10. Poor communication
11. Scope creep

All the above challenges and issues can be shown to be directly or indirectly related to intercultural variations of values and structures (Ahmed, 2008d). Developing effective leadership, creating acceptance by stakeholders, training of using Web 2.0 applications and services, change management training and proper evaluation are some of the solutions proposed to tackle these challenges. For detailed proposed solutions to tackle these challenges, see the solutions proposed by (Ahmed, 2008a, 2008d). Another important thing, to stress here, is that intercultural variations of values, social structures, and institutional structures should be acknowledged, considered, and planned for during the conception, implementation, and management of Web 2.0 systems.

Right Equilibrium
The tenth proposition of ITAF stresses on achieving the right equilibrium. As Fig. 1 shows:

> **Proposition 10.** A balance should be maintained while customizing, adapting, and altering the ICT systems design and project management/ implementation modalities so that the systems are not altered to the extent that they are implemented just to reinforce the existing institutional values and structures. Right equilibrium should be achieved. System should support those values, which are considered more legitimate and necessary.

In case of implementation of wikis in HE sector of a developing country, care has to be taken that, the oversight mechanism should not be re-designed and enforced to the extent that it poses bureaucratic hurdles and delays for the approval of wiki pages. The process should be transparent, quick, and well documented. Owing to bureaucratic and slow working environments in the institutions of a developing country like Pakistan (Islam, 2004), management and implementation modalities should not be altered to the extent that systems get over timed, over budgeted, and thus failed.

As intercultural variations of values and structures exist between developing countries, therefore quality issues in HE in different developing countries may also vary. Different kinds of customizations, alterations, and adaptation of ICTs, systems and management processes and modalities might be needed in different scenarios and in different countries. Successful implementation and sustainability of ICT system after customization, alteration, and adaption in a HE sector of one developing country cannot guarantee the successful implementation and sustainability of the same system in a HE sector of another developing country. The same analogy might also be true for two HEIs in a same developing country.

We have also discussed that ICTs can enforce existing values or can affect the existing values and structures. It might also be true when ICT systems with certain underlying value assumptions are successfully implemented, used, and sustained in a technology consuming country with cultural variations in values as compared to the value assumptions in ICTs and systems. This can lead to the discussion that ICTs including Web 2.0 services and applications can be used in HE in developing countries to change the degree of variations of those values, norms, practices, and structures, due to which quality issues exist.

RECOMMENDATIONS AND CONCLUSIONS

An indirect capability approach perspective on cross-cultural implementation of Web 2.0 applications and tools discusses that social web can improve the capabilities and functioning at the institutional level and at the stakeholders' level by strengthening the infrastructure, processes, and environment in HE sector of developing countries. Web 2.0 applications and services – that is, social and professional networking web systems, wikis, and blogs – can be used for exchange of ideas and cooperation among different stakeholders of the HE sector of developing countries. This interaction and collaboration can provide helpful ideas for overcoming quality issues in the higher education of developing countries.

ICT is developed with certain underlying assumptions about values, norms, and structures. Indeed technologies never exist in a vacuum: know-how and special skills are embodied and embedded somewhere (Goulet, 1975). People and social systems affect the technological development (Friedman, Kahn, & Borning, 2002) in a given society. Therefore, to introduce and implement an ICT system in a new environment – for example, in a new country or an institution having cultural variations of values and structures – ICTs and the related management and implementation processes have to be customized, adapted, and altered (if required) according to the requirements of new environment.

HEIs in developing countries should learn from the success stories as well as from the failures of experimenting with Web 2.0 in the HEIs of the developed countries. They should benchmark the education information systems of HEIs of developed countries and follow the implementation of ICT projects best practices; however, at the same time, they should be customizing, altering, and adapting the systems according to local needs and their cultural variations of values and structures. Otherwise, ICTs and systems might result in creating more quality issues than resolving the existing ones.

The HEIs should be careful in investing newer technologies and tools because Web 2.0 can burst like the dot-com bubble; and it matters to HEIs if resources and data are invested in new and untested applications, which are not subsequently supported adequately or are backed by companies that eventually fail (Anderson, 2007). Web 2.0 technologies are also changing at the rapid pace. Therefore, HEIs should be careful in investing the Web 2.0 technologies and application so that return on investments and efforts could be made possible.

In the end, we stress that technology can act as an enabler, and to be effective, as noted by Gordon (2005), it has to be a part of a comprehensive solution, which must also address organizational, management and, last but not least, legal and regulatory issues. The potential benefits of adopting e-technology can only materialize when technology is introduced as part of well-planned and properly supported social and cultural environment (Asgarkhani, 2005) keeping in mind the leadership, political, and infrastructural situation of the specific developing country.

REFERENCES

Adam, L. (2003). Information and communication technologies in higher education in Africa: Initiatives and challenges. *Journal of Higher Education in Africa*, *1*(1), 195–221.

Ahmed, M. A. (2008a). Developing parliamentary web portals for citizens, MPs and related groups – Challenges and proposed solutions. Paper presented at the IEEE International Symposium on Technology and Society, 2008 (ISTAS 2008).

Ahmed, M. A. (2008b). Improving practicum and internship through ICT in developing countries. Paper presented at the International Conference on Transforming Teacher Education: Improving Practicum and Internship, Lahore, Pakistan, March 26–28.

Ahmed, M. A. (2008c). Information technology transferring from developed to developing countries – technology alteration: A basic framework. Paper presented at the Technology, Management and Policy Graduate Consortium.

Ahmed, M. A. (2008d). Management of ICT projects to strengthen public sector institutions in developing countries: A proposed methodology. Paper presented at the Comsats International Conference on Management (CICM), Lahore, Pakistan.

Ahmed, M. A. (2010a). A capabilities approach perspective on aid assisted e-government projects. Paper presented at the WORLDCOMP'10 – The 2010 World Congress in Computer Science, Computer Engineering, and Applied Computing.

Ahmed, M. A. (2010b). Equilibrium for CMC systems' alteration – An intercultural perspective. Paper presented at the IEEE International Symposium on Technology and Society.

Ahmed, M. A. (2010c). Improving information capabilities of parliamentary stakeholders through ICTs in developing countries. Paper presented at the WORLDCOMP'10 – The 2010 World Congress in Computer Science, Computer Engineering, and Applied Computing.

Ahmed, M. A., & Hoven, J. V. D. (2008). Cultural variations of values – Challenge for information and communication technology transferring projects in the globalizing world. Paper presented at the SAICON, 2008 South Asian International Conference 2008 – Globalisation & Change: Issues, Concerns & Impact Bhurbun, Pakistan.

Alexander, B. (2006). Web 2.0: A new wave of innovation for teaching and learning? *EDUCAUSE Review*, *41*(2), 32–44.

Anderson, P. (2007). What is Web 2.0? Ideas, technologies and implications for education. *JISC Technology and Standards Watch*, February. Available at http://www.jisc.ac.uk/media/documents/techwatch/tsw0701b.pdf

Asgarkhani, M. (2005). The effectiveness of e-service in local government: A case study. *Electronic Journal of e-Government*, *3*(4), 157–166.

David, E. M., & Martin, R. (2006). Web 2.0: Hypertext by any other name? Paper presented at the Proceedings of the seventeenth conference on hypertext and hypermedia.

Ebner, M., Holzinger, A., & Maurer, H. (2007). Web 2.0 technology: Future interfaces for technology enhanced learning? In C. Stephanidis (Ed.), *Universal access in human–computer interaction*. 4th International Conference on Universal Access in Human–Computer Interaction, UAHCI 2007, held as part of HCI International 2007, Beijing, China, July 22–27, 2007, proceedings (pp. 559–568). Berlin: Springer.

Ess, C. (2008). Culture and global networks: hope for a global ethics? In: J. V. D. Hoven & J. Weckert (Eds), *Information technology and moral philosophy* (pp. 195–225). Cambridge: Cambridge University Press.

Franklin, T., & Harmelen, M. V. (2007). *Web 2.0 for content for learning and teaching in higher education*. Available at: www.citeulike.org/group/1572/article/1378679

Fredland, R. A. (2000). Technology transfer to the public sector in developing states: Three phases. *The Journal of Technology Transfer*, *25*(3), 265–275.

Friedman, B., Kahn, P., & Borning, A. (2002). Value sensitive design: Theory and methods. Technical Report 02-12-01. Department of Computer Science and Engineering, University of Washington, Seattle, WA.

Gordon, S. (2006). Rise of the blog [journal-based website]. *IEE Review*, *52*(3), 32–35.

Gordon, T. F. (2005). Information technology for good governance. Paper presented at the French-German Symposium on Governance, Law and Technology, University of Paris.

Goulet, D. A. (1975). The paradox of technology transfer. *Bulletin of the Atomic Scientists*, *31*(6), 39–46.

Heeks, R. (2003). Most egovernment-for-development projects fail: How can risks be reduced? Paper no. 14. Manchester: Institute for Development Policy and Management, University of Manchester.

Hofstede, G. (1991). *Cultures and organizations*. New York: McGraw-Hill.

Hofstede, G. (2010). Cultural dimensions. Geert Hofstede BV. Velp, Netherlands. Available at http://www.geert-hofstede.com/

Islam, N. (2004). Sifarish, sycophants, power and collectivism: Administrative culture in Pakistan. *International Review of Administrative Sciences*, *70*(2), 311–330.

McLoughlin, C. (2008). *Web 2.0 in higher education in Australia*. New York, UK: Franklin Consulting.

Nussbaum, M. C. (2000). *Women and human development: The capabilities approach*. New York: Cambridge University Press.

Oldervoll, J., Boge, C., & Stre, S. K. (2009). KARK: A learning tool at the University of Bergen, Norway. Paper presented at the INTED 2009-International Technology, Education and Development Conference, Valencia, Spain.

Penenberg, A. L. (2005). Like it or not, blogs have legs. Available at http://www.wired.com/culture/lifestyle/news/2005/01/66336?currentPage=all. Retrieved on May 18, 2009.

Pulman, A. (2008). *Blogging @ BU: IHCS case studies*. Working Paper. Poole: CEMP, Bournemouth University. Available at http://www.cemp.ac.uk/downloads/CEMP-PAPERS-Blogging.pdf

Richardson, W. (2006). *Blogs, wikis, podcasts, and other powerful web tools for classrooms*. Thousand Oaks, CA: Corwin Press.

Sen, A. (1999). *Development as freedom*. New York: Knopf.

Sife, A. S., Lwoga, E. T., & Sanga, C. (2007). New technologies for teaching and learning: Challenges for higher learning institutions in developing countries. *International Journal of Education and Development using Information and Communication Technology*, *3*(2), 57–67.

UNESCO. (n.d.). Background and evolution – universities and information and communica-
    tion technologies. Available at http://www.unesco.org/iau/icts/index.html. Retrieved on
    May 18, 2009.
Ward, R. (2006). Blogs and wikis: A personal journey. *Business Information Review*, *23*(4), 235–240.
WVS. (n.d.). World values survey. Available at http://www.worldvaluesurvey.org. Retrieved on
    May 18, 2009.

PART II
PROCESSES IN LEARNING
AND INSTRUCTION WITH
SOCIAL MEDIA

A SOCIAL MEDIA APPROACH
TO HIGHER EDUCATION

Marlyn Tadros

ABSTRACT

With the majority of the educated younger generations increasingly connected and forming online communities, formal education finds itself competing for their attention. Not only that, but online activities have a profound effect on student learning behaviors and capabilities. The importance of engaging students in new and emerging technologies in education cannot be overemphasized because it is, in essence, a worthwhile investment into their futures. Technology creates a more engaging and innovative classroom experience that makes students more interested in the learning process if the correct tools are used.

Social media tools give students the ability to think critically and creatively. More significantly, they allow student engagement with their teachers and more effective and engaging collaboration with their peers, and perhaps even outreach across cultural divides.

This chapter discusses the benefits of using social media for both students and teachers as well as some of the drawbacks and obstacles. The chapter also presents several examples of using social media in the classroom.

Educating Educators with Social Media
Cutting-edge Technologies in Higher Education, Volume 1, 83–105
Copyright © 2011 by Emerald Group Publishing Limited
All rights of reproduction in any form reserved
ISSN: 2044-9968/doi:10.1108/S2044-9968(2011)0000001007

Non scholae sed vitae discimus
                                              – Seneca, 1st-century philosopher

INTRODUCTION

The importance of engaging students in new and emerging technologies in education cannot be overestimated. Using social media creates a more engaging and innovative classroom experience if one is to see education as a life experience that engages students in the process of their own learning rather than making them knowledge databases or receptacles. In his *Pedagogy of the Oppressed*, Freire (2000) calls this latter method the "banking concept of education" where "students are the depositories and the teacher is the depositor. Instead of communicating, the teacher issues communiques and makes deposits which the students patiently receive, memorize, and repeat." Freire views this as master–slave relationship where

> knowledge is a gift bestowed by those who consider themselves knowledgeable upon those whom they consider to know nothing. Projecting an absolute ignorance onto others, a characteristic of the ideology of oppression, negates education and knowledge as processes of inquiry. The teacher presents himself to his students as their necessary opposite; by considering their ignorance absolute, he justifies his own existence. The students, alienated like the slave in the Hegelian dialectic, accept their ignorance as justifying the teachers existence – but unlike the slave, they never discover that they educate the teacher. (2000)

Freire also finds that this method is "based on a mechanistic, static, naturalistic, spatialized view of consciousness, it transforms students into receiving objects. It attempts to control thinking and action, leads women and men to adjust to the world, and inhibits their creative power" (Freire, 2000).

On the contrary, engaging students in the learning process means getting students to relate what they have learned to their real lives, encourages critical thinking and nurtures self-motivation. Social media has the potential to achieve this goal and to substantially alter the learning process. If, as Seneca says, we learn for life not for school, then integrating technology into the classroom to help students learn through the medium they feel most comfortable with is of utmost importance.

But what is social media? In my view, social media are any media that help integrate technology into the lives of people for the purpose of communication. While many view it as only computer-mediated communications, it is also applicable to mobile technology such as mobile phones, book readers, and other handheld devices.

A casual discussion with instructors and professors will immediately reveal the depth of the on-going debate and the excitement and concerns regarding social media. The spectrum spans from the total technophobes on the one hand to the tech-savvy on the other, with many others in between. Among the on-going debates, the following questions arise: how should the classroom respond to the overwhelming distractions of constant connectivity? Should the pedagogy change? Should faculty continue to compete for student attention and hang on to prevalent methods of teaching or should they learn the new media themselves and reinvent their teaching methodology? Even if there is agreement as to the need for using social media, some question whether one would be sacrificing depth for breadth. This chapter attempts to provide some insight into the benefits of using social media as well as the challenges that this use creates in a 21st-century classroom. It will also provide four examples of social media usage in education using web 2.0 tools.

FORSAKING THE TRADITIONAL?

The traditional role of academia, as correctly summarized by Richard Katz (2009), lay primarily in it being an artisan and elite community isolated from society organized around scarcity of resources where academic activities are bundled and where they are physically present in a geographical place. Traditionally therefore, colleges and universities were purveyors and collectors of knowledge. Universities provided a regimented physical space that focused on knowledge dissemination.

When a high school principal decided to ban Facebook and asked parents to stop their children from social media web sites because it encouraged bullying, many parents unthinkingly complied (Portnoy, 2010). The fact that technology has become so ubiquitous makes it hard to believe that students will not find a way to access computers or to access their favorite networking sites especially if they have been banned from them. Some teachers ban laptops and cell phones in class. For those teachers, social media constitutes a grave distraction and affects behavior. Banning those devices might be a not-so-unpopular solution, and in many cases, there is consensus about banning them. Those teachers tend to hang onto traditional methods of teaching, which are largely lecture-based sometimes adding discussions and interactive play, in themselves very worthy causes.

They use blackboard and chalk or whiteboard and markers, provide a written syllabus, use and encourage the use of libraries, provide quizzes and/ or multiple-choice questions, and sometimes require one or two projects as final assignments. Many use PowerPoint presentations. Students are asked to use notebooks, pens, highlighters and books. Needless to say, a large number of students also prefer this method of teaching and learning because it is more linear and structured, and they do not do well in nonlinear and more randomized constructs.

Networked students, on the contrary, use MySpace, Facebook, Twitter, YouTube, and text messaging among others to communicate. They also communicate through graphically rich animations and simulations from synthetic worlds such as World of Warcraft to Second Life. Even more intriguingly, they almost speak an alien language and no longer conform to grammatically correct sentences or to regular spell-checkers. They have their own devised "sign language" that consists of short-handing words and using what is known as "emoticons" to denote facial expressions. As many more social networking sites and opportunities emerge every day, their very social landscape is changing as well as how their brains are wired (Hotchkiss, 2009; Manfield, 2009; Prensky, 2001). University professor and renowned writer Howard Rheingold (2009) put it succinctly:

> I face university students in my classes on a regular basis who are gazing at their laptops while I or another student talks. As far as I can tell, these screen-tropic students might be taking notes or they might be rallying their guild in "World of Warcraft" or changing their Facebook status to "it's complicated."

Should we then abandon the traditional method of teaching and instruction in favor of new media that students are more familiar with? My answer would be an emphatic no because (a) social media is an alternative to some but not all current classroom environments (b) from personal experience, some students continue to prefer the old method of teaching and (c) because social media are just tools to further education and not a goal in themselves. Educators should not take for granted that all our students are digital natives: as Howard (2009) puts it "age is not the measure [of being a digital native], it's knowledge, application, and understanding that defines the immigrant. Everyone else is a digital alien, regardless of age." Those students need to be brought into social media-focused education at a much slower pace.

Social media puts the role of educators in a completely different light to correspond with the new paradigm shift from teacher/curriculum-centered education to learner/student-centered education with "students sharing their own knowledge and opinions and forming their own conclusions about the issues" (Buckingham, 2003). Educators, as Buckingham rightly notes, "can no longer see themselves as 'legislators,' imposing the values and norms of official culture. The best they can hope for is to act as 'interpreters,' making available 'multiple realities' and diverse forms of perception and knowledge" (2003). Much to our chagrin, educators cannot be guardians of language either. When students devise their own language this is a natural progression of language to correspond with the changing times – from linear to nonlinear reading and writing methods:

> What will change – what already is changing, in fact – is *the way we read and write*. In the past, changes in writing technologies, such as the shift from scroll to book, had dramatic effects on the kind of ideas that people put down on paper and, more generally, on people's intellectual lives. Now that we're leaving behind the page and adopting the screen as our main medium for reading, we'll see similarly far-reaching changes in the way we write, read, and even think. (Carr, 2010)

What the principal who banned Facebook and others like him have lost sight of is that the new generation, otherwise known as digital natives (Prensky, 2001), the Millennials (Howe & Straus, 2000), Gen Y (Anderson, 2010), the Nomadics (Reynard, 2008), or the Net Geners (Tapscott, 2009), among others, cannot cope with traditional methods. Born and raised in the information overload age where data is ubiquitous and information no farther than a click of the mouse, they have developed characteristics and habits that are profoundly different from the traditional student of old times. Tapscott (2009) calls those characteristics the 8 norms of Net Geners:

1. they want freedom in everything they do, from freedom of choice to freedom of expression
2. they love to customize, personalize
3. they are scrutinizers
4. they look for corporate integrity and openness when deciding what to buy and where to work
5. they want entertainment and play in their work, education, and social life.
6. they are the collaboration and relationship generation
7. they have a need for speed – and not just in video games
8. they are the innovators

Needless to say, previous generations had those same desires as well, but the difference is that they did not have the same opportunities or the means to achieve them. The Net Geners however being "bathed in bits" (Tapscott,

2009) have the means to achieve those norms at their fingertips. It is true that students had always come from specific cultural and social backgrounds with pre-determined ideas and environments, and educators have had to improve upon existing pedagogies. Nevertheless, students in the digital age bring with them additional layers of complexity:

> an extensive network of information input, peer connections, and the potential of a wider scope of application than what has been the case until now. The negative side of things is the challenge of "managing" not only the multitasking of the students but their insistence upon continual connectivity even when participating in a physical learning space with an instructor and other physical peers around them. (Reynard, 2008)

In addition to the above, students of the net generation are also carving for themselves a public sphere that is different from that of their pre-decessors, one in which they are able to express their views, be widely heard and receive peer criticism and support. This creates a blurring between their public spheres and their private spheres as they seek to find a place and identity in their newly discovered social spaces. Anderson (2010) goes as far as to say that "a fundamental shift is occurring in human identity and activity in communities" spurred on by mobile devices, where

> the benefits to people of sharing information and disclosing details about themselves are becoming more evident. These perceived benefits will change over time as Millennials' interests change, but the general pattern for disclosure will remain. The historic pattern is for each generation to change the boundaries of privacy and identity.

This invasive technology is explored but not fully comprehended by the Net Geners. They may consciously publish images online that may affect their future employment prospects or they may inadvertently publish images that were not intended for "public consumption." In fact, the net generation online often "renegotiate" what is public and what is private and "push at, explore and transgress established norms of public and private. They relish the potential of the media to offer the flexible tools and the free spaces within which to construct their individuality and relationships" (Livingstone, 2005). In spite of this, they are not always conscious of its implications.

While not necessarily tech-savvy in the sense of being able to understand the technology they are using nor use it to its educational potential, they are nevertheless connected in such ways as to make them think differently and acquire different problem-solving techniques:

> Information-age learners prefer doing to knowing, trial-and-error to logic, and typing to handwriting. Multitasking is a way of life for them, staying connected is essential, and there is zero tolerance for delays. Further, modern literacy includes not only text but also

image and screen literacy – it involves navigating information and assembling knowledge
from fragments. (Jones & Pritchard, 2000)

In addition, at risk of unscientific generalization, and from pure
observation as a teacher, I will venture to say that with information coming
at them in quick succession and in seemingly chaotic sequences through
hyper-linking, they have become impatient learners with short attention spans
who need instant gratification. When looking at students in a classroom, there
is what one may term "mass ADD," or as Rheingold (2009) noted "attention
going wild" caused by the abundance of digital media and information
coming at us from all those screens. This relatively new connectivity brought
with it open resources that are affecting accessibility to previously scarce
resources. Instead of going to a library and doing extensive research,
information is readily accessible online at the click of a mouse. This creates an
impatience that has the tendency to lead to a level of superficiality when it
comes to research and academic achievement.

But "academic achievement" is not exactly what those students are
looking for. While they do seek to have well-paying jobs and positions, they
do not view this as something they will get from structured education.
Educators must not lose sight of the fact that a good portion of their students
are more knowledgeable about technology than their teachers and hence
view education as just a required certificate for a job application. Their real
learning curve lies through the path they choose for themselves online,
whether it is social networking sites, online tutorials, peer learning and
reviews, or any other.

Students' experiences are forcing changes that even the most reluctant
naysayers among educators will have to embrace to continue to be relevant.
The dominant culture – in this case the constant connectivity – cannot be
ignored. Watkins (2009) rightly states,

Young people's persistent and innovative engagement with technology is forcing
educators across the country to rethink a host of issues including, for instance, the role
of technology in curriculum design, the personal use of technology on campus ... and
what digital media and technology means, more generally, for the social, emotional, and
educational development of school-age students.

A great example of the digital media mindset is Dan Brown, a former
student at a distinguished college, who produced a video of himself and
posted it to YouTube calling it *An Open Letter to Educators*. In this video,
he announced that he dropped out of college and decided to teach himself
whatever he wanted because, according to him, information is now cheap
and "the monetary value of education equals zero" (Brown, 2010). In a

response to him on his message board, one student wrote, "The younger generation just realize(sic) that you can learn more about the world in your room on your computer than from your parents." While there was an overwhelming support on the message board for Brown's video, one student who also concurred provided an alternative:

> It is entirely possible to sculpt the classroom into a learning process that benefits from the "digital rewiring", and this is an infinitely(sic) better process for enhancing today's society's required competences, than the lectures of old.

Although every generation has its dropouts who believe they are better informed than their teachers or peers, the difference in this case is that Brown managed to publicize his opinions on a larger scale and gain a wide audience through his peers' most accessed and one of the most popular sites, hence generating debate and gaining peer-respect. Educators also became involved in responding to him and consequently an important and note-worthy debate ensued and continues to this day.

Not all students are Dan Browns. Nevertheless, the Dan Browns in this digital age are in abundance and are increasing. To remain relevant, in lieu of banning social networking sites, educators must do what Rheingold (2009) suggested in his series on Attention: "awaken a literacy of attention in classrooms and elsewhere" because it is not about seeing information but "about being in charge of which information we pay attention to." In addition,

> if we don't actively construct, tune, and manage our own information filters, the raw flow of info, misinfo, and disinfo around us will take charge. It's up to each consumer of information to make personal decisions about what to pay attention to and what to ignore. That decision-making is a mental process that all humans have always deployed in the world, but the world that we evolved in through pre-digital eons has been hyper-accelerated recently through our use of the media we've created. We need to attune those native attention filters to our contemporary needs. (Rheingold, 2009)

Educators also need to engage students in constructive dialog. The question that needs to be asked is the following: what do social networking sites and accessibility to them bring to students that we cannot bring them? One suggestion is that it brings connectivity and "relationship":

> In the parlance of internet marketing speak, there is a distinction between the web as principally an awareness media versus a relationship media. The idea being that people want to use the internet not principally as a reference library, but as a way to meet, and talk to, a reference librarian. It is not smart TV, but smart telephony. (Hallis, 2000)

Traditional methods should be revised and educators need to reconfigure relationships with students and with the technology they use that now redefines their social identities. In a paper presented at an MIT conference, one student wrote that rather than viewing social media as tools to bring into the classroom "educational technology more accurately represents a bridge, which enables engagement, exchange, and empathy between communities of learners" (Gonzalez-Appling, 2009). Social networking is therefore not just a tool but a culture of its own that educators need to recognize and embrace.

FORESEEABLE TRENDS AND NEW PEDAGOGIES

In its annual report entitled *IFAP World Report 2009*, UNESCO's *Information for All Program* lists cultural trends affecting the future of education. Among them are the emergence of 3D browsing and the merging of virtual worlds with reality; the use of smartphones and Googlephones; standardized web connectivity in new televisions with 3D technology; spread of e-readers; and finally increased "blog democracy."

Specifically, according to the report, new "breakthrough" trends have begun affecting information for all, not least among them is social networking:

> Social networking is creating a 'cultural revolution' whereby individuals behave in a cooperative way, facilitates the formation of communities, self-organization and self expression as well as social interaction and feedback: "All of this is carried out in a horizontal structure without an institutional framework, sub- and superordination and control. This is all a kind of new cultural revolution: technology is ever more easy to use and man eventually enters the limelight, increasingly translating itself, its communities and society into an online world, which is thus becoming ever more integrated into everyday life. (IFAP, 2010)

Similarly, in the *Horizon Report*, Levine, Smith, and Stone (2010) named four key drivers of technology adoptions for the period 2010 through 2015. They are as follows:

1. The abundance of resources and relationships made easily accessible through the Internet, which is increasingly challenging us to revisit our roles as educators in sense-making, coaching, and credentialing.
2. People expect to be able to work, learn, and study whenever and wherever they want.

3. The technologies we use are increasingly cloud-based, and our notions of IT support are decentralized.
4. The work of students is increasingly seen as collaborative by nature, and there is more cross-campus collaboration between departments.

What does this mean for educators? Many books and articles have been written about what makes a great teacher. This criterion does not change regardless of the technology used. Kincheloe (2005) writes,

> the very teachers who we think are amazing, life affirming, intellectually challenging agents of a democratic education are viewed as threats by the advocates of standardization in this repressive era. These are teachers who seek out diverse perspectives, confront students with conflicting information and different interpretations of the same data. They have the audacity to raise questions in the minds of their students and colleagues about the nature and purpose of what's going on in their schools.

More recently, Andrew Churches provided eight characteristics of the 21st-century teacher: being a risk taker, a collaborator, a model, a leader, a visionary, a learner, a communicator, and an adaptor (2008). New tools of engagement may be used to achieve those same results but with student engagement and collaboration. Educators may ask themselves how, if at all, could students benefit from bringing social media into the classroom? What could new media offer that is not found in the traditional method of instruction?

> networked environments thrive on abundance and complexity. The more people use them, tag them, mash them up, and remix them, the more useful they become. In many ways this is the opposite of what happens in institutional environments trying to manage scarce resources. For example, lectures enable one expert to teach many; office hours schedule scarce faculty time; curriculum and course syllabi standardize content; class schedules pace interactions; and credit hours standardize outcomes. OER and Web 2.0 are creating an abundance of what has been scarce in the past while enabling us to manage the growing complexity. (Geith, 2008)

New media offers self-expression, problem-solving skills, networking, expertise, communication, freedom, democracy [wikis and blogs], and the expansion of horizons beyond the classroom into the community and beyond. Alternately, one needs to think what traditional methods of education offer technology-based education? Perhaps, it can offer depth, critical thinking, systematic logic, and controlled chaos in lieu of randomness.

The new pedagogy should also include information literacy in a world immersed in ubiquitous data. However, it should also take into consideration the type of students who attend college and should be able to change and adapt to the existing cultural and social environments. Teaching should shift to be more student-centered, encouraging student-engagement, critical thinking, with abundance of activities and project-based assignments.

Educators and learners will need to learn how to participate effectively in an abundant data world. New ways of seeing, knowing, and communicating will redefine learning environments, roles, and even forms of knowledge, knowing, and assessment. (Knowledge Works Foundation, 2009)

CHALLENGES

Because integrating social media in the classroom has an interdisciplinary nature, many educators are understandably resistant to it. In using social media, there is a combination of literature with technology skills; copyright, intellectual property, and privacy issues with media in all its forms such as video and photography; and freedom of speech and politics as well as possibly writing and research with blogging and online digital rights. The following are other obstacles that impede the use of social media in higher education – some with short-term and others will long-term repercussions:

- Not all Millennials are tech-savvy in a constructive way. Some students who use mobile phones, texting, e-mail, and video games, even though born and raised surrounded by technology may not necessarily be tech-savvy and may not be able to use a computer. Those students are multitasking students, but nevertheless, they are easily distracted and need some informed instruction (Scanlon, 2009; Howard, 2009). In addition, students who have the skills for gaming and texting may not necessarily have the skills to use new media.
- Social media creates a new digital divide because those students who do not have access to computers in the first place have no access to anything and not just education. They will fall behind more creating a wider digital gap as the world becomes increasingly dependent on social media.
- Social media could create an instructor digital divide between those who know the technology and can use it and those who cannot. Some instructors are technophobes and others simply not willing to learn or do not have the time to learn or devise new methods of teaching. When adopting technology in the classroom, teachers begin to assume new roles that they are perhaps far from ready to adopt.
- Perception of loss of control: "Having a blog to begin with in higher education can be controversial, and opening up the comments feature to allow two-way dialog can be frightening" (Reuben, 2008).

- The web has an ephemeral nature: everything is changing. It will negatively affect scholarly work.
- How do the "norms and rules of real-world student-faculty relationships fit the world of online social media and online campus culture" (Alemán & Wartman, 2009)?
- The proliferation of online social media tools which makes it difficult to remain current with the most recent tools or to find the tools one would need for teaching a specific topic.

In Watkins (2009), a school principal who was interviewed rightly noted that in using social media, the real challenge is education: "educating staff, faculty and parents about the use of digital media ... it's a great tool when used responsibly." That same principal said that failing to educate students about the digital world they are so immersed in is like failing any other area of their academic and "personal development."

In social media-based instruction, educators need to have a flexibility and fluidity in syllabi structure and need to rethink presentation methods and student assignments. Faculty needs to have extensive conversations about interdisciplinary collaboration and about their technology needs. Cooperation between the tech-savvy and lecture-based instructors might be one solution. For example, for an English literature teacher, a tech-savvy instructor may introduce some technologies that would enhance the classic teaching environment including creating a digital map of some timeline, or a history professor could use digital maps to trace the journey of historic figures.

REACHING BEYOND THE CLASSROOM

The following are suggestions for paving the way to using social media in the classroom:

1. Encouraging debate and discussion of real world topics related to the issue at hand. Social media allows younger people to engage in debates and discussions on topics of their interest and one can use this to encourage this type of interaction.
2. Eliminating multiple-choice quizzes. Although they facilitate grading for teachers, they do not show the strengths nor weaknesses of a student. They are dry and are mostly based on guess work. They test only what a student can digest or remember in his/her superficial memory – material

that disappears as soon as that quiz is over. According to Beetham (2007),

> the current generation of digital technologies is better suited to open ended outcomes than the technologies of the instructional design era. Simulations and virtual environments are used to foster exploration rather than a linear progression through materials. Individual learning logs and e-portfolios allow learners to collate evidence towards broadly defined learning goals, and to reflect on their progress. Collaborative technologies and VLEs can be used to capture dialogue, bringing to light the processes as well as the outcomes of learning.

Such a curricular design will be "learner-centered" but, as Beetham warns, "only if there are sufficient teaching resources to support them effectively."

1. Basing activities in class on teamwork skills and strengthening collaboration between students. Instructors can begin by using collaborative technologies such as wikis and blogging.
2. Creating connections (Gonzalez-Appling, 2009): How is what we are studying now connected to a student's real life? How is it connected to life in general; to the past, present, and future? McLaren (2003) calls this the "macro objectives" that are designed to

> enable students to make connections between the methods, content, and structure of a course and its significance within the larger social reality. This dialectical approach to classroom objectives allows students to acquire a broad frame of reference or worldview; in other words, it helps them acquire a political perspective. Students can then make the hidden curriculum explicit and develop a critical political consciousness.

In a study by the Florida Online Reading Professional Development (2004), the author suggested bringing up connections by using the following sentences:

This part reminds me of …

I felt like … (character) when I …

If that happened to me I would …

This book reminds me of … (another text) because …

I can relate to … (part of text) because one time …

Something similar happened to me when …

SOME POTENTIAL MEDIA TOOLS

A good start for many teachers is to use blogging or wikis with their students. Blogging is the earliest form of social networking and perhaps the most popular among faculty. Wikis are newer but they are collaborative software that enable students to create online material through team work. The following are concrete examples of using diverse social media tools that might be more engaging to students:

Wikipedia

Many instructors reject *Wikipedia* as a source of reliable information. Based on crowd-sourcing, Wikipedia, these instructors claim, is an example of superficiality and the abundance of erroneous data on the web. Crowd-sourcing is not about "wisdom of the crowds" but about misinformed people adding unreliable information. According to this rationale, it is bound to lower the conventional standards of research and education. In addition, given its ephemeral nature, it is not the best resource for citation.

Like it or not, *Wikipedia* is being widely used by students. Ask the majority of students about anything and they will pull up a *Wikipedia* definition especially because it is ranked higher in search engine results. If not used for a full research, it is used to gather initial information and data on a topic before conducting a full research and, at the very least, is used "in combination with other information resources" (Head & Eisenberg, 2010). Conventional libraries and encyclopedias no longer meet student expectations of fast, retrievable information. Head and Eisenberg noted that "*Wikipedia* meets the needs of college students because it offers a mixture of coverage, currency, convenience, and comprehensibility in a world where credibility is less of a given or an expectation from today's students." *Wikipedia* is an encyclopedia of the people by the people. Why then could we not channel that resource into an educational experience?

Following the advice of a presenter at a conference organized by the New Media Consortium, I asked students in a few of my classes to make a *Wikipedia* entry or edit an existing stub. The purpose was not only to demonstrate *Wikipedia*'s reliability as a resource but also to encourage them to conduct research and become producers instead of consumers of information. Many students dismissed the notion that crowd-sourcing would work or that peer-to-peer information-sharing was worthy when it comes to significant topics. Toward the end of the semester, each student had created an entry or edited an existing page. The following are some of the results:

- Many students were surprised they had to learn some code to post to Wikipedia and enjoyed checking out the code created in other postings and imitated them.
- Students were amazed at how much research they had to do before posting to Wikipedia.
- Students who posted without proper research or without correct citation had their entries removed by others within 24 hours of posting.
- Students who tried to post images had to verify that the image belonged to them or that it was in the public domain.
- Students found themselves engaged with others, sometimes half way across the globe, discussing why or why not an entry was good or bad, working on editing, and refining their work in a collaborative manner.
- One particular student from Chad wrote about Chadian music and was actually contacted by singers and producers within two weeks of posting who interviewed him as an "authority" on the issue. This increased his self-confidence and sense of achievement in many ways.
- Although students initially had doubts about the assignment, many stated that they would continue refining their entries even after the semester was over.

This is an example of how one can channel what students are most familiar with into an informative and challenging assignment. Needless to say while most students created excellent entries, there were some who faltered and the assignment had no particular interest for them.

Twitter

According to a Pew Center research (Lenhart, 2009) nearly one in five (19%) online adults ages 18–24 used Twitter or updated a status online, as have 20% of online young adults ages 25–34. Nevertheless when I suggest Twitter to students, they treat it with disdain because they do not quite understand why they need to write about "what are you doing now." That motto in Twitter has changed to "what's happening" and when we begin looking at Twitter from that angle, it slowly begins to make sense. I have explained to my students that one can also Twitter by cell phone and began listing the many ways twittering was a more effective way of transmitting brief and concise information than other networking sites.

What would happen if Hamlet or Macbeth had Twitter? This is a question I asked students based on a book I read entitled *Twitterature*, written by two students at the University of Chicago who rewrote many of the classics in 20 tweets or less. An example of such tweets from *Hamlet* in *Twitterature* (Aciman & Rensin, 2010) is as follows:

> Gonna try to talk some sense into Mom because boyfriend totally killed Dad. I sense this is the moment of truth, the moment of candour and –

> The gravedigger's comic speech isn't funny at all. It's heavy and meaningful. Just send me YouTube vids instead, pls. I am so borrredddd.

As Carr (2010) noted about language usage in the digital age:

> What we've learned about digital media is that, even as they promote the transmission of writing, they shatter writing into little, utilitarian fragments. They turn stories into snippets. They transform prose and poetry into quick, scattered bursts of text.

I found the concept fascinating and it was a great assignment for students to experiment with language. This concept was taken one step further by the Royal Shakespeare Company's production of *Romeo and Juliet* (2010) in Twitter, which they entitled *Such Tweet Sorrow*. It was undoubtedly a ground-breaking experiment that used social media for a production. The script was written for the six actors who played the major roles in *Romeo and Juliet*, and they tweeted themselves for a period of five weeks and watched what may become of it. The production was accompanied by a web site that brought it all together. An example of a tweet from the production is the following:

> Wherefore art thou, @Romeo?

> But soft! What tweet through yonder iPhone breaks? It is the east, and @julietcap16 is the sun.

This could be a fun, funny, interdisciplinary assignment for students that could last an entire semester. It could bring up issues of language, art, creativity, innovation, literature, technology, and much more.

Naturally, Twitter could be used for much more than that. Because it limits each tweet to 140 characters, it could help students write concise information that matters without introductions or long essays. This would help students formulate ideas and express them clearly. In addition, Twitter could connect students through their mobile phones as reminders of assignments, last-minute changes, classroom chat on topics related to class, peer-to-peer information exchange beyond the classroom, conference participation, and more. Students may even be encouraged to "follow" a renowned author or poet or media personality (dave, 2008). This would create an enriching and engaging environment for exploring diverse topics in many disciplines.

Mapping and Data Visualization

Many assignments can be transformed through maps and data visualization. Whether the discipline is geography, technology, biology, or even literature and the humanities, one can always ask students to create a map or to digitally visualize data. There are many types of maps and one that is very simple to use is Google Maps. One can trace the history of a famous poet or the migration of birds, and one may even create timelines for inventions or historical events.

A prominent yet more complicated example is Google Lit Trips (http://www.googlelittrips.org/), which was created as an "experiment in teaching great literature in a very different way" (Burg, 2006). Using Google Earth, students discover where in the world the greatest road trip stories of all time took place (Fig. 1). This is complicated only because it requires coding

Fig. 1.   Google Lit Trips.

Fig. 2. A Wordle Screenshot.

knowledge to be able to do it in Google Earth. Using simple Google Maps or any other maps would accomplish almost the same effect.

Data visualization is "the use of tools to represent data in the form of charts, maps, tag clouds, animations, or any graphical means that make content easier to understand" (Educause Learning Initiative, 2009). One may use Wordle (at wordle.net) to generate discussion on various topics or make connections between concepts. One may use a more complex software such as Vue or "Visual Understanding Environment" (http://vue.tufts.edu/), which was created as an open source software by Tufts University to support educators visualize data (Fig. 2).

Through using mapping and data visualization, students find it easier to learn. By creating it themselves, they have the additional advantage of engaging in the process of their own learning.

Digital Storytelling

A digital story is defined by the University of Houston, *The Educational Uses of Digital Storytelling* (2010), as "the practice of using computer-based tools to tell stories." A digital storyteller is "anyone who has a desire to document life experience, ideas, or feelings through the use of story and digital media." To use digital storytelling in education, one may ask students to create a digital story that "ranges from personal tales to the recounting of historical events, from exploring life in one's own community to the search for life in other corners of the universe, and literally, everything in between."

Asking students to present a point of view or opinion or expression of emotion through digital storytelling is a great way to help them express themselves and helps them become more creative and effective communicators.

Second Life

Using augmented reality or an immersive environment is not always a successful endeavor. Based on experience in the classroom, it is my belief that augmented reality could be successful in the future, provided there is some killer education application that will move it to the next level. I have seen many uses of virtual worlds and instructors have told many success stories (Atkins, 2008). Nevertheless, this has not been my experience. Students who engage in online games such as the graphically rich World of Warcraft would not touch Second Life. Indeed, they find it particularly distasteful not only in terms of graphics but also in terms of purpose and objectives. Those who play online games are used to having specific difficult goals set for them with obstacles along the way. However in Second Life, it is open-ended with no goal and no obstacles unless the instructor creates a goal. Although this may seem interesting and flexible, I have yet to see a truly successful model. It is my belief however that in the future, 3D technology will develop further and have the desired educational impact. Currently, that is not the case.

CONCLUSION: THE SOCIAL MEDIA APPROACH

Social networking sites have profoundly changed not only methods of learning and accessing information but also have had far-reaching impacts on both culture and society. If one is to make any progress in student education, one has to take those changes into consideration. Educators must not only react to new trends and their social impacts but must also develop new ways of teaching and construct new pedagogies. To meet the challenges the net generation pose and the changing nature of the educational and learning landscape, critical shifts in thinking about education methods and pedagogy have become imperative. Adaptability is key to this process. There is a need to embrace the new technology and channel it into a constructive pedagogy if only because social media is not a "fad" and is not going anywhere any time soon as trend forecasters have made clear (Anderson, 2010).

Whereas there continues to be many great, effective and memorable educators who are unfamiliar with technology or with social media, future trends suggest that current students have acquired a different attitude and different expectations from the existing learning process. The issue is primarily not the tools themselves but the implications of those tools that include the values of collaboration, creativity, and innovation. Implementing social media with all the challenges it poses will only prepare students for a world that continues to be increasingly connected. Digital education is only important if used correctly: Media literacy helps critical thinking and encourages democratic participation, innovation and creativity, problem-solving, and reflection and exploration:

> Engagement, rather than enhancement must serve as the driving force behind educational technology. The incorporation of new educational tools does not magically improve learning any more than cellular phones, text messaging, and make everyday conversations more interesting. (Gonzalez-Appling, 2009)

The implications of moving toward social media are vast and rewarding in many ways. It includes the abundance of opportunities as we witness the convergence of the traditional and the modern. Resistance to change is an unacceptable and alternative and using traditional methods is unsustainable. Education methods are changing because digital natives think differently. Educators need to seize the opportunity of this milestone and utilize it in the interest of students. Together, we are all in a learning phase that will determine the future of teaching because after that the digital natives will take over and it will be they who will be the teachers of the future.

REFERENCES

Aciman, A., & Rensin, E. (2010). *Twitterature: The world's greatest books in twenty tweets or less*. USA: Viking and Penguin Book.
Alemán, M. M., & Wartman, K. L. (2009). *Online social networking on campus: Understanding what matters in student culture*. New York: Routledge.
Anderson, J. (2010). *Millennials will make online sharing in networks a lifelong habit*. Washington, DC: Pew Internet and American Life Project. Available at http://pewinternet.org/Reports/2010/Future-of-Millennials.aspx. Retrieved on July, 10, 2010.
Atkins, C. (2008). Virtual experiences, observations on second life. In: M. Purvis, T. Bastin & R. Savarimuthu (Eds), *Computer-mediated social networking: First international conference, ICCMSN*. New Zealand: Springer.
Beetham, H. (2007). An approach to learning activity design. In: H. Beetham & R. Sharpe (Eds), *Rethinking pedagogy for a digital age: Designing and delivering e-learning* (p. 30). New York: Routledge.
Brown, D. (2010). An open letter to educators. Available at http://www.youtube.com/watch?v=-P2PGGeTOA4&feature=related. Retrieved on June 10, 2010.
Buckingham, D. (2003). *Media education: Literacy, learning, and contemporary culture*. UK: Polity Press.

Burg, J. (2006). Google Lit. *Trips*. Available at http://www.googlelittrips.com/GoogleLit/ Home.html. Retrieved on May 10, 2010.

Carr, N. (2010). The rapid evolution of "Text": Our less-literate future. encyclopedia britannica blog, January 28. Available at http://www.britannica.com/blogs/2010/01/the-rapid-evolution-of-%E2%80%9Ctext%E2%80%9D-our-less-literate-future/. Retrieved on July 10, 2010.

Churches, A. (2008). Eight habits of highly effective 21st century teachers. Interface: supporting the use of ICT in learning, July 15. Available at http://www.interfacemagazine.co.nz/ articles.cfm?c_id = 10&id = 28. Retrieved on May 5, 2010.

dave. (2008). Twitter for Academia, January 23. *AcademHack*. Available at http://academhack. outsidethetext.com/home/2008/twitter-for-academia/. Retrieved on July 10, 2010.

Educause Learning Initiative. (2009). 7 things you should know about data visualization II. Available at http://net.educause.edu/ir/library/pdf/ELI7052.pdf. Retrieved on July 10, 2010.

FOR-PD. (2004). Making connections, October. Available at http://www.be.wednet.edu/ Departments/TeachingAndLearning/Literacy/Comprehension%20Strategies/Making%20 COnnections/Making%20Connections%20Packet.doc. Retrieved on May 5, 2010.

Freire, P. (2000). *Pedagogy of the oppressed* (30th Anniversary ed.) (M. B. Ramos, Trans.). New York: The Continuum International Publishing Group Inc. Available at http:// books.google.com/books?id = xfFXFD414ioC&printsec = frontcover&dq = PEDAGOGY + OF + THE + OPPRESSED&hl = en&ei = R9wxTPyQEuWfnwess9m2Aw&sa = X&oi = book_result&ct = result&resnum = 1&ved = 0CCsQ6AEwAA#v = onepage&q&f = fals. Retrieved on May 5, 2010.

Geith, C. (2008). Teaching and learning unleashed with web 2.0 and open educational resources. In: R. Katz (Ed.), *The tower and the cloud: Higher education in the age of cloud computing* (p. 222). Berkeley: Educause, University of California. Available at http:// net.educause.edu/ir/library/pdf/PUB7202.pdf. Retrieved on May 5, 2010.

Gonzalez-Appling, J. (2009). Engagement, not enhancement: Building bridges in the 20th century classroom. *MIT6 Conference Paper*. Available at http://web.mit.edu/ comm-forum/mit6/papers/Appling.pdf. Retrieved on May 5, 2010.

Hallis, M. (2000). Relationship media, story and civic culture, March 25. Available at http:// www.storycenter.org/stanford/relate.html. Retrieved on May 5, 2010.

Head, A. J., & Eisenberg, M. B. (2010). How today's college students use Wikipedia for course-related research. *First Monday*, *15*(3). Available at http://firstmonday.org/htbin/cgiwrap/ bin/ojs/index.php/fm/article/viewArticle/2830/2476/. Retrieved on June 20, 2010.

Hotchkiss, G. (2009). The wiring of the digital native. *Search Engine Land*, April 3. Available at http://searchengineland.com/the-wiring-of-the-digital-native-17140. Retrieved on July 5, 2010.

Howard, S. (2009). Digital natives are just geeks. millennials may not qualify. *Learning Solutions Magazine*, May 25. Available at http://www.learningsolutionsmag.com/ articles/41/digital-natives-are-just-geeks-millennials-may-not-qualify. Retrieved on May 5, 2010.

Howe, N., & Straus, S. (2000). *Millennials rising: The next great generation*. New York: Vintage Books.

IFAP, T. (2010). *Information society policies: Annual World report 2009*. Geneva: UNESCO. Available at http://portal.unesco.org/ci/en/files/29547/12668551003ifap_world_report_ 2009.pdf/ifap_world_report_2009.pdf. Retrieved on May 5, 2010.

Jones, D. R., & Pritchard, A. L. (2000). The distance education debate: An Australian view. *Change*, *32*(6). Available at http://www.eric.ed.gov/ERICWebPortal/search/detailmini. jsp?_nfpb = true&_&ERICExtSearch_SearchValue_0 = EJ620002&ERICExtSearch_Search Type_0 = no&accno = EJ620002.Retrieved on July 5, 2010.

Katz, R. (2009). The gathering cloud: Is this the end of the middle? In: R. Katz (Ed.), *The tower and the cloud: Higher education in the age of cloud computing*. Berkeley: Educause, University of California. Available at http://www.educause.edu/thetowerandthecloud/ PUB7202d. Retrieved on May 5, 2010.

Kincheloe, J. L. (2005). The curriculum and the classroom. In: J. L. Kincheloe (Ed.), *Classroom teaching: An introduction* (p. 86). New York: Peter Lang.

Knowledge Works Foundation. (2009). 2020 Forecast: Creating the future of learning. Available at http://www.futureofed.org/driver/pattern-recognition.aspx. Retrieved on May 5, 2010.

Lenhart, A. (2009). *Twitter and status updating: Demographics, mobile access and news consumption* (October 8, Available at http://www.pewinternet.org/Presentations/2009/ 44–Twitter-and-status-updating.aspx. Retrieved on July 5, 2010). USA: Pew Research Center.

Levine, J. L., Smith, R., & Stone, S. (2010). *The 2010 horizon report*. Austin, TX: The New Media Consortium.

Livingstone, S. (2005). On relations between audiences and publics. In: S. Livingstone (Ed.), *Audiences and publics: When cultural engagement matters for the public sphere* (Vol. 2). UK: Intellect Books. Available at http://books.google.com/books?id = ESVm6KiOvh UC&printsec = frontcover&dq = Audiences + and + publics: + when + cultural + engage ment + matters + for + the + public + sphere&source = bl&ots = j9qdsG-nfL&sig = RQExkd UTV5imHiulpMbPFUwm. Retrieved on May 5, 2010.

Manfield, L. (2009). This is your brain on technology: Are digital technologies actually changing the way your brain works? Some neuroscientists say yes. *Backbone Magazine*, January 26. Available at http://www.backbonemag.com/Magazine/E_Trends_01260901. asp. Retrieved on July 5, 2010.

McLaren, P. (2003). Critical pedagogy: A look at the major concepts. In: A. Darder, M. Baltodano & R. Torres (Eds), *The critical pedagogy reader*. New York: Routledge. Available at http://books.google.com/books?id = a2bvKJ6S-L8C&pg = PA182&dq = new + teaching + pedagogy + for + social + media&hl = en&ei = 4Lw5TMW_GYHUtQOjzohS& sa = X&oi = book_result&ct = result&resnum = 5&ved = 0CD4Q6AEwBDgK#v = onepage &q = new%20teaching%20pedagogy%20for%20social%20media&f = false. Retrieved on July 5, 2010.

Portnoy, S. (2010). New Jersey principal wants to keep middle school kids off facebook – Do you agree? *ABC World News*, April 29. Available at http://abcnews.go.com/WN/ ban-facebook-middle-school-kids-world-news-question/story?id = 10507174. Retrieved on July 5, 2010.

Prensky, M. (2001). Digital natives, digital immigrants, part II: Do they really think differently? Available at http://www.marcprensky.com/writing/Prensky%20-%20Digital%20Natives, %20Digital%20Immigrants%20-%20Part2.pdf. Retrieved on May 5, 2010.

Reuben, R. (2008). The use of social media in higher education for marketing and communications: A guide for professionals in higher education. *EduGuru*, August 19. Available at http://doteduguru.com/wp-content/uploads/2008/08/social-media-in-higher-education.pdf. Retrieved on May 5, 2010.

Reynard, R. (2008). Mobile learning in higher education: Multiple connections in customized learning spaces. *Campus Technology*, April 23. Available at http://campustechnology.com/articles/2008/04/mobile-learning-in-higher-education.aspx. Retrieved on May 5, 2010.

Rheingold, H. (2009). Is multitasking evil? Or are most of us illiterate?, December 8. Encyclopedia Britannica Blog. Available at http://www.britannica.com/blogs/2009/12/is-multitasking-evil-or-are-most-of-us-illiterate/. Retrieved on July 10th 2009.

Royal Shakespeare Company. (2010). Such tweet sorrow. Available at http://www.suchtweetsorrow.com/. Retrieved on May 5, 2010.

Scanlon, C. (2009). The natives aren't quite so restless. *The Australian*, January 21. Available at http://www.theaustralian.news.com.au/story/0,,24939539-25192,00.html. Retrieved on May 5, 2010.

Tapscott, D. (2009). *Grown up digital: How the net generation is changing your world.* New York: McGraw-Hill.

University of Houston. (2010). The educational uses of digital storytelling. Available at http://digitalstorytelling.coe.uh.edu/

Watkins, C. (2009). *The young and the digital: What the migration to social network sites, games, and anytime, anywhere media means for our future.* USA: Beacon Press Books.

CREATING AN ECOSYSTEM FOR LIFELONG LEARNING THROUGH SOCIAL MEDIA: A GRADUATE EXPERIENCE

Stella C. S. Porto, Lisa Blaschke and Gila Kurtz

ABSTRACT

Social media – and how to use it within online educational environments – has become an immediate challenge for today's educator. Deciding on the right social media tool to adopt and its purposes in the classroom are decisions that must be approached with great care and reflection. This chapter provides examples of how social media tools are being used within the Master of Distance Education and E-learning (MDE) program at the University of Maryland University College to create and sustain an ecosystem of lifelong learning, student support, reflection, and practical research within the MDE.

INTRODUCTION

The Master of Distance Education and E-learning (MDE) at the University of Maryland University College (UMUC) is in a unique position to fully

Educating Educators with Social Media
Cutting-edge Technologies in Higher Education, Volume 1, 107–134
ISSN: 2044-9968/doi:10.1108/S2044-9968(2011)0000001008

experiment with social media tools. Adult students not only work toward their master's degree completely at a distance, but the program also focuses on preparing these students to be managers and leaders in distance education and e-learning within various settings, including higher education, government, not-for-profits, and private corporations.

Thus, social media tools have become both a means and a mission for the MDE. It is part of our mission because MDE students, as future professionals in the area of e-learning, need to acquire experience with social media tools to be able to utilize them as e-learning resources within the workplace. Social media is a means, as these media have been used in diverse ways for accomplishing learning activities and have also served as an important instrument in supporting students outside of the virtual classroom by creating an online community and providing the vehicle for many collaborative initiatives. Besides continuously using social media tools as part of instructional activities and assignments, new and current students are kept continuously interconnected beyond the instructional course-based environment and have access to an immediate support system using program-managed and moderated social software tools. As an added advantage, social media sustains the network of MDE graduates, keeping alumni closely involved with the program and exposing both graduates and current students to new opportunities for lifelong learning. Additionally, social media has supported MDE faculty members in becoming increasingly involved with the program in a more holistic way. Thus, web 2.0 technologies have had a direct impact on the MDE program, creating a synergy among all stakeholders.

This chapter discusses the use of social media tools within the MDE experience in the virtual classroom and throughout the MDE online community, as well as providing lessons learned from this rich experience. More specifically, the chapter discusses in detail the different uses of wikis, blogs, social networking sites, and collaborative environments such as Google docs both as part of learning activities in different courses of the masters program and as for extracurricular activities involving MDE students and alumni. The projects to be described throughout the chapter include collaborative knowledge-bases for important topics related to distance education, the MDE hub serving as a one-stop shop for information about the program, an MDE student mentoring program, an MDE internship program, MDE student e-portfolios, student journals, and group assignments.

USING SOCIAL MEDIA IN THE MDE

Social media technologies place great emphasis on user-generated content, content sharing, and collaborative work, all of which add significant value to deeper learning processes. Whether interacting in a virtual world like Second Life (www.secondlife.com), facilitating knowledge through Wikipedia (www.wikipedia.com), networking through Facebook (www. facebook.com), sharing video delivered through YouTube (www.youtube. com), or developing an e-portfolio using a blog, instructors and students use these innovative Web 2.0 technologies to interact, share, and build a learning community (Harris & Rea, 2009). In this chapter, we discuss the social media applications – namely wikis, blogs, podcasts and vodcasts, live web meetings, and social networking sites – that are being used within the MDE ecosystem: the classroom, the program, and the community.

THE ONLINE CLASSROOM

By incorporating social media into MDE courses (http://www.umuc.edu/ mde), we not only introduce students to currently available technology, but we also give them an opportunity to experience firsthand how social media tools can be used pedagogically and innovatively. With this modeling approach, we teach students how to teach and lead by example, promoting and sustaining the motto of: *our means is our mission and our mission is our means.*

We believe that incorporating the social media concept into online teaching helps to elicit learner participation beyond standard textual responses and enables us to engage students as *interactive learners* in a way that has been nearly impossible up to now. In fact, we find that using social media can help students create for themselves new contexts for learning and communication. As Harris and Rea (2009) stated: "Students become part of the lesson"! (p. 141). To maximize these interaction levels, we utilize social media for a variety of purposes within the MDE classroom (Table 1).

In the following sections, we discuss each of these social media initiatives and how MDE instructors use these as teaching aids and for assignments.

Social Media as a Teaching Aid

Social media plays an important role in building online communities and is useful for motivating and supporting online collaboration. In these online communities, learners work together to share information, construct knowledge, and establish social networks (Harasim, Hiltz, Teles, & Turoff, 1998). Overall, we believe that the hybridization of social media tools with the current teaching aids [e.g., the learning management system (LMS)]

Table 1.   Social Media within the MDE Classroom.

Type of Social Media	Uses
Audio and video, live and recorded sessions (e.g., Wimba, Skype)	Project management, document sharing and discussion, information distribution and visual presentation, student feedback
Wikis	Project management, document sharing, discussion, information gathering, student interaction
Blogs	Information distribution and sharing, student feedback, student interaction
Textual chat	Discussion, student feedback, project management
Document sharing	Student feedback ("coaching"), information gathering, and sharing
Mashups	Information gathering and sharing, visual presentation, knowledge construction

serve as a means for using *new tools* to give students *new experiences* that help to increase their learning success and meet their professional needs.

Here's how we use social media tools to serve our pedagogical purposes.

Textual

Within the MDE classroom, *synchronous chat* functionality is built into the WebTycho platform, UMUC's proprietary LMS (www.tychousa.umuc.edu/). Students use the chat function to maintain contact with each other and the instructor, to discuss course content, establish frameworks for course projects (e.g., project schedule, responsibilities, action items, and due dates), and to discuss feedback on course assignments. As instructors, we use the chat function to provide feedback on assignments and student performance, as well as to generally keep lines of communication open with students. In an online, asynchronous environment, students may feel lost out in cyberspace. The chat function, together with the classroom awareness function, allows us to easily strike up a conversation at any time with any student who is online – and vice versa – as shown in Fig. 1.

We believe that this immediate feedback supports the individual learning experience. As one student observed:

> We are an instant gratification world and this includes the classroom. I recall nothing more frustrating than leaving a class not understanding because either there was no time to ask questions or the environment wasn't conducive to do so. Having a mechanism in place for this purpose alone would make the classroom setting much more effective. (MDE Student)

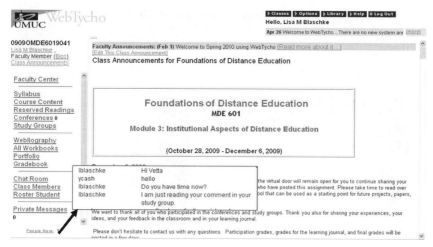

Fig. 1.   Using Chat Within the LMS Environment.

Audio

We use *audio* in the form of podcasts and voice boards (e.g., www.wimba. com). Audio files are used to introduce students to the classroom environment, as well as to course content. Audio has also been used as a form of advance organizer, providing students with an overview of module and/or course content (Holmberg, 2005). Students have responded positively to the use of audio introductions in the classroom and have found that the introductions help reduce the psychological distance that can arise from the separation of student and instructor in online environments. These audio introductions make instructors and visiting experts more familiar to students and help students "put a voice" to the instructor/expert with whom they are interacting.

As a standard feature of *OMDE603* (*Technology in Distance Education and E-learning*), we purposefully guide students' use of social media applications to facilitate their multimedia skill development. Podcasts, generated by either students or instructors, have been used to help share multimedia knowledge and information (Bonk, 2008). To support this effort, we have created audio tutorials and use sites such as *YouTube*, *Teacher Tube* (www.teachertube.com) to post these lessons for easy student access (see Fig. 2 for an example).

Video

The inclusion of synchronous instruction helps in creating a greatly enhanced teaching and learning experience through active engagement and

Fig. 2.   An Audio Tutorial on Cognitive Mapping.

spontaneous exchanges (Agosti, Cavalli, Gnudi, Lorenzi, & Malvisi, 2006). We use Wimba Live Classroom (www.wimba.com/products/wimba_classroom/), for example, to present course content and to introduce and discuss class-related topics, activities, and assignments. The Wimba Live Classroom session is synchronous and incorporates graphics, application sharing, audio, video, and chat. The sessions can also be recorded so that students have the choice of visiting the sessions synchronously or asynchronously.

Within *OMDE603* and *DETC630* (*Synchronous and Asynchronous Learning Systems in Distance Education*), we also use live audio and video meetings to discuss topics relevant to courses. For example, we conduct live discussions on the digital divide using Wimba (Fig. 3).

Student feedback on the use of video has been positive:

Synchronous collaboration with group was great and

I enjoyed and learnt a lot from, hands-on sessions ... which added to our understanding of the technology used in synchronous modes. (MDE Students)

Document Sharing
Document sharing allows students to collaborate in the development and construction of knowledge. Students use free web applications, such as Google Docs (www.docs.google.com/) and Adobe Buzzword (https://www.adobe.com/acom/buzzword/), to share documents and to simultaneously

Quick Links ... EDM300 Spring 2010 > Group Area > **10**

Group Area

10 AM: 4 (Natural Disasters) (permalink)
last edited by *Chelsea* on Wednesday, 04/14/2010 11:31 AM

WE ARE DONE!!! THE PROJECT HAS BEEN SUBMITTED!!!! GREAT JOB EVERYONE!

Group members:

1. Angelica
2. Chris
3. Chelsea
4. Stephanie
5. Stephanie

Team Attendance:

date	3-31	4/7 10am	4/9 10:00am	4/12	4/14 10am	date	date	date	date
1	here	here	here	here	here				
2	here	absent!	absent!	here	here				
3	here	here	here	here	here				

Fig. 3. Video Live Meeting (Instructor Screen).

edit and discuss (using chat and/or audio) document content. The ability to share and discuss course assignments synchronously and asynchronously supports students not only in information sharing but also in constructing new knowledge.

Within the *OMDE670* (*Capstone* course), we also use document sharing applications to collaborate with students on their final research projects. Using document sharing allows us to track student progress without invading their privacy and helps us ensure that important project milestones are met along the way. Document sharing also supports in synchronous assessment of work, specifically in providing the student guidance in improving his or her research project. The student invites us to his or her document, and we work together online with the student in reviewing the research project content and progress. We also use the document sharing function asynchronously, providing context specific feedback to the student work using document commenting functionality.

Within *OMDE603*, we use document sharing mainly for administrative purposes. For example, students share their blog URLs in Google Docs and register for synchronous activities.

MashUps
A mashup is "Web page or application that uses and combines data, presentation or functionality from two or more sources to create new services"

[retrieved from http://en.wikipedia.org/wiki/Mashup_(web_application_hybrid), para 1]. Mashups can be used for information exchange and collaboration to create new information in an open learning environment (Auinger, Ebner, Nedbal, & Holzinger, 2009). Within *OMDE601* (*Foundations of Distance Education and E-Learning*), we use Google Maps (www.maps.google.com) and combined class research to create a mashup of new information. Students create the mashup by "pegging" distance education institutions on a Google Map. The resulting map, which includes the institutional web sites, provides students with a visual impression of the global presence of distance education institutions and direct access to the institutional web page from the map.

Feedback from students on the use of this mashup has been positive, with one student writing:

> This is a neat exercise. When I first decided to apply at UMUC I was ignorant of how far the reach of distance education spreads. Then, when I was researching schools for the class assignment, I was amazed with the scope and number or distance education institutions throughout the world. The map brings it into focus and really solidifies the idea of distance education being global. (MDE Student, 2009)

Social Media for Assignments

Blogs

Blogs, as online journals, serve the purpose of allowing students to process and personalize information. Ideally, long-term blog assignments allow students to become capable of taking charge of their own learning, and they eventually develop into independent lifelong learners (Pang, 2009). Blogging has also been found to reduce students' sense of isolation and increase their feelings of connectedness (Wolf, 2008). In addition, blogging can support student reflection, as well as writing style development (Pulman, 2007).

Within *OMDE603*, students are asked to create a blog (textual or video) as their second course assignment. The purpose of the activity is for students to reflect on their personal viewpoints regarding the course readings and their ideas related to the class. They are also asked to write or record blog posts about topics not covered in class discussions or other activities. Each student is assigned a critical friend (a fellow classmate) to give feedback on the student's posts. The last blog posting is a reflection on the critical friend activity.

For most of the students, blogging is a new experience different from what they have known before. As one of the students shared:

> I have learned much while working on this project and have gained a growing respect for this format of communication. It is very unique. It proved to be a good tool for reflection. I found that I was challenged to examine new ideas from different perspectives. Putting my thoughts in print often helped solidify new concepts and encouraged a better understanding of complex ideas. It required that I examine and refine my opinions. (MDE Student)

Wikis

Wikis can be used in the online teaching setting to facilitate shared knowledge building among and by students (Meishar-Tal, Tal-Elhasid, & Yair, 2008). Students perceive wikis as positively supporting collaboration efforts and effectively supporting learning and engagement (Hughes & Narayan, 2009; Kurtz & Bar-Ilan, 2010). In *OMDE603*, students are asked to work in a wiki as a group to create an annotated class glossary of distance education (DE) terms relevant to the course. Each group of students chooses one term to contribute to the glossary. This is an ongoing activity as students can choose any term that they like as long as it is relevant to the course and has *not* been contributed in earlier classes. This way we combine past and present collaborative knowledge. Although students value the group work, a number of them report modest perceptions of the wiki activity supporting their learning, mainly due to the need for "getting together" as a working group. Students have found it difficult to hold other students accountable in the online classroom (as compared to face-to-face) and have recommended incorporating synchronous technology within the wiki activity.

Overall, students understand the value of the wiki activity:

> I want to thank Professor Kurtz and Professor Rawson for getting me out of my comfort zone and giving me (the class) the opportunity to work with Blogs and Wikis. I admit that I did not understand why we were doing those assignments until a few weeks ago. I finally realized that learning takes on a variety of methods. I want to work in education and be an instructor (Professor at some point in time), and I need to be open to a variety of teaching methods. The current generation that is attending and will be attending higher education has grown up playing games on XBox, Playstation, etc. The teaching methods have to be a little more exciting than in the past to keep students interested. (MDE Student)

In addition to using wikis for collaborating on coursework, students provide feedback to each other on the student wiki content, including the navigation and structure of the wiki. This only occurs, however, when a student is invited to the wiki by the wiki's creator. As instructors, we also post feedback directly into the wiki, for example, as a response to an entry in the wiki and/or within the discussion area of the wiki page.

The E-Portfolio
A cornerstone of the MDE program is the *e-portfolio*. At the start of the program, each student creates a wiki, which becomes the home of the e-portfolio. The e-portfolio is an evolving student creation, and as the MDE student progresses through the MDE program, the student uses the e-portfolio to capture and store experiences, reflections, and artifacts.

In *OMDE601*, the first course for newly registered MDE graduate students, we initially introduce students to the wiki and the e-portfolio. First, we assign students to groups of two (dyads) and ask them to collaborate together in researching and evaluating at least three different wiki providers (e.g., Wikispaces, Wetpaint, Pbworks). During this evaluative process, students identify their personal requirements (or desired features) for the wiki. On the basis of the results of their research, students then choose a wiki for use in storing their individual, personal learning journal. Students can decide whether or not to invite fellow students to the wiki. We use the dyad activity as an "ice-breaker" activity, which encourages students get to know each other while learning about wikis.

Within the wiki, we ask each student to maintain an individual, reflective learning journal. By incorporating online learning journals into the classroom, we introduce students to Web 2.0 technologies, as well as encourage them to think critically and reflectively about what they have learned within the course. Completion of a personal learning journal is done by each student, and we encourage students to expand upon their learning journal wikis with each course of their graduate program – continuously reflecting on their learning experiences and the knowledge they have gained through their experiences.

Each course is a building block within the learner experience. Together, the MDE courses create a continuum of each student's personal and professional development while in the MDE program. The student's continuous work on the e-portfolio ultimately serves as the basis for the student's final MDE capstone project. During the capstone project, the student is required to submit both a research project and the final version of his or her e-portfolio. It is this e-portfolio that the students take with them into the professional work environment as evidence of student accomplishments (Fig. 4).

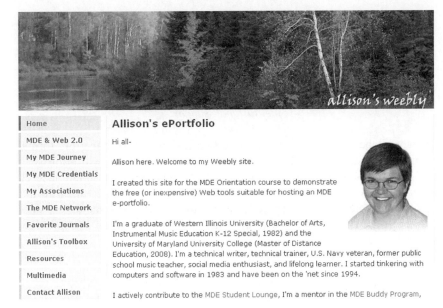

Fig. 4.   Example of a Student Portfolio (http://akipta.weebly.com/).

THE COMMUNITY

Social Media for Support Functions and Online Communities

Several learner support activities such as orientation, personal counseling, peer tutoring, and alumni organizations depend on the existence of student communities (Brindley, Walti, & Zawacki-Richter, 2004). According to Palloff and Pratt (2005), the sense of belonging and community come from the "creation of a sense of shared values and shared identity" (para 1). In this chapter, supporting functions are those that are distinct from the virtual classroom-based functions of teaching and learning. Supporting functions are nonetheless vital to learner success. We also include among these functions those that help faculty members execute their job more effectively and efficiently. Moreover, support functions also include activities that are offered to learners after they have formally completed their programs. It contains an intrinsic connection to lifelong learning, since these functions offer stakeholders a meaningful connection to their learning community.

This section discusses how the MDE community has used social media to deal with the challenges imposed by distance (Mason & Rennie, 2008) and to provide support to students, faculty, and alumni in an innovative fashion that stretches beyond the standardized services already provided by the institution. Before we delve into the details of MDE ecosystem, we discuss institutional support functions offered for all online programs.

Institutional Support

It would be a mistake to underestimate the importance of formal institutional support in the online learning setting. In an institution such as UMUC, institutional support has reached a reliable and sustainable level, offering students a wide variety of administrative functions, which do not require the student to ever come to the institution. By the same token, since most of the faculty cadre is also at a distance, the institution also provides extensive faculty support.

Three main channels are used to access such functions:

UMUC website (http://www.umuc.edu). The UMUC website offers extensive information about academic programs, processes and procedures, and several supporting resources such as the online library and the writing center.

UMUC portal (http://www.umuc.edu/myumuc). The portal is the main gateway for students and faculty to execute administrative functions such as admissions, registration, posting grades, credit transfer, and access to student records.

WebTycho (UMUC's proprietary LMS) platform (http://tychousa.umuc.edu). The WebTycho platform, which students and faculty use to access the virtual classrooms, is reserved mainly for teaching and learning activities.

One other important support function to students and faculty is the Information and Library Services (ILS), which provides a full spectrum of library and information resources and services. The ILS promotes information literacy throughout the institution, while managing an extensive online digital library.

UMUC also promotes professional development through its Center for Teaching and Learning (http://wwww.umuc.edu/ctl), which offers online workshops and initial training for online teaching. To aid course development and design as well as distance delivery operations, UMUC counts on a comprehensive cadre of professionals as part of their Office of Instructional Support and Services (http://www.umuc.edu/oiss). In the last year, UMUC has taken a few steps in the use of social media to connect with its stakeholder community. UMUC has an established presence on Facebook and LinkedIn and has created a blog that reports on the latest institutional news. A detailed discussion of UMUC support is beyond the scope of this chapter, but the links provided here provide an impression of the broad spectrum of support functions provided at an institutional level.

The MDE, however, has always understood that such institutional support functions do not provide students, faculty, and alumni with a real sense of community and therefore are not able to create a more tightly-knit support network, usually available among groups of people who have a closer relationship and a common goal. It has always been a focal point for the program to create this sense of community and from there enable the rise of new supporting services, specifically tailored to the needs of all MDE stakeholders. We describe and discuss each of these initiatives as they compose the MDE ecosystem, highlighting their purpose, functionality, effectiveness, and important traits about the social media tools that were chosen in each case.

MDE Student/Alumni Program-Level Support

While UMUC provides a general infrastructure for supporting an MDE ecosystem, social media has become a key component for feeding into and sustaining this ecosystem. Strong relationships to support learning and academic success are at the heart of the study by Blackmun and Thibodeau (2004) on learning communities. These cultivate a blend of challenge and support "wherein students may exchange ideas and experiences with both professors and peers" (p. 146). The understanding that online students benefit from communities outside of the classroom is naturally derived from the benefits perceived in traditional campus life (Smith & Drago, 2004). Although most of the students in online programs are adults, who might have had traditional campus experiences in the past or may not desire collegial camaraderie, it is still true that online students tend to demonstrate feelings of isolation and are in need of a supporting network when studying at a distance. Moreover, surveys have demonstrated that online students are in fact interested in many of the services available to students in traditional environments (Fu, Hintz, Ruggles, & Miller, 2008). The lack of a campus life imposes difficulty in keeping students and graduates connected beyond the ties of the online classroom. Thus, social media provides the potential for bridging the gap and offering support services from admissions to graduation, further on through alumni services.

Each of the MDE support social media initiatives have been created and slowly developed over time, according to the needs of the program's stakeholders. In many cases, as technology evolves, it is clear that certain tools should have been used for specific purposes; however, they were not available or unknown of that time. This caveat in itself provides us with an important lesson from this process: the tool chosen for a specific function is never optimal. It might be the best at the moment given a certain context. Thus, it is usually unfair or simply unsuitable to assess choices made in the past. Many options could serve the same purpose, and choices might end up being made based on ease of use to the individual in charge. Changes in the adopted tool might make sense, but cost-benefit factors such as the amount of time and effort in getting a new environment up to speed for the entire community need to be carefully assessed. We believe that when pioneering in this arena, one has to combine some rational decision-making skills, with a good dose of courage and subjectivity and take the risk to move forward. We hope that the discussion of the following projects serves as inspiration and also motivation to those wanting to experiment with this new and ever-growing gamut of social media tools.

Throughout the community-related initiatives (extra curricular activities) involving social media tools within the MDE, the responsibility for creating content, updating information and making evolutionary changes, for the most part, has relied on the actions of the program manager. In some instances, for specific initiatives, the responsibility has been delegated to graduates of the program and a few students (who in some cases use the initiative as part of their final capstone research project). What is significant to report is the fact that the accountability of such efforts is not in any way tied to planned efforts, financial support, or administrative control by the institution. This has a dual, somewhat opposite, effect. On one hand, having responsibility and account-ability at the program level gives the program manager flexibility and freedom to act swiftly in creating new projects, in disseminating important information, and in calling its stakeholders for action. On the other hand, there is an extra burden placed on management, and in many cases the lack of necessary support to make things happens in an effective and broad manner. One example of this is the use of free social media tools for most of the initiatives. This can be a point of contention and might put the program manager in a delicate situation without the needed technological support and backup. The dimension of this effort needs to be considered by those who will be in charge of such initiatives in their institutions. Taking into consideration policies and procedures as well as institutional culture is a proactive way to avoid unwelcome surprises down the road.

The MDE HUB

The MDE Hub (http://mdeprogram.weebly.com) (Fig. 5) is currently the one-stop shop for the MDE, created after many of the initiatives described here were well underway. The hub came about due to the proliferation of different projects and supporting initiatives and attempted to aggregate and organize information for the MDE community. For this project, we used Weebly (http://www.weebly.com). The ease of the interface, with drag-and-drop elements for composing website pages, is one the most attractive features of this environment. It also allows the use of different background styles/layouts for the site and various different webpage templates to be used within the same site. The latter characteristic is an important asset when planning a site that will work as a one-stop shop, since you might want to create pages that will serve different functionalities (e.g., a blog page, aggregation of RSS feeds, forms) (Russell, 2008; Wright, n.d.; Weebly Team, n.d.). In the case of the MDE hub, the focus was on aggregating both institutional information and links to other MDE Web 2.0 (O'Reilly, 2005)

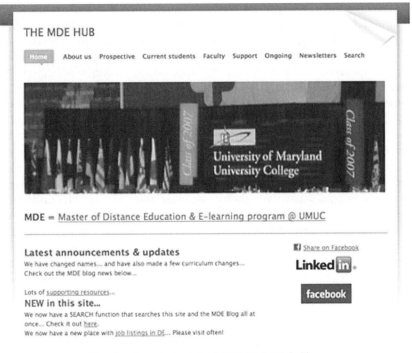

Fig. 5.   Snapshot of the MDE Hub Web Site.

support initiatives. One important choice is not to replicate information, since replication will duplicate maintenance efforts. Thus, use everything the institution provides and add to it instead of replicating it. The key word here is "added value." If there is no "added value," stick with what the institution has given you, even if style and wording are not the best choice. This will reduce immensely any problems with inconsistency.

The MDE Student Lounge
The student lounge (http://groups.google.com/group/MDE-Lounge) is by far the most effective and utilized environment of the MDE community. Building virtual communities with students and alumni has been a known challenge for those managing online programs. The lack of a campus life imposes difficulty in keeping students and graduates connected beyond the ties of the online classroom. The MDE early on recognized this need. In many presentations about the MDE social media tools, people frequently ask exactly that: If you had to pick one tool, which one would you say is the most important in your entire arsenal? The answer comes out without a doubt: the student lounge. It is probably the simplest tool and provides very little space for creativeness when it comes to creating content and design, but it is the tool that keeps the members of the community together and allows for collaboration to take place. Our initial efforts to form a student lounge involved using a virtual classroom shell within UMUC's LMS. Later, a proprietary solution was designed specifically for alumni use. However, this environment was not supportive to our busy alumni, who needed to first log into the LMS environment to check for messages. Also, the initiative did not support an ongoing relationship between current students and alumni (http://elearningtech.blogspot.com/2006/07/do-you-want-lms-does-learner-want-lms.html; http://tychousa.umuc.edu/). Before the alumni network was integrated into the current MDE student lounge, a survey was conducted with those who were part of the existing lounge, asking about their perceptions of building a community outside the institutional walls. There was some insecurity, especially when it came to sharing personal information. One would think that this would not happen within a group of professionals or "wanna-be" professionals in the online world, but fear is well spread out among all groups, and the cyber world still carries some of the mythical threats especially for those from the pre-Internet era. Some traits were important in the selection of the online environment for this prospective online community of practice: privacy, security, immediacy, and simplicity. At the time, it made sense to choose Google Groups as the platform. Besides the usual level of security and

privacy of an online group, Google Groups has a simple interface, which allows you to "choose whether you want to read and post messages online, or to just use your current email account to read and respond" (http://groups.google.com/intl/en/googlegroups/tour3/page2.html). It is possible to create pages, add files and all the basic functions of a discussion forum, but the most important characteristic is the ability it gives each participant to configure his or her own account to receive online posts as emails or email digests. Moreover, users can sign up to the group using their own email addresses, without having to create a new address to participate. This simplicity and straightforward mode of operation has created a thriving environment within the MDE community and has enabled the advancement of other social media activities.

The MDE Blog

The MDE blog (http://mdeblog.blogspot.com) was the first attempt at using social media within the MDE (Fig. 6). At the time, there was no way to

Fig. 6.   Snapshot of the MDE Blog.

reach out to students, other than trying to acquire email lists from enrollment management units at UMUC. This meant that as an administrator of the program, there was no way we could send out information to current students, alumni, or even prospective students. The blog, therefore, became the venue for diffusing program information: an announcement page readily available for the program manager to reach out to stakeholders directly. This is somewhat different than the way most blogs are used, or at least are tailored for. Blogs in general function as journals and reflection tools (http://googleblog.blogspot.com/). Since the MDE blog was the first vehicle of information dissemination and since blogs have become increasingly versatile, allowing users to add all sorts of structured pieces of information beyond the reverse chronologically ordered posts, the MDE blog also went through a significant period of time in which it became the repository of all MDE information through its side bars and available widgets. The advent of the MDE Hub was thus a game changer and helped clean up the MDE Blog, returning it to a state of being a simple blog once again, where posts work as announcements for program stakeholders and related groups. Important here is to notice the evolution in the use of a certain tool and the impact of changes on stakeholders. It is clear that the current setting-having the MDE Hub as the one-stop shop and a separate blog for major announcements, easily linked to the hub-works best. However, in the process of getting to that final situation, decisions had to be made carefully, taking into consideration how best to balance the workload (moving and editing data) and the need to communicate to the community and to possibly change their habits. This decision-making process does not always support moving forward with change, which may initially make sense both technologically and cosmetically. This was certainly the case for the MDE. For a long time after the blog was created, it was evident that we were stretching its use. It became more difficult to edit the side columns, and information was definitely becoming cluttered within the available static/ permanent spaces. Visually, posts were becoming harder to find, and as much as reorganization was possible, it just was not working. Moreover, new possibilities such as Google apps and wikis began to appear. There were many instances when it just made sense to plunge and work on the big change. It happened as a consequence of several students and alumni using Weebly as their e-portfolios and finding it useful and sharing this with the rest of the community through the MDE Student Lounge. But, here again, a learning moment ... Was Weebly the best choice ever? Would no other tool work? No. It was a constellation of events and circumstances. A tool that seemed easy enough, that provided the envisioned flexibility and a moment where there were hands to do the work and make it happen. The thriving for the perfect choice can paralyze us ... But, one needs to have the time....

The MDE Peer-Mentoring Program

One interesting initiative that resulted from the use of social media tools is the MDE Peer-Mentoring Program (Fig. 7). The peer-mentoring program is run entirely by an MDE alumnus and its purpose is to match new students to senior students or graduates of the program. It is voluntary for both mentors and mentees, and the manager of the project matches mentors and mentees by considering possible commonalities of background and shared interests. It is a project with a clear mission of retention and support to new students, who are usually in need of extra orientation, support and motivation. New students are often returning to school after many years of no academic activity, or might be career changers, or are simply new to the online environment and have never taken classes while fulfilling the demands of family and work, all at the same time. The first few semesters might be the most challenging ones. It is during those semesters that students tend to drop out because of external events, temporary setbacks or

Fig. 7. Snapshot of the MDE Peer-Mentoring Program Website.

a simple lack of encouraging academic results. The latter can be a significant problem for students coming from undergraduate experience, where they might have never had their work seriously critiqued or received detailed feedback about essential skills in graduate level education, such as writing, information literacy, and critical and analytical thinking. To succeed in the program, students need to be able to overcome these initial barriers and difficulties during the first semesters. The level of readiness of students in an open admission school is definitely a major hurdle for instructors and supporting staff. The peer-mentoring program has already proven itself as a success.

Remarks about this program include:

> The mentoring really made the difference, and I am grateful to you for setting up this element of the program! Thank you! (MDE Student)

> This was an excellent part of my introduction to online education. Even though I have completed 5 degrees ... I was paired with a mentor whose profession and interests were similar to mine and he was *very* helpful. I would recommend it to all who are new to online education. (MDE Student)

> Thank you ... for taking the time to talk me through the rough spots this semester. It really helped. I think the program helps distance students who might feel kind of, 'out there (MDE Student)

Social Networking Sites

In a push for greater visibility of the program, as well as for broadening the opportunities for accessing information by students and especially alumni, the MDE created groups inside well-established social networks, namely LinkedIn and Facebook (Fig. 8). LinkedIn was a natural choice given its professional focus, and the existing networking among working adults in related fields of interest. The Fan/Group page within Facebook was a natural consequence from the existing number of students, alumni, and faculty with Facebook accounts. There is no hard data about the amount of access there is to such pages, but there is anecdotal information that shows the appreciation from students and alumni for the presence of the program in both environments.

MDE New Technologies Wiki

In early 2007, when MDE management was pushing the use of social media tools both as a supporting function for the program as well as an important dimension in teaching and learning within several program courses, it was clear that faculty members had a need for more readily available

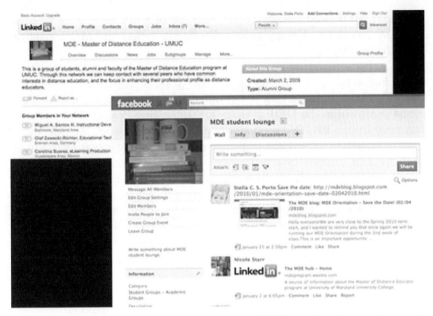

Fig. 8. Snapshot of the MDE Linkedin Page and MDE Student Lounge Facebook Page.

information. This sparked the creation of the MDE New Technologies wiki – http://mdewiki.wetpaint.com. This wiki served as an aggregator of information concerning social media tools and Web 2.0 technologies. The focus was not to create new information but to aggregate what was already available on the web, mostly quick and just-in-time visual information explaining concepts and demonstrating through practical examples the use of distinct technologies. This was in fact the first wiki we developed for the MDE, and in this case, we adopted Wetpaint (http://www.wetpaint.com). Wetpaint is a "wiki farm" (http://webtrends.about.com/od/glossary/g/ wikifarm_def.htm), and as with other wiki farms, Wetpaint will allow a user to have multiple wikis with the same account. Wetpaint wikis are offered in a free version and is easy to use. They can be made private or public; the administrator/creator can also add other writers, editors or simply readers of the wiki. There is a possibility to create a wiki for educational purposes – without advertisements – despite being free. Wetpaint defines itself as an online community, because the wikis include functionalities such as social networking and blogs, besides the typical content creating and collaboration, typical of wikis in general. This particular MDE wiki has served the purpose of working as a knowledge-base and has not had many collaborators, other than the MDE manager and a few students.

MDE Internships
One important initiative that has resulted from the extensive use of social media tools within the MDE is the MDE Internship Project. This initiative was born from a two-fold motivation: provide a framework for students to acquire hands-on experience in distance education and e-learning and get students and alumni involved with ongoing program-related activities, helping the program move forward and in different directions, including technology innovation, curriculum update and enhancement of the community of practice. This project has provided students with a diverse set of opportunities, including: designing new projects (such as the MDE Buddy Program), research positions, and e-book editing (http://www.mde.uni-oldenburg.de/40574.html-Volumes).

The technology used to list the internship offerings was Google Sites, which is a generic web page generator by Google. It allows the easy development of web pages, but has less functionality than those in Weebly (used for the MDE Hub, Fig. 5).

MDE Social Bookmarks
The most recent addition to the MDE social media suite is the MDE social bookmarking environment created using Diigo (http://groups.diigo.com/group/MDE_research). Diigo is an online, social bookmarking community environment, where a user with an account can create groups, join other groups, all of which exist with the purpose of sharing online bookmarks. Bookmarks can be tagged and annotated, which become then helpful in more thematic searches. Users can also add comments about bookmarks that have been added by peers within the same group. In the case of the MDE, the social bookmarking group has a twofold goal: to collect and annotate research projects done by MDE community members, and collect, tag and share online bookmarks in the field of distance education and e-learning that can be useful to the entire community. Tagging and annotating are an important piece of this initiative. For now, there are only a few contributors, but there is a hope that bookmarks from many of the stakeholders will be collected into this unique set. Diigo goes beyond just bookmarking and in fact creates a social networking environment that can be used to share thoughts and reflections related to the field. This is seen as an important component of a strong and thriving community of practice.

The MDE Capstone Wiki

The capstone course (OMDE 670 – http://www.umuc.edu/programs/grad/courses/omdecat.shtml#omde670) entails a study of distance education and training designed to demonstrate cumulative knowledge and skills through two major projects: an e-portfolio and a research project (http://mdecapstone.pbworks.com). The personal e-portfolio documents credentials and accomplishments to date and also serves as an ongoing resource and record of continuing professional development. The research project that focuses on a distance education/training program, organization, or important research topic, involves indepth analysis of the setting and application of concepts and strategies to enhance practice and performance in distance education and training. A full wiki was developed to provide information concerning these two major projects to be completed at the end of the program. For the capstone wiki, the wiki farm that was chosen was Pbworks (http://www.pbworks.com). Pbworks is similar to the tools offered through Wetpaint, but has a clearer interface, and offer the possibility of interaction through comments from wiki participants, creation of pages, and attachment of files. A user is allowed to create several different wikis and register and invite other participants as editors, writers, or readers. Wikis can also be public or private. In the case of the MDE, all wikis mentioned were created for free, are public and, because the wikis are for educational purposes, have no advertisements. This wiki has been used during the capstone course, as part of the MDE orientation and can be accessed by any student and any time, interested in understanding the requirements and expectations of the final course in the program.

It was clear that beginning to build the e-portfolios at the end of the program was not adequate for students to capture the essence of their individual MDE journeys. Out of this need was born the MDE Orientation. The orientation started in Fall 2008 as a one-week workshop, delivered through the WebTycho platform in a course format. Since then it has been delivered every term, always during the second week of classes. Students participate voluntarily and can take part in the workshop as often as they want. The orientation has expanded to include discussion of the final research project, which is also developed during the capstone, as well as the advising of new students in the program. We have anecdotal information concerning the value of the orientation, and it indicates that is has made a significant difference in the level of readiness of students when they reach the capstone course. However, given the fact that the orientation is voluntary, there are still many students who do not take advantage of this extra support, although it does not represent any additional cost.

SOCIAL MEDIA AND THE MDE FACULTY

The MDE faculty is, in every sense of the word, international. Faculty come from and are located in all corners of the world: Australia, Germany, Israel, South Africa, the United Kingdom, Canada, Brazil, and the United States. It is not uncommon for students to have two instructors on different continents within one course (and a teaching assistant on another!). To coordinate instructional activities, whether research, planning, development, or teaching, instructors make use of a wide assortment of social media tools. Skype (www.skype.com) is a common social media tool used within the MDE, as teams of instructors meet at the start of each semester to prepare for the next cohort of their courses.

The faculty counterpart to the MDE Student Lounge is the MDE Faculty Forum, which is something of a faculty coffee break area, using the online Google Groups setting (http://groups.google.com/group/MDE-faculty). It is here where faculty members exchange ideas, hold ongoing discussions about current trends and issues in the field of distance education, and spar over a variety of program-related topics (e.g., the role of adjunct faculty).

While the student lounge was able to create a real community of practice, as well as social network for the MDE students and alumni, communicating with faculty, when it came to administrative and pedagogical issues, was not addressed through this environment. It was a no-brainer to take the concept used for the student lounge and bring it to life for faculty (exclusively) as well. This community followed the same trajectory as the MDE Student Lounge, in which faculty also initially had an environment for discussion using a WebTycho classroom. The same pitfalls addressed in the case of student lounges were true for this faculty setting as well: low interaction and interest levels, lulls and then bursts of activity. We swiftly moved to a Google Group for faculty, following the experience with the student lounge, this time around with a different purpose, but benefiting from the same advantages: privacy and immediacy.

From a managerial perspective, the addition of the MDE Faculty Forum made program operations more effective and efficient, enabling immediate communication of policies, procedures, events, deadlines, and scheduling. Instead of simple emailing, the information shared with faculty was registered in the online environment and could be easily found. At any given time, the program manager has to deal with adjunct faculty, who might be in different states of involvement with the program (currently teaching, scheduled to teach in an upcoming semester or just taking a break from teaching). Information takes a different level of importance for such distinct groups of faculty. A forum gives important support in this varied communication. It also gives faculty the ability to configure how they want to receive information. This is important for adjunct faculty, who in many cases might want to have their email 'inbox' dedicated to the information they receive related to their primary job. The forum has promoted better communication of administrative and managerial issues, as well as greater exchange of thoughts related to teaching practice and pedagogical issues. It provides faculty with a sense of belonging, which is crucial for adjunct faculty teaching at a distance, who seldom meet.

Social media also sustains the MDE faculty in ongoing research efforts. Using wikis, faculty members meet to discuss the latest in technology developments and the potential pedagogical application of the technology within the classroom. We also use wikis and document sharing tools to gather and prepare research, as well as write and rewrite articles and chapters for publication in scholarly journals and non-periodicals. Adobe Buzzword, Dropbox (https://www.dropbox.com/), and Skype were all used in preparing this chapter for publication. Wikis were used during the preparation of the EFMD-CEL re-accreditation self-assessment report. The use of the wiki enabled several people from the MDE community as well as other people who provide service to the program, to understand the nature of the report and provide input and feedback.

FINAL REMARKS

The chapter has discussed extensively the use of social media tools within the MDE at UMUC. We have described and analyzed the benefits and challenges of using such tools in various settings, including teaching aids, class assignments and learning activities, professional development, networking, and student advising and support. These different approaches and endeavors have created a mesh of interconnected experiences, which have created *an ecosystem for lifelong learning through social media*. Our experience in the design, development, and use of these social media tools within the teaching and learning environment has enabled us to become not only more comfortable with trends in Internet technology, but also to become enablers and motivators for our students in their own pursuit and journey in the learning of and through technology.

The future of online education is intrinsically tied to the continuous change and advancements in the digital technology landscape. Therefore, those leading, managing, and teaching within this educational setting need to be in the driver's seat of such shifts, ensuring that the pedagogy remains at the forefront when choosing and adopting new technologies. The focus must remain on student access, learning, and achievement. Within the MDE program, we realize this by making our mission is our means, and our means as our mission. This synergistic mix of mission and means creates an enormous potential for learning through action with social media.

This chapter demonstrates the need to carefully consider instructional design and adult learning and student support issues when planning and managing any projects and activities using social media. Overall, it is apparent that the road ahead is not clear of obstacles and intriguing challenges. However, the outcomes and lessons learned confirm that this is a path of no return. Technologies like social media are here to stay – and are evolving rapidly. It is time to embrace them within a controlled experimentation process and acknowledge and absorb the invaluable potential they bring to all stakeholders in higher education, in particular to this specific program. It is without doubt that we recognize that this program has changed in nature and form due to the influences of social media tools. A rich ecosystem for lifelong learning has been unleashed, and its evolution will be a ride full of surprises, but is definitely not one to be missed.

ACKNOWLEDGMENTS

We would like to recognize the work of other members of the MDE community, who have greatly contributed to several of the projects we have described in this chapter, namely Allison Kipta, Julie Rozzi, Jim Rawson, and Christine Walti.

REFERENCES

Agosti, G., Cavalli, E., Gnudi, A., Lorenzi, A., & Malvisi, L. (2006). The virtual classroom within blended learning: Using synchronous conferencing as a support tool. A paper presented at the Annual European Distance Education Network (EDEN), Vienna.

Auinger, A., Ebner, M., Nedbal, D., & Holzinger, A. (2009). Mixing content and endless collaboration – MashUps: Towards future personal learning environments. In: *Universal access in human-computer interaction: Applications and services, 5616* (pp. 14–23). Heidelberg: Springer Berlin.

Blackmun, E., & Thibodeau, P. (2004). Learning communities. In: J. Brindley, C. Walti & O. Zawacki-Richter (Eds), *Learner support in open, distance and online learning environments* (pp. 145–156). Oldenburg, Germany: Bibliotheks- und Informationssystem der Carl von Ossietzky Universitat Oldenburg.

Bonk, C. J. (2008). YouTube anchors and enders: The use of shared online video content as a macrocontext for learning. Paper presented at the American Educational Research Association (AERA) 2008 Annual Meeting, New York, NY. *Learning*. Available at http://www.publicationshare.com/SFX7EED.pdf

Brindley, J., Walti, C., & Zawacki-Richter, O. (2004). The current context of learner support in open, distance and online learning: An introduction. In: J. Brindley, C. Walti & O. Zawacki-Richter (Eds), *Learner support in open, distance and online learning environments* (pp. 9–28). Oldenburg, Germany: Bibliotheks- und Informationssystem der Carl von Ossietzky Universitat Oldenburg.

Fu, S., Hintz, S., Ruggles, L., & Miller, R. (2008). Best practice in creating an online academic community for non-traditional students. In: *Proceedings of the 4th US-China forum in distance education* (pp. 202–211), July 2008. Adelphi, MD: University of Maryland University College.

Google Groups Tour: Discuss online or over email. (n.d.). Available at http://groups.google.com/intl/en/googlegroups/tour3/page2.html. Retrieved on August 29, 2010.

Harasim, L., Hiltz, S. R., Teles, L., & Turoff, M. (1998). *Learning networks: A field guide to teaching and learning online*. Cambridge, MA: The MIT Press.

Harris, A., & Rea, A. (2009). Web 2.0 and virtual world technologies: A growing impact on IS education. *Journal of Information Systems Education*, *20*(2), 137–144. Retrieved from ABI/INFORM Global (Document ID: 1755224731).

Holmberg, B. (2005). *The evolution, principles and practices of distance education*. Oldenburg, Germany: BIS-Verlag der Carl von Ossietzky Universität.

Hughes, J. E., & Narayan, R. (2009). Collaboration and learning with Wikis in post-secondary classrooms. *Journal of Interactive Online Learning*, *8*(1). Available at http://www.ncolr.org/jiol/issues/PDF/8.1.4.pdfJ. Retrieved on August 29, 2010.

Kurtz, G., & Bar-Ilan, J. (2010). Usage of Wiki technologies as a collaborative studying environment. A paper presented at the Second Wiki Academy Conference, Israel.

MAshup (web application hybrid). (2010). In wikipedia, the free encyclopedia. Available at http://en.wikipedia.org/w/index.php?title=Mashup_(web_application_hybrid)&oldid=378536230. Retrieved on August 29, 2010.

Mason, R., & Rennie, F. (2008). *E-learning and social networking handbook*. New York: Routledge.

Meishar-Tal, H., Tal-Elhasid, E., & Yair, Y. (2008). Wikis in academic courses: An institutional perspective. In: Y. Eshet, A. Caspi & N. Geri (Eds), *Learning in the technological era* (pp. 79–83). Chais Conference on Instructional Technologies Research, Ra'anana, Israel: Open University of Israel.

O'Reilly, T. (2005). What Is Web 2.0 Design patterns and business models for the next generation of software. Available at http://www.oreillynet.com/lpt/a/6228. Retrieved on January 31, 2007.

Palloff, R., & Pratt, K. (2005). Online learning communities re-visited. In: *Proceedings of the 21st annual conference on distance teaching and learning*, August 2005. Madison, WI: University of Wisconsin. Available at http://www.uwex.edu/disted/conference/Resource_library/proceedings/05_1801.pdf. Retrieved on August 29, 2010.

Pang, L. (2009). Application of blogs to support reflective learning journals. Available at http://deoracle.org/online-pedagogy/teaching-strategies/application-of-blogs.html

Pulman, A. (2007). Blogging @ BU: IHCS case studies. Centre for Excellence in Media Practice. CEMP Work in Progress, Bournemouth University, UK. Available online at: http://eprints.bournemouth.ac.uk/5731/1/CEMP-PAPERS-Blogging.pdf

Russell, K. (2008). Webspace: Weebly. *Click*, February 8. Available at http://news.bbc.co.uk/2/
    hi/programmes/click_online/7243271.stm. Retrieved on April 15, 2010.
Smith, L. J., & Drago, K. (2004). Learner support in workplace training. In: J. Brindley (Ed.),
    Learner support in open, distance, and online learning environments (pp. 193–201).
    Oldenburg, Germany: Bibliotheks-und Informationssystem der Universität Oldenburg.
Weebly Team. (n.d.). Weebly featured review. *000Webhost.com*. Available at http://www.
    000webhost.com/directory/reviews/weebly.com/. Retrieved on April 15, 2010.
Wolf, K. (2008). A blogging good time: The use of blogs as a reflective learning and feedback
    tool for final year public relations students. In: Australian Collaborative Education
    Network (Ed.), *Proceedings of world association for cooperative education-Australian
    collaborative education network Asia pacific* (pp. 649–656). Australia: Australian
    Collaborative Education Network.
Wright, S. (n.d.) Website reviews: Weebly.com. *Helium*. Available at http://www.helium.com/
    items/1191856-is-the-free-personal-website-creation-service-weebly-any-good. Retrieved
    on April 15, 2010.

THE *NETWORKED CLASS* IN A MASTER'S PROGRAM: PERSONALIZATION AND OPENNESS THROUGH SOCIAL MEDIA

Lina Morgado

ABSTRACT

Social media have been a powerful source of social and cultural change in the past few years, reframing the ways in which we communicate, interact with information, and build knowledge. In a higher education context, they have had a significant impact in breaking down the walls of traditional classrooms and closed online environments (LMSs). By combining formal and informal contexts and interactions, and enabling the dialog with wider audiences, they bring affordances such as transparency, real-life communication, meaningful tasks, and conversations, which result in a stronger engagement on the part of the students and a better, more diversified learning experience.

In this chapter, I describe the ways in which social media were used in an online master's degree on e-Learning Pedagogy, at Universidade Aberta, Portugal, in an effort to move toward the networked class. *Tools and services used include Twitter, Facebook, Delicious and Diigo, blogs,*

Educating Educators with Social Media
Cutting-edge Technologies in Higher Education, Volume 1, 135–152
Copyright © 2011 by Emerald Group Publishing Limited
All rights of reproduction in any form reserved
ISSN: 2044-9968/doi:10.1108/S2044-9968(2011)0000001009

*wikis, and Second Life, among many others that students have been using
to perform their tasks and publish their work.*

SOCIAL SOFTWARE AND SOCIAL MEDIA

Social media have been a powerful force of change in the past few years,
reframing the ways in which we communicate with one another, interact
with information, and build knowledge. Yet, despite the social, economical,
cultural, and educational impact they have had, it is hard sometimes to
distinguish this concept from others with which it is closely related and,
more often than not, identified, like Web 2.0 (also occasionally labeled
"social web") or social software.

Clay Shirky is generally acknowledged as being the first to use the term
"social software" in our contemporary context, when organizing the Social
Software Summit in November 2002, defining it then as "all uses of software
that supported interacting groups, even if the interaction was offline" (Boyd,
2006). He later simplified his definition to "software that supports group
interaction" (Shirky, 2003). Coates (2005), in his *An addendum to a definition
of Social Software*, tried a more extended description, characterizing it as
follows:

> Social Software can be loosely defined as software which supports, extends, or derives
> added value from human social behaviour – message-boards, musical taste-sharing,
> photo-sharing, instant messaging, mailing lists, social networking.

Generally speaking, one can say that the concept refers to the use of
technology-mediated communication that fosters the sharing of information
and knowledge as well as the formation of communities. In practice, it is
supported by Web applications that provide users with the possibility of
contributing with information in exchange for something (Peña, Córcoles, &
Casado, 2006). According to this perspective, a complex system emerges
from the sum of these contributions, revealing a collective intelligence
labeled by Surowiecki (2004), "the wisdom of crowds," developing socially
and culturally in cyberspace (Lévy, 2002). The development of this collective
intelligence represents to O'Reilly's (2005) one of the key factors in the
success of the "new web" that he popularized as "Web 2.0."

Anderson (2006, 2008) takes a different approach. For him, it is hard to
define the concept of social software, mainly because of two reasons: firstly,
because it includes a great variety of technologies, and secondly, because it is
the social aspects that emerge when these different technologies are combined.

For Boyd (2006), social software brings profound changes in terms of how these technologies are designed, how they conceptualize participation, and how individuals behave. Dron (2007) and Dron and Anderson (2009), while considering that there is no clear definition of social software, offer an interesting description of what it means to him: organic, self-organizing, and evolutive, replicating what is successful and reducing what is not. Romaní and Kuklinski (2007) take a similar perspective, contending that people often do not use Web 2.0 tools for the end they were created, rebuilding it according to their needs and social practices, thus causing the best tools to thrive.

Moore (2007) highlights the fact that when we look at the most common descriptors used to talk about Web 2.0 tools, social software and user-generated content come at the top. These two descriptors together create a clear distinctive characteristic when compared to previous technologies: The power of users to work together in the creation of content through multiple authorship, whether it be text, audio, or video artifacts. In his view, this results in the rise of a third key characteristic – open access to the content created in this manner.

Anyway we look at it, when trying to describe, social media people end up talking about social software or, at a more general level, Web 2.0. The focus that matters must be set on the social affordances it brings, on the way it changes the relationship between consumers and producers of content, and on the user empowerment it supports in a context that has become highly interactive, participatory, and cooperative.

Education (Davidson & Goldberg, 2010), and particularly online education (Anderson, 2008), has no choice but to respond to these new realities in an engaged and effective way. Learners have now new needs and expectations concerning their learning process and are used to new ways of interacting with other people and with information and knowledge, all of which require new modes of facilitating and supporting their learning (Alleman & Wartman, 2009).

Furthermore, personalization and control of their own learning become key issues, with learners having a very active role in the process, as the participatory culture of the Web requires participatory pedagogies.

Finally, the networked experience enabled by social media (Dron & Anderson, 2009), based on conversations, sharing, and cooperation, calls for contexts in which learning has a strong social dimension and interaction and cooperation are fostered (Siemens, 2008, 2010; Downes, 2006).

In the next section, I describe the effort in the e-Learning Pedagogy Master's program, at Universidade Aberta (UAb), to be up to the challenges that online learning faces today and to find new and effective ways of promoting learning in the networked society.

THE CASE OF A MASTER'S PROGRAM

Introduction

UAb, the Portuguese Distance Education University, is going through a profound process of change that involves the virtualization of teaching and learning supported by a new pedagogical model for online education (Pereira, Mendes, Morgado, Amante, & Bidarra, 2008). Based on pedagogical and sustainability considerations, the pedagogic model adopted implies, for postgraduation courses, the constitution of virtual classes where groups of students work collaboratively under the constant orientation and supervision of a teacher, with high levels of interaction (Morgado, Pereira, & Mendes, 2008), while for graduation courses, the pedagogic model implies more limited levels of group work and considerable time for individual study, with the possibility of interaction and some collaboration among students and interaction with the teacher at predefined moments during the course.

One of the most challenging tasks in this process of migration to online learning was to give the proper training and support to the teachers who were going to embody this change and put UAb's new pedagogical model into practice. In the context of Distance Education, both students and teachers, as well as other mediators in the learning process, have been socialized according to models heavily based on self-learning. In the context of a pedagogical change such as our model entails, it was important to create supporting mechanisms for the various actors so that a *resocialization for interaction* and a new learning culture could take place (Mendes, Morgado, & Amante, 2008). It should not, however, be merely added to the course contents, but constitute an integral component of the learning experience through the design of significant activities, helping to overcome resistance to new forms of learning, to technology, and to a new kind of pedagogical relation.

The Pedagogical Foundations of the Master's Program

The Master's program in e-Learning Pedagogy was created in 2005, as a response to a growing need for training and specialization in distance education, more specifically the need to establish a solid pedagogic foundation in e-learning for those working in teaching, training, instructional design, content creation, or research in the field. At the same time, it sought to meet the challenges of a tight and effective integration of information and communication technologies in Education and of educating individuals for the knowledge society.

Since its inception, the Master's has followed UAb's pedagogic model (Pereira et al., 2008), based on the principles of flexibility, autonomy, interaction, and collaboration. It has also focused heavily on innovating and exploring new paths, based both on the relentless technological advances (and the cultural and social changes associated to them) and on the growing research in the field.

The base virtual learning environment used is Moodle (the platform adopted by UAb), combined with a host of social media tools and services. The program is taught completely online and resorts mainly to asynchronous communication.

The learning process is activity driven, with students performing significant, real-life tasks and producing digital artifacts that they publish using in the process various tools and services such as blogs, wikis, podcasts and videos, social bookmarking (Lee, Miller, & Newnham, 2008), Slide-Share, VoiceThread, Facebook (Boon & Sinclair, 2009; Piscitelli, Adaime, & Binder, 2010), Twitter (Huberman, Romero, & Wu, 2009; Ebner, Lienhardt, Rohs, & Meyer, 2010), or Second Life (McKerlich & Anderson, 2007; Warburton, 2009; Edirisingha, Nie, Pluciennik, & Young, 2009; Salmon, 2009), to name the most relevant. The students work individually, in pairs, or in small teams, according to the task or, sometimes, to their own will. Cooperation in the form of sharing (ideas, resources, and reflections), peer feedback, and peer review are strongly encouraged and occasionally designed in the task. The fact that students publish their work on the Internet allows for interaction and dialog with a wider audience, which results in greater meaning and motivation in the learning process, as they become part of a "networked class" and move far beyond the virtual classroom walls of a private garden like Moodle.

Personalization and Openness
Personalization of the learning experience happens in various ways (Downes, 2007; McElvaney & Berge, 2009). A number of students coming into the e-Leaning Pedagogy Master's already have an online presence, although in most cases, it is not very developed. Students in this situation are encouraged to continue using the tools and services through which they already interact with people and information online, along with other tools

that are necessary for their work in the course. Students who are at a lower stage in their online presence are given guidance in how to start using some core tools and services necessary for their learning and encouraged to add their own preferred ones as they get more proficient on the Web. They also benefit greatly from the experience of their more seasoned colleagues and from the experimenting and sharing of new ideas and processes that keeps going throughout the course.

The result is that these students end up creating or developing their own personal learning environments (Downes, 2007; Attwell, 2010), mostly tailored according to their individual preferences and characteristics, that they use to conduct their learning, publish their work, maintain an e-portfolio, gather, and organize relevant information. Their Personal Learning Environment (PLE) is, in these circumstances, a very effective bridge between the more formal aspects of their learning and the rich, informal interactions they have with other people and resources they are connected to on the Internet.

Personalization also manifests itself by a certain degree of flexibility in the curriculum of the curricular units and by the choice of individual, pair, or team work. There are core contents to be studied by everyone, but students are also given a choice of exploring or deepening areas that are more relevant to them or more in line with what they need at this moment of their learning process. On the contrary, because students produce artifacts as part of their learning process, they are contributing with resources and contents to the course that may be (and often are) used by other students to learn new things. Although some tasks are designed with a specific type of work required (individual, pair, or team), students are given some opportunities for choosing how they would like to perform certain activities according to their preferences and considering how they want to approach the task – sometimes working alone will fit best what they want to do, some other times a team, or a pair will make more sense to them.

Openness is another major element when you are trying to achieve a "networked" class, and it is highly encouraged and practiced in the Master's program (Mott, 2010). Most of the materials and resources used to support the learning of contents are freely available online. Furthermore, as I have mentioned earlier, the artifacts produced by students in the course of the activities to demonstrate what they have learned and the competences they have acquired are published online and become, thus, learning resources for their colleagues. Students are also encouraged to publish their work using a Creative Commons license, so that it may be used by others to learn or reused for teaching or training in other contexts. This way, a relevant part of the knowledge created throughout the learning process and the objects resulting from it are made available as open educational resources for the wider community of users who may benefit from them and are not lost or archived away once the course ends.

We believe this transparency is very valuable in any educational context, because it helps students and teachers achieve a better learning experience. In an online context, this is made easier and more powerful due to the social technologies that allow for easy publication, access, and interaction, with the additional affordance of having a much wider audience when you publish and communicate outside the virtual classroom, as often happens in our Master's.

The fact that a student's work is made available for the others to see and comment upon deepens the social dimension that learning should have and provides more opportunities for learning with and from the other students and other people, greatly fostering cooperation and dissemination of relevant information and knowledge. It also helps contextualize and understand the teacher's actions and decisions, providing, at the same time, a broader feedback, because the comments made to somebody's work might be really helpful to many others.

Assessment
Assessment in the e-Learning Pedagogy Master's is based on the evaluation of the tasks performed by students during their learning process. These tasks are diversified and lead to, in most cases, the production of digital objects or artifacts that constitute, as a whole, a student's e-portfolio, that is, a showcase of what they have learned and of the competencies they have developed, often along with some sort of reflection (global or for certain tasks) on the process they have experienced. These tasks are done individually, in pairs, or in teams, sometimes according to the instructions given, some other times according to the students' choice.

Students get timely feedback during the tasks to help them adjust their work and overcome difficulties that may arise. Individual grades per task and the descriptive evaluation that accompanies them are not made publicly available, but because the work is available online and peer feedback is encouraged, students know their colleagues' work and often comment on it or review it. In some curricular units, students get to grade their colleagues in some tasks, and their assessment represents a percentage of the final grade in that task.

A recurrent question concerning assessment in online learning, and a very important one, is "How do we know that it is the student, in fact, who did/is doing the work, and not someone else?" As happens with other educational contexts, online education is not immune to fraud. People cheat in face-to-face tests, exams, and individual or group assignments, and the same happens in assessment situations online. We need to accept the fact that there will always be a minority of people who will beat the system, because no system is 100% fraud-proof. Our effort needs to concentrate on keeping the numbers very small and guarantee that these are rare exceptions.

We need to look at this issue relating it to the pedagogical approach (the type of activities and tasks students are asked to perform) and to the kind of assessment strategy is put in place (how students have to demonstrate their knowledge or competence). Moreover, we need to check how the assessment activities are related to the learning tasks.

If the online learning experience

- is based on memorizing and reproducing content,
- encompasses little interaction or the teacher has little or no presence in that interaction,
- requires no collaboration among students,
- is not transparent at all, that is, students do not have to publish their work, and
- does not require students to regularly perform tasks and produce some sort of artifact that demonstrates or illustrates what they have learned or have become capable of doing then you will need some sort of face-to-face assessment or sophisticated authentication technologies to guarantee the identity of the student assessed and the validity of their knowledge, because it is almost impossible to identify most cases of fraud.

If, on the contrary, the online learning experience

- is based on developing skills and competences,
- has a high level of interaction and the teacher participates regularly in that interaction,
- requires students to collaborate or cooperate throughout the learning process,
- is transparent, that is, requires students to publish their work,
- requires students to perform tasks regularly and produce artifacts that demonstrate or illustrate their knowledge of the contents studied and their skills and competences in applying them in specific situations and the assessment activities,
- requires a personal elaboration of the contents,

- is related to the tasks performed, drawing on material and reflections produced in the process,
- is multiple and diversified, and
- is specific, that is, requires the application of knowledge and skills to specific situations as we believe happens in our Master's program, then the chances for fraud are pretty low.

It is not impossible that students find someone who, for any strange reason, would be willing to work endless hours to do a course like this for them, but it seems highly improbable. Furthermore, the high levels of interaction and the strong social dimension characteristic of this pedagogical approach enable the development of effective interpersonal relationships that allow people to know each other relatively well.

Organization

Since 2008 (third edition), the Master's program follows the Bologna process principles. The Master's program is divided in two semesters with four curricular units each, for a total of eight curricular units. Each unit lasts for about 20 weeks and the 4 curricular units in each semester are taught simultaneously. The class has an average of 25 students. The study plan is as follows:

- First semester (*all four curricular units are taught simultaneously*), *Note:* * indicates Students choose 2 of these 4 optional curricular units.
  Learning and Technologies (Optional*) – 6 European Credit Transfer System (ECTS)
  Materials and Resources for e-Learning (Optional*) – 6 ECTS
  Educational Communication – 8 ECTS
  Education and Networked Society – 8 ECTS
  Models of Distance Education – 8 ECTS
- Second Semester (*all four curricular units are taught simultaneously*)
  Design and Assessment in e-Learning (Optional*) – 6 ECTS
  Psychology and Internet (Optional*) – 6 ECTS
  Virtual Learning Environments – 8 ECTS
  Pedagogical Processes in e-Learning – 8 ECTS
  Research Methodologies in e-Learning – 8 CTS

The Master's is supervised by a coordinator, who participates in its design and implementation, both with respect to organization, articulation, and teacher support, and with respect to the pedagogical aspects involved, to assure the quality of teaching and learning. This coordinator also plays an important role in the relationship with the students, being in charge of the introductory familiarization module, where students get in touch with some relevant tools and processes to be used in the course, and responsible for moderating a coordination space throughout the two semesters. Only students have access to this space and it is where they can get help with any problems they might be having in their learning process not related to the contents of the curricular units.

Typical Use of Social Media in the Master's Program

There is a wide variety of social tools and services used in the Master's program. The core set used in most activities includes blogs, wikis, and social bookmarking, but to produce and publish their work students resort to a very diversified range of possibilities, according to their needs and preferences. I describe the typical uses of the most relevant tools and services in the following sections.

Blogs (Blogger, WordPress)
This is, perhaps, the most important tool because of its role as a student's personal place of publishing and of aggregating an online presence. Students use it to publish some of the assignments required for the course, but most of them also share their ideas, reflections, and experiences about the learning process or resources they find interesting, along with more personal posts about any subject they feel inclined to write about. Students also use their blog to link to work they have published elsewhere.

This and the fact that they follow other people (and are followed, in the case of Blogger) receive comments both from fellow students and from other Internet users, and comment on other students' blogs both creates an integrated online presence, that can also serve the purpose of an e-portfolio, and develops their personal learning network.

One of the interesting points in the use of blogs is how, in some circumstances, formal learning and somewhat "forced connections" (their fellow students) mingle with informal learning and the personal connections that students have or create on the Internet. The use of blogs by students has, at least in some cases, promoted active participation and dialog on the Web well beyond any course considerations.

Therefore, we could say that blogs are at the centre of students' PLE and play an important role as far as their personal online presence and the bridging between formal and informal learning are concerned.

Wikis *(PBWorks, Wikispaces)*

Wikis are sometimes used as a "whiteboard" for brainstorming or gathering everyone's ideas about any given topic, but, from a teaching point of view, they are mainly used in team activities, where it is important, on the one hand, to provide a flexible and effective environment for collaboration and, on the other hand, to be able to monitor individual contribution to the team effort.

Because of its flexibility and ease of use, wikis are often the choice of students when they want to publish their work and feel their blog is not best suited for it. Some students also use it to aggregate the work they have published in different places, making it easier to access the different artifacts they have produced. Most of them will still link to this wiki from their blog, which is their most personal presence on the Web.

Social Bookmarking *(Diigo, Delicious)*

Delicious is the preferred service used by students for bookmarking relevant resources, because it is the most known and widely used. However, because of some characteristics that have a greater educational potential, like groups, highlighting, notes, and comments, Diigo is the service we use for formal course-related tasks. Therefore, whereas in Diigo, the bookmarks collected are course content related, associated with comments or brief discussions in the Diigo group forum, Delicious is used by students in a much more personal perspective. Some of the bookmarks may relate directly or indirectly with material relevant for the course, but the majority of them reflect students' personal interests and explorations on the Web. Again, this is an interesting case of formal and informal learning coming together through the use of social media.

Media Hosting Services

By media hosting services, I mean sites that host multimedia objects such as videos, presentations, podcasts, screencasts or mash-up multimedia objects. YouTube, SlideShare, Prezi, Scribd, PodOmatic, and VoiceThread are the most commonly used to host these objects, but due to the degree of choice students have in many circumstances and the variety of artifacts they choose to produce, there are many other services used. These objects are generally embedded in students' blogs or wikis when that option is available, which is the case in most of the services used.

Twitter

We still have not devised a productive way of using Twitter for course-related work, that is, it is not currently used for teaching or required for learning tasks, but many students and teachers use it to exchange information and resources relevant to the course, along with their regular, personal, or professional use of this service.

Twitter is currently used by the Master's coordination to disseminate information related to the course, relevant events taking place, resources that are shared by teachers and students, or any other piece of information that is perceived as having a potential interest for the students or teachers in general.

A very positive experience with Twitter was the publicizing and following of the Master's Annual Conference, MyMPeL2010.[1] Information about the conference before it and a live account of the presentations and discussions taking place during the conference were shared on Twitter by students and other participants and disseminated (retweeted) by their followers, generating a high flow of information about the conference and a prominent online presence. The hashtag used was *#mpelconf* and it was the top subject on Twitter in Portugal on that day.

Facebook

Facebook, much like Twitter, is not currently used for teaching or required for learning tasks. However, is has been used with success by the coordination and some students in the course.

The coordination created an account on Facebook that is "befriended" (in both directions) with students and teachers of the Master's, but also with other people who come through *friends'* personal or professional networks.

The main goal is the sharing of information relevant to the course, but also the creation of communication and interaction channels in the network that open the course community to outsiders. The sharing of content (materials, resources, media, such as photos, videos, or presentations), the comments made, the publicizing of events, or self-revealing messages about personal feelings, interests, likes, and dislikes all facilitate the establishment of connections of a more interpersonal or emotional nature.

Another interesting aspect resulting from this is how public and private, personal and professional, local, and global aspects of people's online experience often mix in this environment, as happens with Twitter and, to a lesser extent, the aforementioned blogs.

Although Facebook has not been widely used by students to support their formal learning, there have been situations in which they have utilized the service effectively to get comments and feedback from the wider community regarding their work on an ongoing task, either through the creation of a group or through polls to gather their audience's opinions.

Tagging

Tagging is an important aspect in a process where so many different tools and services are used, where students' work, cooperation, and interaction are spread throughout so many different places and where course-related, formal activity is mingled with personal, informal online activity.

Tags are especially relevant in the case of blogs, social bookmarking, and Twitter (the term here is "hashtags"), where the mix between formal and informal or personal is stronger, to easily identify and retrieve the elements that are part of the course work or directly related to course contents and resources. Generally, a global tag is agreed upon at the beginning of the Master's program and used in the services where it applies. Sometimes, for specific tasks, additional tags are arranged between students and their teacher in the curricular unit involved.

Virtual Worlds – Second Life

Some people may find it hard to consider Second Life as part of the Web 2.0, and we would not absolutely disagree, although it is not a clear-cut judgment to make. When it comes to social media, however, and considering how it is broadly defined, we think it falls under this notion. The reason we deal with it in a section of its own has to do with the particular characteristics of the environment.

The number of students who already use Second Life before the Master's is very low. In the current edition (fourth), only one had a Second Life (SL) account and an avatar. Therefore, and taking into account the learning curve typical of this environment, Second Life is introduced and explored right at the start of the Master's, during the familiarization module (the two-week introductory model), to be later used in some curricular units for course work or by students to perform some tasks or present their work. The use of Second Life is coupled with Moodle for instructions, some online discussions and support.

The learning activities designed to explore Second Life at this time have their foundation on Salmon's five-stage model of online learning (Salmon, 2009). The data is recorded in Moodle forums and chat logs, all in written

Table 1. Exploring Second Life in the Familiarization Module.

Moodle Activities Forums	Second Life Activities	Description: Activity, Objectives, and What was Accomplished
Help and feedback forum Individual presentation (Real Life (RL) and photo)	Activity one Session 1 in-world	Welcome to SL and encouragement; Ice-breakers; Creating the group and adding all the participants; Communicating in SL; Setting the rules/netiquette Sharing the difficulties
Second Life System Requirements Accounts of first time in SL Doubts and difficulties about SL navigation Summary of the in-word meeting	Activity 2 Sessions 2 and 3 in-world	Improving communication in SL; Analysis of the interface (Friends, in particular); Creating a notecard; Finding Linden dollars for free
Second Life Individual presentation of the avatar (photo postage using Flickr and SL name) Issues related with SL Sharing reflections about SL exploration	Activity 2 Session 3 in-world	Expressing doubts and exposing difficulties; Going shopping; Commenting on one another's appearance and see individual improvements; Sharing positive and less positive SL experiences Buying things and saving them in the inventory; Editing appearance and changing clothes

text (Table 1). All the resources needed to develop the activities are made available in Moodle. In the following is a description of the type of work that takes place with SL during the familiarization module.

Afterwards, during the course, SL is used in some curricular units, either to host conferences (some of which are a collection of presentations done by students) or to perform tasks in which students have to design learning activities for Second Life (Macedo & Morgado, 2009a, 2009b). Although this does not happen often, sometimes, SL is the students' environment of choice to show/present their work in certain activities.

CONCLUSION

I have tried to outline and describe the ways in which we are trying to accomplish the notion of a "networked class" in the Master's in e-Learning Pedagogy at UAb, through the extended use of social media to support learning. I have also put forward the pedagogical framework in which the Master's operates and given examples of the typical use of such tools and services by students and teachers, other than UAb's e-learning platform, Moodle.

Key elements for us are personalization and openness, because they are central to the development of personal learning networks and environments and to the formation of meaningful connections to other people and resources. They are also nuclear to foster cooperation and sharing, creating the basis for a strong social dimension in the online learning process that is, in our view, one of the great affordances social media provide us.

The degree of choice at several levels (contents, tools, and collaboration) and the possibility of communicating, sharing, and interacting outside the class empowers students relatively to their learning process and brings their learning closer to real life, resulting in a more significant and contextualized experience. Furthermore, the possibility of interacting with and getting feedback from a wider audience and experts in different fields, with whom they engage in real conversations, also enriches their learning and makes it more effective and rewarding. By publishing their work openly online, students become also authors, and the artifacts they produce in their learning tasks can later be used by others as resources for learning.

One of the most valuable consequences of using such a distributed, open, and personalized environment for learning is the degree to which the different circles of students' activity as individuals (formal and informal, personal and professional), traditionally separated, come together and mingle, how their experience of formal education – taking a master's degree at a University – can be connected to and incorporate their other activities online, becoming seamlessly part of their lifelong learning process and of their development as individuals.

NOTE

1. Information available at http://mpel.crowdvine.com.

REFERENCES

Alleman, A. M., & Wartman, K. (2009). *Online social networking on campus: Understanding what matters in student culture*. New York: Routledge.
Anderson, T. (2006). Higher education evolution: Individual freedom afforded by educational social software. In: M. Beaudoin (Ed.), *Perspectives on the future of higher education in digital age* (pp. 77–90). New York: Nova Science Publishers.
Anderson, T. (2008). Social software to support distance education learners. In: T. Anderson (Ed.), *Theory and practice of online learning* (pp. 221–241). Canada: AU Press, Athabasca University.
Attwell, G. (2010, March). *The affordances of Web 2.0 and the development of personal learning environments*. Pontydysgu: Bridge to Learning. Available at http://www.pontydysgu.org/2010/03/the-affordances-of-web-2-0-and-the-development-of-personal-learning-environments
Boon, S., & Sinclair, C. (2009). A world I don't inhabit: Disquiet and identity in second life and facebook. *Educational Media International, 46*(2), 99–110.
Boyd, D. (2006). The significance of social software. BlogTalk Reloaded, Vienna, Austria, October 2. Available at http://www.danah.org/papers/BlogTalksReloaded.pdf
Coates, T. (2005). An addendum to a definition of social software. Plasticbag.org (blog). Available at http://www.plasticbag.org/archives/2005/01/an_addendum_to_a_definition_of_social_software/
Davidson, C., & Goldberg, D. (2010). *The future of thinking: Learning institutions in a digital age*. Cambridge, MA: MIT Press.
Downes, S. (2006). Groups vs networks: The class struggle continues. Presentation to eFest Conference, Wellington, New Zealand. Available at http://www.downes.ca/presentation/53
Downes, S. (2007). Learning networks in practice. *Emerging Technologies for Learning, 2*, 19–27. Available at http://partners.becta.org.uk/page_documents/research/emerging_technologies07_chapter2.pdf
Dron, J. (2007). Designing the undesignable: Social software and control. *Educational Technology & Society, 10*(3), 60–71.
Dron, J., & Anderson, T. (2009). How the crowd can teach. In: S. Hatzipanagos & S. Warburton (Eds), *Handbook of research on social software and developing community ontologies* (pp. 1–17). Hershey: IGI.
Ebner, M., Lienhardt, C., Rohs, M., & Meyer, I. (2010). Microblogs in higher education – A chance to facilitate informal and process-oriented learning? *Computers and Education, 55*, 92–100.
Edirisingha, P., Nie, M., Pluciennik, M., & Young, R. (2009). Socialisation for learning at a distance in a 3-D multi-user virtual environment. *British Journal of Educational Technology, 40*(3), 458–479.
Huberman, B., Romero, D., & Wu, F. (2009). Social networks that matter: Twitter under the microscope. *First Monday, 14*, 1–5.
Lee, W., Miller, C., & Newnham, L. (2008). RSS and content syndication in higher education: Subscribing to a new model of teaching and learning. *Educational Media International, 45*(4), 311–322.
Lévy, P. (2002). L'intelligence collective et ses objets. samizdat|biblioweb. Available at http://biblioweb.samizdat.net/article42.html

Macedo, A., & Morgado, L. (2009a). Learning to teach in second life. *Proceedings of EDEN seventh open classroom conference*, Oporto. Paper award leading innovative practice. Available at http://www.eden-online.org/contents/conferences/OCRCs/Porto/AM_LM.pdf

Macedo, A., & Morgado, L. (2009b). Socialisation and social presence in distance education using virtual environments. *Proceedings of XI symposium on computers in education*, Coimbra (pp. 120–126).

McElvaney, J., & Berge, Z. (2009). Weaving a personal web: Using online technologies to create customized, connected, and dynamic learning environments. *Canadian Journal of Learning and Technology*, *35*(2). Available at http://www.cjlt.ca/index.php/cjlt/article/view/524/257

McKerlich, R., & Anderson, T. (2007). Community of inquiry and learning in immersive environments. *Journal of Asynchronous Learning Networks*, *11*(4), 35–52. Available at http://sloanconsortium.org/sites/default/files/v11n4_mckerlich_0.pdf

Mendes, A., Morgado, L., & Amante, L. (2008). Online communication and e-learning. In: T. Kidd (Ed.), *Handbook of research in instructional systems and technology* (pp. 927–943). Hershey: Idea Group Inc.

Moore, M. (2007). Editorial – Web 2.0: Does it really matter? *American Journal of Distance Education*, *21*(4), 177–183. Available at http://www.informaworld.com/10.1080/08923640701595183

Morgado, L., Pereira, A., & Mendes, A. Q. (2008). The "contract" as an instrument to mediate learning. In: A. Mendes, R. Costa & I. Pereira (Eds), *Computers and education towards educational change and innovation* (pp. 63–72). Amsterdam: Springer Science.

Mott, J. (2010). Envisioning the post-LMS era: The open learning network. *EDUCAUSE Quarterly*, *33*(1). Available at http://www.educause.edu/EDUCAUSE+Quarterly/EDUCAUSEQuarterlyMagazineVolum/EnvisioningthePostLMSEraTheOpe/199389

O'Reilly, T. (2005). What is Web 2.0: Design patterns and business models for the next generation of software. *O'Reilly*. Available at http://www.oreillynet.com/pub/a/oreilly/tim/news/2005/09/30/what-is-web-20.html

Peña, I., Córcoles, C. A., & Casado, C. (2006). The 2.0 teacher: Teaching and research from the web. UOC Papers, no. 3. Available at http://www.uoc.edu/uocpapers/1/dt/cat/mas.pdf

Pereira, A., Mendes, A., Morgado, L., Amante, L., & Bidarra, J. (2008). *Universidade Aberta's pedagogical model for distance education*. Lisbon: Universidade Aberta. Available at http://repositorioaberto.univ-ab.pt/handle/10400.2/1295

Piscitelli, A., Adaime, I., & Binder, I. (2010). *El Proyecto Facebook y la posuniversidad. Sistemas operativos sociales y entornos abiertos de aprendizaje*. Barcelona: Ed. Ariel.

Romaní, C. C., & Kuklinski, H. P. (2007). Planeta Web 2.0. Inteligencia colectiva o médios fast food. GRID-UVic. Flacso Mexico. Barcelona/México DF. Available at http://www.flacso.edu.mx/planeta/blog/index.php?option=com_docman&task=doc_download&gid=12&Itemid=6

Salmon, G. (2009). The future for (second) life and learning. *British Journal of Educational Technology*, *40*(3), 526–538.

Shirky, C. (2003). A group is its own worst enemy. Available at http://www.shirky.com/writings/group_enemy.html

Siemens, G. (2008). New structures and spaces of learning: The systemic impact of connective knowledge, connectivism, and networked learning. Comunicação apresentada no *Encontro sobre Web 2.0*, Universidade do Minho, Braga. Available at http://elearnspace.org/Articles/systemic_impact.htm

Siemens, G. (2010). Teaching in social and technological networks. *Connectivism* (blog). Available at http://www.connectivism.ca/?p=220

Surowiecki, J. (2004). *The wisdom of crowds*. London: Little Brown.

Warburton, S. (2009). Second life in higher education: Assessing the potential for and the barriers to deploying virtual words in learning and teaching. *British Journal of Educational Technology, 40*(3), 414–426.

PART III
DESIGN OF INSTRUCTION
WITH SOCIAL MEDIA

FUTURE SOCIAL LEARNING NETWORKS AT UNIVERSITIES – AN EXPLORATORY SEMINAR SETTING

Nina Heinze and Wolfgang Reinhardt

ABSTRACT

Even if there are heavy transformations in technology, science, and society taking place in recent years, university courses often still emphasize head-on teaching methods with classic learning tools and resources. At the end of a course, students have then often acquired second hand knowledge, which is often detached from experience-based, constructive learning. The use of new media, the process of working in teams with application of these services, and problem-solving scenarios remain out of students' grasp. In this contribution, we illustrate a participative and cooperative seminar setting between two German universities that tries to overcome those limitations. We describe the pedagogic design and the practical implementation of the course, list objectives and intentions and describe the organizational structure of the seminar.

Educating Educators with Social Media
Cutting-edge Technologies in Higher Education, Volume 1, 155–172
Copyright © 2011 by Emerald Group Publishing Limited
ISSN: 2044-9968/doi:10.1108/S2044-9968(2011)0000001010

INTRODUCTION

Students today are considered net-savvy, technology-affine persons who feel comfortable using the latest Web 2.0 tools to communicate and collaborate with their peers (Oblinger, 2007). While this may hold true for leisure activities, it is far from vindicable in university settings (Heinze, 2008). Here they are often confronted with buzzwords like Web 2.0 and semantic Web, augmented reality or ubiquitous learning in head-on lectures that are far from the reality they have experience with. Furthermore, they are taught to research these topics and often hold theoretical presentations on these subjects without being able to experience the use, potential and deficits of new technologies themselves. At the end of a semester, they have acquired "second hand" knowledge about the theoretical significance of these tools, which is often detached from real learning experiences. The use of new media, the process of working in teams with application of these services, and problem-solving scenarios remain out of students' grasp. There seems to be a mismatch between students' practical application of social media services and the theoretical framework surrounding these technologies.

We believe that this does not need to be the case. There is great potential for teaching and learning in university settings with social media tools. Theory and practice of these areas can and must be combined to create rich learning experiences. Students' captivation of Web 2.0 technologies and their affinity to technology must be utilized to foster a deep understanding of the subject matter, foster competencies, and provide them with real-life experiences. We would like to describe how existing Web 2.0 services could be used for hands-on collaborative and cooperative learning experiences in formal university settings. To discover and evaluate how social media can be integrated into university courses, we devised a seminar setting that requires two groups of students from two different universities with differing research backgrounds to jointly solve design and implementation tasks from real-world research projects from the field of technology-enhanced learning (TEL) by using social media for collaboration and communication. One group shared the same geographic location, that is, the students were all from the same university and had the possibility to meet online as well as face-to-face while the other group did not share the same location and students could solely meet online and work exclusively with Web 2.0 tools. This chapter describes the theoretical framework and evaluation measures of our course setting and provides an example of how social media can be used in formal learning environments to provide hands-on experience in the field of TEL.

SOCIAL MEDIA IN FORMAL LEARNING SETTINGS – AN EXPLORATORY COURSE DESIGN

During the past years as teachers at the University of Paderborn and the University of Augsburg, both in Germany, we felt that while students use social media frequently they often lack the skills to apply the possibilities of these technologies to their studies. We saw the need to foster students understanding of the potentials and also shortcomings of social media that goes beyond posting the current state of being on Twitter or uploading the latest travel pictures on Facebook. We wanted to design a seminar setting where students had to use social media tools to work with one another collaboratively and engage in practice-oriented problem-solving tasks. The idea for a social learning network between our institutions was born.

Partners

The concept for the course was conceived at the University of Paderborn in the Computer Science Education Group. The group is actively involved in connecting learning communities with communities of practice (Hinkelmann, Holzweißig, Magenheim, Probst, & Reinhardt, 2006; Reinhardt & Holzweißig, 2006) and engaging students with real-life problems. Courses and student projects at this institution always try to involve partners from outside the own organizational boundaries and to work on tasks that are real, hard to solve, easy enough to be solvable and that promise to be motivating and engaging for the students. The seminar is carried out within the master's program in computer science.

The Digital Media Department at the University of Augsburg's Institute for Media and Educational Technology is active in the fields of new technological developments in education as well as interpersonal communication. The potential of media and educational technology for the purposes of information, communication, and education as well as the transfer of academic knowledge is in the focus of the institute. The seminar is being carried within the context of the Media and Education study program, which combines the areas of mass communication, media pedagogies, and media IT.

The two institutions provide an interdisciplinary base for exploring the use of social media in university settings since they complement each other in expertise in research, development, and evaluation of social media and innovative course designs at universities (Heinze & Schnurr, 2010a; Hinkelmann et al., 2006).

Aim of the Seminar

Our intention was to alleviate the shortcomings of head-on education and provide students with the possibilities to actively engage in learning activities, thus enabling practice-oriented knowledge creation within the realm of a formal seminar setting. To achieve this, we designed a flexible learning environment that allows learners to shape their own learning activities while solving real-life problems by situating abstract knowledge in concrete experience. Dewey (1986) describes this as combining what he called primary and secondary learning experiences. In secondary learning experiences knowledge is passed from educator to learner with small association to the learners individual experience or practice. This form of knowledge transfer is exemplary of head-on teaching. Primary learning experiences are evoked by practical interaction with real-life situations.

Both primary and secondary learning experiences are important for acquiring knowledge since probing and experiencing the implications of theory in practice provides significance to the learning process (*ibid.*). Thus, in the described course, we aim at combining theory and practice by providing authentic learning experiences in real-life environments by enabling students to solve actual Web 2.0 and semantic web problems in the areas of media and computer sciences with the use of tools commonly used in these research fields. Learners need to situate their abstract knowledge in concrete experience, which, in turn, will provide them with actual workplace, technical and social skills.

To achieve this, students who are mostly complete strangers have to collaborate with each other in small teams using social media tools to solve scientific problems in the field of TEL, create artifacts like architectures, working prototypes and wikis, and organize their learning and scientific working activities. Topics covered include smart devices for learning, potentials of m- and u-learning, Personal Learning Environments (PLEs), game-based learning, semantic web, and awareness in collaborative learning settings.

Prospects and Objectives

Twelve students participated in the course. Among them were four bachelor students in their 4th semester in the study programme "Media and Communication" with their majors in Mediapedagogics and eight master students with a background in computer sciences and business informatics. The course was split into two groups. One group consisting of two teams of two students shared the same geographic location and students all came from a technical, computer science background. The other group of four teams consisting of two students was separated geographically and students came from the fields of computer sciences and educational sciences/mass communication. It was mandatory in both groups to use social media to display collaboration and communication efforts and progress through a number of tools. In the geographically separated teams with the interdisciplinary background of the members the participants were faced with the challenges of distributed collaboration as well as with the differing approaches of scientific disciplines. Each student had to work on the solution of scientific problems in the field of TEL in collaboration with at least one student from the other university. The course therefore required participants to actively use social media and social networking tools to coordinate tasks, combine their efforts, plan and carry out the development of working solutions and artifacts to their cases that are available to all members of the team and the instructors at all times. The evaluations we carried out before, during and after the course and were intended to show if there were any significant differences between the two groups in terms of challenges and Web 2.0 use. Because of the strong inclusion of social media in the entire course of work we expected that students would be faced with the possibilities and shortcomings of these tools in regards to technology and communication. This should have lead to an increase in information and media literacy through the use of social media tools for problem-solving activities in a scientific context. We also expected that these learning and working conditions would lead to the development of higher communication skills and social competencies by nature of the dense collaboration efforts to jointly produce artifacts in the course of the seminar in (interdisciplinary) teams. In addition, the tools used should have supported the individual learning processes of the learners due to the active use of these technologies during the entire course of the seminar.

To avoid overburdening the students by providing too little guidance in learning outcomes, the course set clear goals by demanding that students produce artifacts in the field on TEL as learning products. At the beginning of the seminar each team was presented with a set of real-world topics and problems that need to be solved collaboratively by the end of the semester. This included the design and development of prototypes, wikis or other media. The topics and projects students were confronted with were connected to the challenges and research areas of the cooperating EU projects MATURE (http://mature-ip.eu) and STELLAR (http://www.stellarnet.eu). These projects are funded by the European Commission and revolve around the integration of technology in organizations and research groups. An inclusion in these projects allowed students to actively engage in current research fields in TEL that are prevailing topics in real-world settings. To ensure that students were coming along in their work and mastering the challenges they were faced with it was necessary for them to present their state of work in ongoing presentations and wikis. This allowed us and the entire team to stay up to date on research and developments and foster skills by providing feedback and input. In addition, students developed skills in working scientifically by showing how they were engaging in the process of working scientifically and managing their knowledge.

In addition to the subject-specific learning goals, the inclusion of external research partners and projects made it necessary for the seminar to be held in German as well as in English. Students did not only have to overcome geographical and research discipline barriers but also had to engage in work that was not carried out in their native language. This in turn increased their language skills and should have let them become more comfortable speaking a non-native language in the future.

Overall we expected students to display a high level of engagement, close-knit collaboration and knowledge management activities by allowing them to choose their topic of interest as well as their final artifact. The challenges they encountered in the course of the seminar should have increased their problem-solving and social skills, provided them with participation in real-life research activities and enabled them to experience the potential and deficits of social media tools. This in turn should also have fostered thinking "outside of the box" of a tightly structured university course and allowed them to develop creativity in the field of working scientifically.

SETTING THE SCENE: SOCIAL INTERACTION IN TRADITIONAL SEMINARS

The social interaction in traditional seminar settings basically takes place in real life only. Usually students and staff meet at the beginning of the semester, select topics to work on from a given list and form groups of two to four people. Often the work within those groups is divided among the group members so everybody can work on a certain facet of the given topic. In focus meetings with the supervisor the group presents their progress and has time to ask questions and to request further input. Most often little interaction takes place between the different seminar groups; they do not share references or ideas and hardly help each other on occurring problems. Very often the single groups stay restricted to their particular topic and do not make use of expertise from outside. However, Siemens (2005) stressed the fact that it is more important who you know rather than what you know because individual knowledge lies in the networks. He introduced connectivism as a new learning theory that presents learning as the social network-forming process with – personal and artificial – artifacts and persons. Moreover, Polanyi (1967) emphasized the importance of dialogues and conversations within communities – for him knowledge is socially constructed. Peer reviews in courses are sometimes used to encourage students to become more responsible, reflective, and socially interactive with their fellow students (Dochy, Segers, & Sluijsmans, 1999; Gehringer, 2001).

In traditional courses the second half of the semester or the end of a block course foresees that all groups present the results of their work. Here the participants mainly receive information without questioning its truth, source, or validity. The supervisors comment on the presentation and grade the final seminar paper together with the quality and clarity of the presentation. More often than not both quality and quantity of social interactions are not part of the grading procedure, leaving room for improvement with regards to the growing demand for reflective learners with high social competence. Here, the use of social media tools can improve learning and lead to richer learning environments. Chatti, Klamma, Jarke, and Naeve (2007) propose to apply the SECI model (Nonaka & Takeuchi, 1995) for knowledge management to learning with Web 2.0 tools. In their vision of a framework for Web 2.0-driven learning the phases of the SECI model (socialization, externalization, combination, and internalization) are supported by social media tools and thus directly influence the interaction between participants in an educational setting. In the following section, we introduce how social media tools can be used to support constructivist learning of students in seminar-like educational designs.

Constructivist Learning with Social Media

While objectivist learning theories (mainly cognitivism and behaviorism) view knowledge as an entity existing independently from the mind of an individual that can be transferred from one person to another, constructivist concepts of learning assume that knowledge is individually constructed by a person (see Jonassen, 1991; Chatti et al., 2007; Jonassen, 1999; Knuth &

Cunningham, 1993). Jonassen (1999, p. 10) describes constructivism in the following manner:

"Constructivism ... claims that reality is constructed by the knower based upon mental activity. Humans are perceivers and interpreters who construct their own reality through engaging in those mental activities ... thinking is grounded in perception of physical and social experiences, which can only be comprehended by the mind. What the mind produces are mental models that explain to the knower what he or she has perceived ... We all conceive of the external reality somewhat differently, based on our unique set of experiences with the world and our beliefs about them." Furthermore Bednar, Cunningham, Duffy and Perry (1991, p. 91) elaborate, that in constructivist learning arrangements "the learner is building an internal representation of knowledge, a personal interpretation of experience. This representation is constantly open to change, its structure and linkages forming the foundation to which other knowledge structures are appended. Learning is an active process in which meaning is developed on the basis of experience ... Conceptual growth comes from the sharing of multiple perspectives and simultaneous changing of our internal representations in response to those perspectives as well as through cumulative experience."

In this sense, knowledge cannot be transmitted; it is constructed in a social context, fostered by communication and collaboration with peers and during the solution of real problems. The seven pedagogical goals of constructivist learning environments design (Cunningham, Duffy, & Knuth, 1993; Knuth & Cunningham, 1993) may help to understand the distinguishing appropriateness of social media to foster co-construction of knowledge and learning in a rich social experience (Honebein, 1996):

1. Provide experience with the knowledge construction process. Students take primary responsibility for determining the topics or subtopics in a domain they pursue, the methods of how to learn, and the strategies or methods for solving problems. The role of the teacher is to facilitate this process.
2. Provide experience in and appreciation for multiple perspectives. Problems in the real world rarely have one correct approach or one correct solution. There are typically multiple ways to think about and solve problems. Students must engage in activities that enable them to evaluate alternative solutions to problems as a means of testing and enriching their understanding.
3. Embed learning in realistic and relevant contexts. Most learning occurs in the context of school whereby educators remove the noise of real life from the learning activity. For instance, word problems in math

textbooks rarely relate to the types of problems found in real life. The result is the reduced ability of the students to transfer what they learn in school to everyday life. To overcome this problem, curriculum designers must attempt to maintain the authentic context of the learning task. Educators must ground problems within the noise and complexity that surrounds them outside the classroom. Students must learn to impose order on the complexity and noise as well as solve the core problem.

4. Encourage ownership and voice in the learning process. This illustrates the student-centeredness of constructivist learning. Rather than the teacher determining what students will learn, students play a strong role in identifying their issues and directions, as well as their goals and objectives. In this framework the teacher acts as a consultant who helps students frame their learning objectives.

5. Embed learning in social experience. Intellectual development is significantly influenced through social interactions. Thus, learning should reflect collaboration between both teachers and students, and students and students.

6. Encourage the use of multiple modes of representation. Oral and written communications are the two most common forms of transmitting knowledge in educational settings. However, learning with only these forms of communication limits how students see the world. Curricula should adopt additional media to provide richer experiences.

7. Encourage self-awareness of the knowledge construction process. A key outcome of constructivist learning is knowing how we know. It is the students' ability to explain why or how they solved a problem in a certain way, to analyze their construction of knowledge and processes.

The seven pedagogical goals of constructivist learning environments design emphasize the need for successful learning arrangements to be constructive, self-organized and embedded in social experience. Social media is all about intrinsic motivated engagement of users. On the basis of the wide variety of existing tools, methods, and technologies, learners can choose those that best fit to their individual learning styles. Social media is even powerful enough to let users create their own structured and connected content that sometimes is of higher quality than expert systems (folksonomies, blogs, social tagging are good examples of the bottom-up power of social media) (Chatti et al., 2007). The application of Web 2.0 tools in learning design leaves enough room for instructor's aid and facilitation upon student's request. Furthermore, those tools simplify and potentially speed-up the assistance. Teaching and learning with social media tools is subjective to yield frictions and errors during the execution of task. There is a steep learning curve in the interaction with social media tools based on real-life experiences and the availability of uncountable tools leaves room for more than one way of solving problems.

The application of social media to learning design always means the work with unfinished tools and maybe a limited set of functionalities (O'Reilly, 2005). Moreover, steady buzz and noise accompanies the actual learning activity and other users of a social media service may join, contribute, or question the treated topics and thus care for the embeddedness in realistic context. Interaction and medial representation in social media is characterized by a rich diversity of formats. Users publish, discuss, and annotate videos, pictures, slideshows, music, text-based messages, and many more different content types. This richness is the foundation for an improvement of developed media literacy and competence of the students enlisted in courses that make use of this diversity of media. Lave and Wenger (1991) strongly emphasize that learning can be understood as the participation in a social process, and Web 2.0 tools are all about social connections. People befriend each other, share experiences and learn from each other. During the use of social media tools the hierarchical restrictions of real-life interaction often get blurred because users in social media are more or less equal. This fact engages students to interact with others, ask for help and provide support on topics they are good in. On the other side, staff needs to be open-minded enough to accept this understanding of being a friendly facilitator rather than the authoritative teacher.

In the era of Web 2.0, it is easy to prove a statement made, check used sources and to give feedback on nearly anything. Educational design can thus make use of these activities and support students in developing a good mechanism of explaining their work in an understandable and verifiable way. Moreover, the application of social media tools to learning designs improves student's abilities to give and handle feedback in an appropriate way.

Educational Design and Organization of the Seminar

The educational design of the course is based on the seven pedagogical goals of constructivist learning environments design described above (Honebein, 1996).

1. Students were provided with experience in the knowledge construction process since they decided on the topics they wanted to work on and were

allowed to choose how they learn and what approach they take during the problem-solving process. The instructors aided and facilitated where needed but did not provide rules or a strict structure of work processes.

2. By having to work with students from another university with a different academic background and different scientific approach to the discipline, students experienced multiple ways of looking at a problem as well as proposing and presenting a solution. This let them enrich their experience and increased their understanding for other disciplines.

3. Moreover, due to the collaboration with MATURE and STELLAR the learning experience of the students was embedded in realistic and relevant contexts. An authentic learning context was created and students had to learn to cope with the complexity of projects that were situated in real-life settings.

4. The strong student-centeredness of the course encouraged ownership and voice in the learning process by allowing the students to decide what and how they want to learn and solve problems.

5. In addition, by fostering collaboration and communication through the project teams students had to work in, learning was embedded in social experience since the seminar was based on the idea of working in a team and actively engaging in learning and solving problems together.

6. The means of collaboration and communication through social media encouraged the use of multiple modes of representation. Rich learning experiences were provided by use of video conferencing, presentation software, audio and video production, and text creation through wikis.

7. Instructors encouraged self-awareness of the knowledge construction process by providing students with feedback during meetings and asking students to reflect on their learning and working processes after their presentations. These seven principles formed the base of the course and provided the structure in which all measures took place.

Several tools were used to allow students to engage in collaboration and communication processes. They were an online social networking site (http://fsln.mixxt.com), Mendeley (http://www.mendeley.com) for creating and sharing their bibliographies, Doodle (http://www.doodle.com) for voting procedures during the seminar, Delicious (http://delicious.com) for social bookmarking, Twitter (http://twitter.com/) for informal message exchange and involvement of external experts, and finally Wikis within the social networking site for an open and ongoing documentation of the students work. Further tools were at the disposal of the students if they wished to use them. In addition, the courses were held simultaneously at both universities with the broadcasting of one classroom to the other. Video and audio are shared real-time, students held presentations together with students from the other university. They researched and prepared using social media only; they never met in real life before. Students gained hands-on experience with new modes of interaction that went beyond leisure, fostered their knowledge of working with social media in university settings, and guided them in their processes of informal learning embedded in a formal instruction setting.

Timeframe

The seminar was held during the course of 15 weeks beginning in mid-April and ending in July 2010. The kick-off meeting provided students with an introduction of the goals and topics of the course as well as the projects students could choose to work in. The second meeting in the following week finalized the project teams. In addition, a keynote was held by a leading researcher in TEL. Students were then given the time from May until the first week of June to coordinate tasks and work on their projects. During this time period, the teams met with the instructors on a bi-weekly basis to report their efforts, reflect on the learning process and discuss problems. The work in this period took place virtually through Social Media tools. In the first week of June, each team must present their prototypes to the instructors and in the first week of July teams handed in the papers describing their work. From mid-July until the end of July three all-day courses were held synchronously through video conferencing between the two universities. During these meetings each team presented their work, showcased their prototype and answered questions regarding the design and development as well as their learning and working process. On July 31, all teams handed in revised versions of their papers including feedback from instructors and the all-day meetings.

Topics

Each topic of the seminar was designed to bear an IT or educational artifact that integrates the core themes of the topic and that outlines the specific strengths and opportunities for future learning arrangements. The topics of the seminar were chosen to be engaging, newsworthy, having a promising future and leaving enough space for creative artifact designs. Topics of the seminar include among others: (1) social media monitoring and learner engagement, (2) smart devices for u-learning, (3) game-based learning, (4) interactive learning objects, (5) real-time cooperative learning, and (6) awareness in learning networks. We presented each topic together with a motivation why it is an interesting and relevant topic within the frame of the seminar, some initial questions that may arise when dealing with the topic and clear goals and exemplary outcome artifacts. The expected artifacts range from learning designs that make use of latest technologies and methods over system architectures and system designs to working prototypes that operate on the seminar's social structure and generated digital artifacts.

Team Forming

In the second week of the course, students were placed in teams of two in which they remained throughout the course. Students were able to choose three projects they would like to participate in order of preference through a Doodle poll. The instructors then decided on the participants of each team on a first come, first serve basis and applied best match strategies according to preference of the students, academic background of each student and home university. It was prerequisite that at least half of the course consisted of geographically separated teams with one student from each university amongst its members. The teams then proceeded to coordinate their efforts.

Specifics of Collaboration in Distributed Teams

Cooperative work and learning in distributed teams is marked by some particularities that do not occur in that manner in local teams. The team members need to define and elaborate a common shared language and shared symbols to ease their communication and to ensure a common ground in discussions. While this is also important for local teams because communication and coordination in distributed teams is always accompanied with an organizational overhead, it is even more important in distributed collaboration. Several studies stress the fact that informal communication is very important in terms of team spirit, information flow and coordinative activities. For the domain of social software engineering there are studies (e.g., Herbsleb & Mockus, 2003; Robillard & Robillard, 2000) showing that ad-hoc communication can make up to 41% of a team members time. Distributed collaboration leaves hardly any opportunity for spontaneous or ad-hoc meetings; there are no water-cooler talks or the option for a quick chat during lunch break. Cherry and Robillard (2004) note that as a consequence problems in coordination and collaboration can occur. Moreover the need for documentation of upcoming and completed tasks, responsibilities, and used resources is significantly higher in distributed teams. Speaking in terms of the SECI model, the results of individual learning processes need to be more explicitly externalized than in local teams to share one's own progress with others. Those artifacts can serve both as external (group) memory (Keil-Slawik, 1992) and as foundation for engagement analysis and other grading purposes.

Grading

Five grading criteria were included in the course. The first aspect was active participation in the seminar, which made up 30% of the grade. It was displayed during the course meetings and by the frequency and quality of the use of social media tools like Twitter, Delicious, Mixxt and so forth. Since the idea of the seminar was to engage students in learning something new by applying something new, it was essential for students to actively engage with each other by means of these tools. Potential and shortcomings of work in distributed, interdisciplinary teams can only be experienced by application. The second criterion was the ongoing work on the paper describing the project, the work processes and the prototype. This made up 20% of the grade. Writing a paper on ones research and development efforts is a major part of working scientifically and leads to an increase in key competencies like information literacy and knowledge management. The third criterion was general engagement and creativity. It also presented 20% of the grade. Since the course is based on constructivist learning assumptions the work in progress was monitored by the instructors and problem solving skills that go beyond the mere following of a text book or the checking off of a to-do list as well as the engagement in team forming activities were an important aspect of the course. The fourth criterion was the presentation of the project and the prototype. This accounted for 15% of the final grade. Students had to show that they understood their problem and had to display how they solved it. These skills are essential in any area of work and provide students with information literacy skills. The fifth and last criterion was quality and creativity of the developed artifact, which also made up 15% of the grade. This part of the final mark was of course related to the skills and competencies students must acquire when studying computer or information sciences.

Evaluation and Feedback Methods Applied

We used several methods to monitor and evaluate the students' engagement, performance, and the overall progress of the produced artifacts. Furthermore, we needed to evaluate the learning arrangement itself to improve the pedagogic design, the tools used and the grading mechanism. Students were also asked to fill out a questionnaire during the first week of the course and at the end. The intention was to analyze what social media tools students have used in the past and for what purposes. Also students were asked to describe their former experiences with work in teams, distributed work, as well as a self-assessment of their skills in the areas of information literacy and social media. The same questionnaire was distributed during the last week of the course. Results were compared to gain insight into the learning experiences of the students to evaluate the quality of the design and improve it based on these measures.

Regarding the use of social media tools for communication and collaboration among students of the seminar we applied Artefact-Actor-Network (AAN) Theory (Reinhardt, Moi, & Varlemann, 2009) to monitor and depict the students' activities, connections and created artifacts.[1] AANs are a theoretical model to connect social networks with so-called artifact networks that make claims about the relation and similarity of online actors and the digital artifacts they interact with. The similarity of artifacts is calculated using different mechanisms from text-based similarity to a comparison of the occurring concepts and external links of artifacts. Mainly we focused on the connection between Twitter and Delicious artifacts and their relations. Especially we were interested in whether students tweeted about their bookmarks and vice versa to inform their fellow students. Further, an engagement analysis was conducted to monitor the work of the students with the social media tools. In line with this effort is the evaluation of the continuous production of the wiki.

During the course, the participants were asked to fill out peer feedback forms on a regular basis (once every two weeks). The intention of those forms was to gain insights in the group processes, occurring difficulties in processing of the teams topics as well as the social climate in the team. Furthermore we asked the students to rate the performance of their fellow students and the learning design during the specific phases. Doing this allowed us to gain rapid feedback from the students, evaluate the learning design itself and obtain clues about the individual performance within the teams.

The above-described combination of qualitative and quantitative measures to evaluate the students' engagement and progress as well as the design of the course will provide insights that can be compared against each other and that will lead to a thorough investigation of the quality of the seminar. This in turn will enable us to improve the setting and develop optimized learning scenarios.

CONCLUSIONS AND OUTLOOK

The above-described seminar setting proposes a student-centered approach to teaching and learning in real-life settings under a constructivist perspective. In addition, much emphasis is placed on the use of social media and its potential for collaboration and communication in (distributed) teams. With this framework we hope to provide students with authentic learning experiences and practice-orientation in regard to digital technology in teaching and learning settings. In our view it is important for the future to broaden the scope of university courses that allow students to engage in real-life work settings to enable them to experience potentials and deficits of tools they have at their disposal that go beyond their use for leisure. The outlined course intends to include the "noise" of working in real-world environments, the challenges of working in (distributed) interdisciplinary teams as well as the strains of these conditions on students own capabilities and limitations to a controlled university setting. Our goal is to facilitate the experience of first-hand knowledge embedded in the theoretical foundation of a university course to foster key competencies, broaden the students view of learning and working environments and increase employability within a structure that allows guidance from an instructor when necessary and leaves room for reflection.

In addition we strongly believe that peer learning should play an important role during the course of students studies. Research has shown that students very often prefer to rely on their peers for help and assistance in informal learning settings (Heinze & Schnurr, 2010b). This preference should be accounted for and its potential needs to be explored further. Hence, the manifold qualitative and quantitative evaluation measures before, during and after the seminar serve to explore the students progress, their learning experiences as well as the structure of the course in general. This data should provide sufficient feedback about the quality of the seminar setting, its strengths and weaknesses as well as its potential for further developments in terms of instructional setting and necessary support. With these means we intend to develop a best-practice example of sustained integration of social media and peer learning in praxis-oriented university courses. We are well aware that the effort that is put into planning, executing, and evaluating the setting is high and such resources are seldom available to most universities. Still we believe there is great potential in the use of social media for teaching and learning that is yet not explored. We hope to provide insight with our results and further educational design in higher education with our framework and its thorough evaluation measures.

NOTE

1. During the seminar the students and the supervisors created among others more than 500 tweets, saved over 350 bookmarks on Delicious and 60 scientific papers in Mendeley. The students had several Skype meetings and used instant messaging tools for informal chats and fine-tuning of their work.

REFERENCES

Bednar, A. K., Cunningham, D., Duffy, T. M., & Perry, J. D. (1991). Theory into practice: How do we link? In: T. M. Duffa & D. H. Jonassen (Eds), *Constructivism and the technology of instruction: A conversation* (pp. 17–34). Hillsdale, New Jersey: Lawrence Erlbaum Associates.

Chatti, M. A., Klamma, R., Jarke, M., & Naeve, A. (2007). *Proceedings of seventh IEEE international conference on advanced learning technologies (ICALT'07)*. (pp. 780–782).

Cherry, S., & Robillard, P. N. (2004). Communication problems in global software development: Spotlight on a new field of investigation. In third International Workshop on Global Software Development. ICSE, 2004.

Cunningham, D. J., Duffy, T. M., & Knuth, R. A. (1993). Textbook of the future. In: C. McKnight, A. Dillion & J. Richardson (Eds), *Hypertext: A psychological perspective*. Englewood Cliffs, NJ: Prentice Hall.

Dewey, J. (1986). Experience and education. *The Educational Forum, 50*(3), 241–252.

Dochy, F., Segers, M., & Sluijsmans, D. (1999). The use of self-, peer and co-assessment in higher education: A review. *Studies in Higher education, 24*(3), 331–350.

Gehringer, E. F. (2001). Electronic peer review and peer grading in computer-science courses. *ACMSIGCSE Bulletin, 33*(1), 139–143.

Heinze, N. (2008). *Bedarfsanalyse für das Projekt i-literacy. Empirische Untersuchung der Imformationskompetenz der Studierenden der Universität Augsburg*. Research Report 19. University of Augsburg, Department for Mediapedagagics.

Heinze, N., & Schnurr, J.-M. (2010a). Integration of a conducive infrastructure to establish new learning cultures at universities. In: *Proceedings of the 2010 ED-MEDIA world conference on educational multimedia, hypermedia & telecommunications* (upcoming).

Heinze, N., & Schnurr, J.-M. (2010b). *Perspektiven des Lebenslangen Lernens-dynamische Bildungsnetzwerke, Geschäftsmodelle, Trends* (pp. 24–35). Berlin: Gito.

Herbsleb, J. D., & Mockus, A. (2003). An empirical study of speed and communication in globally distributed software development. *IEEE Transactions on Software Engineering*, *29*(6), 481–494.

Hinkelmann, K., Holzweißig, K., Magenheim, J., Probst, F., & Reinhardt, W. (2006). Linking communities of practice with learning communities in computer science education. In: D. Kumar & J. Turner (Eds), *Education for the 21st century – impact of ICT and digital resources, IFIP 19th world computer congress, TC-3, education, IFIP computer science* (pp. 83–92). Springer: Berlin.

Honebein, P. C. (1996). Seven goals for the design of constructivist learning environments. In: B. Wilson (Ed.), *Constructivist learning environments: Case studies in instructional design* (pp. 11–24). New York: Educational Technology Publications.

Jonassen, D. H. (1991). Objectivism versus constructivism: Do we need a new philosophical paradigm? *Educational Technology Research and Development*, *39*(3), 5–14.

Jonassen, D. H. (1999). Designing constructivist learning environments, In: C. M. Reigeluth (Ed.), *Instructional design theories and models: A new paradigm of instructional theory* (Vol. 2, pp. 215–239). Mahwah, New Jersey: Lawrence Erlbaum Associates.

Keil-Slawik, R. (1992). Artifacts in software design. In: C. Floyd, H. Züllighoven, R. Budde & R. Keil-Slawik (Eds), *Software development and reality construction* (pp. 168–188). Berlin: Springer.

Knuth, R. A., & Cunningham, D. J. (1993). Tools for constructivism. In: T. M. Duffy, J. Lowyck & D. H. Jonassen (Eds), *Designing environments for constructivist learning* (pp. 163–187). Heidelberg: Springer.

Lave, J., & Wenger, E. (1991). *Situated learning: Legitimate peripheral participation*. New York: Cambridge University Press.

Nonaka, I., & Takeuchi, H. (1995). *The knowledge creating company: How Japanese companies create the dynamics of innovation*. New York: Oxford University Press.

Oblinger, D. G. (2007). Becoming net savvy. *Educause Quarterly*, *3*, 11–13.

O'Reilly, T. (2005). What is Web 2.0 – Design patterns and business models for the next generation of software. Available at http://oreilly.com/pub/a/web2/archive/what-is-web-20.html. Retrieved on September 2005.

Polanyi, M. (1967). *The tacit dimension*. New York: University of Chicago Press.

Reinhardt, W., & Holzweißig, K. (2006). Mobile knowledge experience – Ansätze für die interdisziplinäre Informatikausbildung. *DeLFI 2006, Darmstadt 11*, September 14, pp. 395–396.

Reinhardt, W., Moi, M., & Varlemann, T. (2009). Artefact-actor-networks as tie between social networks and artefact networks. In: *Proceedings of the 5th international ICST conference on collaborative computing: Networking, applications and worksharing* (CollaborateCom 2009), November 2009 (pp. 1–10). IEEE.

Robillard, P. N., & Robillard, M. P. (2000). Types of collaborative work in software engineering. *Journal of Systematical Software*, *53*(3), 219–224.

Siemens, G. (2005). Connectivism: A learning theory for the digital age. *International Journal of Instructional Technology and Distance Learning*, *2*(1), 3–10.

CONNECTING FUTURE TEACHERS WITH THE TEACHERS OF TODAY

Larysa Nadolny

ABSTRACT

The Teachers and Technology CONNECT website was created to connect K-12 teacher candidates with current classroom teachers. This website utilizes social media software and web 2.0 tools in a collaborative and supportive learning community. University teacher education students complete course activities using this website, including creating a video lesson plan. These videos are requested by participating classroom teachers and reflect best practices in using technology in the classroom. This successful project benefits both participating students and teachers, as well posted online for viewing by teachers around the world.

A transformative idea in the preparation and professional learning of educators and education leaders is to leverage technology to create career-long personal learning networks within and across schools, pre-service preparation and in-service educational institutions, and professional organizations. The goal of these career-long personal learning networks would be to make professional learning timely and relevant as well as an ongoing activity that continually improves practices. (Office of Educational Technology, 2010, p. 46)

Educating Educators with Social Media
Cutting-edge Technologies in Higher Education, Volume 1, 173–188
Copyright © 2011 by Emerald Group Publishing Limited
All rights of reproduction in any form reserved
ISSN: 2044-9968/doi:10.1108/S2044-9968(2011)0000001011

The earlier quote from the *National Educational Technology Plan* illuminates one of the great challenges in teacher education today: how to overcome the isolation of the classroom in favor of a connected learning model. A connected model creates powerful learning communities of students, parents, teacher candidates, experts, and the community. In this model, all elements, acting in concert, support student success and a 21st century education. *Teachers and Technology CONNECT*, an online portal developed by West Chester University of Pennsylvania (WCUPA) faculty, utilizes social networking, and web 2.0 tools to address this challenge. Using this site and its tools, education students at WCUPA work together with local teachers to develop expertise and provide support. Although the university students are just beginning their understanding of the art of teaching, they successfully provide resources and video lesson plans in response to classroom teacher requests. This mutually beneficial activity leverages the power of technology within a supportive and educational social network.

TEACHERS AND TECHNOLOGY CONNECT

The *Teachers and Technology CONNECT* website (Fig. 1) was developed in an effort to connect K-12 teacher candidates taking educational technology courses at WCUPA with current classroom teachers. Although the students in these courses maintained some online contact with classroom teachers, this contact did not make use of social media and online communication tools. In 2009, the website was created as a portal for all collaborative activities and communication in these courses. During the 2009–2010 academic year, this website housed two WCUPA student assignments, links to a FaceBook group, a compilation of news from relevant blogs, and a live feed of educational websites. This website is designed with flexibility in mind. As course content changes and technology advances, so will this portal.

The *Teachers and Technology CONNECT* website utilizes best practices in educational technology research in an active learning community. The concept of communities of learners in education is not a new idea (Gabelnick, MacGregor, Matthews, & Smith, 1990). Learning communities can provide support, professional development, community building, and expertise to educators (DeWert, Babinski, & Jones, 2003; Kay, 2006). With the increase of internet access and technology in the classroom, online learning communities are an excellent method for teacher professional

Fig. 1. Teachers and Technology CONNECT Website. http://www.paedtech.com/
teacher.html

development (Lieberman, 2000). Communication technology can bring the education community together, virtually. It can enable learning and support that would otherwise be impractical or financially prohibitive (Gomez, Sherin, Griesdorn, & Finn, 2008).

The *National Educational Technology Plan* calls for a transformation of teaching and learning. Revised from 2004, and in line with the new Obama administration's goals, this plan aims to utilize modern technologies for education reform. The portion of the plan for teaching emphasizes a connected learning model. Teachers should not only be connected to resources and data, but also communities (Office of Educational Technology, 2010). The Teachers and Technology CONNECT website supports this plan. Teachers and pre-service teachers can share knowledge and expertise through social media and educational technology tools. By creating learning communities for educators to meet a variety of needs, the education community can work toward the connected learning model indicated in the plan.

In addition, most teachers are not prepared to teach effectively using technology in the classroom. Although teacher preparation programs vary, most do not succeed at preparing teacher candidates to integrate technology in the classroom (Kay, 2006). A 2009 National Center for Education

Statistics study (NCES) reports that only 25% of teachers agreed (to a moderate or major extent) that their undergraduate teacher education program prepared them to effectively use technology in the classroom (Gray, Thomas, & Lewis, 2010). This lack of preparation is evident through discussion with local school district administrators. One director of technology commented, "[F]rom my perspective, it is totally unacceptable for newly graduating teachers to possess instructional technology skills that are inferior to those of experienced staff members they will be joining or possibly replacing." Teacher education programs must respond to this issue with an increase in relevant and meaningful learning experiences in the field of educational technology.

In addition to a lack of effective preparation, many teachers are not utilizing technology beyond presentation or content delivery (Pellegrino, Goldman, Bertenthal, & Lawless, 2007). Another local director of technology faces this issue in his school district. "Most teachers think that 'presentations' are enough to utilize technology or that instructional software used by students is good. While these items are valuable, they do not encompass the whole of instructional technology." The NCES survey also supports this observation. Teachers reported what types of classroom technology is used directly by the students. Most often, students are using technology for writing, practicing basic skills, and research. Teachers report that their students are least often using blogs and wikis, social networking websites, technology for product design, demonstrations, models, or simulations (Gray et al., 2010).

Teachers and Technology CONNECT addresses both teacher candidate and classroom teacher deficiencies. The university course assignments on this website are authentic in context, created in cooperation with participating teachers. This encourages the university students to make the connection between the realities of the classroom and educational goals, whereas the teachers benefit through resources which exemplify best practices in educational technology.

EDUCATIONAL TECHNOLOGY COURSEWORK

Teacher candidates at WCUPA have experience with classroom technologies throughout their general coursework, as well as an educational technology course. The EDM 300: Introduction to Educational Technology course provides teacher candidates with a supportive, yet challenging environment in which to explore theoretical, practical, and critical issues related to the integration of technology in teaching and learning. Special attention is given to the use of the internet for classroom activities and collaborative tools (e.g., interactive lessons, multimedia resources, blogs, wikis, and virtual worlds). Students typically take this 3-credit course during their sophomore year at the university.

Connecting EDM 300 students to the actual classroom environment is a difficult task. The students have very little experience in the classroom, and some are still deciding whether to continue as a teacher candidate or change majors. They have not had any formal student teacher practice, and they rely on their own experiences in education as a model for technology integration. The course assignments are designed with this in mind; utilizing case studies, videos, and technology-mediated classroom interactions. This is a critical time in their understanding of the teaching profession and the challenges of a career in education.

THE TAKE 2 PROJECT

Overview

The Take 2 project is one of the collaborative activities on the *Teachers and Technology CONNECT* website and illustrates the creation of a "learning community." Local teachers submit requests for technology infused lesson plans. EDM 300 students respond to those requests by creating a 2-min video lesson plan posted on YouTube. The videos reflect course content in educational technology as well as any specific teacher requirements. Once completed, the posted videos are not only available to the requesting teachers, but to teachers around the world.

The Take 2 project addresses several EDM 300 course objectives (see below) as well as the National Educational Technology Standards for Teachers (NETS-T). These standards were recently revised and reflect the essential knowledge and skills for the use of technology in the classroom (International Society for Technology in Education, 2008). Students completing this project will:

- Participate in a learning community and connect with classroom teachers.
  - NETS-T Standard 5(A): Participate in local and global learning communities to explore creative applications of technology to improve student learning.

- Apply content knowledge on technology integration into a classroom lesson.
  - NETS-T Standard 2(A): Design or adapt relevant learning experiences that incorporate digital tools and resources to promote student learning and creativity.
- Use classroom technologies to plan, create, and produce a video lesson plan.
  - NETS-T Standard 3(A): Demonstrate fluency in technology systems and the transfer of current knowledge to new technologies and situations.

Students are given one class period for planning, and three weeks to complete the assignment. During the planning period, students select groups (4–5 students per group) based on common K-12 certification areas and begin the planning process. For the remaining time, student groups meet during class, online, or outside the class time.

Teacher Request Line

The Take 2 project begins with the local teaching community. Using personal contacts, discussions groups, and email distribution lists; local teachers are briefed on the project and notified of the request line. Initially, the lesson requests were entered on a Google form embedded into a webpage. The responses were then stored in Google Docs for review by the course students. After one year of implementation, the request line was moved to FaceBook, a social networking website. The change allows for an increase in participating teachers and the ability for discussion and reflection on the videos.

A requesting teacher is asked for his or her name, email address, comfort level with technology, and topic information. Teachers are asked to provide as much information as possible about their lesson topic when making the request. The requests typically encompass a required teaching unit or standard, and are varied in detail and content area. If there are any questions or concerns, course students are encouraged to contact the teacher via email. In an effort to individualize the project, EDM 300 students are provided an opportunity to review the requests with their group members. If none of the teachers requests relate to their field of study, the student groups are permitted to propose a new topic.

The background information provided by the teachers is invaluable in the development of the lesson plans. Teachers can indicate their comfort with technology as well as any unique classroom issues. One middle school teacher gave insight into her use of advanced classroom technology.

> I have decent technology skills, though everyone has room for growth. I am not afraid to learn new technology. This year, my students have created short videos using PhotoStory, they have e-pals with other classes around the world and we are having a videoconference with another class that is also studying ancient civilizations.

Students preparing for this lesson are able to include more innovative technological applications in response to the readiness of the teacher. In contrast, a high school teacher indicated administrative pressure to use technology. "Our district is pushing for the technology piece and integrating culture into the curriculum." From this quote, students can assume that external factors are driving the use of technology. This teacher may be resistant to technology integration and need a simple, easy lesson plan. With appropriate planning, this teacher may become excited about the initial lesson, and will be willing to expand his or her knowledge in future projects.

Not only are students able to adjust the lesson to respond to the teacher's experience with technology, but any other valuable information presented in the request. Referencing student skills and needs, one teacher mentioned that her class has "many [students] with dyslexia and comprehension issues." This important detail may completely change the lesson as originally envisioned by the student group. Not addressing this element in the design of the lesson would guarantee an unsuccessful learning event for those students.

The teachers are asked to provide topical information to guide the video lessons. The two examples below are brief, but provide enough information for the development of the videos.

> We are studying ancient Rome. Students learn about the land, the daily life of the people, religion, art/technology, the government, architecture, gladiators, roman numerals, ancient roman contributions to our current life and more while they study this unit. Students read the *Magic Treehouse* research guide on ancient Rome as their "textbook".

> The students will research a Spanish dance in the library of the choices that I present. They must talk about the origin, style of dress, key instruments used in this type of dance, the movement etc ... They must also find music and attempt to try and or teach the dance to the class.

Video Production

The Take 2 project is designed to allow students to integrate the knowledge acquired in class into a culminating showcase, the video lesson plans. The video must cover specific areas that are impacted by technology in the classroom: project activities, differentiation, adaptation, and assessment (Fig. 2). In addition to the video, students must include a document with citations and additional resources.

Students are asked to follow the *Code of Best Practices in Fair Use for Media Literacy Education* (Center for Social Media, 2008) when producing their videos. This document provides educators a set of guidelines for classroom use and reuse of media for teaching and learning.

Your video must include the following elements:
- Title
- Overview
  - Appropriate grade levels
  - Content area standards (state or national)
  - ISTE standards for students
  - Estimated time
- The Project
  - Overview of all activities in the project
    - Make sure to include websites or technology tools associated with each activity
- Differentiation
  - 2-3 methods to differentiate the project (content, process or product)
- Adaptations
  - 2-3 methods for general computer or technical adaptations
- Assessment
  - 1 suggestion for assessment using technology
  - 1 suggestion for assessment not using technology
- Credits slide
  - Team members names
  - Course information
- Resources List (as a separate document)
  - Cite all resources used in the video (text, books, software, images, music, etc.) in APA format
  - 5 supplemental resources to support the teacher in the project (websites, software, books, etc.)
  - All resources must meet high quality standards, see "Best of the Web" assignment

Fig. 2. Take 2 Video Assignment. This Figure Illustrates the Required Section of the Video.

Previous to the publication of this document, fair use and copyright with technology-infused literacy projects was murky at best. The five principles described in the document guide teachers in understanding the acceptable use of media in developing 21st century literacy skills.

Particularly relevant to this project is Principle 4: Student use of copyrighted materials in their own academic and creative work. Most students in EDM 300 are not able to determine when a copyrighted work is used to enhance understand or for entertainment purposes. The description of this principle further explains the issue.

> Students' use of copyrighted material should not be a substitute for creative effort. Students should be able to understand and demonstrate, in a manner appropriate to their developmental level, how their use of a copyrighted work repurposes or transforms the original. For example, students may use copyrighted music for a variety of purposes, but cannot rely on fair use when their goal is simply to establish a mood or convey an emotional tone, or when they employ popular songs simply to exploit their appeal and popularity. (Center for Social Media, 2008, p. 13)

Understanding of this document serves two purposes; one, to follow best practices in the Take 2 project, and two, for the students to have the background information to implement these guidelines in their own classrooms.

Students in EDM 300 have access to a variety of technology tools to assist in the creation of the video. The course is held in a computer lab with one Mac computer per student. Each computer is equipped with iMovie, Garageband, Photoshop, and video conversion software. Students also have access to Flip digital video cameras, interactive whiteboards, digital projectors, document cameras, and a wide variety of educational software. With high-speed internet access, webcams, and built-in microphones; the students are able to record their computer screen (commonly referred to as screencasting) for use in the videos. Students are directed to websites such as http://www.screentoaster.com and http://www.jing.com for quick and easy screencasting tools.

The students are prepared for the basics of video production through the completion of several online activities introducing the iMovie software. In the activities, students are asked to view video tutorials for iMovie, as well as video production curriculum from Apple. They also critique videos on teachertube.com for technical improvements and suggestions. Although the students are given extensive support during the project, the formal instruction in video production is minimal.

Group Wiki

As described in the NETS-T (3A), teachers should not only be familiar with a variety of technologies, but also be able to apply those skills. That concept is reinforced throughout the EDM 300 course. Students are asked to demonstrate newly learned skills and techniques during course activities and assignments.

Early in the semester, students learn about widely available web 2.0 communication tools. For the Take 2 project, they have a chance to utilize a *wiki* for group communication. A wiki is a webpage that can be edited by multiple users ("Wiki"). Each group is asked to keep track of attendance during group meetings on the wiki (Fig. 3). This attendance record is also used during peer evaluations and to assign individual grades to the project. Students may also use the wiki to assign tasks and communicate, but this is strictly optional.

Submission and Assessment

The completed videos are provided to the course instructor along with the additional resources document. The videos are uploaded after assessment by

Quick Links   EDM300 Spring 2010 > Group Area > 10

Group Area

10 AM: 4 (Natural Disasters) (permalink)
last edited by Chelsea on Wednesday, 04/14/2010 11:31 AM

WE ARE DONE!!! THE PROJECT HAS BEEN SUBMITTED!!!! GREAT JOB EVERYONE!

Group members:
1. Angelica
2. Chris
3. Chelsea
4. Stephanie
5. Stephanie

Team Attendance:

date	3-31	4/7 10am	4/9 10:00am	4/12	4/14 10am	date	date	date	date
1	here	here	here	here	here				
2	here	absent!	absent!	here	here				
3	here	here	here	here	here				

Fig. 3. Group Wiki. This Snapshot Shows the Group Wiki Area in the Universities Online System.

the instructor to ensure high quality of materials posted online. The videos are assessed on a five point, five category rubric. Categories include requirements, content, organization, mechanics, and teamwork.

The students are responsible for emailing the requesting teacher and notifying him or her of the completed video. The instructor is included on the email to assist in any questions or concerns. The instructor also follows up with the teacher, requesting feedback for the students.

With large groups of students, it can be a challenge to accurately assess individual contribution to a project. The teamwork category on the rubric is assessed through a peer-review process. All students are asked to report on the contributions of team members (attendance at meetings, completion of tasks, etc.) and their own contributions. This evaluation is not designed to rank students within a group. It can provide important feedback to the instructor on students who performed above and beyond requirements, and those who did not contribute.

STUDENT PERSPECTIVE

In order to gain insight into the effectiveness of the project, EDM 300 students were surveyed after the completion of the project in spring 2010. The survey explored topics such as satisfaction, effectiveness, and impact of the Take 2 project. The survey contained Likert items (strongly agree, agree, neither agree nor disagree, disagree, strongly disagree) and open-ended questions. The majority of students (90/102) completed the survey for an 88% response rate.

Students were overwhelmingly satisfied with the design and implementation of the Take 2 project. The students indicated that they enjoyed creating a video lesson plan as well as gained technical expertise (Fig. 4). Students enjoyed creating a usable product that benefited real-world teachers rather than the more routine student assignment. Mark, one of the students, commented, "I liked how it was a new spin on creating a lesson plan. Everything I do is just sitting in front of a computer doing research so it was nice to get out and actually say what I am thinking rather than having to put it down on paper." Another student, Samantha, agreed that she "liked this assignment because it was a non-traditional assignment. This assignment wasn't the common 5 page paper or 20 slide PowerPoint."

The students indicated that the project achieved its goal of making the connection to the realities of the classroom. When asked about what they enjoyed about the project, Jodie reflected on her experience creating a video

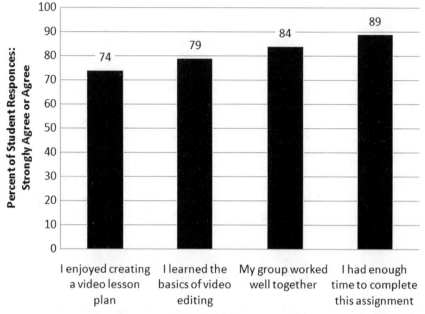

Fig. 4.   Take 2 Student Survey. Students who Selected Strong Agree or Agree for
Each Question.

lesson plan. "I enjoyed thinking creatively and realistically about a unit
for my future students. This gave me the opportunity to get a feel for
what it might be like to create a unit assignment for students, and exposed
me to the potential frustration of having to work around standards."
Amanda also appreciated the classroom connection. "The assignment gave
me a chance to feel like a teacher and get a small taste of what it will be
like to have my own classroom. When you are in charge of class, the
students expect you to make the least interesting topics fun and exciting for
them. This assignment challenged me and as an individual and an aspiring
teacher."

Students who did use the wiki for organizing tasks utilized the tool in
different ways. Some groups used it as a discussion board, responding to
each other's comments; whereas others used it as a task list or storyboard.
When asked about the group wiki area on the survey, only 44% of students
agreed or strongly agreed that it was helpful. The other students had no
opinion (34%) or did not find it helpful (20%). Participation in the wiki was

State Standards	I am having a lot of trouble finding a standard that relates specifically to constellations. This standard, for 4th graders, seems to fit the best. 3.3.4.B1: Identify planets in our solar system and their basic characteristics. Describe the earth's place in the solar system that includes the sun (a star), planets, and many moons. **Recognize that the universe contains many billions of galaxies and that each galaxy contains many billions of stars.**
Big dipper story	I have the story.
oriions belt story	Yes. The only thing is that there is no actual story with the belt but with the actual hunter, so that's what I used.
differention 1	Giving students different ways to approach the assignment: 1. using powerpoint to create a small slide show 2. using comic life to make a small comic about stars 3. using paint to create drawings of stars and then adding text.
	website:
differention 2	Using black construtions paper, white chalk and silver or gold star stickers, students can map out their constellation.Students will write their stories of their constellations.
Comments?	Jess-- so for the ISTE standards I picked the numbers I felt fit out lesson plan. I left out number 2 which is communication and collaboration, because from our discussion in class on Monday, I felt that students will technically be doing the constellation assignment individually. Also, I wanted to ask any of you if you think I should keep all of the sub-categories under each big standard. Some of them I feel do not apply to what our lesson wants to accomplish, but I'm not sure myself if technically we are allowed to leave out parts under each standard.
	Let me know what you all think? Thanks! see you in class Monday-- have a great Easter (or just the weekend :))

Fig. 5.   Task Keeping in the Wiki. This Snapshot Shows One Group Discussion.

not a requirement of the project, and some students did not enter any information other than attendance. The groups who did utilize the wiki showed evidence of careful thought and communication (Fig. 5).

When asked if classroom teachers would benefit from the YouTube videos, the students were very positive. Brenda believed that the videos were motivating for teachers. "I definitely think that classroom teachers will benefit. Our lesson was so informative and thought out that we had a lot of trouble fitting everything into two minutes. It is also a more interesting way to see lesson plans than just reading them online." Edward agreed, "Absolutely. Some teachers are a little outdated with their work, and having the opportunity to see what young college students think would be appropriate for a lesson plan would be very beneficial to them." Jessica made a connection to her own teaching career. "I definitely believe classroom teachers will benefit from these videos. I know that when I start my career in less than two years, I will rely on many different sources when creating my lesson plans."

Students were asked to indicate improvements for the project on the survey. Most notably students mentioned more training on the iMovie software and the ability to view videos from previous students. Although the students were given online assignments which explored iMovie tutorials, they felt limited by their basic skills in that application. This issue can be addressed by including a short video assignment at the beginning of the semester. By incorporating video into a different topic in class, students will have more exposure to the program before the major assignment. Several students requested access to other student videos which were not posted online. Students were purposefully not shown other videos in order to spark creativity and unique expression of the lesson plans. Chris suggested to "show the YouTube videos in class and allow peers to critique the videos in order to see how they can improve."

TEACHER PERSPECTIVE

After the videos are completed and posted online, the participating teachers are able to provide feedback to the students groups. The informal feedback is requested through an email originating from the course instructor. The responses varied, with some teachers providing a detailed evaluation and others no response at all.

Overall, teacher responses have been positive and encouraging. It is apparent that the teachers appreciate the time and effort put forth by the teacher candidates. The most frequent response is a short, "thank you" or "good job." One middle school teacher was surprised at the wealth of information in the video. "I've never seen any of these websites before. Thank you! I can't wait to see what the kids think of them." Another teacher reflected on her own abilities to use the lesson. "I didn't know my students could create something on Google Earth. I'll have to figure it out myself first though, to make sure I can help them."

RECOMMENDATIONS

The *Teachers and Technology CONNECT* portal has the ability to impact the growth and development of educators and work toward a connected learning model. One indication is the success of the Take 2 project. This course assignment demonstrates the power of social media and web 2.0 tools to bring together teachers and teacher candidates in a mutually beneficial learning community. However, much work still remains to be done:

- In order to fully realize the connected learning model of the National Educational Technology Plan, the website must be able to create "career-long personal learning networks" (US Department of Education, 2010,

p. 46). This can be achieved by including graduate students, school administrators, as well as members of professional organizations. This will improve the quality of online interactions with multiple perspectives on educational technology.

- Data collection and assessment, beyond the current antidotal evidence, must be included for replication and application of this model. Future developments include a detailed survey for teacher participants as well as follow up to see if the lessons plans were implemented in the classroom. With the addition of the FaceBook community, university students can be followed through their career as they participate as practicing teachers.

Although this community of learners is only once piece of the educational technology puzzle, it can provide the skills, knowledge, and support for educators to impact student learning with the power of technology.

REFERENCES

Center for Social Media. (2008). *The code of best practices in fair use for media literacy education.* Available at http://www.centerforsocialmedia.org/

DeWert, M. H., Babinski, L. M., & Jones, B. D. (2003). Safe passages: Providing online support to beginning teachers. *Journal of Teacher Education, 54*(4), 311–320.

Gabelnick, F., MacGregor, J., Matthews, R. S., & Smith, B. L. (1990). Learning communities: Creating connections among students, faculty, and disciplines. In: R. E. Young (Ed.), *New directions for teaching and learning, number 41* (pp. 5–18). San Francisco: Jossey-Bass Inc.

Gomez, L. M., Sherin, M. G., Griesdorn, J., & Finn, L. (2008). Creating social relationships: The role of technology in preservice teacher preparation. *Journal of Teacher Education, 59*(2), 117–131.

Gray, L., Thomas, N., & Lewis, L. (2010). *Teachers' use of educational technology in U.S. public schools: 2009 (NCES 2010-040).* Washington, DC: National Center for Education Statistics, Institute of Education Sciences, U.S. Department of Education.

International Society for Technology in Education. (2008). *National educational technology standards for teachers.* Available at http://www.iste.org/

Kay, R. (2006). Evaluating strategies used to incorporate technology into preservice education: A review of the literature. *Journal of Research on Technology in Education, 28*(4), 383–408.

Lieberman, A. (2000). Networks as learning communities: Shaping the future of teacher development. *Journal of Teacher Education, 51*(3), 221–227.

Office of Educational Technology. (2010). National Educational Technology Plan 2010: Transforming American education: Learning Powered by technology. Available at http://www.ed.gov/technology/netp-2010

Pellegrino, J. W., Goldman, S. R., Bertenthal, M., & Lawless, K. (2007). Teacher education and technology: Initial results from the "What Works and Why" project. *Teacher Education and Technology*, *106*(2), 52–86.

U.S. Department of Education. (2010). *National Educational Technology Plan*. Washington, DC: Office of Educational Technology, U.S. Department of Education.

DEVELOPING A PEDAGOGY: THE ROLE OF THE TUTOR IN ENABLING STUDENT LEARNING THROUGH THE USE OF A WIKI

Martina A. Doolan

ABSTRACT

This chapter clarifies the role of the tutor in enabling collaborative learning through assessment using technology as part of a blended learning framework. This is achieved through a practical example of using Wikipedia and the Collaborative Learning through Assessment and Technology (CLAT) pedagogical model.

INTRODUCTION

This chapter intends to clarify the role of the tutor in enabling student learning through the use of a wiki application. Such clarification firstly establishes that there is a clear role for the tutor in establishing a wiki learning environment to support collaborative learning through assessment. Secondly, this chapter provides guidance on how this role can be enacted as this area of practice develops further. This is achieved through a practical

Educating Educators with Social Media
Cutting-edge Technologies in Higher Education, Volume 1, 189–205
Copyright © 2011 by Emerald Group Publishing Limited
ISSN: 2044-9968/doi:10.1108/S2044-9968(2011)0000001012

example of using the "Collaborative Learning through Assessment and Technology" (CLAT) pedagogical model, which is underpinned by social constructivism and the principles of "good teaching and learning practice." The argument is made that a wiki when used in this way is a learning resource to support collaborative learning.

This chapter helps the reader to understand the wiki concepts and their potential to enhance collaborations, knowledge development, and transfer. Furthermore, this chapter presents the key concepts to prepare learners for using a wiki within a blended learning framework. This includes the use of the CLAT model when considering the learning design and adaption to curriculum to achieve the concepts and practices that are necessary in collaborative learning through the use of a wiki application in higher education.

WHAT IS A WIKI?

The wiki concept was born in 1995 by BoLeuf and Ward Cunningham (Leuf & Cunningham, 2001). A wiki is an example of one of a group of social networking technologies known as Web 2.0. The Web 2.0 term was developed in 2004 by Dale Dougherty of O'Reilly company (O'Reilly, 2005a, 2005b). The name is based on a Hawaiian term "wiki," which means to "hasten" or "quick." A wiki has no fixed structure and provides pages that can be constructed and authored by any user, and access rights to do this can be granted, therefore allowing a wiki to be private or public. The structure is defined by users, group dynamics, and establishment of social rules and norms. The dynamic nature of a wiki means accessibility to technology from any place, at any time through various traditional and mobile technologies.

Visually, a wiki looks similar to web pages; however, unlike a web page, a wiki provides the facility for adding new content and to edit this as part of a collaborative process unlike a discussion forum, which does not allow contributions to be edited. The exchange is asynchronous, all communications and edits are recorded providing learners with an opportunity to collaboratively build, develop, and exchange knowledge online; for instance, through coediting documents. This differs to the World Wide Web, where an individual learner is a "read-only" participant of information.

Wikipedia (www.wikipedia.com) is a well-known online free encyclopedia that anyone can edit.

Coverage of Web 2.0 learning focuses on the social, collaborative, and community building aspects of the technologies providing the freedom and opportunities for individuals to work in groups, socialize, and collaborate using technologies such as blogs, wikis, video sharing, and podcasting (Anderson, 2007). There are many wikis on the market; some are standalone whereas others are embedded within institutional resources. Most modern wikis support the embedding of media such as audio and video. wikis also have a history feature that allows previous versions to be revisited and a rollback feature that restores previous versions. These features are useful in tracking the progression of knowledge development and monitoring and facilitating learner's works.

WHY USE A WIKI?

A wiki can be used for a range of individual or group-based tasks. Individual tasks include developing reflective practice by writing a diary and enhancing this with photographs and links to useful online resources. As a learning resource, wikis support learners and educators to engage in the creation of artifacts and materials such as audio, video, documents, and presentations. These can be uploaded to the wiki at the push of a button. As a group, a wiki may be used as a learning repository to share and receive feedback on assessment or works in progress. From these, a learning resource can be collectively created to revisit year on year. Furthermore, a wiki may be used as a faculty resource such as an intranet or to develop an institutional web site.

What is particularly useful about a wiki for educational purposes is that with guidance and support, its ease of use in creating content and in defining structure presents opportunities to develop a personalized dynamic learning space consisting of pages that can be coconstructed and coauthored by learners and educators alike to best suit the needs of the learner, educator, and of learning design. A wiki allows the networking of pages, and therefore, pages may be linked to other pages or linked to other web sites and content, including images, sound, video, documents, and PowerPoint presentations. Using a wiki in this way has been found to support learners in creating dynamic learning environments (Doolan, 2007a, 2007b).

THE CLAT MODEL

This section introduces the CLAT pedagogical model; the focus on this model is on the role of the tutor and technology using a blended learning approach that combines activities through innovative online and the

Table 1.   The CLAT Strategies.

The CLAT *Strategies*	Principles
Relationship with students and teaching philosophy	1, 2, 3, 4, 6, 7
Approach taken	
Encourage students to produce learning resources	2, 3, 4, 7
Learning activities/tasks. Active learner engagement	2, 3, 4, 5, 6, 7
Learner and tutor-generated content – deep learning approach	
Technology – coauthor, collaborate	2, 7
Structure – public area open to all learners and private group areas	
Establishing the culture, preparing students	1, 2, 6, 7
Setting and communicating clear directions/expectations	
Communicating clear directions/expectations	1, 2, 4, 7
Clear boundaries, that is, trust, respect, share, and scholarly practice	
Supporting social presence, nurturing student relationships	1, 2, 6, 7

traditional practices using Web 2.0 technologies to supplement class-based activities. The most effective practice will be based on the tutor style, learners, discipline, and methods in addition to the availability and access to the relevant technology. The role of the tutor in the integration of blended learning can be viewed as a microcosm of the development of the Internet. Through this and based on empirical research into practice for over a period of five years (Doolan, 2006, 2007a, 2007b, 2009, 2010), the CLAT model defines four roles into which blended learning educators fit and which directly relate to the conceptual usability of the World Wide Web.

The CLAT model is underpinned by social constructivism (Vygotsky, 1978) and the principles of "good teaching and learning practice" (Chickering & Gamson, 1987) as illustrated in Table 1.

CLAT CONCEPTUAL FRAMEWORK

The social constructivist perspective is supported by the model through the use of a wiki technology where learners collectively engage in learning activities through a wiki to coproduce artifact. In so doing, learners collaborate and collectively share and build knowledge. At the same time learn how to work and relate to peers while engaged in the collaborative learning activities. The learning design by the tutor is set to encourage collaborative learning by engaging learners in learning activities that require interaction intergroup and intragroup, peer-to-peer support, and critical analysis of others' works, which culminate into a coproduced artifact.

Interaction between learners is a vital ingredient in social and collaborative learning. The interactions are designed with an emphasis on collaboration, negotiation, debate, and peer review. This is central to the social constructivist learning theory (Vygotsky, 1978) and the CLAT model by forming relationships (Lave & Wenger, 1991) with others based on the foundation that learning is a social activity (Wenger, 1998).

Collaborative learning has been shown to engage learners in knowledge sharing providing supportive environments where learners not only build relationships but can also depend on one another to negotiate and manage their learning needs (Tu, 2004; Doolan, Thornton, & Hilliard, 2006). Knowledge construction is a social process that occurs through collaborations within learning environments that situate learners in authentic contexts (Barab & Duffy, 2000; Collins, Brown, & Newman, 1989).

Using a wiki and the pedagogical model in this way has resulted in a shift in the emphasis from the tutor and places this firmly in the hands of the learner. The tutor becomes one of a Guru of learning as illustrated in Fig. 1.

In this way, the Guru through the learning design sets up the learning and steps back leaving the learners to actively engage in their learning through the use of a wiki when used to support collaborative learning through assessment. This has resulted in empowered learners to take ownership of their own learning, while managing and supporting peers when engaged

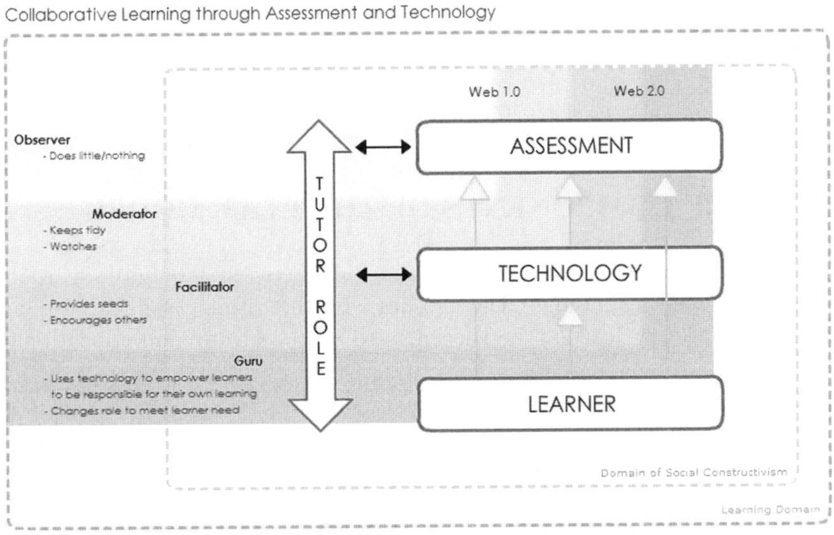

Fig. 1. The CLAT Pedagogical Model.

collectively with learning activities. This practice has further resulted in learners socially constructing their agreed learning space, with learners personalization of learning in terms of where, how, and when students learn (Doolan, 2006). Given the unstructured nature of a wiki, learners have been shown to construct their own learning environment; learners have also been shown to produce "truly" dynamic learning environments (Doolan, 2006, 2007b). Using a wiki and learning designed by the tutor and supported by the "CLAT" model has also been shown to provide a greater range of opportunities for learners to interact with each other outside the classroom boundary (Doolan, 2006, 2007a, 2009, 2010).

DEVELOPING THE CLAT PEDAGOGY

Developing pedagogy in this context is paying attention to the practices employed in learning and teaching in Higher Education while purposively building a relationship between the practice of learning and teaching and between learner and teacher, learner and learner, and teacher and learner. This has led to the development of the CLAT model. Hence, the pedagogical model presented in Fig. 1 is deeply rooted in educator's experiences in partnership with learners of using a blended social constructivist approach; the blended approach combines technologies outside of the classroom with face-to-face class-based activities (Doolan, 2009; MacDonald, 2006). This blended approach brings together a rich educational experience based on five years practice and the evaluation of that practice in partnership with learners (Doolan & Barker, 2005; Doolan, 2006, 2007a, 2007b, 2009, 2010).

THE COMPONENTS OF THE CLAT MODEL

The CLAT model illustrates the relationship between the tutor, learner, assessment, and technology. The emphasis on the tutor is in defining their role in supporting learning and learners to meet learning and educational objectives.

The learning design in this model is the process of maximizing the effectiveness of learning materials, technology, and learner experiences and progression to meet the needs of the learner both individually and as an outcome of benefitting from learners in engaging with their study such as developing understandings, skills, or competencies. In this way, the learning design seeks to increase and optimize the potential to empower the learner to take ownership of learning and motivate to perform and succeed. The CLAT pedagogical model as in Fig. 1 presents the learner with a challenge through their learning experiences to go beyond information retrieval and absorption.

Web 1.0 defines the period from the inception of the World Wide Web in 1991 up until the rise of the Web 2.0 phenomena in 2003. Web 1.0 is a model of the Web where content is consumed as a passive medium.

At the heart of the CLAT pedagogy is the role of the tutor in the learning designs. In addition to the aforementioned is a key to the design by tutors in ensuring student ownership, engagement, and to foster a learning community with the emphasis on the domain of social constructivism (Doolan, 2006, 2007c, 2009, 2010). Online activities should be considered in terms of the overall student learning experience and blend, combining face-to-face sessions with online learning to maximize on the pedagogic opportunities afforded by both approaches.

THE TUTOR ROLES

The four roles are not mutually exclusive and may overlap. The model is not based on a fixed set of competencies but allows for the tutor role to be flexibly determined to fit with any of a variety of educational aims and learning outcomes. How learners will be supported online and the appropriate role for a tutor will be determined using the criteria described below.

Observer

The observer is one where the technology is available; however, in this role, the technology is perceived as a reference point, for example, by reading content in a discussion forum. At the same time, the observer favors traditional pedagogical approaches to learning. The technology may be available to the observer, for example, through institutional technological resources. By referencing works, this role may encourage the tutor to reflect on practice or reflect while being in practice. By observing the technological content, the observer reflects on practice and learner contributions, evaluates the experience with learners, with the intention of building knowledge and confidence to progress to a moderator or facilitator of learning.

Moderator

In addition, to the role of observer, the moderator role sees the tutor make use of institutional technology, for example, a discussion forum. Using this technology, the moderator posts and responds to postings. The concept of a moderator is discussed by Salmon (2002) who relates the moderator role to an "e-tutor." The model in Fig. 1 defines the moderator in a blended learning context and sees this role as providing a clear framework for learning with little or no learner choice. However, learners may act as moderators under the guidance of a tutor.

Facilitator

The facilitator provides encouragement for active learner engagement, providing seeds, and prompting and encouraging learners to participate using technology. The facilitator designs the learning and provides learning activities for learners; some may be completed individually such as a "learning contract" set as the first learning activity intended to engage the learner in learning and build a working relationship with peers. Learning activities may take the form of collaborative writing, providing tips and feedback on learners input as the writing progresses. The facilitator style is interactive, nudges and nurtures where learners are encouraged to interact, and engages fully in their learning. Learners are nudged to actively contribute and are reassured that what they say matters, drawing on contributions and responding as appropriate. Using this style, it is helpful to the learner to provide in advance of using technology such as a wiki, an indication as to when facilitation will take place. Individual learners need to feel supported, safe, and sheltered, where learners feel able to contact the tutor, this is a multidimensional dialog between student–tutor, student–tutor, tutor–faculty, student–faculty, faculty–student, and student–student.

Guru

The "guru" style is upfront and then the tutor steps back. This requires a high level of experience, confidence, and upfront resources. The guru has a particular way of blending technology to accommodate learners to socially construct their own learning and dynamic learning environment to empower and support learners in personalizing their learning (Doolan, 2007b, 2009).

The guru role comprises a stepping-back approach enabling learners to engage with each other without tutor intervention, online facilitation, guidance, or support. This might seem risky, but this is kept to a minimum by spending time up-front and a careful design of the student learning experience as presented in the example in this chapter. Key to this approach is the need to communicate clear expectations to the students from the outset and to ensure that these are fully understood as in the CLAT model strategies defined in Table 1.

The tutor preparedness is high supported by the creation of a relaxed atmosphere (Ramsden, 1992) where the participants are at ease to feel frightened and to express this. The tutors' role is in motivating and supporting learners to become autonomous learners away from tutor dependency. To this end, learners are stimulated by encouraging them to adopt an open and inquisitive approach to their learning, indeed are partners in the learning design and intellectual development, a skill that they can use throughout their lives. The tutor communicates responsibility to learners as their tutor, and learners are encouraged to communicate theirs to the tutor, and each other. These engagement protocols have been shown to help learners to take responsibility for themselves, and their own learning, while being sensitive to the needs of others in their group (Doolan, 2006, 2008). The boundaries for engagement need to be made clear as illustrated in Table 1. The engagement between tutor and learner and learner and tutor is limited, while the learners are engaged in their learning. In this case, this needs to be built into the learning design. Doolan (2006, 2009) takes an approach that sees the tutor set up the learning design and step back leaving the learners to engage in individual and group-based assessed tasks using a wiki and underpinned by the model in Fig. 1.

No matter the role adopted by a tutor, the key aspects to consider are as follows: the careful design and implementation of learning activities in the learning design and a partnership approach to learning between learner and teacher, learner and learner, and teacher and learner. The technology supports the learning design in this example a wiki was used to support the collaborative experience. To ensure students are adequately prepared for the online experience through introductory sessions, perhaps via a lecture and tutorial and to ensure that students fully understand what is expected of them, it is important set clear expectations and boundaries as denoted by the strategies in Table 1.

As illustrated in Fig. 1 the CLAT model and its strategies in Table 1, it is also important for the tutor to clarify to students from the outset exactly what the tutor role will be in supporting them online; for example, if they are to act as observer, moderator, facilitator, or guru. The latter empowers learners to interact with one another without tutor intervention. In the study presented in this chapter, the tutor's role is one of a guru, to step back and allow learner–learner interaction. This has resulted in the building of a learning community (Doolan, 2007) fostering ownership, social interaction, and a task-driven focus (Doolan, 2006).

PRINCIPLES AND STRATEGIES

The CLAT model strategies extend the seven principles of good practice in undergraduate education (Chickering & Gamson, 1987) given in the following, and extended strategies are outlined in Table 1.

Principle	Good Practice
1	Encourages contact between learners and faculty
2	Develops reciprocity and cooperation among learners
3	Uses active learning techniques
4	Gives prompt feedback
5	Emphasizes time on task
6	Communicates high expectations
7	Respects diverse talents and ways of learning

The CLAT pedagogical strategies provide a context for the tutor to consider both in the design and in the implementation process when introducing the use of technology such as a wiki with learners and identify what this means in "good "practice when using the CLAT model.

OVERVIEW OF RESEARCH INTO
PRACTICE – THE STUDY

This section presents an overview of the CLAT model in practice while using a wiki to support educators, and specifically, in their role as tutor in terms of helping them to create an online learning environment using a wiki with a focus on developing collaborative task-driven learner–learner interactions.

Course and Context

Ninety-six second-year undergraduate students studying on a combined modular degree in information systems undertook this module. The module is built around information systems case studies, providing an insight into realistic company environments. The overall aim is for students at all stages to develop their skills in building computer-based, user-friendly information systems. The development of problem-solving skills was encouraged, replacing the current paper-based system with a computer-based system.

This "real-world" approach included a problem-based learning assessment methodology. Students were divided into groups and required to carry out a thorough analyses and design of a computer system using the wiki learning environment, to complete individual and group work activities according to the needs of the community. The overall learning objective is for students to apply the principles and techniques of system development in a team environment, thus fostering and developing collaborative working skills. The students are also expected to use appropriate engineering practices to make informed decisions about best approaches to an information system development. This requires students to move from problem identification through to implementation and evaluation processes, requiring decisions to pursue chosen approaches within the context of a collaborative working environment.

Learning Activities: The Face-to-Face and Online Blend

Active student engagement requires the chosen activities to be shared equally within and across the group, with an emphasis on learning by doing (Kolb, 1984) and an emphasis on understanding and a deep approach to learning (Biggs, 2003). Moreover, the activities in this study were set to enhance information sharing within groups and across groups, personalized learning and autonomy (DfES, 2005), encouraging learners to create their own learning environment, take control, and to feel ownership for their own learning. Therefore, the assessment activities were chosen specifically to be shared and jointly owned within each group. This is an important motivational factor, with the aim of encouraging collaboration between learners to build a learning community. To create a shared responsibility for group learning and to foster individual responsibility, the problem presented needs to involve each leaner with a specific and structured job to complete

(Crook, 2003). Students were provided with all of the relevant templates required to undertake the activities for the assessed learning activities, and all associated activities were based on the case study. By completing the learning activities, this enabled students to complete the assessed report for the module, and the wiki provided an environment to complete the learning activities. The assessed report consisted of solutions to five sets of activities and included Eliciting and Documenting Requirements and Group Commitment, Support for Project Stakeholders, Evaluation, Reflective Journal, and Peer Review.

The face-to-face blend with online learning was carefully designed into the module and maximized the learning opportunities provided by each approach (Doolan & Barker, 2005). To ensure students were adequately briefed and understood the requirements of the learning activities, a lecture provided the most appropriate method for introducing the online wiki environment, through a live demonstration. A tutorial prepared students for the online group work learning activities, taking students from a familiar face-to-face tutorial situation, and leading them into an online collaborative environment through a simulated interactive exercise. Both the importance of team working and the need to see this as an important life skill were emphasized; the face-to-face sessions were key factors in fostering student engagement and to prepare them for the online activities. This was achieved by providing a short report from industry outlining skills shortages faced by employers, helping learners to make the connection between this and the syllabus and to emphasize the importance of team working, collaboration, and the development of problem-solving skills.

The online experience complemented and took forward the initial face-to-face lecture/tutorial approach by providing an environment for students to build a task-driven, individual, and group-owned learning community. This required commitment from each group member to seed the community and to take ownership of the learning. To provide an initial context for the online process, students were required to distribute contact details and confirmation of their membership to the rest of the group; a photo of an animal, object, or movie star to represent the group member; three sentences about themselves, an understanding of the ground rules; and a brief project plan. Therefore, the design of the learning experience required careful planning and up-front commitment and investment from the tutor. Students who came late into the group or had difficulties were supported by other group members and no tutor intervention was required. This takes the role of the tutor to a guru beyond that of a facilitator or e-moderator (Salmon, 2002) as is often the learning context created with group discussions delivered through an institutional Virtual Learning Environment (VLE). wiki technology allows the tutor to adopt a different role, exploring new approaches to support personalized student learning.

SUMMARY OF RESULTS

The results were derived from learners own reflective blogs in which the students highlighted their perception of their experiences while engaged in collaborative learning and assessment. Content analysis was performed on the texts deriving categories such as "People" as noted in Table 2, and these

Table 2.   How Did the Wiki Support Group Assessment?

People
"The ability to review who has written what and who has changed" g.1
"Quickest way each member could express their ideas" g2
"We used Wiki to post up the questions we were stuck on" g2
"Ensure that participation in the project was free from intimidation" g3
"Gave group members an added sense of confidence and encouraged them to further participate
     without worrying about making mistakes" g3
"Able to function as a team" g10
"Only our group can put all our ideas up" g12
"Ask members for their opinions" g13
"Put and share useful ideas, resources, use it to chat to members, solve problems" g7

Task
"Someone can work on any task at any time" g2"
"To help keep up-to-date with the progress of the project" g3
"Great area to support our assignment" g4
"Attach documents, presentations, images, journals and web links" g7
"Add more detail on the learning activities" g13
"Can post attachments of their own work" g15
"Hyperlinks and simple text for creating new pages and cross links between pages" g16
"keeps track of changes" g13
"Has proven instrumental to the completion of the module work" g11
"The most helpful part of Wiki is that someone can work on any task at any time" g2
"To help keep up-to-date with the progress of the project" g3
"Great area to support our assignment" g4
"Allows user to attach documents, presentations, images, journals and web links" g7
"Add more detail on the learning activities" g13
"Can post attachments of their own work" g15
"Hyperlinks and simple text for creating new pages and cross links between pages" g16
"Keeps track of changes" g13
"Has proven instrumental to the completion of the module work" g11

Table 3.   Summary of Key Issues for Wiki Use.

Importance of developing a strategy and communicating this to students

Students should be perceived as a community with a focus on both *people* and the *learning activities* set

The approach should be people oriented, providing the opportunity to interact with others through peer to peer support for learning

Students value the opportunity to manage their own learning and learning environment citing usefulness of editing, inputting, and deleting information collaboratively, ease of use, creating hyperlinks to pages, and new pages with cross linking. This was particularly evident in the students whose rationale for community was task orientated

Students felt *safe* and *sheltered*, reporting that participation in the project was free from intimidation with an added sense of confidence and felt encouraged by their group members to participate. They were not overly concerned about making mistakes and indeed reported they felt that other group members would be willing to correct their mistakes

Educators/tutors can influence the way a learning community develops and empower students to take ownership of their own learning

Students are indeed a valuable resource: they are *people* and do amazing things

were illustrated using quotes from the text in the key categories using the learners' own words.

Table 2 presents examples of student feedback in relation to the categories "people" and "task" and how wiki use supported learners in undertaking group-based assessment learning activities (the group number is specified alongside each response in the table).

This study has emphasized the need to consider the role of the tutor in designing and implementing an online learning community of undergraduate computing students through the use of wiki technology. Table 3 summarizes the key issues arising from this specific experience of introducing wiki technology to computer studies students. Although these specifically relate to the context outlined in this chapter, many of the issues will apply equally to other disciplines.

Overall, this study has shown that a wiki offers a major opportunity to personalize the student learning experience in a system of mass higher education, and technologies such as wikis not only provide new learning opportunities, but they are also relatively easy to set up and use. What has been found to be a key in ensuring quality of the learning experience is the role and approaches adopted by the tutor and resulted in the iterative development of the CLAT model as shown in Fig. 1.

DISCUSSION AND CONCLUSION

The CLAT model was developed based on educators' experiences while engaged in learning design to support collaborative learning through assessment. In this chapter, a wiki application was presented as used by tutors and students to support collaborative learning through assessment. While setting up the wiki environment in practice, the tutor sought support initially from the technical staff. It is important to ensure that the learners' works were protected given the collaborative nature of the learning in assessment. It was also important that only those students belonging to the cohort of students would have access to the wiki environment. Therefore, there is a need for initial training on wiki use and technical support at least during initial use by tutors.

The preparedness of tutors and learners alike is a key to active engagement in learning while using a wiki when used to support collaborative learning through assessment. As discussed in this chapter, active learner engagement requires the chosen activities to be shared equally within and across the group, with an emphasis on learning by doing and nurturing within learners a deep approach to learning. In this chapter, the learning activities were set to enhance information sharing, understand, and skills development while enabling autonomy and ownership of learning by encouraging learners to create their own dynamic learning environment while using a wiki.

A wiki enables and challenges learners to copersonalize their learning by codeciding and codesigning their own learning space and ways to manage their learning. It provides convenience as learners can decide remotely and collectively on how, when were, and when to learn. When used to support collaborative learning, there are no more physical group meetings; people who work can still engage and learners can fit collaborative learning into their lifestyle and commitments. By using a wiki, learners were encouraged to complete learning activities that push exploration, a need to know, show, and share findings for cocritical analysis and coreview. Thus, learners together progressively coconstruct, coproduce, and cobuild their knowledge, understanding, and perhaps skills under the guidance of the tutor depending on the role adapted: observer, moderator, facilitator, or guru – real social constructivism. Once learners are seated at the computer, they may look up articles, find resources, and populate the wiki collectively. At the same time learners can engage in discussion while simultaneously completing the wiki work, learners can also check facts, information, understandings and validate quality too. In contrast, if the learning is paper based, this means trips to libraries, meeting schedules, on campus, costly phone calls, and so on.

Finally, this chapter has clarified the role of the tutor and shown that the role the tutor is a key to ensuring motivation and engagement amongst learners while learning collaboratively through assessment using technology such as a wiki. Such clarification has firstly established through the CLAT pedagogical model that there are four roles that maybe adapted by the tutor: observer, moderator, facilitator, and guru in establishing a wiki learning environment to support collaborative learning through assessment. What the CLAT pedagogy has shown is when adapting a role that content alone uploaded to technology is not a motivator for learning; when considering the tutor role, there needs to be a mechanism in place to support active and purposive learning: information processing, knowledge construction, and building understanding and possibly skills. Secondly, this chapter has provided guidance on how this role can be enacted as this area of practice develops further. This was achieved through a practical example of using the CLAT pedagogical model. The argument was made that a wiki when used in this way is a learning resource to support collaborative learning.

REFERENCES

Anderson, P. (2007). What is Web 2.0? Ideas, technologies and implications for education, February. Available at www.jisc.ac.uk/media/documents/techwatch/tsw0701b.pdf. Retrieved on April 30, 2010.

Barab, S., & Duffy, T. (2000). From practice fields to communities of practice. In: D. H. Jonasses & S. M. Land (Eds), *Theoretical foundations of learning environments* (pp. 25–55). Mahwah, NJ: Lawrence Erlbaum.

Biggs, J. (2003). *Aligning teaching for constructive learning*. New York: The Higher Education Academy Press.

Chickering, A. W., & Gamson, Z. F. (1987). Seven principles for good practice in undergraduate education. *AAHE Bulletin*, 3–7.

Collins, A., Brown, J. S., & Newman, S. E. (1989). Cognitive apprenticeship: Teaching the crafts of reading, writing and mathematics. In: R. Glaser & L. B. Resnick (Eds), *Knowing, learning, and instruction: Essays in honor of Robert Glaser* (pp. 453–494). Hillsdale, NJ: Lawrence Erlbaum.

Crook, C. (Ed.) (2003). Editorial changing times. *Computer Assisted Learning*, *19*(4), 399–400.

DfES. (2005). Harnessing technology: Transforming learning and children's services, March 15. The Department for Education and Skills. Available at http://www.dfes.gov.uk/publications/e-strategy/. Retrieved on July 8, 2008.

Doolan, M. A. (2006). Effective strategies for building a learning community online using wiki. *Proceedings of the 1st annual blended learning conference 2006*, Hatfield, University of Hertfordshire (pp. 51–63).

Doolan, M. A. (2007a). Our learners are the net generation growing up in a digital world. How then do we engage with and support this type of learner? *ECEL 2007: The 6th European conference on e-Learning*, 4–5 October 2007, Copenhagen, Denmark, ECEL (pp.159–172).

Doolan, M. A. (2007b). Setting up online collaborative learning groups using Wiki technology – A tutors' guide. *SEDA Staff Development Magazine* (April) 12–14.

Doolan, M. A. (2007c). Collaborative working: Wiki and the creation of a sense of community. In: *Proceeding of the 2nd international blended learning conference 2007*, 14 June. University of Hertfordshire, Hatfield, Hertfordshire (p.70).

Doolan, M. A. (2008). Bridging the gap: Adapting curriculum design and teaching practice to engage the net generation learner in an online learning community. In: *Proceedings of the 3rd Annual Blended Learning Conference 2008*, 18–19 June. University of Hertfordshire, Hatfield.

Doolan, M. A. (2009). *Developing a pedagogy using Web 2.0 to engage the net generation learner. ICERI 2009*. Madrid: ICERI.

Doolan, M. A. (2010). *The role of the tutor: Developing a pedagogy using audio to support collaborative assessment EDULEARN 2010* (6–8 July). Barcelona: EDULEARN.

Doolan, M. A., & Barker, T. (2005). Evaluation of computing students performance using group based learning online and offline. *Proceedings of the 9th CAA international computer assisted assessment conference*, July 5–6. Loughborough, Leicestershire, Loughborough University.

Doolan, M. A., Thornton, H. A., & Hilliard, A. (2006). Collaborative learning: Using technology for fostering those valued practices inherent in constructive environments in traditional education. *Journal for the Enhancement of Learning and Teaching*, 3(2), 7–17.

Kolb, D. A. (1984). *Experiential learning: Experience as the source of learning and development*. Englewoood Cliffs, NJ: Prentice-Hall.

Lave, J., & Wenger, E. (1991). *Situated learning legitimate peripheral participation*. Cambridge: Cambridge University Press.

Leuf, B., & Cunningham, W. (2001). *The Wiki way: Quick* collaboration *on the Web*. Boston: Addison-Wesley.

Mac Donald, J. (2006). *Blended learning and online tutoring: A good practice guide*. London: Gower Publishing.

O'Reilly, T. (2005a). Web 2.0: Compact definition, October 1. Available at http://radar. oreilly.com/archives/2005/10/web-20-compact-definition.html. Retrieved on April 27, 2010.

O'Reilly, T. (2005b). What is Web 2.0: Design patterns and business models for the next generation of software, September 30. Available at http://oreilly.com/web2/archive/what-is-web-20.html. Retrieved on April 28, 2010.

Ramsden, P. (1992). *Learning to teach in higher education*. London: Routledge.

Salmon, G. (2002). *E-moderating: The key to learning and teaching online*. London: Kogan Page.

Tu, C. H. (2004). Electronic community of practice. In: M. Silberman (Ed.), *The 2004 training and performance sourcebook and the 2004 team and organization development sourcebook*. Wappingers Falls, NY: Inkwell Publishing.

Vygotsky, L. S. (1978). *Mind in society*. Cambridge, MA: Harvard University Press.

Wenger, E. (1998). *Communities of practice: Learning, meaning and identity*. Cambridge: Cambridge University Press.

TECHNOLOGY INTEGRATION CAN BE DELICIOUS: SOCIAL BOOKMARKING AS A TECHNOLOGY INTEGRATION TOOL

Gloria Edwards and Barbra F. Mosley

ABSTRACT

This chapter addresses the needs of ongoing educational reform and presents the merits of social bookmarking as a technology integration option for pre-service teachers. Delicious, a social bookmarking tool, was introduced as a Web 2.0 tool that assists in tracking websites that hold the potential to contribute toward the meaningful learning of students. Delicious and other social bookmarking tools give 24/7 access to tagged websites from any computer anywhere in the world as long as Internet access is available. Numerous emerging technologies are making their way into the classrooms. As such, K-12 schools and post-secondary institutions of higher learning bear the responsibility for preparing all students to successfully use them to compete in this global economy. During fall 2009 and spring 2010 semesters, the authors piloted use of Delicious in seven mandatory teacher education technology-based courses. Specific instructions were provided for selecting interactive,

Educating Educators with Social Media
Cutting-edge Technologies in Higher Education, Volume 1, 207–225
Copyright © 2011 by Emerald Group Publishing Limited
All rights of reproduction in any form reserved
ISSN: 2044-9968/doi:10.1108/S2044-9968(2011)0000001013

user-friendly websites with content that would complement lesson plan content and thereby contribute toward greater learning potential. A total of 106 graduate and undergraduate pre-service teachers located, standardized, and began sharing their tagged Delicious bookmarks as part of a major course project for integrating technology into a classroom. The websites were documented within full and abbreviated lesson plans that detailed the rationale for use of each technology resource/tool. Approximately 300 websites that met specifically defined criteria were located by the pre-service teachers who also benefited from the merits of collaboration and sharing through social bookmarking with Delicious. They simultaneously experienced how ready-access to quality technology resources/tools could positively impact the learning opportunities of their K-12 students. Access to the Delicious database collection is available by contacting the authors.

INTRODUCTION

Educational reform has been the driving force behind ongoing change in K-12 schools and post-secondary learning environments since the 1957 Soviet Union launching of Sputnik (Garber, 2007, para. 1), when teachers in the United States were charged to improve their preparation of students for future jobs with emphasis in the content areas of math, science, and technology (Flynn, 1995). Over four decades later, *The No Child Left Behind Act* (2001) served to remind us that several items, including technology integration, were still on the educational reform agenda (Cowan, 2008). Aside from having never reached a consensus of agreement on its definition, technology integration remains somewhat of an abstraction in institutions of higher learning charged with preparing teachers to meet the technology integration mandate (Belland, 2009). Should the focus be on instructing pre-service teachers in the use of specific hardware and software tools or primarily involving them in creatively exploring options on what to do with such tools within the classroom (Oliver, 2007)? Perhaps a fresh focus is needed in pre-service teacher education and in-service teacher professional development in light of technology integration barriers that include high stakes testing needs, lack of resources, and negative teacher beliefs (Belland, 2009). Best practices endorse a most palatable direction: establish opportunities for pre- and in-service teachers to interact with and model the behavior of technology-using teachers (Boulos & Wheelert, 2007; Oliver, 2007).

Teacher education faculty bear the primary responsibility to educate and train pre-service teachers and provide ongoing professional development opportunities to in-service teachers through outreach. Because of their consistent interactions with pre- and in-service teachers, teacher education faculty must endeavor to be within the top ranks of technology-using teachers. They must model the use of various technologies for the K-12 and higher education classrooms, explain and demonstrate how these technologies are linked to and affect learning outcomes, and assist in the decision-making process of identifying those technologies that contribute toward meaningful learning.

The purpose of this chapter is to support the ongoing educational reform agenda of technology integration in the K-12 classrooms. It is the contention of the authors that one way to accomplish this is through the education and training of pre-service teachers based on best practices suggestions. The following "one-shot" case study addresses the technology integration problem and documents how two teacher education faculty are: (1) using Delicious, a social bookmarking tool (Delicious.com, 2010), to model the use of a new and emerging technology to pre-service teachers, and (2) educating and training pre-service teachers in the use of this technology tool which when used appropriately can help meet the mandate of preparing K-12 students for the future through meaningful learning experiences. This chapter would be of interest to teacher education faculty, pre- and in-service teachers, and educators looking for simple, yet effective ideas, resources, and tools that can be modeled and/or used within K-12 and higher education classrooms.

The case study is documented in four sections. Pedagogical Foundations present the literature and theoretical position of the case study. Teaching Technology Integration describes the mandatory technology integration course, knowledge and skill survey, the Delicious project, and the serendipitous twist that led to the answer of a question that was never asked. Meeting the Technology Integration Need is a discussion of how the course project developed into an external project with the potential to reach beyond pre-service teachers to in-service teachers. Looking to the Future offers concluding remarks and informs the reader of future plans for the Delicious project.

PEDAGOGICAL FOUNDATION

The literature and theoretical foundation of this chapter speaks to three primary areas: technology integration, social bookmarking, and cognitive thinking.

Technology Integration

A definition of technology integration is necessary if teachers are to understand what the modeled behaviors of technology-using teachers look like. Belland (2009, p. 354) offers an intriguing 21st century definition for consideration – "the sustainable and persistent change in the social system of K-12 schools caused by the adoption of technology to help students construct knowledge." Research continues to suggest that technologies, when appropriately used in the classroom, help to facilitate meaningful, student-centered learning. Teacher education faculty have been considering and/or piloting the inclusion of texting, blogging, and wikis as technology integration options with mixed results (McPherson, Wang, Hsu, & Tsuei, 2007; Richardson, Dec. 2005/Jan. 2006). Even so, the possibility remains that inclusion of these and other tools into the K-12 classroom hold the potential of offering meaningful learning opportunities to students (Mosley, Smith-Gratto, & Jones, 2008). The appropriate use of technologies mandates that users stay abreast of new and rapidly emerging technologies. Therefore, technology integration promotes constant change – change in the way teachers teach and change in the way students learn – change that requires a constructivist perspective and solid commitment toward the use of emerging technologies that hold the potential to offer students meaningful, classroom, learning experiences (Jonassen, Howland, Marra, & Crismond, 2008).

Understanding technology integration beckons a brief look backwards into the previous century. Looking back, learning had its foundation in the three R's – reading, writing, and arithmetic. Although the three R's still serve as the basis of learning, additions have been made to that foundation. Computers, as tools to facilitate learning and assist in technological literacy, were just the tip of the iceberg. The Internet forced us to reconsider where knowledge could be acquired. Moving forward into the 21st century, Web 2.0 AKA (also known as) the Read/Write Web offered a radical shift in our educational perspective of how and where learning could and would occur.

K-12 schools and post-secondary institutions of learning are accountable for preparing each generation to successfully compete in the global economy. A commitment toward technology integration is necessary to ensure that ALL students receive opportunities to mature into lifelong learners who possess the full complement of 21st century skills necessary to meet the employment needs of the future. Beyond knowledge in core subjects, students must receive ample opportunities to become critical thinkers, problem solvers, effective communicators, experienced collaborators, information and technology literate, flexible and adaptable, globally competent, and environmentally literate (Partnership for 21st Century Skills, 2009). Richardson (2007) calls it a "C change" and linked teaching and learning to a new skills set of seven C's: *communication, connection, collaboration/ cooperation, creation/contribution, community, continual learning,* and *culture.* Standards have since been approved and put in place to inform and guide teachers and students in meeting established educational technology goals, especially as they pertain to the purpose and plan of technology integration (International Society for Technology in Education, 2008). It is through the use of varying technologies that the 21st century skills set can be fully understood and learned.

As emerging technologies increase and find their way into the workplace, they have profound implications within K-12 and post-secondary institutions of learning. In both these environments, students are being prepared for entry into the workplace. Technology integration ideas emerge and are tested to determine their effectiveness. Such is the case with the Web 2.0 culture of social networking and community building, especially as it pertains to support the social interactions among teachers and students (Churchill, Wong, Law, Salter, & Tai, 2009).

The Web 2.0 environment has exploded into one of the favorite meeting places of the century. Young and old alike connect, communicate, collaborate, create content, contribute opinions, form communities based on common interests, learn 24/7, and make discoveries; all at the click of a button. Participants routinely blog, wiki, podcast, tweet, stay informed with real-time news and weather, share their lives through Facebook and Flickr, network in LinkedIn, and devotedly watch the world go by in YouTube (CMO.com, n.d.). Because the Web 2.0 environment has gained a captive audience, the authors believe that consideration should be given to including the seven C's within those technology integration initiatives that center around the Web 2.0 social media landscape; which is a rich, diverse environment of places, resources, tools, and services where interacting, publishing, and sharing have quickly becoming the norm.

A captive audience presents a tremendous opportunity to implement change, so colleges and universities with teacher education programs are on board for a positive shift in technology integration perspectives. A number of curricular changes are aggressively being discussed with particular care not to reinvent the wheel (Cowan, 2008) but to consider multiple components that together hold the potential to prepare the next generation of technology-proficient new and practicing teachers (Duran, Fossum, & Luera, 2007). Of particular importance is the need for teacher education faculty to take a leadership role in this change paradigm by modeling meaningful technology use and by establishing a structure of collaboration capable of functioning at the center of such changes (Belland, 2009; Duran et al., 2007).

Social Bookmarking

Social bookmarking is an online, Web 2.0 tool that lets users save (or bookmark) web addresses to their very own personal online account. Social bookmarking tools are more sophisticated than similar options within browser like Internet Explorer or Mozilla FireFox which simply add/save websites to your Favorites or Bookmarks. No cost is imposed for this service, however, users must register. Social bookmarking tools provide 24/7 access to saved websites on any computer from anywhere in the world as long as Internet access is available. Additionally, social bookmarking tools give users the power to organize websites through "tags" and "notes." Tags assist in the development and implementation of an indexing/keyword system so websites can be appropriately categorized, sorted, and viewed separately from others in the collection. Notes provide information that describes the website in greater detail than its title. An important benefit is that users can collaborate online with other users and share their websites with individuals having similar interests.

A number of social bookmarking tools are available on the Internet including, but not limited to, Delicious (http://www.delicious.com), Digg (http://www.digg.com), and StumbleUpon (http://www.stumbleupon.com). Each has its own special features. Potential users are encouraged to investigate each one carefully to determine which will meet their specific needs. Owing to its simplicity, Delicious was the social bookmarking tool of choice for this case study.

Cognitive Thinking

The use of Web 2.0 tools in conjunction with the collaborative nature of society form an interesting partnership with the push to improve literacy skills, particularly information literacy and digital literacy (Collins, 2009). Users of social bookmarking tools, like Delicious, have many opportunities to improve their literacy skills by simply using the tool. Additionally, the level of interaction with social bookmarking tools can be mapped to the cognitive, affective, and psychomotor domains of learning. Of particular interest to the authors is the connection of social bookmarking to the cognitive domain or what has come to be known as Bloom's Digital Taxonomy (Churches, 2009). For teacher education faculty, the goal is to progressively move learners along the continuum from low to high such that problem-solving and critical thinking skills are ultimately in full use. When the generic skills of social bookmarking are mapped to the cognitive domain of learning, they spread across all six levels from the lowest thinking skill of remembering through the highest thinking skill of creating; with collaborative opportunities offering the greatest impact toward meaningful learning (Table 1).

Social bookmarking lends itself well to the retrieval of information. Since it is impossible for today's learners to remember the enormous volume of information that continues to increase exponentially, the simple act of bookmarking puts users at the first level of the cognitive domain hierarchy (Table 1). The power of social bookmarking, however, is in the tags and the notes. The process of tagging and including notes moves users along the cognitive domain hierarchy to the next taxonomy level of understanding where construction of meaning takes place. Frequent use of social bookmarking tools lend themselves nicely toward users reaching the higher levels of thinking that comes with the procession from tagging, to searching, to collaborating and sharing. Information and digital literacy skills can be improved by consistently interacting with social bookmarking tools and mastering the skills therein.

Table 1. Cognitive Domain and Social Bookmarking (Using Delicious) Skills.

	Domain Levels	Social Bookmarking Skills
Low	Remembering	Adding a website(s) without tags and notes
↑	Understanding	Adding a website with well-structured tags and/or notes
	Applying	General tag searches
	Analyzing	Specific tag searches and external searches (Yahoo, Google, etc.)
↓	Evaluating	Selecting of most appropriate website(s) based on search results
High	Creating	Creating professional category systems (folksonomy) and establishing collaborative connections of mutual interests

TEACHING TECHNOLOGY INTEGRATION

The authors have direct responsibility for teaching a mandatory 15-week technology integration course intended to help pre-service teachers gain practical experience in including technologies in the curriculum that help to facilitate meaningful student learning. The rigors of the course must be maintained with appropriate technologies; therefore, the course is project-based, which provides the flexibility to remove projects and develop new ones that include emerging technologies. The authors have consistently tracked, through survey, the technology knowledge and skills of graduate and undergraduate pre-service teachers taking these courses. Fall 2009 and spring 2010 semesters were no different. The 13-item menu/matrix-type survey, created by the authors, was distributed to the students through ZapSurvey, an online survey tool, on the first night of each course so that individual and overall class profiles of technology knowledge and skills could be obtained. The ID coded surveys made inquiry into their generation of birth (Boomers, Gen X, or Millennials), frequency of use and comfort level with generic hardware and software applications, and their knowledge of and interaction levels with common Web 2.0 tools. The data was then exported to Statistical Package for the Social Sciences (SPSS) and analyzed by the authors (IBM Corporation, 2010).

Over the past four years, the same survey has been distributed with minor modifications and updates pertaining primarily to the inclusion of new technologies. The data have consistently been used by the authors to (1) verify the appropriateness of the technology projects, (2) determine what software application training was necessary, (3) identify those students with skills deficiencies who without additional support would in all likelihood perform poorly in the course, and (4) help in determining when instructional changes in projects were necessary.

Participants

A total of 106 pre-service teachers from 7 courses (3 undergraduate; 4 graduate) during fall 2009 (54 students) and spring 2010 (52 students) responded to the survey. Only 5 of the 106 pre-service were male; one from fall 2009 and four from spring 2010. Whereas the research suggests that students will most likely overestimate their knowledge and skill levels (Dunning, Heath, & Suls, 2004), it also recommends that survey developers and/or proctors implement procedures to encourage honest responses from

Table 2. Fall 2009 Frequency Count of Online and Related Skills.

Skill	Boomers		Gen X		Millennials		Total
	No	Yes	No	Yes	No	Yes	
Blogging	3	1	18	5	16	11	54
Chatting	3	1	5	18	2	23	54
Email	0	4	0	23	0	27	54
Facebook/MySpace	4	0	4	19	1	26	54
Instant messaging	2	2	4	19	0	27	54
Online library research	2	2	5	18	3	24	54
Surfing the web	0	4	0	23	0	27	54
Texting	3	1	17	6	22	5	54
Twitter	1	3	2	21	0	27	54

survey takers. Over the years before the release of the online surveys, the authors have consistently encouraged survey takers to be honest in their responses as their answers would also be used to confirm that decisions for the projects correlated well with the necessary skills and abilities to complete them, to determine what training would be provided, and for future instructional improvement.

The fall 2009 survey data were sufficient to confirm the authors' decision to implement the new technology project (Table 2). The results suggested that, in general, students were comfortable on the Web, possessed sufficient online skills, and were adequately prepared to handle the project. One-on-one support was provided to those whose profiles indicated deficiencies, and as expected, the millennial generation of students seemed more involved in the social networking community than those of other generations (Table 2).

The Delicious Project

The same four progressively challenging technology projects were required in each of the courses both semesters. Only the Delicious project is pertinent to this chapter; therefore, discussion of the projects will be limited to it. The Delicious project was third in the sequence and took place between weeks 6 and 10 of each of the courses. It was also a new technology integration project and required pre-service teachers to select one grade level and a maximum of three content areas in which to develop three full or abbreviated lesson plans, according to the standardized lesson plan formats of the university. Of importance to this chapter was the requirement that each lesson plan contain a feasible, online technology integration component, preferably within a Web 2.0 environment.

Both the graduate and the undergraduate pre-service teachers were asked to search for, locate, fully interact with, and ultimately select what they believed were the three best websites to integrate within their K-12 lesson plan. The technology integration component had to match some element of the content requirements of the lesson plan, be user-friendly (easy to operate interface, easy to understand navigation, and low learning curve), and interactive (ongoing exchange of information, especially audio, video/animation, and/or feedback). A one or two paragraph rationale explaining why each website was selected and the benefits of its use had to be thoroughly explained within the lesson plans. The pre-service teachers would also have the opportunity to demonstrate what they believed was their best of the three technology integration components to the class. Since many of them were involved in field experiences, another goal was to help them obtain technology-appropriate resources that their cooperating teachers would allow them to include within their practice lessons.

Most Internet users know that on any given day webpages and websites appear and disappear exponentially. Formal keyword and webpage naming rules are not always applied during the website design process, which can make locating websites for technology integration purposes very time consuming and frustrating. There are untold numbers of websites that possibly meet the established criteria for inclusion within the technology integration project lesson plans; however, finding them in some cases defaults to happenstance. The authors possessed a small collection of 16 websites that fully demonstrated the quality of websites pre-service teachers were expected to locate. The most expedient way to provide students with access to these resources was to bookmark the websites within Delicious and provide the pre-service teachers with access to it. The processes of the website discoveries were shared in a 30-minute orientation. One of the websites was specifically used as part of an in-class demonstration and discussion of quality (Fig. 1).

The rationale of using Delicious to view bookmarked website collections was well received. Pre-service teachers were guided through the process of obtaining their own Delicious accounts and given access to the authors' collection. The 30-minute training session included an explanation that assessment of all bookmarked websites would be made through each Delicious account with the authors being granted access to all collections of bookmarks. It was at that time that their excitement about being able to bookmark websites, share their findings, and have 24/7 access to them really began to escalate.

Fig. 1. User-friendly, Interactive Weather Website that Meets the Quality Criteria. *Source:* Edheads Weather: Activate Your Mind (2010). http://www.edheads.org/activities/weather/index.htm

A standardized list of tags was developed by the authors and given to the pre-service teachers as part of a mandatory task. Its purpose was to help in the process of tagging. It was not, however, meant to lock users into a rote process of tag selections. On the contrary, it provided them with a small set of logical tags that would help in constructing tags of their own. For every bookmark from the standardized list pre-service teachers included within Delicious, a maximum of two tags of their own could also be included. This facilitated the process by which meaning was given to their bookmarks through the construction of new tags. Additionally, it facilitated the process by which additional tags were added to the standardized list of tags.

Similar to tags, the inclusion of notes within Delicious was mandatory and meant to help facilitate understanding. Pre-service teachers added notes that made sense and then used the decision-making process to search Delicious and select those websites they believed would be most beneficial to use based upon the tags and notes. This is a particularly powerful process which helps in moving pre-service teachers to the higher levels of thinking in the cognitive domain taxonomy. Pre-service teachers transfer their knowledge of the process to familiar search engines (Google, Yahoo, Bing, etc.) to more strategically explore the Internet for additional website discoveries. This helps clarify how collaborating and sharing through Delicious move users to the highest levels in the taxonomy.

Internet Safety and Privacy Issues

A few students in the course were overheard discussing how Delicious could really simplify their lives with all their online accounts. Some were contemplating the input of personal logins and passwords for banking and charge card accounts. When discouraged from doing so, one student remarked that the input would be safe if designated as "Private." Yes, bookmarks can be marked as "Private," however, such designations do not guarantee the security of sensitive information. Social bookmarking websites cannot and do not offer firewall protection or encryption security of confidential information. These systems can be easily hacked into. Warnings and frank discussions, although not previously considered, took place following a decision that such information needed to become a mandatory part of the orientations provided as Delicious accounts were obtained. Users must understand that the benefits of Delicious do not take precedence over Internet safety rules. The authors therefore strongly recommended that sensitive account logins and passwords NOT be placed within any social bookmarking tool including Delicious.

A Simple, Yet Exciting Discovery

The momentum of using Delicious continued the second week following orientation to the project as the pre-service teachers gave classroom demonstrations of their bookmarked websites. This resulted in multiple, informal, collaborative interests as they began sharing via Delicious their websites with one another. By week 3, a training session was implemented to further orient students to the benefits of social bookmarking through Delicious, especially privatizing bookmarks and adding or deleting users. By week 4, when the project was due, students had located websites that seemingly met the criteria of the project. Some students were even overheard remarking that they were not even looking for "that" website, but stumbled upon it while performing searches for other assignments. Apparently, their information literacy skills were kicking in.

The following week, the authors assessed each student's lesson plans and Delicious bookmarks using an assessment rubric. A larger than expected number of exceptional websites that met the defined criteria were received. Additionally, many of the accessed Delicious accounts contained more than the required three bookmarked websites with tags and notes. Some had begun to use Delicious for their own personal uses and many had established collaborative connections with other students identified as "fans" within their accounts. The serendipitous twist is that the simple social bookmarking assignment, which was never meant to arouse such interest, had rapidly turned into an informal collaborative project among pre-service teachers. Additionally, the project as originally designed was not created to address the technology integration barriers in K-12 environment. Irrespective, while nearing the end of the 15-week semester and after close tracking by the authors, the authors began looking at the Delicious project from the perspective of weakening technology integration barriers. A possible answer seemed to be looming without having even asked the question: Can the simple task of bookmarking website addresses according to a standardized set of rules have any impact on the technology integration barriers voiced by in-service teachers?

MEETING TECHNOLOGY INTEGRATION NEEDS

By the end of fall 2009, the authors reflectively reviewed what had transpired with the technology integration project. It was believed that improvements to the project would yield benefits capable of extending beyond the technology integration course. Understandably, the pre-service teachers could continue to collaborate with one another; however, the collaborative spirit needed to be passed on. Two technology integration barriers in-service teachers consistently voice regarding their reluctance to integrate technology into their classrooms include (1) the lack of appropriate resources and (2) the lack of time to actually find what they need IF it's even out there on the Internet (Belland, 2009). Ironically, the project appears to have weakened these barriers through the collaborative efforts of pre-service teachers.

The opportunity to outreach, specifically to in-service teachers, was knocking at the door. Conversations between the authors to revamp the project to accommodate the long-term needs of both pre- and in-service teachers turned into planning sessions. Suggestions for restructuring included (1) enforcing formal guidelines for bookmarking websites, (2) linking the project to pedagogical thought, (3) establishing an exclusive Delicious account to house the "best of the best" bookmarked websites, (4) assigning an administrator for on-going maintenance of the Delicious account, (5) extending an open invitation to pre- and in-service teachers everywhere to freely access the growing compilation of websites, and (6) welcoming collaborative suggestions from pre- and in-service teachers for the inclusion of additional websites they believe meet the defined criteria of being quality, user-friendly, interactive websites.

Each suggestion for restructuring the project was carefully analyzed. With total agreement that the Delicious environment would be an acceptable home for the project, the first hurdle was crossed. One of the authors volunteered to establish an exclusive Delicious account into which the "best of the best" websites would be housed and to be the interim administrator for the account. The procedures for formally bookmarking the websites and the need to identify the pedagogical foundation upon which the project would stand were immediate priorities. The remaining suggestions were put on hold pending establishment of the Delicious environment as a fully functional database.

Procedures for Bookmarking Websites

The next semester (Spring 2010), graduate and undergraduate pre-service teachers were again surveyed. The profiles of skills again suggested that, overall, the participants possessed the necessary skills to successfully complete the project (Table 3). They were formally oriented to the restructured technology integration project in a one-hour training session and responded favorably to searching for and fully interacting with at least three, quality, user-friendly, interactive websites that they would consider using within their classrooms.

This time, formal guidelines were mandatory. No one would use the system default of just bookmarking the URLs and accepting the website default titles. Instead, they would standardize their bookmarks using four of the five formal elements provided within the Delicious environment (Fig. 2). After students obtained their free Delicious account, they received instructions for properly adding websites:

1. URLs would be added using the Delicious "Saving a new bookmark" link or toolbar button. Typing full URLs into the Delicious environment

Table 3. Spring 2010 Frequency Count of Online and Related Skills.

Skill	Boomers		Gen X		Millennials		Total
	No	Yes	No	Yes	No	Yes	
Blogging	0	2	14	6	17	13	52
Chatting	0	2	6	14	2	28	52
Email	0	2	0	20	0	30	52
Facebook/MySpace	0	2	3	17	0	30	52
Instant messaging	1	1	4	16	4	26	52
Online library research	0	2	1	19	3	27	52
Surfing the web	0	2	0	20	0	30	52
Texting	1	1	16	4	24	6	52
Twitter	0	2	0	20	0	30	52

Fig. 2. Structure for Creating the Bookmark in Delicious.

was prohibited; however, copying and pasting URLs was the preferable method. This was to ensure that typographical errors did not contribute toward initial broken links.

2. A specific rather than the default title was now required such that, at a glance, a potential user would know exactly what the website was.

3. User-friendly notes of approximately one to three sentences of pertinent information about the webpage/website and/or how it could be used to contribute toward meaningful learning were mandatory.

4. They were each responsible for formally tagging their webpages/websites using the standardized list of tags, created and distributed by the Delicious administrator. The list consisted of two categorical choices: grade level and content. Students were required to select a minimum of one choice from each category but no more than five total

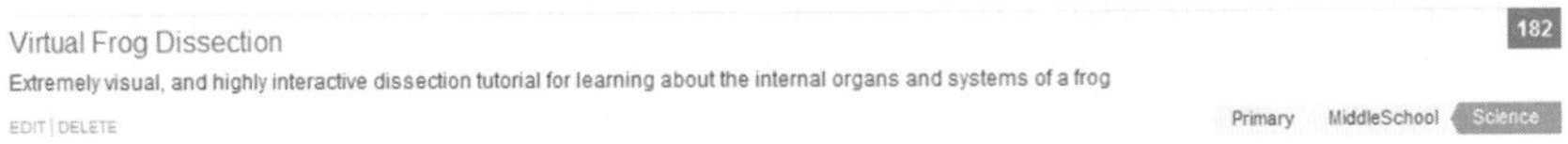

Virtual Frog Dissection   `182`
Extremely visual, and highly interactive dissection tutorial for learning about the internal organs and systems of a frog
EDIT | DELETE   Primary   MiddleSchool   Science

Fig. 3.   Final Appearance of Saved Bookmark within Delicious.

choices. The list was not exhaustive; therefore, students could add a maximum of two tags of their own that could help facilitate successful Delicious searches. The saved bookmark would be a small, yet informative search result (Fig. 3)

Depending on the course (graduate or undergraduate), pre-service teachers followed specific instructions for providing the Delicious administrator with access to their bookmarks. The undergraduates emailed their full Delicious user link to the authors. The graduates added the administrator as a "fan" through "Add a user to Network." This process allowed the administrator to keep a manageable number of fans clustered in the Delicious account. The authors retained full authority for the decision to include within the separate, formal Delicious database only the most appropriate of the bookmarked websites based upon the established course criteria. The culminating activity for the Spring 2010 project was completion of an abbreviated lesson plan which included their detailed rationale for integrating the technology into a classroom.

LOOKING TO THE FUTURE

During two semesters (Fall 2009 and Spring 2010), 106 graduate and undergraduate pre-service teachers contributed over 300 websites that they believed were quality, user-friendly websites that they would consider using within their classrooms. The Delicious administrator reviewed and evaluated their choices. Some bookmarks were rejected, some were eliminated as duplicates; however, approximately half of the submissions received a "thumbs up" for possible inclusion within the "best of the best" Delicious database collection. Interestingly, following the course a number of students continued to add websites to their Delicious account; some of which are also under consideration for inclusion in the collection. The final pilot of the project will take place during Fall 2010 with four courses of pre-service teachers making contributions as part of the technology integration project. A minimum of 300 quality websites are estimated to populate the Delicious collection by the end of the Fall 2010.

Sharing the Delicious Experience

Following the final pilot, the next stage of the project will begin. By spring 2011, the project will be totally standardized as an ongoing technology integration project for the pre-service teachers at this east coast university. Students within the School of Education at a second university are expected to join the project as in-service teacher users of and hopefully contributors to the Delicious collection. Their interactions will be tracked to determine the volume of use and specifically which websites (content and grade levels) seem to generate the most interest for integration into the classrooms. Of particular interest to the authors will be whether pre- and in-service teachers appear to be targeting specific grades and/or content areas for integration and if perhaps other content and grade areas are deficient within the collection. Additionally, the authors plan to unveil the collection at upcoming education conferences to generate interest in the project, particularly amongst in-service teachers. Anticipation is high that there will be interest in not only using the collection but also providing workshops on how to effectively integrate the websites into the curriculum and use Delicious.

The Next Delicious Slice

The size of the Delicious database of cataloged websites that pre- and in-service teachers would consider using within their classrooms will always be small in comparison to the potential websites on the Internet as yet unfound. As the collection grows, the job of maintaining it will require more than an interim administrator. It will require someone to perform weekly monitoring to ensure that links are working and broken bookmark links are found or removed from the collection. Consideration is being given to linking the Delicious database to the library of the east coast university and soliciting assistance in its maintenance.

Maintaining the database is just the beginning. Once the collection is unveiled to in-service teachers, it would be beneficial to communicate with them to determine how helpful the resources are, if teachers are sharing the resources with one another, and if they would like to make contributions to the collection. The compilation of such information must be formalized and would definitely open the door for research opportunities on collaboration and sharing.

As the "best of the best" collection expands, the authors anticipate new directions for collaboration between pre-service and in-service teachers.

One future project under consideration is providing in-service teachers with professional development opportunities so that they can establish and maintain their own Delicious collections. Access to the original Delicious database collection will always be available; however, there are partnership opportunities that can be established between teachers in different K-12 schools, districts, and universities which are as yet unexplored. What started as a single idea to address the educational reform agenda by facilitating the use of a Web 2.0 tool in a technology integration course blossomed into a plethora of ideas for ongoing learning experiences that validate the merits of collaboration and sharing through social bookmarking. The door remains open to implement best practices: establish opportunities for pre- and in-service teachers to interact with and model the behavior of technology-using teachers.

Unveiling of the database is scheduled during Spring 2011. Interested individuals may contact the authors via email for access to the Delicious Best-of-the-Best Education Websites: gedwards@georgian.edu OR mosleyb@ncat.edu

REFERENCES

Belland, B. R. (2009). Using the theory of habitus to move beyond the study of barriers to technology integration. *Computers & Education*, *52*(2), 353–364.

Boulos, M. N. K., & Wheelert, S. (2007). The emerging Web 2.0 social software: An enabling suite of sociable technologies in health and health care education. *Health Information and Libraries Journal*, *24*(1), 2–23.

Churches, A. (2009). Bloom's digital taxonomy. Available at http://www.scribd.com/doc/13442504/Blooms-Digital-Taxonomy-v30. Retrieved on April 17, 2010.

Churchill, D., Wong, W., Law, N., Salter, D., & Tai, B. (2009). Social bookmarking – repository – networking: Possibilities for support of teaching and learning in higher education. *Serials Review*, *35*(3), 142–148.

CMO.com. (n.d.). The CMO's guide to the social media landscape. Available at http://www.cmo.com/social-media/cmos-guide-social-media-landscape. Retrieved on April 9, 2010.

Collins, S. (2009). How digital tools prepare students for the 21st century: A Collins consults white paper prepared for inspiration software, Inc. Available at http://www.inspiration.com/sites/default/files/documents/How_Digital_Tools_Prepare_Students_for_the_21st_Century.pdf. Retrieved on April 5, 2010.

Cowan, J. E. (2008). Strategies for planning technology-enhanced learning experiences. *The Clearing House*, *82*(2), 55–59.

Delicious.com. (2010). Web 2.0 social bookmarking tool. Available at http://www.delicious.com

Dunning, D., Heath, C., & Suls, J. M. (2004). Flawed self-assessment: Implications for health, education, and the workplace. *Psychological Science in the Public Interest Journal*, *5*(3), 69–106. Retrieved from the Academic Search Complete database.

Duran, M., Fossum, P. R., & Luera, G. R. (2007). Technology and pedagogical renewal. *Computers in the Schools*, *23*(3), 31–54.

Flynn, P. (1995). Global competition and education: Another sputnik? *The Social Studies*, *86*(2), 53–55.

Garber, S. (2007). Sputnik: The fiftieth anniversary. Available at http://history.nasa.gov/sputnik/. Retrieved on June 29, 2010.

IBM Corporation. (2010). About SPSS Inc. Available at http://www.spss.com/corpinfo/faqs.htm. Retrieved on November 2, 2010.

International Society for Technology in Education (ISTE). (2008). National educational technology standards. Available at http://www.iste.org/Content/NavigationMenu/NETS/ForTeachers/2008Standards/NETS_for_Teachers_2008.htm. Retrieved August 17, 2009.

Jonassen, D., Howland, J., Marra, R., & Crismond, D. (2008). *Meaningful learning with technology*. Upper Saddle River: Pearson.

McPherson, S., Wang, S., Hsu, H., & Tsuei, M. (2007). New literacies instruction in teacher education. *TechTrends*, *51*(5), 24–31.

Mosley, B. F., Smith-Gratto, K., & Jones, A. (2008). Tech toys of the net generation: Possible implications for colleges. *Teaching with Compassion, Competence, and Commitment*, *2*(2), 8–21.

Oliver, K. (2007). Leveraging Web 2.0 in the redesign of a graduate-level technology integration course. *TechTrends*, *51*(5), 55–61.

Partnership for 21st Century Skills. (2009). The MILE guide: Milestones for improving learning and education. Available at http://www.p21.org/documents/MILE_Guide_091101.pdf. Retrieved on April 5, 2010.

Richardson, W. (2007). The seven C's of learning. *District Administration*, *43*(4), 97 [Electronic Copy]. Retrieved from the Academic Search Premier databases.

Richardson, W. (Dec. 2005/Jan. 2006). The educator's guide to the read/write web. *Educational Leadership*, *63*(4), 24–27.

U.S. Department of Education. (2001). The *no child left behind act*. Pub. Law No. 107-110. Available at http://www.ed.gov/policy/elsec/leg/esea02/index.html. Retrieved on April 2, 2010.

PUBLIC ISSUES, PRIVATE CONCERNS: SOCIAL MEDIA AND COURSE MANAGEMENT SYSTEMS IN HIGHER EDUCATION

Jeremy Sarachan and Kyle F. Reinson

ABSTRACT

Social media and their changing nature present compelling public and private dilemmas for higher education. Instructional delivery faces obstacles to effectively reaching students who often prefer online communities and spend considerable recreational time using these social networking sites. CMS has limited appeal as an inviting space for students. An effective learning environment provides a communal place for student–professor interactions and an accessible and interactive space for collaboration and global knowledge distribution. This chapter focuses on some considerations educators should take into account as they manage courses through an increasingly socially mediated landscape.

Higher education's traditional delivery of course content takes place in closed systems, but when information can be exchanged with great speed and reach as it can with social media, the notion of forcing students to sit in the classroom while an instructor distributes photocopies and reading lists

Educating Educators with Social Media
Cutting-edge Technologies in Higher Education, Volume 1, 227–244
Copyright © 2011 by Emerald Group Publishing Limited
ISSN: 2044-9968/doi:10.1108/S2044-9968(2011)0000001014

of books to purchase seems grossly antiquated. Academia has been either slow to adapt to new media or has imposed the same closed system to its digital delivery via course management systems (CMS). College and university instructors whose pedagogy has been shaped in traditional educational environments are facing an emerging generation of students with mobile devices in their hands and search engines at their fingertips. More importantly, these students are less inclined to value an instructor's unique expertise if, in fact, the Internet can more readily deliver the same content.

Couple the reliability of search engines like Google with a powerful and authentic social network of students engaging in the same coursework and the proverbial sage on the stage is more vulnerable than ever before, unless she embraces experimenting with the technology. The most engaging conversations are taking place on the Internet because people can communicate in whatever medium fits the content most effectively, whether it is video, images, or hyperlinked text. The massive library of information available through social media and information networks changes the rules of the learning environment – and educators who explore the possibilities may find new ways to engage students in broader, richer discussions. Course management systems are unable to fulfill the expectations of a networked society since by definition it is a closed system that tries to keep up with rather than lead innovation in educational and media technology.

EDUCAUSE, a nonprofit association that promotes the intelligent use of information technology in higher education, published *The Tower and The Cloud: Higher Education in the Age of Cloud Computing* (Alexander, 2008). The edited volume addresses many of the concerns educators should apprehend as they contemplate deconstructing and reconstructing instructional design. Bryan Alexander, who directs research for the National Institute for Technology and Liberal Education, warns that: "A virtual learning environment consisting solely of students and instructor ... cannot partake of these network effects. One way forward for higher education is to nudge more digital content into the open web, combining our honed wariness about privacy and security with our awareness of the full-blown social web" (Alexander, 2008, p. 199). Students will benefit from gaining experience in analyzing and critiquing the collaborative knowledge on the Internet (whether academic or from supposedly "questionable" sources like Wikipedia) and be encouraged by the responsibility that comes from making their own work part of this collective knowledge. Higher education will soon face a crucial moment in which students will either accept or reject its importance in society. Closed systems will be unable to keep up with the abundance of information available and how educators react will define the next generation of higher education.

TECHNOLOGY TODAY: EMPOWERMENT TOMORROW

In a socially mediated course management structure, the characteristics of a traditional classroom will change considerably. Social media successfully and sustainably integrated will shape the pedagogical terrain of the future. If higher education ignores the habits of early adapters, it will do so at its own peril. As Marshall McLuhan observed in reaction to the emerging media of the 1960s

> One-room schools, with all subjects being taught to all grades at the same time simply dissolve when better transportation permits specialized spaces and specialized teaching. At the extreme of speeded-up movement, however, specialism of space and subject disappears once more ... Centuries of specialist stress in pedagogy and in the arrangement of data now end with the instantaneous retrieval of information made possible by electricity. (McLuhan, 1964, p. 346)

With the increasing abundance of reliable, publicly accessible information readily available via the Internet, academia runs the risk of closing itself off to mainstream conversations and dragging itself into marginal spaces if adjustments are left unexplored. How educators will straddle public access and intellectual property issues and address the traditionally private teacher–student relationship with respect to grading and feedback depends on how a CMS is modeled.

OPENING THE SYSTEM

In a closed system, much of a course's value arguably rests in its expert instructor guiding students through important concepts and objectives. The nature of access to course content is changing, and the prospects for open systems that make quality information and content available are much greater than once thought. The Massachusetts Institute of Technology launched its OpenCourseWare (OCW) program nearly a decade ago with the goal of improving teaching methods and sharing knowledge all over the world. Reactions were mixed. As David Diamond notes, "At a time when most enterprises were racing to profit from the Internet and universities were peddling every conceivable variant of distance learning, here was the pinnacle of technology and science education ready to give it away. Not the degrees ... but the content" (Diamond, 2003). Even with this increasing availability, the hegemony of a bricks and mortar university is far from being displaced by OCW. However, as of 2009, more than 200 higher education institutions across the world offer some form of OCW (Bays et al., 2009); examples of this more liberating philosophy come from various universities that offer learning modules or entire courses online for any learner to view or instructor to utilize. Connexions (cnx.org) offers learning objects and Opencourseware Consortium (ocwconsortium.org) offers courses from an extensive list of universities (Hafner, 2010). This openness serves at least two purposes: a global distribution of course materials that leads to an expansion of knowledge to anyone with web access and a showcase of a given college's role as a leader in technological innovation, contributing to enhanced educational practice within a Web 2.0 system and an increased understanding of how learning is likely to be affected by digital technology in the coming years.

Truthfully, any university (with proper funding) could adapt a similar practice of sharing its materials. Little is just "given away." Consider that tuition covers a degree and opportunities for student interaction, guidance, and instruction by professors. Course materials, while prepared through a considerable effort and time commitment by professors, are nonetheless not what they are specifically paid to do; this is only a means to an end of their professional responsibilities. Opening learning materials to a larger audience showcases the intellectual strength of a university and even would allow current students at the university to more knowledgably select courses. Even openly available course websites could achieve this specific objective through basic information dissemination.

The rising costs of American higher education are largely shouldered by students, either through tuition increases or cuts in funding that force educational programs to be viewed based on the return students will receive on their investment. If a student simply wants to learn through self-directed programs of study, it is possible that creative content gathering from online syllabi could yield a rich understanding of a subject, even without the sticker price of the degree. Through social media, learning too, becomes a social process where common spaces must be negotiated. Closed systems are simply not part of the conversation. Knowledge increasingly exists in other spaces that are free and easily shared, with or without peer-review. The epistemology of social media may be in its infancy, but open learning environments and the potential for conversations that can build knowledge are worthy of exploration.

COLLABORATION AND THE "PERSONAL BRAND"

Perhaps the most promising reason for blending social media into CMS is the opportunity for true collaboration, breaking down the educator–student dynamic of one-to-one instruction and replacing it with the more Web-realistic opportunities for crowd-sourcing and transparency. Students enrolled in a course that employs social media should recognize that they have access to the work of not only their peers in the classroom but to global subject-matter experts as well. The course work students complete is also easily contributed to or accessible via the Internet, so their own "personal brand" is at stake as part of these potential collaborations. The personal brand is also a key component for educators to consider because student work on the Web can also reflect on the instructor.

For many college students, social interaction and identification is perhaps a more important part of the experience than the education itself. One study of social connectedness and student cell phone use suggests that users who tended to be *more lonely* or *less socially connected* acquired cell phones for their symbolic values of fashion and status, not because it made them less lonely – or even because they found the phones useful for their communication needs (Wei & Lo, 2006). One's personal brand is created and enabled easily through social media because it is a means for self-identification and fulfillment. German sociologist Ulrich Beck (2001) argues "the creator of an individual identity" is "the central character of our time" (p. 165). This ethic of self-fulfillment suggests that students will choose, decide, and shape themselves in virtual settings and the basics of personal branding through collaboration are a real world skill for communicating across disciplines.

Students prefer to be comfortable and social, but higher education is not always well equipped to offer such spaces. Instead, students are forced into the unnatural setting of a classroom at a time when their consumption of media is largely happening somewhere else. Shifting paradigms in CMS clearly will encounter experiential questions of student comfort and social utility and educators should be cognizant of the places where students will feel most comfortable.

CMS PLACES AS NO PLACE

The problem with CMS Webware today is that it fails to offer a sense of place. It also neglects to take into consideration identity and community, merely serving as a repository for locked-down course materials and a mixed bag of Web 2.0 tools packaged neat but not so pretty, like so much technological pabulum. What these systems do offer are secure course materials and the convenience of an all-in-one package; therefore professors continue to use commercial CMS despite a marked difference between this expensive Webware and easy-to-use and immensely popular social networking tools like Facebook. Although Web 2.0 definitions typically include interactivity and user-generated content, authentic Web 2.0 tools also can lead to the development of a more personal and creative system that allows the user to fully engage with technology (Song, 2010).

Considering Facebook as the primary example, another roadblock comes from students who reject the educational use of Facebook as an invasion into their social lives and from a desire to keep their social networking activity and the learning process separate. The number of people using CMS represents a fraction of the number of people who use Facebook and other popular social networks. This difference in use is reflected by the success of the Facebook interface (after all, who needs training in how to use Facebook?) and the sense of community it creates. Ultimately, whether one looks at Facebook or another social networking tool, qualities that create an effective educational environment: trust, collaboration, and constructivist learning, are better reflected by social media. "Web 2.0 applications that encourage social construction of knowledge ... are freely available and may provide more creative instructors with better options than any LMS [Learning Management System] currently available" (Lane, 2008, p. 6). Lane adds that various sites need to be "cobbled together" to fulfill all needs. In fact, this synthesis of materials is what students will have to do as professionals in myriad fields. "7 things you should know about ... Personal Learning Environments," a document produced by the Educause Learning Initiative (2009), describes the concept of a PLE which encourages students to pull together writings and other personal content creation from appropriate websites, while Campbell (2009) discusses the possibilities of a "personal cyberinfrastructure" where students would gain skills in basic server administration to better build the own virtual identities. Meanwhile, while CMS Webware is capable of many functions (including blogging and creating wikis), it tends to be used for faculty convenience to organize materials by type (Word documents, PDFs, videos) within a digital folder rather than for using tools that could lead to positive changes in pedagogy (Lane, 2009).

THE THIRD PLACE OF FACEBOOK

Ray Oldenburg (1999) wrote about the nature of the Third Place in *The Great Good Place*. The First Place is one's home and the Second Place is the place of work, but the Third Place reflects one's "home away from home" (Oldenburg, 1999, p. 38). This may range from a bowling alley to a local bar or coffee house. Much has been written about how virtual worlds can create a Third Place (Steinkuehler & Williams, 2006; Moore, Gathman, & Ducheneaut, 2009). In particular, Second Life offers its inhabitants the ability to visit its 3-D coffee houses, dance clubs, and concerts, although it is the totality of the virtual space that functions as a Third Place. Online multiplayer games, even those designed for education, also offer an obvious metaphor for an engaging virtual space (Carron, Marty, & Heraud, 2008). Collectively, these virtual locations create a singular sense of familiar space not obtainable in the real world. The reach of the virtual third place is multigenerational, and includes spaces created for children through such sites as Club Penguin and Webkinz.

However, 2-D spaces like Facebook also easily satisfy the requirements of a Third Place. The first requirement is the creation of a "neutral ground" which allows people to engage with each other without getting too immersed in each other's lives – clearly Facebook creates enough virtual distance between "friends" to accomplish this. The second requirement is of a "leveler," giving each participant equal status. Again, this is achieved as student, teacher, author, and athlete may all become Facebook friends on equal par. The third requirement is that "conversation is the main activity" and that is the main purpose on Facebook whether it be through synchronous conversation via the chat function or an asynchronous conversation through the News Feed. Fourth, there is "accessibility and accommodation": Facebook is available 24 h a day to offer the companionship of others whom are signed on simultaneously. Other characteristics include the *presence of regulars*: the friends who post to the wall the most; *a low profile*: Facebook's standard template contrasts with the flash and gaudiness of MySpace; *a playful mood*: satisfied by the games and quizzes; and finally a *home away from home*, which Facebook certainly provides (Oldenburg, 1999, pp. 20–42). It is this familiarity that may create the strongest draw for users.

This idea of meaningful community is supported by the notion of "normative space," whereby a room or other location offers meaning besides its mere function (Stromer-Galley & Martey, 2009, p. 1050).

Facebook creates meaning through labeling portions of its visual layout. For example, "the Wall" functions as a place for meaningful but unrestrained commentary, not unlike graffiti in the real world. A degree of community and place also is created within 2-D environments like MySpace, LinkedIn, and other community-based sites. But in a very deliberate way, Facebook creates this sense of place by the careful and simple placement of the News Feed as the predominant feature of the page. Imagine a house party with all of your friends stopping in to say how they are doing. The ability to blog with the notes feature or speak synchronously with friends online all serve to create a place of connection that's both welcoming and comforting as it reduces barriers of time and place through the integration of close friends and acquaintances (and sometimes strangers) from the past to the present.

IDENTITY AS THE KEY TO COMMUNITY

Facebook is able to create meaningful exchanges because it embraces the users' full identities in a familiar space. The ability to post favorite movies, book, or quotes may appear to be banal but actually encourages users to reveal much personal information. Users posting their "favorites" indirectly sketch a literal representation of their personality and the choice of profile picture encourages visual creativity and a snapshot of an authentic and meaningful moment in time, a contemporary example of Roland Barthes' theory of the *punctum* (Sarachan, 2010).

Students value the effect space has on their identity and development during the turbulent years of adolescence and college. "Such instability and uncertainty have rendered space and territory of particular importance to young people, whether as the source of relative safety and stability, or as a means of reflexively mapping and making sense of one's identity and transitions or as a facilitator of social networks" (Hodkinson & Lincoln, 2008, p. 29). This definition of space carries over from the real world to the Internet, and whether this space is real or virtual, a sense of space to "map" one's self may help both social and academic development.

Social networking has become a ubiquitous method of maintaining connections and even sustaining friendship. If social networks like Facebook embody aspects of one's life and identity, the current positioning of Facebook as "only" a social space irresponsibly repositions its potential power as an educational tool to the sidelines in deference to student demand to have a place to relax.[1]

The best college classrooms attempt to create a feeling of community and sharing. Online communities do the same – as defined by their strategy for attracting and retaining members (Buss, 2009). Students already use Facebook as an aid for social acclimation to college (Madge, Meek, Wellens, & Hooley, 2009). The application of Oldenburg's Third Place within social networking sites allows that aura of community to also permeate the educational setting created within the space, which could exceed what is obtainable in all but the most ideal classroom settings.

THE PROBLEM WITH CMS

CMS such as Blackboard seemingly offer an ideal educational environment, including a broad selection of collaborative tools, flexible navigation/ organizational structure, and "locked-down" security for the professor and the course content (Fig. 1).

The organizational structure of CMS courses, with *Assignments, Readings, Syllabus,* or other headings, allows for easy creation of a course with multiple media types (Microsoft Word documents, PDF files, videos, podcasts) that are available for students in a coherent manner. (Of course, much of the same organization could be created using a free or college-hosted wiki site.) However, materials are only available to enrolled students for the semester. This limitation is troubling. Mott and Wiley discuss the

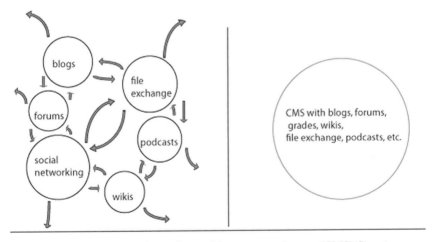

Fig. 1. Social Network vs. Course Management System (CMS) Structure.

artificial limitations created by this course architecture, citing Campbell's (2008) proposition that students (and instructors) desire "cognitive prints" that represent the desire to leave a permanent record of work (which is the perceived reality of Web 2.0 sites as Facebook and WordPress, even if this permanence is illusory.) In a "locked-down" environment, students lose access to course materials after the end of the semester. This has the effect of limiting extended learning and encouraging the all-too-common practice of forgetting materials at the end of a class. When a professor allows materials to be available indefinitely, students (and even alumni) have the option to return to these materials as desired. This would lead to an ongoing repository of learning. This ability to search for and revisit knowledge is another characteristic of an information literate society that places greater emphasis on critical analysis over rote learning.

Furthermore, the CMS package creates obstacles for building community and establishing a global-centric approach to education. The collaborative tools are comprehensive: blogs, wiki tools, chat, "drop boxes," etc. However, they usually offer fewer opportunities for personalization or the open communication offered by Web-based tools. Even if a professor progressively engages Web 2.0 tools for students to comment on a given reading assignment, a CMS blog is still a closed environment. Potentially, an open blog (hosted on WordPress or Tumblr or Blogger) invites outsiders who stumble upon the blog to comment, potentially opening up the discussion to wider debate (as in two cases that this chapter's authors' classes have experienced, class discussion included the authors of assigned books.) As Web 2.0 is defined to include collaboration and content creation, then in some ways the visual and collaborative limitations of CMS Webware suggests that these tools function as Web 2.0 in name only, lacking some of the elements that define their more flexible counterparts on the web. Mott and Wiley (2009) suggest that the CMS systems as they are typically used are linked to archaic pedagogical methods that assume that the instructor must provide all information (through lecture or posted content) rather than helping students become information literate and able to investigate a given topic, allowing them to discuss and analyze material collaboratively.

Certainly, a CMS lacks the conditions to create a successful "Third Place." Hierarchal roles of professor and student are accentuated since the professor has control over all settings, while a Web 2.0 environment may be more readily "turned over" to the students. Even if a professor retains administrative control of a Facebook page or Wiki, at least the semblance of leveling may be achieved. Web 2.0 tools are more likely to encourage conversation because this behavior already occurs there. Despite the presence of chat tools in CMS, there exists a mindset of "getting in and getting out" in order to complete a given assignment. Perhaps more significantly, CMS will never function as a "home away from home," whereas educational embedding into social media may more successfully achieve that objective. Certainly, the campus climate may have some effect on how important this objective becomes. With a small campus where the personal touch is more highly valued, such an online environment parallels the classroom. In a large university, such expectations may be lower, although student may see an online "Third Place" as providing what is typically unobtainable in a large lecture class.

Conversely, the locked-down, password-protected nature of CMS destroys any sense of community. Regardless of the features built into more advanced (and potentially costly) systems, Blackboard, and other systems create an isolated space for a particular university, creating an unrealistic cocoon that tries to make the Internet protected and simplistic, but leaves students to their own devices when it comes to creating strategies for using the Web to its fullest extent for personal and professional responsibilities that follow graduation. The acquisition of knowledge is as easy as a course management system makes it seem to be, and while there are certainly advantages in keeping elements of a course in one place, there are venues to do so (websites, blogs, wikis, etc.) that will expose students to uses they can apply elsewhere.

FACEBOOK: THE DISAPPEARANCE OF THE CREEPY TREEHOUSE

Facebook is on the edge of being accepted as an educational tool. In fact, Facebook contains groups to discuss uses of Facebook in education. One obstacle has been the accusation that using Facebook for education purposes is a prime example of the "Creepy Treehouse," a concept that has received significant press, including an article in the *Chronicle of Higher Education* (Young, 2008). In this instance, the "Creepy Treehouse" specifically refers to the unwanted intrusion of faculty members into what students see as their social space. Perhaps more reasonably, applications like Blackboard Sync that offer a mash-up of Facebook and Blackboard have received the same accusations and labels. Multiple solutions have been offered, ranging from maintaining professor–student interaction in Facebook Groups or Facebook Pages, or even letting students create the groups for class projects and work, thereby taking the administrative control (and power) away from the instructor. One study conducted at a single U.K. university suggests that Facebook was used by 10% of students for daily educational work and by 23% of students to learn daily about social events. Student educational use focused on student-to-student initiated questions and discussion rather than top-down uses by professors (Madge et al., 2009, p. 148). In the same study, 50% of respondents either disagreed or strongly disagreed when asked to respond to the question of whether Facebook helped them academically. (Most of the students found it to be a distraction.) Yet, 53% of the respondent thought it acceptable if Facebook was used for educational purposes (Madge et al., 2009, pp. 149–150). This suggests that while Facebook immersion for social purposes may be unavoidable, time spent with the site could also be strategically structured for a more educationally positive effect. Different strategies may encourage more effective usage, including transparency about why it is being used and allowing students to create groups for their own group work (Jones, 2010). Another study suggests that the activity of university librarians on Facebook has been deemed more acceptable due to their lack of power (i.e., lacking the responsibility to assign grades) (Connell, 2009). As social networks continue to expand, students may more fully accept faculty presence, although faculty and students will have to manage the interactions appropriately (Staton, 2008). One study suggests that a presence on Facebook can enhance teacher credibility if the online persona matches the classroom style (Mazer, Murphy, & Simonds, 2009). Although a student-specific demographic reflects users in the early history of the site, for new students beginning high school now, that institutional memory will fade and the notion that it is a place for everyone will most likely seem less "creepy."

All of these activities suggest inevitability: that a social space as popular and ubiquitous as Facebook will eventually embrace more and more social structures. Given Facebook's hopes to make its "Open Graph" the focus of the web experience by using "like" buttons to monitor user interests, rather than users engaging search engines directly (Schonfeld, 2010), it is likely to eventually (and unavoidably) embrace educational needs. Of course, there are other alternatives to Facebook, including Wikis and Blog sites, which may or may not be hosted by a college. Each provides its own specific features and limitations.

Regardless, all of these spaces offer the advantages of multisemester survivability, optional public access, and applicability to the professions. These sites permit public access, allowing the content created by students and professors to have an effect on the world outside the Ivory Tower. Students who develop the skills to use various Web 2.0 tools, including wikis and social networking construction sites, may more effectively apply them to their professional practice in business, education, the arts, or the health professions. By using these tools, students will have to deal with the issues that engage academics and professionals using these tools, including questions of privacy, copyright, netiquette, ethics, identity formation, and access across economic barriers. These are challenges faced by anyone using social media in education, but discussion of these issues will help students better navigate them in their post-collegiate years. Although many companies use internal communication systems, others demand familiarity with social media. Employers would expect to train new employees in their own systems, but might have greater expectations that they already understand the technical and strategic uses of publicly available resources.

STRATEGIES FOR SOCIAL MEDIA IN EDUCATION

Although not geared toward education directly, Facebook's Page feature allows students to become a fan of a given educational enterprise: a course project, an entire course, or a university as a whole. Pages allow for either collaborative or one-way communication between students in a class and an instructor. On this page, one can post text, links, videos and photographs, write "Notes" (blog), publicize events, and add a large number of Facebook applications to further increase functionality. Students and instructors need not "friend" each other, minimizing any unwanted personal connections.

Although not as complete as a CMS, a professor could use the Notes feature to display the syllabus, readings, and assignments, the Discussions area for class interaction and the Wall for general questions and announcements. Furthermore, the presence of the students' pictures under "People [who] Like This" allows the professor and students to learn names more easily, more quickly creating a sense of community (although this places pressure on students to choose their profile picture with some caution). Facebook's familiar layout and highly intuitive navigation allow users to be more comfortable using the space and to feel more at "home." Students do not require training in using these features for social networking objectives. Some educational applications may require explanation, although the most effective uses will not stray too far from the expected function. Although a complex course may be weakened by the inability to contain course documents in folders and other organizing structures, a more straightforward class could benefit from an easy-to-navigate course management system contained within a real world social networking site.

More conservatively, professors may leave the creation and administration of a Facebook group to students, instead encouraging the use of groups for group project coordination and study group collaboration. A somewhat more active approach is to allow for a group dedicated to discussion that is created by a professor but positioned as an optional activity, as suggested by Madge et al. (2009).

The growing number of online classes and programs leads to the question of whether an online course could be fully developed on Facebook. At present, this might be difficult. Many features of a traditional CMS are not available and professors who use traditional CMS Webware tend to use multiple features (Jones & Jones, 2008). But, this fact suggests two courses of action: creation of increasingly Web 2.0-style CMS, although as aforementioned, the very nature of such closed systems prevents a satisfying solution; or alternatively, the synthesis of Web 2.0 sites that could be combined to create a flexible and powerful personal learning environment (Educause Learning Initiative, 2009).

Currently, websites exist for posting syllabi and assignments (WordPress, LiveJournal, and Blogger), manage grades (Engrade), write collaboratively (PBWorks, Wetpaint, Google Docs), collect assignments (Mediafire), practice social bookmarking (Delicious), share images and videos (Flickr, YouTube), participate in online chat (Meebo, AIM), and utilize easily accessible group tools (Facebook Google Apps). The primary obstacle of using all of these tools is simply keeping track of all of them and asking students to do the same, and certainly this will prove a deterrent for some. However, the use of the sites (and few professors would need all of them for every class) would offer many benefits, including allowing students to become familiar with various Web-based tools that they can carry over to their careers and simply become more versatile in learning digital technologies. At this point, so-called digital natives do not have a familiarity with as many different tools as generally believed (Burhanna, Seeholzer, & Salem, 2009). Using these tools would allow professors in a range of disciplines to address the demands for increasing digital literacy.

Perhaps one shift we need to make, then, is in our expectations. If we begin by expecting that our students will be online as part of their daily lives, and engaged in multimedia communication, then teaching them how to act to their advantage within physical and cyberspace networks becomes less optional and more imperative. Our findings reveal that social software's advantages for academic and career networking are not as clear to students who most need them as they could be. (Greenhow & Robelia, 2009, p. 136)

The other advantage is the ability to make available professors' and students' intellectual work to the global Internet community (through the use of blogs, wikis, and specialized sites like iTunesU). The ability to add to and utilize the collective intelligence of professors and students on a global scale will lead to a greater chance that we will deserve the label of *information society*. Furthermore, the acceptance that "virtual geographies are founded upon a fluid premise of evolving connectivity, [that] are situational and not static" (Papacharissi, 2009, p. 216) will ease the way for further acceptance of multiple-site course management networks.

OTHER SOCIAL MEDIA ALTERNATIVES

Fortunately, if the mixed bag scenario proves to be too intimidating for professors, there are numerous tools to create a self-contained (if somewhat simple) social network. Other more sophisticated tools require a fee, including Social Text and Ning, which eliminated free accounts in the summer of 2010. This action may suggest an inevitable trend away from feature-rich, free sites, whether the payment comes in the form of dollars (Ning) or loss of privacy (Facebook). Even with these fees, the costs are still considerably less than licensing commercial course management systems. Regardless, such continually emerging sites allow educators to create a specialized space that, while not naturally part of the global community, may be left open for worldwide viewing and allows a degree of specialization and simplicity while still creating a "Third Place." Experimental spaces like Howard Rheingold's (n.d.) social media classroom offer hosted sites and downloadable free software to allow educational institutions to experiment with social media in a more intuitive and open setting.

Some of these Web-only sites may eventually disappear while an established CMS offers reliability and sustainability. Yet any company can fail. Familiarity with multiple systems offers safeguards against such occurrences and as long as an instructor retains digital copies of materials, the ability to move between online offerings corresponds to the need for students to learn to adapt to an ever-changing digital landscape.

FREEDOM FOR LEARNING

Changes in web applications and an increasingly digitally literate culture will force changes in instructional models. In a decade's time, current 5-year-olds may correctly deserve the label digital natives, whereas current college students do not. Current CMS will begin to resemble DOS programs of decades past, as it is likely that attempts to make a one-style-fits-all product will increasingly slow down Webware development while the survival-of-the-fittest, ever-changing landscape of Web 2.0 sites will continue to evolve to match users' latest needs. Such tools offer the best means to engage students. Fear of infringement into students' private spaces (at least on the Web) will be dismissed by growing interconnectedness of identities inhabiting Web spaces. Students may not even see the distinction of public/private, given the willingness to share information to social networking friends that already exists. Rather, their space may better be defined as "personal," which more readily allows visitors into a given space (Lewis & West, 2009, p. 624). This willingness to share information continues the predictions made by Howard Rheingold (1994) in his discussion of Jeremy Bentham's Panopticon. Now, the "prisoners" (Facebook users) offer up their personal information to those "friends" who would watch them. Whether this change leads to increased openness or a dangerous lack of personal space, the careful insertion of education materials into the mix will make little difference in this paradigm shift. What does matter is the purposeful placement of learning opportunities into active and popular online spaces as they become a crucial place for interaction and community. In this way, public intellectual discourse may have a chance to reach new levels of significance.

NOTE

1. In May 2010, Facebook made significant changes to its privacy policies that angered many users, although a call for a boycott had no more effect than ripples in a pond. Whether or not these changes redefine the concept of privacy too much (too soon?) is being debated, but ironically, for educational purposes and this chapter's call for openness, the changes are not necessarily troubling or relevant beyond providing a topic for a class discussion about ethics in the digital age. For one informed view of the debate, see Singel (2010).

REFERENCES

Alexander, B. (2008). Social networking in higher education. In: R. Katz (Ed.), *The tower and the cloud: Higher education in the age of cloud computing* (pp. 197–201). Boulder, CO: Educause.
Bays, T., Carchidi, D., Carter-Galvan, S., Chambers, P., Fons, G., Gooding, I., Hardin, J., Kleymeer, P., Smith, R., & Weeramuni, L. (2009). Code of best practices in fair use for

opencourseware. From centerforsocialmedia.org: http://www.centerforsocialmedia.org/ocw. Retrieved on April 29, 2010.

Beck, U. (2001). Living your own life in a runaway world: Individualisation, globalisation and politics. In: W. Hutton & A. Giddens (Eds), *On the edge: Living with global capitalism* (pp. 164–174). London: Vintage.

Burhanna, K., Seeholzer, J., & Salem, J. (2009). No natives here: A focus group study of student perceptions of Web 2.0 and the academic library. *Journal of Academic Librarianship*, 35(6), 523–532.

Buss, A. (2009). *Online communities handbook: Building your business and brand on the Web.* Berkeley, CA: New Riders.

Campbell, G. (2008). Cognition prints. *Gardner Writes.* Available at http://www.gardnercampbell.net/blog1/?p = 635. Retrieved on June 28, 2010.

Campbell, G. (2009). A personal cyberinfrastructure. *Educause Review*, 44(5), 58–59.

Carron, T., Marty, J., & Heraud, J. (2008). Teaching with game-based learning management systems: Exploring a pedagogical dungeon. *Simulation & Gaming*, 39(3), 353–378. doi:10.1177/1046878108319580.

Connell, R. (2009). Academic libraries, Facebook and Myspace, and student outreach: A survey of student opinion. *Portal: Libraries and the Academy*, 9(1), 25.

Diamond, D. (2003, June 30). MIT Everyware. From Wired.com: http://www.wired.com/archive/11.09/mit_pr.html. Retrieved on April 25, 2010.

Educause Learning Initiative. (2009). 7 Things you should know about…personal learning environments. Available at http://www.educause.edu/Resources/7ThingsYouShould-KnowAboutPerso/171521. Retrieved on June 28, 2010.

Greenhow, C., & Robelia, B. (2009). Informal learning and identity formation in online social networks. *Learning, Media and Technology*, 34(2), 119–140. doi:10.1080/17439880902923580.

Hafner, K. (2010). An open mind. *The New York Times*, 16–18 and 32–33, April 18. New York.

Hodkinson, P., & Lincoln, S. (2008). Online journals as virtual bedrooms? Young people, identity and personal space. *Young*, 16(1), 27–46. doi:10.1177/110330880701600103.

Jones, G., & Jones, B. (2008). Web-based course management software: An empirical study of faculty usage. *International Journal of Instructional Media*, 35(3), 251–260.

Jones, J. (2010). The Creepy Treehouse problem. *ProfHacker.* Available at http://chronicle.com/blogPost/The-Creepy-Treehouse-Problem/23027/. Retrieved on April 9.

Lane, L. (2008). Toolbox or trap? Course management systems and pedagogy. *Educause Quarterly*, 31(2), 4–6.

Lane, L. (2009). Insidious pedagogy: How course management systems impact teaching. *First Monday*, 14(10). Available at http://firstmonday.org/htbin/cgiwrap/bin/ojs/index.php/fm/article/view/2530/2303. Retrieved on June 28, 2010.

Lewis, J., & West, A. (2009). 'Friending': London-based undergraduates' experience of Facebook. *New Media & Society*, 11(7), 1209–1229. doi:10.1177/1461444809342058.

Madge, C., Meek, J., Wellens, J., & Hooley, T. (2009). Facebook, social integration and informal learning at university: 'It is more for socialising and talking to friends about work than for actually doing work.' *Learning, Media and Technology*, 34(2), 141–155. doi:10.1080/17439880902923606.

Mazer, J., Murphy, R., & Simonds, C. (2009). The effects of teacher self-disclosure via Facebook on teacher credibility. *Learning, Media and Technology*, 34(2), 175–183. doi:10.1080/17439880902923655.

McLuhan, M. (1964). *Understanding media: The extensions of man.* New York: McGraw-Hill.

244   JEREMY SARACHAN AND KYLE F. REINSON

Moore, R., Gathman, E., & Ducheneaut, N. (2009). From 3D space to third place: The social life of small virtual spaces. *Human Organization, 68*(2), 230.
Mott, J., & Wiley, D. (2009). Open for learning: The CMS and the open learning network. *In Education, 15*(2). Available at http://www.ineducation.ca/article/open-learning-cms-and-open-learning-network. Retrieved on June 25, 2010.
Oldenburg, R. (1999). *The great good place: Cafés, coffee shops, bookstores, bars, hair salons, and other hangouts at the heart of a community.* Cambridge, MA: Da Capo Press.
Papacharissi, Z. (2009). The virtual geographies of social networks: A comparative analysis of Facebook, LinkedIn and ASmallWorld. *New Media & Society, 11*(1–2), 199–220. doi:10.1177/1461444808099577.
Rheingold, H. (1994). *The virtual community: Homesteading on the electronic frontier.* New York: HarperPerennial.
Rheingold, H. (n.d.). Social Media Classroom. *Social Media Classroom.* Available at http://socialmediaclassroom.com/. Retrieved on April 29, 2010.
Sarachan, J. (2010). Profile picture, right here, right now. In: D. Wittkower (Ed.), *Facebook and philosophy: What's on your mind?* (pp. 51–64). Chicago, IL: Open Court Publishing.
Schonfeld, C. (2010). Zuckerberg: "We are building a web where the default is social." *The Washington Post.* Available at http://www.washingtonpost.com/wp-dyn/content/article/2010/04/21/AR2010042103555.html
Singel, R. (2010). Facebook's gone rogue; It's time for an open alternative. *Wired.com.* Available at http://www.wired.com/epicenter/2010/05/facebook-rogue/. Retrieved on June 24.
Song, F. W. (2010). Theorizing Web 2.0. *Information, Communication & Society, 13*(2), 249–275. doi:10.1080/13691180902914610.
Staton, M. (2008). Debunking the Creepy Treehouse: The functional mall. *Edumorphology.* Blog. Available at http://www.edumorphology.com/2008/08/debunking-the-creepy-treehouse-the-functional-mall/. Retrieved on April 9, 2010.
Steinkuehler, C. A., & Williams, D. (2006). Where everybody knows your (screen) name: Online games as "third places." *Journal of Computer-Mediated Communication, 11*(4), 885–909. doi:10.1111/j.1083-6101.2006.00300.x.
Stromer-Galley, J., & Martey, R. M. (2009). Visual spaces, norm governed places: The influence of spatial context online. *New Media & Society, 11*(6), 1041–1060. doi:10.1177/1461444809336555.
Wei, R., & Lo, V. (2006). Staying connected while on the move: Cell phone use and social connectedness. *New Media & Society, 8*(1), 53–72. doi:10.1177/1461444806059870.
Young, J. (2008). When professors create social networks for classes, some students see a 'Creepy Treehouse.' *Chronicle of Higher Education.* Washington, DC. Available at http://chronicle.com/blogPost/When-Professors-Create-Social/4176

PART IV
DELIVERY OF INSTRUCTION
WITH SOCIAL MEDIA

WEB 2.0: INFORMATION LITERACY, LIBRARIES, AND PEDAGOGIES

Beth Martin

ABSTRACT

Social media allows students and faculty to research and display information in innovative new ways. Research methods courses – when developed by faculty members and librarian/instructional technologists – can move beyond database navigation and PowerPoint presentations when incorporating social media. This chapter discusses two Information Literacy case studies, one for a junior seminar in the hard sciences and the second for a class on the history of African-American Mathematicians. The courses were developed at a private, four-year Historically Black College/University (HBCU) through a faculty/library collaboration. These classes used a variety of Web 2.0 and social media tools including Google Maps, Flickr, Delicious, Yahoo Pipes, Meebo, YouTube, iTunes U, and the Moodle Learning Management System. Each case study will define and describe how each tool was used and the collaboration between faculty and librarians/technologists to implement social media. Student and faculty assessment of the program as well as anecdotal evidence is discussed for each study and implementation tips are provided. These case studies provide the practitioner ways to create an interactive, collaborative learning experience for students and faculty while alleviating library anxiety.

Educating Educators with Social Media
Cutting-edge Technologies in Higher Education, Volume 1, 247–259
ISSN: 2044-9968/doi:10.1108/S2044-9968(2011)0000001015

October 2009 was designated National Information Literacy Awareness Month by Presidential Proclamation. President Barack Obama, in the proclamation, called "upon the people of the United States to recognize the important role information plays in our daily lives, and to appreciate the need for a greater understanding of its impact" (Presidential Proclamation National Information Literacy Awareness Month, n.d.).

Information Literacy (IL) is a widely used phrase that is considered of special import in our knowledge society. An information literate person should contribute to the knowledge society – which is a society where knowledge and information is the major "capital." The Association of College and Research Libraries (ACRL), a member of the American Library Association (ALA), states that an information literate person

> must be able to recognize when information is needed and have the ability to locate, evaluate, and use effectively the needed information. Producing such a citizenry will require that schools and colleges appreciate and integrate the concept of information literacy into their learning programs and that they play a leadership role in equipping individuals and institutions to take advantage of the opportunities inherent within the information society. Ultimately, information literate people are those who have learned how to learn. They know how to learn because they know how knowledge is organized, how to find information and how to use information in such a way that others can learn from them. They are people prepared for lifelong learning, because they can always find the information needed for any task or decision at hand. (ACRL, n.d.)

The ACRL statement is often cited when discussing IL instruction at colleges and universities. Essentially, the statement suggests that "learning how to learn" is composed of understanding knowledge organization, displaying information-seeking skills, and critical information use because these skills prepare people for lifelong learning. Most IL is taught during one or two library sessions in a student's freshman year, although some university libraries have created a one-credit course that students are required to take before they graduate. Traditional library instruction taught students how to use the library resources – books, databases, and technologies – as well as citing sources, copyright issues, and using appropriate keywords/search terms.

IL instructors must hone their critical information consumer skills by understanding the forces shaping the information landscape. IL instructors must also understand how students seek and use information – a skill that may vary due to race, socioeconomic status, and geography among many other variables.

This chapter provides the practitioner ways to incorporate IL into their classes using free Web 2.0 tools. These tools include Google Maps, Flickr,

Delicious, Yahoo Pipes, Meebo, and YouTube. In addition, the studies show how to use Learning Management Systems (LMS) such as Moodle and Clickers. Clickers are "small, handheld devices that allow students to respond to questions asked verbally, on paper or on screen and enables you to instantly assess their comprehension of your lessons" (*eInstruction*, 2010). LMSs allow educators to store and display classroom information as well as process grades and take attendance. Moodle and Blackboard are two popular LMSs.

LITERATURE REVIEW

Mandy Lupton researched IL as a situated component within an essay research and writing class (2008). She argues that while IL is often taught as a generic skill set, educators are better served to examine IL as a "learning activity situated within a topic, course and discipline" (Lupton, 2008). Lupton devised a phenomenological study that examined student habits during the research and writing process. Phenomenography investigates the relationship between people and phenomena through which Lupton states that the "world does not exist independently of the person; rather, it is constituted by the person who experiences it" (2008). Her study found that universities err when they present IL as only a generic skill that is divorced from context.

Andrews and Patil situated IL instruction in an engineering class, which maintained the classroom context. The assignments called for an annotated bibliography, a list of "credible" sources, and a class on locating materials in the library such as books and articles (Andrews & Patil, 2007). The library services were evaluated with a survey and the professors graded the annotated bibliographies. The annotated bibliographies were used to assess critical thinking skills, and the librarians focused on teaching research techniques using the databases and catalogs.

Context refers to not only refers to the classroom but also the personal space occupied by the student or information seeker. Personal ideologies, race, and socioeconomic status among other variables all encompass the contextual experience of information seeking. IL research has done little to address the needs of different groups beyond economics. The majority of IL research appears in health and medical literature. This research does address the digital divide or the role economics plays in information access as well as information on different ethnic groups. Brodie et al. (2000) performed a study on medical information-seeking behaviors that examined the digital divide through the lens of education and race.

Shirley Brice Heath, in her book *Ways With Words*, examined the information gathering/disseminating behaviors of groups in an effort to understand the learning differences among two cultures – black and white (1983). She studied two communities in the Carolina Piedmont region: Trackton, a working class black community, and Roadville, a working class white community, to better understand their communication behaviors. While this study focused on language use and acquisition among children, it provides interesting insight into the literacies of different races. The Trackton community members read and learned socially in that they read aloud news and letters for community members. Heath found that those in Trackton who "read alone" were considered antisocial. Heath stated that Trackton community members found that "in general, reading alone, unless one is very old and religious, marks an individual as someone who cannot make it socially" (1983). Reading as a community offers information sharing and a place to create knowledge through the narratives. In Roadville, reading is taught as a solitary endeavor and community members derive meaning from the authority of the writing, not from the interaction about writings. The Roadville community conforms to writing genres to learn, such as newspapers and textbooks, whereas the Trackton community conforms to verbal genres of storytelling to learn.

WHILE each group is social and participate in social events – even learning – there are distinct differences in their styles. In Trackton, stories may be embellished or exaggerated, but learning occurs just as in the solitary "read alone" community in Roadville. Learning through narrative is an important part of the Trackton community, whereas "just the facts" is the preferred learning method in Roadville. The white community learning style is a type of "scientific method" where there are certain rules to follow to create knowledge. Knowledge is created in the Trackton community in a more socially engaging manner – by those who learn through their verbal communication and narratives with members of their community.

The social aspect of learning in Trackton provides an interesting segue into creating information practices for millennials – a group considered very social, especially digitally social. Considine, Horton, and Moorman (2009) describe millenials as the "children who have grown up since the emergence of the world wide web and the assortment of related digital technologies" (2009). Their research discusses the need for various literacies – particularly media – to educate this group. Millenials, or digital natives, are very social with approximately 83% belonging to an online social group. Earlier generations are considered digital immigrants who learn digital technology as a second language. Digital natives are used to communication technologies to create their social sphere. Considine et al. also discusses their engagement as content creators as well as consumers (2009). The amount of information available for consumption brings its own pitfalls because "without the ability to question, analyze, and authenticate information found online, in print or in any media format, Millenials are open to manipulation and misinformation" (Considine et al., 2009).

THEORY

Michel Callon and Bruno Latour examined micro- and macro-actors in an effort to describe society (1981). Traditionally, sociologists defined micro-actors as "individuals, groups, families" and macro-actors as "institutions, organizations, social classes, parties, states" (Callon & Latour, 1981). Traditional research focused on either micro- or macro-actors as separate entities; however, Callon and Latour argued that researchers should not differentiate between micro- and macro-actors; instead, actors should be considered holistically. In essence, all actors such as institutions, organizations, individuals, groups, and artifacts work together to create a macrostructure – Callon and Latour refer to their ideas as Actor-Network Theory (ANT). The macrostructure becomes a unified structure known as a "black box" (Callon & Latour, 1981). This box is a collection of ideas, information, and artifacts that becomes so ubiquitous that individual actors do not need to understand how the box functions. A personal computer is an excellent example of a black box. The user does not need to understand all the actors involved in the computer – who created the computer, the economics of the creation, and the technology in the device – the user just needs the computer to function. The black box exists until a need forces it open – perhaps a societal need or change. Actors promote change through their black box interactions to create new changes such as the move to mobile computing. The interactions continue until another black box is formed or destroyed.

ANT appears in education theory, research, and practice in several ways. Scott Waltz discusses the "missing discourse of non-humans as social actors" in education (2006). Technology's shaping of the education landscape is ongoing, and Waltz argues it must be considered when discussing social change. Waltz describes the human/nonhuman interactions using a boy and a girl. A boy and a girl are not just defined by their human aspects, but also through their "apparel … bodily comportment and adornments, and speech" among other nonhuman artifacts (Waltz, 2006).

ANT is portrayed as laying the "groundwork for a productive description of the socio-technical links grounded in careful observations of researchers and the particularities of textual records" (Waltz, 2006, p. 65). Students can be portrayed through demographics, but also through their community interactions and their technology interactions. These sociotechnical interactions – going to the spaces where the students reside – shape the way individuals and institutions educate.

Habib and Wittek used ANT to analyze student portfolios in learning activities. The portfolios are the artifact that acts upon the students and in turn shapes the students conception of learning. Students "appropriate" the portfolios at different levels, in this example, nursing students are given portfolio guidelines and their use of the guidelines is examined. Nursing students who "relate" to the guidelines "in a very literal manner might feel insecure about what they are supposed to do," whereas those who have appropriated the guidelines as tools "allow themselves to interpret (translate) them in such a way they feel free to color their assignments according to their own intentions and interests" (Habib & Wittek, 2007, p. 279). The actors shape their learning based on their abstraction of the assignment – the ability to act upon the artifacts allows for greater knowledge creation.

THE FIRST WEB 2.0 CLASS

Our university periodically offers a course on African-American Mathematicians – this course gives our students a unique perspective on the contributions of African-Americans to the field. A faculty member approached the library and asked for a library instruction class so that students could learn how to navigate library resources. The professor had information resources from previous classes and I decided to try some new techniques in the classroom. As a librarian, I wanted the information to be arranged in a way that enhanced the information itself, not just display a series of links. The visual display of information can be as informative and students may not be aware of the tools at their disposal that can enhance their assignments. I decided to use Google Maps along with the Internet and library resources that were already available. I placed the map "pins" on locations where the mathematicians went to work or ended their careers. When the students clicked on a particular pin, they found links to information resources about the mathematicians.

The information display showed a heavy concentration of mathematicians along the east coast with a few scattered across the country. The map could be used as a starting point for class discussion – such as why did many of the mathematicians choose to settle along the east coast? These types of questions lead into discussions of where African-Americans could obtain work and what was happening during the period these scholars were looking for work.

In addition to Google Maps, the library created a Delicious account. Delicious is a "social bookmarking service, which means you can save all your bookmarks online, share them with other people, and see what other people are bookmarking" (*Delicious*, 2010). Delicious is an excellent tool for libraries in that web sites can be vetted by librarians, and faculty then placed in a single location for our student body as well as the public. Each pin on the Google map had a link to the Delicious site that contains web resources regarding African-American Mathematicians and access to other library resources.

The students were then able to research from a new environment that not only displayed information but also served as a place for knowledge creation. The images provide new ways for them to interpret and understand the information before them.

LESSONS LEARNED

The reference class was designed to display information and provide resources in a new and engaging manner. However, the pedagogy was not adjusted to the new tools. For example, instead of delving into the reasons for the map and how it can provide information just by examining the placement of pins, the map was used as a place to aggregate links. This is similar to creating a webpage of the links and directing the students to the page; therefore, a chance for knowledge creation was lost.

The professor and I did not spend a lot of time discussing the new ways students could talk about their research using tools such as Google Maps or Delicious. The maps can be integrated into other assignments with the library research class serving as a springboard. When creating the class, I should have spent more time working with the faculty on the new tools as well. During the semester, it is hard for faculty to find time to use these tools; therefore, we created a new class for faculty development on Web 2.0 tools. The professors can learn about the new tools as they choose to experiment with presentations and research delivery in their classrooms.

We did not ask for student feedback or give any type of assessment after the course. Therefore, we do not know the impact on the students or if they had suggestions for improvement. In future courses, we will add an assessment component.

THE SECOND CLASS

All of the seniors have to write a senior thesis in their major, and a faculty member wanted to have a refresher research course. The course was for physical science majors in the second semester of their junior year. The students were asked to create their thesis proposal as the final assignment for the course as well as complete short assignments that tested their research skills. The first four weeks of the course were dedicated to various research topics such as how best to search a database, how to use the five areas of web site evaluation, the difference between peer-reviewed and other types of journals, information on plagiarism and citations, as well as information on ethics in scientific research. The courses were placed in a Moodle learning management system – "Moodle is a course management system designed to help educators who want to create quality online courses" and "is open source and completely free to use" (*Moodle*, 2010). This allowed us to experiment with an embedded librarian feature that meant I added resources directly into the professors LMS course and made myself available to the student's on-demand. Acting on-demand means that I was available through instant messenger 7:30 AM until 5:00 PM and one evening Monday through Friday, e-mails were returned within 24 hours, and students could stop by my office as needed. The professor and I had worked together before on a one-time research class for rising seniors that discussed research techniques. The professor found the class successful and wanted to expand the class to several sessions for second-semester juniors. Working together, we created several new techniques for placement in Moodle course.

The main university Moodle page already incorporated several library resources such as database and catalog services (Fig. 1).

The main page also provides access to our "Ask-A-Librarian" service that uses the Meebo Instant Messaging Service. Meebo is an excellent communication tool that "integrates all social network and communication channels into a single, simple-to-use interface, users can easily share content and communicate in real time" (*Meebo*, 2010). Students can access research tools within their learning management system without having to jump to a

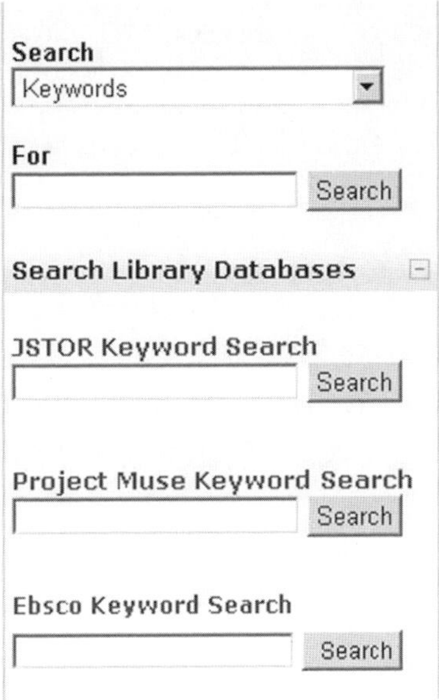

Fig. 1. Library Resource Access in Moodle.

new page. In this instance, the ask-a-librarian feature is monitored by the reference librarian on duty.

The professor had a series of topics she wanted to discuss and part of her class dealt with ethics in scientific research. We searched YouTube EDU to find lectures on this topic and added them to the Moodle sites. Students can watch the videos as an out-of-class assignment, then there can be a class discussion based on the videos.

Drawing on the success of library integration in the main Moodle page, I took it a step further and added information into the specific Moodle class. Using Moodle, I divided the course into several weeks with one topic per week (Fig. 2).

In addition, I added a Meebo client that went directly to my account. This allowed me to serve as a research specialist within the class – I was available during my on-duty hours through the instant messaging service.

Just as in the course for African-American mathematicians, we added links to the library Delicious web site. However with the proliferation of tags, I felt it may become less user-friendly for our students and faculty. To alleviate this, I used Yahoo Pipes to limit the searches and what displays in the Delicious site. A Yahoo Pipe is "a powerful composition tool to

Fig. 2. Library Information Literacy Course in Moodle.

aggregate, manipulate, and mashup content from around the web" (*Yahoo Pipes*, 2010). The free tool from Yahoo allows you to manipulate and gather information from other Web 2.0 resources such as Delicious. In this case, I tagged all the sites appropriate for the course with the course number and then created a pipe to filter based on that number. I then placed a link to the pipe within the Moodle course; therefore, when a student clicks on the link, only the appropriately tagged sites appear. The site is easy to update because we can just add new tags within delicious while maintaining the current code. It is also easy to change or add tags as needed to update different Moodle sites.

   In addition to the sites specifically designated for the course, I also used Yahoo Pipes to filter-based on a keyword search. Users can perform keyword searches with Delicious itself; however, it is helpful to embed a pipe in Moodle; therefore, the students just see another keyword search from within their course. This provides the students a similar search environment to Google – basic keyword search – within their course. The students type in the keyword and click "run pipe" and are then given the output based on their keyword search.

LESSONS LEARNED

Student input was positive – I passed out evaluations in the course created in conjunction with the professor. In addition, the professor and I discussed the course – she found it useful and believes the students research methods improved. Student comments stated that they found the online component and the interactive research course useful for their research. We ended the course with a "jeopardy" style game that covered the material – the students scored very well. They even suggested that we add more interactive tools to the Moodle site as well as to the classes. The clicker software was purchased – however, we are looking at Web 2.0 software that will allow us to accomplish the same task without purchasing new hardware. We will be able to use the student's phones or a web site to play the jeopardy game.

HOW TO CREATE THESE TOOLS

The first step in creating some of these tools is to create a Google Account and the easiest way to do this is with a Gmail account. A Google account provides access to Google maps. Upon logon to Google maps, enter the create maps under My Maps, then add a title and determine your privacy settings. For the purposes of our classes, we chose the satellite view; however, one can switch between satellite and map as fits the pedagogical situation. Upon map creation, I then add pins to the appropriate areas, click "done" and the new Google Map is complete. One can then add the map into a web site, LMS, or any other digital pedagogy tools. Delicious is an easy tool to setup; to join, visit the delicious web site and complete the login information. One can then add web sites appropriate to a class with various tags to help students locate the information. The tags can be especially useful for classes, if the web site is tagged with the course name or a professor's name, whichever is more appropriate for the students.

A Delicious site is also helpful to create the Yahoo Pipes for a LMS or web site. To create a Yahoo Pipe, one must first create a Yahoo account. Upon account creation, login to Yahoo Pipes and watch the tutorials to help get started. The pipes may seem a little daunting at first; however, the pipes are open source, which makes it easy to find code that fits a specific need. Once logged into Yahoo Pipes, perform a search based on the appropriate pipe function such as a Delicious lookup. To create pipes for my classes, I browsed Yahoo Pipes using the keyword Delicious. I found several pipes that fit my needs and explored their code. I found the ones that appeared the easiest to customize and added them to my pipes. I always give credit to the source and share my pipe so that others can use them. Upon completion, save the pipe and embed the link into a LMS or web site.

Meebo is an instant messaging tool that aggregates instant messaging accounts and allows for a widget placement into your website or LMS. Create a Meebo account by visiting meebo.com and completing the sign in information. Create a Meebo widget by clicking create widget, then add your account name and customize the colors. When the widget information is complete, it is easy to copy the code and place in a LMS or web site.

CONCLUSION

Web 2.0 tools are often easy to use and can be incorporated into the appropriate pedagogies with a little time and effort. Tools like delicious and Google Maps may also be useful for student's presentations/ research, whereas Meebo allows students to reach you during your digital office hours. While many of these tools incorporate easily into a LMS, the professor or librarian may need to work with an information technology administrator to customize the site. The pedagogies must be considered along with the course goals, but the new tools can be engaging and useful to students as they begin to display their knowledge in new ways.

These tools are also useful to use in conjunction with library resources for research purposes. The library may already have a delicious site that faculty can add information too and use in the LMS systems. This may also curb library/research anxiety among the students.

I did take the experiment with Google maps and create a mashup that combines information from our Flickr archives with a campus map. Visitors to the library site can tour the campus through archival images – it is an interesting tool derived from our in-class experiment. Just as with the mathematician map, visitors can click on a pin and learn more about the institution as well as link to our Flickr archives. There are many ways to use Web 2.0 to enhance your pedagogy and your student research capabilities – these tools provide an excellent start.

REFERENCES

ACRL. (n.d.). Information literacy competency standards for higher education. Available at http://www.ala.org/ala/mgrps/divs/acrl/standards/informationliteracycompetency.cfm. Retrieved on October 25, 2009.

Andrews, T., & Patil, R. (2007). Information literacy for first-year students: An embedded curriculum approach. *European Journal of Engineering Education*, *32*(3), 253–259.

Brodie, M., Flournoy, R. E., Altman, D. E., Blendon, R. J., Benson, J. M., & Rosenbaum, M. D. (2000). Health information, the Internet, and the digital divide. *Health Affair*, *19*(6), 255–265.

Callon, M., & Latour, B. (1981). Unscrewing the Big Leviathan: How actors macro-structure reality and how sociologists help them to do so. In: *Advances in social theory and methodology: Toward an integration of micro- and macro-sociologies* (p. 325). Boston: Routledge & Kegan Paul.

Considine, D., Horton, J., & Moorman, G. (2009). Teaching and reading the millennial generation through media literacy. *Journal of Adolescent & Adult Literacy*, *52*(6), 471–481.

Habib, L., & Wittek, L. (2007). The portfolio as artifact and actor. *Mind, Culture, and Activity*, *14*(4), 266–282.

Heath, S. B. (1983). *Ways with words: Language, life, and work in communities and classrooms* (p. 421). Cambridge: Cambridge University Press.

Lupton, M. (2008). Evidence, argument and social responsibility: First-year students' experiences of information literacy when researching an essay. *Higher Education Research and Development*, *27*(4), 399–414.

Presidential Proclamation National Information Literacy Awareness Month. (n.d.). The White House. Available at http://www.whitehouse.gov/the_press_office/presidential-proclamation-national-information-literacy-awareness-month/. Retrieved on October 25, 2009.

Waltz, S. B. (2006). Nonhumans unbound: Actor-network theory and the reconsideration of "things" in educational foundations. *Educational Foundations*, *20*, 51–68.

WEBSITES

Delicious. (2010). Available at http://delicious.com/. Retrieved on April 20, 2010.

eInstruction. (2010). Available at http://www.einstruction.com/. Retrieved on April 20, 2010.

Meebo. (2010). Available at http://meebo.com/. Retrieved on April 20, 2010.

Moodle. (2010). Available at http://moodle.org/. Retrieved on April 20, 2010.

Yahoo Pipes. (2010). Available at http://pipes.yahoo.com/pipes/. Retrieved on April 20, 2010.

SOCIAL ANNOTATION TO ENHANCE LEARNING AND ASSESSMENT IN HIGHER EDUCATION

David G. Lebow, Dale W. Lick, Hope J. Hartman, Campbell Dalglish and Oliver Grundmann

ABSTRACT

Social annotation products make the thinking of learners transparent, visible, and easily accessible for sharing with others, self-reflection, and feedback. This is accomplished by enabling almost any number of users to have threaded discussions linked to selected sections of a page. Three professors share their experiences with the use of a social annotation product, HyLighter, to enhance teaching, learning, and assessment activities in three different areas of the college curriculum. One teaches screenplay writing. He describes how he used HyLighter to improve students' writing and critical review skills. A second teaches online graduate-level courses in pharmaceutical and forensic sciences. He describes the application of HyLighter to help students learn about chemical structures and related analytical principles. A third is a professor of educational psychology. She discusses her use of HyLighter to implement an alternative multiple-choice assessment approach in

Educating Educators with Social Media
Cutting-edge Technologies in Higher Education, Volume 1, 261–278
Copyright © 2011 by Emerald Group Publishing Limited
All rights of reproduction in any form reserved
ISSN: 2044-9968/doi:10.1108/S2044-9968(2011)0000001016

*educational and developmental psychology courses. The chapter concludes
with thoughts on the potential of social annotation technology to shift the
focus of learning systems from content to be learned to what is going on
inside the minds of learners.*

Collaborative or social annotation products enable users to have threaded
discussions linked to selected sections of a page. This capability is in
contrast to wikis that enable easy co-creation and editing of web pages but
are limited for purposes of discussion. By making the thinking of learners
transparent, visible, and easily accessible for sharing with others, self-
reflection, and feedback, social annotation tools have the potential to shift
the focus of learning systems from content to be learned to what is going on
inside the minds of learners. After a brief description of *HyLighter*, a
browser-based social annotation product developed by HyLighter LLC (see
www.hylighter.com),[1] three professors describe their experiences using this
product in their classes followed by concluding comments.

DESCRIPTION OF HYLIGHTER

In the Middle Ages, the manuscript served as a type of low-tech social
annotation medium. Scholars used the margins and spaces between lines of
manuscripts to engage in dialogue with other readers. The same physical
copy of a manuscript was passed around a community, and readers used the
margins to correct errors, debate interpretations, and learn from the
annotations left behind by previous readers. In a sense, the manuscript was a
medium for knowledge-production distributed between readers and writers
(Wahlstrom & Scruton, 1997; Wolfe, 2008).

Today, hundreds of systems exist (e.g., Google Sidewiki, Reframe It, and
Webnotes) that allow users to annotate web-based or other data through the
web or other Internet protocol. However, despite the proliferation of these
products, two problems with annotation interfaces have stood in the way of
realizing the potential of social annotation for teaching and learning. First,
the margins of the page provide limited space for placement of commentary
and extended threaded discussions. As more participants add more
annotations, the challenge for the designer is how to keep commentary
aligned with targeted text or objects without creating separation between the
two and adding cognitive effort for the user. Second, as more participants

add highlighting and other markup to the primary text or image, the accumulating markup (i.e., highlighting, strikethroughs, and other marks – often with different colors to represent different contributors), may overwrite the document and create a confusing mass of metadata (e.g., as is the case with software programs such as Microsoft Word Track Changes or Acrobat Connect).

HyLighter solves the problems of how to manage accumulating and overlapping markup and limited space for displaying commentary through (a) its color-coding mechanism for "mapping" the intellectual travels of reviewers through a document or source (e.g., HTML, Word, Excel, PowerPoint, PDF, JPEG, and GIF), (b) its capacity to align commentary in the margins with related sections of a page, despite the limited real estate available, and (c) various methods for organizing, analyzing, and editing input. The approach enables almost any number of individuals (e.g., an instructor and online class of 30 or more students) to engage in collaborative conversations tied to specific sections of a source without overwriting the primary source or cluttering the margin.

Fig. 1 shows the unique approach of HyLighter to map the distribution of highlighting (i.e., areas emphasized and commented on by readers) through a document. An area highlighted by you (the logged in user) but not by anyone else appears in yellow; areas not highlighted by you, but marked by one or more contributors, appear in shades of blue (the darker the shade, the more overlapping interest for that fragment); and areas highlighted by you and others appear in various shades of green. The margin on the left shows comments linked to the highlighted areas. Threaded comments (i.e., responses to existing comments) appear indented under the original comments. To see comments linked to highlighted text, you click in the text. The author bars (i.e., the bar above a comment that displays the name of the author) of all related comments are highlighted. To see the highlighted text to which a comment refers, you click a *Jump to Marker* icon in the author bar. To add a comment, you select a block of text using click-and-drag or other standard methods to select text and the comment box editor opens. To add a reply to an existing comment, you click *Action* and select *Add Reply*.

As participants engage in discussions, HyLighter provides various "views" for working with the group input including (a) a table showing highlighted excerpts and associated comments with various sort and search options and (b) a split-screen format for editing that displays the HyLighter session on the left in a horizontal format (i.e., the margin panel is placed under the highlighted source instead of vertically along the side) and the source document in its native application on the right.

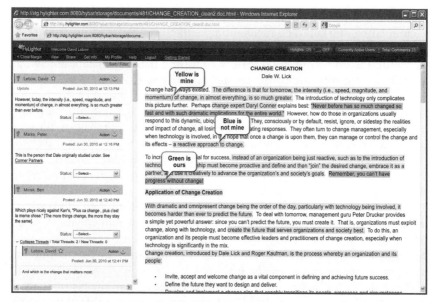

Fig. 1. The HyLighter Screen. The Browser Displays the HyLighter Tool Bar below the Browser Tabs. The Screen is Split into Two Panels. The Right Panel Holds the Source with Various Color-Coded Sections. The Left Panel Shows Comments and Related Information Submitted by Contributors.

The design of HyLighter embodies certain conjectures about learning and social context drawn from the existing research and theory base of the learning sciences. For example, this includes social constructivism (Lave & Wenger, 1991), the theory of expert performance (Ericsson, Krampe, & Tesch-Römer, 1993) and knowledge-building communities (Scardamalia, Bereiter, McLean, Swallow, & Woodruff, 1989). Three key conjectures from the learning sciences that have guided the HyLighter design effort are:

- Design activities that make the thinking of learners visible and articulated to themselves and others. This is based on the premise that the thoughts that go on in the heads of students are most important (Leamnson, 1999).
- Provide students with frequent opportunities to reflect on and adjust their thoughts and arguments and engage in discussions with their peers and the instructor. By providing timely feedback, students have opportunities to clear up their thinking before misconceptions settle in for good and are further motivated to engage in the learning process.

- Promote development of metacognitive skills (i.e., capacity to monitor one's thinking process, be aware of what one knows and does not know, and reflect on what one has learned) and a positive disposition toward learning. Ability to learn, including self-regulation and self-assessment skills, is one of the most important outputs of the educational system.

To summarize, HyLighter tightly binds online asynchronous or synchronous discussions to specific sections of a text or image and helps to extract value from the collective thinking and interactions of contributors. Much as in the tradition of scholars during the Middle Ages, HyLighter blurs the line between authors and readers and brings rich social interaction and multiple perspectives to formerly static environments. From the broad perspective of the learning sciences, HyLighter enables three key functions:

1. Makes the thinking of teachers and students that are ordinarily hidden, become transparent and easily accessible for sharing with others, self-reflection, and feedback.
2. Allows users to continuously compare their developing understanding to others, assess performance, and monitor progress.
3. Supports efforts to organize, integrate, and synthesize ideas from multiple sources and perspectives.

FACULTY EXPERIENCES

Three professors shared their experiences with HyLighter-enhanced learning and assessment activities in three different areas of the college curriculum. Their reports are part of an informal action research project aimed at evaluating HyLighter across the curriculum to improve classroom instruction and educational effectiveness. In this context, action research is defined as classroom-based studies initiated and conducted by teachers who systematically reflect on their teaching or other work and collect data that will answer their questions (Zuber-Skerritt, 1992).

Campbell Dalglish teaches screenplay writing at City College of New York (CCNY). He described how he used HyLighter to improve students' writing and critical review skills. Oliver Grundman is in the Department of Medicinal Chemistry at the University of Florida, where he teaches graduate-level courses in online Forensic Science and Pharmaceutical Chemistry programs. He described the application of HyLighter to help students learn about chemical structures and analytical principles in pharmaceutical and forensic sciences. Hope Hartman is a professor of education at CCNY. She described her use of HyLighter to implement an alternative multiple-choice assessment approach in her educational and developmental psychology courses (Hartman, 2010).

CRITICAL REVIEW OF SCREENPLAYS

Writing a screenplay is one of the most complicated forms of creative writing. Anyone who dares take on this arduous task knows that critical review is essential in the development of a script. HyLighter was first tested in second semester college English classes to develop skills in analyzing, discussing, and writing responses to argumentative essays and strengthening skills in writing persuasive arguments (Lebow & Lick, 2003). This suggested the idea of using HyLighter to facilitate the screenplay writing process and support teaching and learning of this complex activity.

A writer must navigate through five stages (two of them coming with a Writer's Guild price tag) to produce the first draft of a screenplay. Once a first draft is completed, contracts are signed, production elements attached (e.g., input from producers, directors, actors, script doctors, and sometimes co-writers), and another process begins. This involves an entire development team working with the writer to create what is called the "production script." In the business, this exchange is often referred to as "development hell." The sharing of notes back and forth and rewrites from the author can all add up to many years of hard work, with potentially nothing achieved at the end in terms of a movie.

Between the first draft and the production script, the screenplay receives "coverage," a two- to five-page document that evaluates the script in multiple ways. This allows a production company to quickly assess and decide whether or not they want to make the film or video without having to read the script. Coverage has three parts: (1) the "top page," which contains a log line (i.e., a one or two sentence description designed to create interest in the project), the specifics of the script in terms of authorship, agency, genre, page length, copyright, and, most importantly, a critical grid that has six parts: (a) theme, idea, and premise, (b) character, (c) plot/structure, (d) dialogue, (e) visual description, and (f) production value (quantitative and qualitative); (2) a summary, without opinion or commentary that simply reports the plot and characters; and (3) a critical commentary that embellishes the six elements of the critical grid, supporting why the reviewer "recommends, maybe recommends, or passes" on the script. This three- to five-page "tool" is what gets passed among people in the industry and can determine whether a screenplay gets a second read.

As a teacher of screenplay writing for the past 24 years, I have found that getting my students to read and critically evaluate each other's work is a challenge. Before computers and projectors for electronically displaying content became available, I would bring multiple copies of students' scripts to class to share with others a week before a scheduled workshop. When computer technology arrived, I could project a script up on a screen, but still, students had to handout copies of their scripts the week before to get everyone's feedback. At the end of class, students walked out with 15 copies of scripts from 15 students, and one from me with notes written all over them. I had no way of telling who was saying what to the writer, and I could not imagine being the writer having to sort through all those notes.

At the end of the year, the most frequent negative comment of students was that either they didn't get enough feedback, or the feedback they were getting from classmates was not helpful. I had no practical way of reading what they were writing on each other's scripts unless, of course, I was willing on a weekly basis to collect and read all 225 copies myself (for my 3 classes during a semester that would have meant reading 9,450 scripts), review them with comments, and then hand them back to the writers so they could continue revising.

In the fall semester of 2006, when I visited the Center for Excellence in Teaching and Learning at CCNY and asked Hope Hartman, the director, for a better way to review the work of my students, she introduced me to David Lebow and HyLighter. Immediately everything changed. Within weeks, I had students using this software to review each other's exercises and scripts. Students were able to get feedback instantly, I was able to read what they were saying to each other and comment on that, and suddenly the class was hopping with excitement. When we had our workshops, I could display the document from HyLighter on an LCD screen in class, hide all comments, have actors read through the script, and then bring up all the comments and have a real live critical review of the script with everyone participating. The dialectics that came up over what does and does not work began before class even started, and everyone was able to add to the comments during the class.

As a result of implementing various HyLighter-enabled practices, our class discussions took on a whole new level of relevance, meaning, and expeditious review. Classes became communities of inspired writers who shared a common commitment to the value of critical revision. Since the fall of 2006, I have never read another teacher evaluation where a screenplay writing student complained about not getting enough feedback. One student, who never spoke in class because English was her second language, wrote more on the scripts of her fellow students than anyone else in the class. Students loved her.

In addition to creating a sense of community and shared purpose, HyLighter provided a mechanism to increase the value of the coverage grid mentioned previously. Reviewers were able to annotate throughout the script where they thought weaknesses existed and add tags to their comments by selecting from a drop down menu of grid descriptors. Once a script is marked up, writers can retrieve all comments made on a particular coverage area – the dialogue, the theme, the structure, or the visual writing – and get the benefits of aggregating all the inputs by coverage category as they work on the rewrite. In sum, HyLighter has been responsible for enhancing our learning experiences, relationships with and among students, and, most importantly, the work of students, so that they feel confident when they go into the difficult world of getting a script brought to the big silver screen.

ONLINE GRADUATE CLASSES IN PHARMACEUTICAL AND FORENSIC SCIENCES

Online platforms for the delivery of course content provide a broader spectrum of course content delivery and assessment options than traditional approaches. A recent report prepared for the US Department of Education entitled, "Evaluation of Evidence-Based Practices in Online Learning – A Meta-Analysis and Review of Online Learning Studies" (Means, Toyama, Murphy, Bakia, & Jonbes, 2009) focused on new approaches to teaching and learning that build on the capabilities of online platforms and advanced instructional tools. One of the findings of the report was that learners who were able to utilize interactive tools and control their learning process performed better than learners who used static tools that were instructor-controlled. Also, students who engaged in self-reflection by assessing their answers in comparison to other students in an online chemistry class benefited (Bixler, 2008).

The application of online and distance education courses that involve complex relationships such as chemical structures and analytical principles in pharmaceutical and forensic sciences is challenging. However, the aforementioned meta-analysis and studies provide evidence that abstract principles can be successfully transferred into an online setting. The interactive and self-reflective features that HyLighter provides are ideal for student–student interactions, as well as for a collaborative approach to answer questions related to pharmacological, structure-based, and analytical problems.

The HyLighter tool was utilized as an additional assessment tool for student assignments in two graduate-level distance education courses at the University of Florida (www.forensicscience.ufl.edu and www.pharmchem. cop.ufl.edu). The courses were administered as asynchronous, text-based modules with animated and static graphics for illustration of chemical and analytical processes such as drug–receptor interactions or generation of mass spectra. The student demographics varied both in educational background (all students were required to have a Bachelors degree, preferably in a natural science such as biochemistry, chemistry, medicine, or related) and work experience (ranging from students having just finished their undergraduate degree to those working in the field for over 10 years). The classes utilized for implementation of HyLighter were "Fundamentals of Medicinal Chemistry (PHA 5433)" and "Forensic Toxicology 1 (VME 6613)." Both classes were taught by different instructors and during different terms without an overlap of students being enrolled in both classes.

The HyLighter assignments for both classes were scheduled toward the end of a respective module on mass spectrometry for Forensic Toxicology 1 and the end of the semester after all modules were released to students for Fundamentals of Medicinal Chemistry. Students were asked to either (a) comment on an area highlighted by the instructor or (b) highlight an area and write a comment or explanation themselves.

For the Forensic Toxicology 1 assignment, 14 students were asked to interpret mass spectra of the illicit drugs cocaine and methamphetamine. Interpretation of mass spectral data is an integral part of the everyday work of a forensic toxicologist, and, therefore, students need to acquire a basic understanding in this area.

In this first application of HyLighter, the instructor imported PowerPoint slides that included mass spectra images. He highlighted specific sections of various slides and added questions as *sticky posts* (i.e., comments that always appear at the top of a discussion thread in the HyLighter margin). Although HyLighter provides the instructor with the option to set permissions for independent review (i.e., students can see the instructor's sticky posts and their own responses but not the responses of other students), the instructor set permissions to make all comments visible to all students throughout the exercise. The rationale for allowing students to see each other's comments was to encourage them to engage with each other before submitting their answers. Also, the instructor wanted to compare this open approach to a two-part approach that required independent responses from students before allowing students to share and discuss their responses.

Students answered and discussed the questions associated with highlighted areas and came to conclusions for each. This was accomplished online in both real-time discussions and asynchronously. The conclusions of students were either approved or corrected by the instructor. Self-assessment by students was provided on a grading scale ranging from 0 to 10. The self-assessments of students at the end of the exercise for the mass spectra interpretation were different than the instructor's grading and revealed that students may be overconfident but can improve their skills by learning from their mistakes. This observation is consistent with research on metacognitive knowledge monitoring that evaluated how well students distinguish between what they know and do not know. Results suggested that accurate monitoring is an important variable in school learning (Tobias, Everson, & Laitusis, 1999).

The second course in which HyLighter was used as an educational tool combined the knowledge acquired by students after finishing all required module assignments. The exercise was intended to provide 23 students enrolled in the course with the opportunity to apply and transfer their theoretical knowledge into an actual practical example. The HyLighter assignment was mandatory. The course "Fundamentals of Medicinal Chemistry" introduced basic concepts related to the physicochemical properties of a drug structure as well as principles of what the body does with a drug (pharmacokinetics) and what the drug does to the body (pharmacodynamics). Similar approaches have been evaluated for online medicinal chemistry courses offered to pharmacy students (Alsharif & Galt, 2008).

After students worked on individual homework assignments and completed online timed quizzes, the HyLighter assignment was used to summarize the concepts of the course and then make students apply their knowledge to a new structure. All instructional material was prepared as PowerPoint slides and imported into HyLighter as images. Unlike the Forensic Toxicology 1 assignment where students could see all comments from the beginning, this second HyLighter assignment was split into two parts. The first part required students to independently respond (i.e., students could not see the responses of their peers) to the teacher's sticky-post questions followed by a second part that allowed students to see all responses and discuss their answers.

The instructor posted questions in the margins linked to highlighted areas of each slide and provided initial instructions on how to use the HyLighter tool. Students initially gave individual responses without seeing the responses of other students. After a deadline had passed, the instructor changed HyLighter permissions to reveal all comments and encouraged discussions among students. Students were able to comment on each other's responses using HyLighter's reply feature and many recognized and acknowledged if they initially had made a mistake. The instructor also provided feedback to students and evaluated them based on their initial responses and contributions to follow-up discussions. This process was supplemented with chat sessions within the platform used for module and assignment administration. Fig. 2 shows a slide from the "Fundamentals of Medicinal Chemistry" activity.

During chat sessions, students provided positive feedback about the HyLighter assignment. They were able to apply acquired knowledge and experience and see the relevance of their new knowledge to the drug

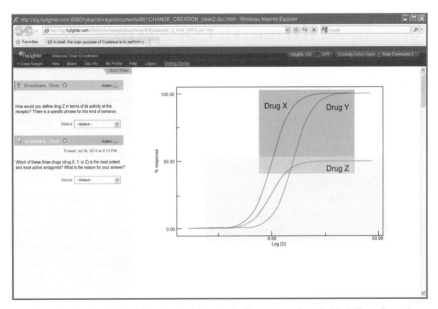

Fig. 2. A PowerPoint Slide in HyLighter. The Instructor has Added Two Questions Linked to Different Sections of the Graphic. Students Independently Respond to the Questions and are Able to See the Responses of their Peers and the Instructor When the Instructor Changes Hylighter Permissions.

development process. The HyLighter assignment also helped in reviewing material from undergraduate classes such as basic analytical techniques, physicochemical properties of chemical structures, basic applications of chemistry to the drug design process, and biotransformation processes.

In conclusion, the main advantages of using HyLighter as an instructional tool in distance education courses as administered in the pharmaceutical and forensic sciences programs at the University of Florida were:

1. HyLighter was an effective tool for students and instructors to transfer knowledge acquired in written modules into practical examples and authentic assessments.
2. Students were able to evaluate and compare their own answers with those of their peers, which provided additional discussion incentives and increased engagement.
3. HyLighter enabled collaborative student approaches for alternative assessment activities that complemented quizzes and individual assignments.

HYLIGHTER-ENHANCED MULTIPLE-CHOICE TESTING

Multiple-choice tests have a long but not always illustrious history in education across the curriculum and levels of schooling. Teachers often like them because they are easy to administer and score. Students often like them because the answer is given to them to recognize, so they do not have the more intellectually demanding task of recalling the answer. Also, if they do not know the answer, they can always guess and usually have at least a 25% chance of getting it right.

On the contrary, many educators have pointed out a limitation of multiple-choice items – no credit is given to alternative answers to questions. A student might get the "wrong" answer, but for good reasons, such as a creative approach to thinking about the question or problem, or because the question itself is vague or ambiguous. In other words, wrong can sometimes be right and right can sometimes be wrong. A student can get the "right" answer by guessing while not knowing the material or by having a completely wrong or only partially correct understanding of the material.

As a cognitive psychologist teaching educational and developmental psychology to pre-service and in-service teacher education students, I wanted to (a) probe the reasoning underlying students' answers to multiple-choice items and (b) model for teachers an alternative approach to multiple-choice testing.

Consequently, I uploaded multiple-choice tests in HyLighter and used the comment feature to require students to explain the reasons for their answers. Students received equal credit for both their answers and the reasons underlying their answers. Each test had 20 items, so each question was worth 5 points. Two and a half points were awarded for the correct answer and the same for good reasoning. In some cases partial credit was given for students' reasoning.

Enhanced multiple-choice testing allowed me to obtain a better understanding of what students knew, misunderstood, confused, or failed to grasp. The approach also revealed patterns of errors and misconceptions. This feedback guided my subsequent instruction with particular classes soon after the tests and guided my plans to teach some material more effectively in the future. This procedure also forced students to think about and learn the material more deeply than they would have for a typical multiple-choice test. It also helped students reflect on their own thinking and learning so they could study more effectively for future tests.

In addition to the feedback I received about students' learning and the effectiveness of my teaching, students received feedback about their own and each others' learning. Immediately after taking the test, students were able to click on questions to identify the correct answer. Shortly after the whole class had finished their test, students were able to see models of good explanations of answers by their classmates. During a subsequent class, I discussed the forms and functions of feedback obtained through this enhanced, multiple-choice testing and identified specific misconceptions students had about the material in the course.

The second time students engaged in enhanced multiple-choice testing through HyLighter, they were much more successful for a number of reasons. They were better able to study at the level of depth and with methods needed to master content well enough to produce good reasons for their answers. They knew more about themselves as learners and test takers. They had learned from their peers how to provide more accurate and thoughtful explanations of their multiple-choice selections. Students were also more successful the second time because I provided them with feedback about the types of explanations that were made on the first test. In class, we discussed successful and unsuccessful answer explanations. This helped them to plan their subsequent test preparation with these potential problems in mind.

   Successful explanations often involved a combination of categories such as explanation/description and elaboration and example. This is illustrated by the response of one student to the question: How does the nature of the learning environment affect teacher learning?

a. Learner-centered environments emphasize teachers learning how to transmit important information to students.
b. Knowledge-centered environments encourage teachers to rethink how they teach particular subjects.
c. Assessment-centered environments indicate that classroom teacher feedback is greatly overrated in importance.
d. Community-centered environments emphasize the importance of teachers' independent thinking, learning, and problem solving.

The correct answer, b, was successfully justified by one student with:

> Just because you are an expert does not mean you will be able to teach material. Just because you are a skilled pedagogue does not mean you will be able to teach any subject. There needs to be a balance between subject knowledge and pedagogical content knowledge. A knowledge-centered environment will encourage teachers to reexamine strategies they have used in the past. In such an environment, a physics teacher might realize that his/her instruction could be improved by focusing on big understandings rather than individual equations.

   Common unsuccessful combinations were explanations including categories such as misconceptions, personal opinion, and part/whole. This is illustrated by the response of one student to the question: According to *How People Learn*, one of the most important features of the new learning technologies is:

a. The ability to develop students' basic skills.
b. The ability of learners to interact with others.
c. An emphasis on the traditional curriculum
d. They build on students' prior experiences with technology.

   The correct answer is b, because a recurring theme of the book's chapter on technology was that technologies have valuable uses as contexts for social interactions that support learning, and many examples of this were given. An example of a wrong answer is d, and a given unsuccessful student explanation is as follows.

> The use of technology in the classroom has to be built upon their prior knowledge. The proper scaffolding needs to be in place so a student can achieve & narrow his ZPD [i.e., the zone of proximal development is the difference between what a learner can do

without help and what he or she can do with help] with the help of the teacher & the use of technology in the classroom.

On the contrary, a student received partial credit for the wrong answer d, because of demonstrating understanding of the social interaction benefits of technology.

> Though community aspects of choice b are somewhat true, and there are several projects that have shown the benefit of e-based cooperations & collaborations, I tend to think that technology is best employed when it facilitates the learner-centered environment.

On the second test, many answers were developed more fully and some students referred to the enhanced multiple-choice procedure as involving a combination of multiple-choice and essay methods. In one case, students' explanations of their answers revealed that a test question was problematic because so many students misunderstood it. Consequently, the enhanced multiple-choice testing procedure helped me to prepare more effectively for the second test by facilitating metacognitive question construction (i.e., taking into account what makes sense to students when formulating test questions).

At the end of the second test, as an option, students were able to provide feedback on their reactions to the experience of taking the enhanced multiple-choice test through HyLighter. Following are examples of students' comments, both positive and negative:

Positive
- I thought this worked very well. I liked the fact that it made one think in depth about the answers and try to justify them.
- This was the most progressive test taking experience I have ever been involved in. It's amazing how little straight multiple-choice tests reflect regarding students' conceptions.
- The whole process of highlighting made me very critical of my answers and also made me read each word carefully in the answer choices.
- Responding to the test was kinda cool. And I think as a teacher I would like to have the ability to see inside my students' heads at the time they take the exam. So overall I would say a good experience.
- Would be especially good for math tests where students can guess the answer or cheat without actually knowing the concepts.
- Provides an opportunity to easily assess students' progress.
- I thought this worked very well ... It allowed me to see gaps in my thinking and knowledge.

Negative
- This test was difficult. I started out strong but felt weaker at the end. Some of the questions were more detail oriented than I expected, and it took much longer than I expected ... This must take hours to correct!
- I wasn't exactly sure to what extent we were to explain ourselves and that might have been helpful to know.
- It should be practiced first. Surprises aren't good, especially when you're taking a test.

Enhanced multiple-choice testing through HyLighter was a powerful experience for my students and me. During class discussion many of them reported wanting to do something similar with their own students, as they valued the window into the thinking and reasoning of students provided by social annotation technology. In the current era of high stakes multiple-choice tests, gaining insight into students' thoughts and knowledge while engaged in multiple-choice testing not only has important educational implications but also political, social, and economic implications too.

CONCLUSION

Three cases have illustrated uses of social annotation to promote student-to-student and teacher-to-student interaction tied to different types of content or source materials. In screenplay writing classes, students engaged in a type of reciprocal peer review of their drafts. By establishing an environment where rich feedback from peers and the instructor was the norm, students experienced the value of giving and receiving constructive feedback. In online Forensic Science and Pharmaceutical Chemistry classes, students engaged in collaborative learning and assessment activities that helped promote self-assessment, increased engagement with complex concepts, and support of transfer. Finally, HyLighter-enhanced multiple-choice testing in pre-service and in-service teacher education classes, facilitated error analysis, and provided scaffolding for students to transition from lack of knowledge or understanding to mastery of material deep enough for transfer of learning. In sum, HyLighter-enhanced practices fostered self-efficacy, thereby resulting in cognitive, affective, and social benefits for students and improved quality of instruction for teachers.

Brown, Collins, and Duguid (1989) have pointed out that documents not only deliver information but also build and maintain social groups. From their perspective, the document is a medium for the negotiation of meaning, and, on this basis, they have recommended developing technology to improve the means of negotiation. Social annotation applications satisfy this criterion through three key functions:

- Makes the thinking of teachers and students that are ordinarily hidden, become transparent, visible, and easily accessible for sharing with others, self-reflection, and feedback.
- Allows users to continuously compare their developing understanding to others, assess performance, and monitor progress.
- Supports efforts to organize, integrate, and synthesize ideas from multiple sources and perspectives.

However, what we understand about how to implement and manage social annotation systems across disciplines is relatively limited. To realize the full potential of this form of social media for education more research is required on how to adapt technology and practices for various contexts of use.

Broad goals of the next phase in development of HyLighter include (a) develop new functions to increase versatility and integrate with other social media and learning management systems and (b) modify and improve HyLighter and related practices based on feedback through a collaborative relationship with practitioners in the field. In sum, HyLighter is an emerging set of tools and methods that support various document review practices to harness the cognitive and social interaction potential of knowledge-based social networks and accelerate learning, creativity, and improvements in performance of members. At its core, HyLighter builds on the principle that our own views grow and are enhanced by remaining open to the views of others.

NOTE

1. The development is led by two of the co-authors, David G. Lebow and Dale W. Lick and a dedicated team of programmers led by Kamal Muthuswamy.

REFERENCES

Alsharif, N. Z., & Galt, K. A. (2008). Evaluation of an instructional model to teach clinically relevant medicinal chemistry in a campus and a distance pathway. *American Journal of Pharmaceutical Education, 72*(2), 31.

Bixler, B. A. (2008). *The effects of scaffolding student's problem-solving process via question prompts on problem solving and intrinsic motivation in an online learning environment.* PhD Dissertation. The Pennsylvania State University, State College, Penn.

Brown, J. S., Collins, A., & Duguid, P. (1989). Situated cognition and the culture of learning. *Educational Researcher, 18*(1), 32–42.

Ericsson, K. A., Krampe, R. T., & Tesch-Römer, C. (1993). The role of deliberate practice in the acquisition of expert performance. *Psychological Review, 100*(3), 363–406.

Hartman, H. (2010). Windows into teaching and learning through social annotation practices. In: M. S. Khine & I. M. Saleh (Eds), *New science of learning: Computers, cognition and collaboration in education* (Chapter 21, pp. 427–450). New York: Springer.

Lave, J., & Wenger, E. (1991). *Situated learning: Legitimate peripheral participation.* Cambridge: Cambridge University Press.

Leamnson, R. (1999). *Thinking about teaching and learning: Developing habits of learning with first year college and university students.* Sterling, VA: Stylus Publishing.

Lebow, D. G., & Lick, D. W. (2003). Medieval scholarship meets 21st century technology. Part two: The interactive annotation model. *Online Classroom* (5), 4–5.

Means, B., Toyama, Y., Murphy, R., Bakia, M., & Jonbes, K. (2009). *Evaluation of evidence-based practices in online learning: A meta-analysis and review of online learning studies.* Washington, DC: U.S. Department of Education.

Scardamalia, M., Bereiter, C., McLean, R. S., Swallow, J., & Woodruff, E. (1989). Computer supported intentional learning environments. *Journal of Educational Computing Research, 5*, 51–68.

Tobias, S., Everson, H. T., & Laitusis, V. (1999). Towards a performance based measure of metacognitive knowledge monitoring: Relationships with self-reports and behavior ratings. Paper presented at the Annual Meeting of the American Educational Research Association, Montreal, Quebec, Canada, April 19–23.

Wahlstrom, B., & Scruton, C. (1997). Constructing texts/understanding texts: Lessons from antiquity and the middle ages. *Computers and Composition, 14*(3), 311–328.

Wolfe, J. L. (2008). Annotations and the collaborative digital library: Effects of an aligned annotation interface on student argumentation and reading strategies. *International Journal of Computer-Supported Collaborative Learning, 3*(2), 141–164.

Zuber-Skerritt, O. (1992). *Action research in higher education: Examples and reflection.* London: Kogan.

OUR HEAD IN THE CLOUD: TRANSFORMING WORK ON COLLEGE COMPLETION

Diana D. Woolis and Gail O. Mellow

ABSTRACT

Global Skills for College Completion (GSCC) offers transformative use of social media – a Guided Digital Environment – a unique set of online tools and processes to capture, consolidate, and advance the effective faculty classroom work. The ambition of GSCC is to achieve a quantum increase in the historically low pass rates of basic skills students in American community colleges. The goal is to produce a rate increase so dramatic, consistently 80%, that it is "visible to the naked eye." This increased success rate in basic skills would have the effect of accelerating remediation and increasing the probability of college completion. We believe community college basic skills faculty possess all the wisdom necessary to figure out how to improve these rates, given the right tools. In this chapter we describe the GSCC project, the Guided Digital Environment and the Tools and Routines provided to faculty to allow them to be research-practitioners in the project, and the research we drew on to build it. We include early information and observations on the essential design elements for identifying effective basic skills pedagogy. We also describe the innovative technological tools used to create an engaged community and leave a digital trail for analysis. GSCC is funded

Educating Educators with Social Media
Cutting-edge Technologies in Higher Education, Volume 1, 279–301
ISSN: 2044-9968/doi:10.1108/S2044-9968(2011)0000001017

by the Bill and Melinda Gates Foundation through a grant to the League
for Innovation as part of its goal to double the number of young adults in
the United States with a postsecondary credential by 2020.

CHAPTER OVERVIEW

The ambition of Global Skills for College Completion (GSCC) is to achieve
a quantum increase in the historically low pass rates of basic skills students
in American community colleges. Our goal is to produce a rate increase
so dramatic, consistently 80%, that it is "visible to the naked eye." This
increased success rate in basic skills would have the effect of accelerating
remediation and increasing the probability of college completion. GSCC
is funded by the Bill and Melinda Gates Foundation as part of its goal
to double the number of young adults in the United States with a
postsecondary credential by 2020.

GSCC's ambitious goal involves two distinct but interrelated elements.
The first is using social networking technology to create both an environment and a process for practitioner-driven innovation. The second is
applying this optimal environment and process to the pedagogy of basic
skills, making it possible to create an evidence-based overarching basic skills
pedagogy that identifies the essential design elements of effective practice
for the first time.

At this writing, 4 months into a 28-month-long project, the experiment is
still in progress. Yet we have already learned a great deal and can report
promising work.

We define basic skills as those reading, writing, and math competencies
required for students to maintain a "C" or better grade in college level work.
At U.S. community colleges, a large percentage of students (with national
estimates of between 40% and 60%) enter with high school credentials but
lacking "college ready" basic skills. These students require compensatory
classes to obtain the necessary foundations in reading, writing, and/or math.
Unfortunately, almost half of the students needing these classes either do
not enroll, do not complete, or fail the basic skills class, effectively ending
the promise of college completion.

We believe community college basic skills faculty possess all the wisdom
necessary to figure out how to improve these rates, given the right tools.
GSCC offers these pioneers the transformative use of a particular social
media environment – a specific set of online tools and processes to capture,

consolidate, and advance their most effective classroom work. Two of the Co-Principle Investigators (GSCC is funded through grant to the League for Innovation in the Community College) and authors of this chapter, together with their team, designed what we term a *Guided Digital Environment*, in which the faculty work is taking place. In this chapter we describe the GSCC project, the Guided Digital Environment, and the research we drew on to build it. We include early information and observations on the essential design elements of effective practice basic skills pedagogy.

Our dual-pronged research task – involving both social media and basic skills pedagogy – is daunting, but no more so than many other education research projects. The theme of the 2010 American Educational Research Association's national conference, *Understanding Complex Ecologies in a Changing World*, suggests that responding to complexity must be considered part of the current education research agenda. The conference website reads:

> Education research sits inside what Donald Stokes calls "Pasteur's Quadrant," referring to the dual focus of building basic theory while simultaneously improving practice ... Our attempts to understand and influence such learning often try to strip away complexity for presumed efficiency ... Ubiquitous technologies empower and encourage all forms of communication and movement within and across all kinds of borders; an ecological focus encourages education researchers to draw on interdisciplinary constructs and theories, complex research designs, and multiple methods of data analysis ... (AERA, 2010)

We conclude this chapter by sharing our view of how social media can transform work on college completion, based on what we are already seeing, because it can embrace the lived complexity of the educational environment.

INCREASING COLLEGE COMPLETION RATES: AMERICA'S ELUSIVE GOAL

Fewer than 30% of community college students complete an associate's degree. Between 40% and 60% of all community college students require developmental education to achieve a college-ready skill level, but fewer than 60% of low-income young adults pass these classes. Indeed, for 30 years or more, the pass rates of the large numbers of community college students who require basic skills to succeed have not changed.

Developmental education – providing effective instruction to high school graduates who lack the basic skills in reading, writing, or mathematics necessary for college level work – has been a formidable challenge. Methods of teaching in college have not been given the attention they require to address the disproportionately high levels of need of both students and faculty for support. To date, attempts have occurred faculty-by-faculty and discipline-by-discipline, inching along with publications of best practices but without a concerted attempt to link the multidimensional aspects of the problem and without the benefits of research conducted with advanced technologies. Advanced technologies are particularly important because they help the researcher see more clearly and on a granular level what works, for whom, and why.

President Obama's proposal of an American Graduation Initiative to have 5 million more individuals graduate with a credential beyond high school, the Bill and Melinda Gates Foundation's Double the Numbers initiative, the Lumina Foundation's Achieving the Dream and Getting Past Go, among others, are focused on college completion. Together they represent an unprecedented focus on community colleges. These democratic institutions, now enrolling almost half of all undergraduates in the United States, have become increasingly fundamental to American success in producing a highly educated citizen. But without dramatic increases in the proportion of students who not only enroll but complete a degree, the potential of community colleges will be squandered. It is within this milieu that the researchers conceptualized the GSCC project.

GLOBAL SKILLS FOR COLLEGE COMPLETION:
80% OR BUST

The goal of our 28-month project is to develop a breakthrough scalable pedagogy and curriculum that will support faculty teaching to raise the basic skills pass rate of community college students to 80%. We were advised by many not to use the goal of 80%, at least not publicly, as the odds of success are slim. But we are not looking just to budge the needle on the old Chevy – we are aiming to transform the vehicle. If our rocket does not make it to the moon on the first trip, but we see clearly how the rocket *will* get to the moon, it will be a huge achievement. We can say that at this early stage of the launch the GSCC prototype is holding its own.

How can we justify this ambitious goal?

The Beauty is in the Pattern

The key to the sharply improved pass rates that GSCC envisions is the emergence of correlated pedagogical patterns – ways of teaching basic skills that will work in a wide variety of contexts. The best way to develop these underlying patterns is to begin with an exhaustive culling and codification of successful practices across multiple faculty. There is no shortcut, although social media open up new vistas of data collection and management. We will arrive at winning patterns when they can be reproduced anywhere, not just under special conditions. It is this search that underlies our cross-disciplinary examination of relevant research, theory, and practice.

This idea of pattern detection and its use to establish and grow a pedagogical framework is central to our thinking. If the whole of our work is taking place in largely uncharted territory, the idea of generating pedagogical patterns from the collective work of faculty is at its outer reaches. But it is not without precedent. Some footing can be gained from work taking place in recommender systems,[1] which we discuss later. Also, the private sector has moved aggressively into the land of the terabyte. Pattern Based Strategy™ developed by Gartner[2] seeks patterns from conventional and unconventional sources that can positively or negatively impact strategy or operations, and sets up a consistent and repeatable response by adjusting business patterns. It is "a framework for proactively seeking and acting on the early and often-termed 'weak' signals forming patterns in the marketplace. It's also about the ability to model the impact of patterns on your organization and identify the disciplines and technologies that help you consistently adapt" (Gartner, n.d.).

The identification of patterns depends, first, on very large amounts of "data," or a large record of effective practice. GSCC by its nature makes available for analysis a voluminous and detailed record of teaching practice and impact. Moreover, while GSCC uses established modes of social net-working, these are neither haphazard nor voluntary but rather structured and required. This approach has served to organize faculty's classroom work as they adapt their practice to reflect their role as practitioner researchers. It has also caused a substantial exchange of practices – advancing the conversation on innovation, and adding to the treasures of searchable, collate-able data.

More specifically, the challenges of detecting pedagogic patterns require several different sets of data. We believe they can be obtained by:

- capturing and understanding what successful basic skills faculty do and know;

- understanding the complexities of the context in which these teachers and/
  or specific practices work;
- developing robust methods of reflection;
- extrapolating patterns of successful pedagogy from multiple practices;
- relating pedagogical patterns to student learning outcomes; and
- subjecting individual faculty successes to repeated use over time and by
  others.

It is worth noting that the data points above both begin and end with
faculty expertise, with considerable faculty reflection and iteration along the
way.

Basic Skills Faculty Lead the Way

The GSCC project as a whole proceeds from two underlying assumptions.
First, faculty knowledge and expertise must form the center of any attempt
at massive reformation of educational practices, and second, traditional
education evaluation research must be radically improved to capture the
new complexity of in vivo teaching pedagogy.

As for the first assumption of the centrality of faculty expertise to true
innovation, GSCC predicates its research model on the knowledge that
nationally, community colleges possess a cadre of dedicated professionals
who are passionately committed to student achievement. To tap their talent,
we designed a system of scholarly practice that integrates the doing of
teaching with the research of teaching and that uses student work and
outcomes to substantiate success. Our goal was to engage faculty as co-
designers of the GSCC prototype.

Faculty members as a constituency must become the leaders in
the national goal of increasing student degree completion through higher
basic skills pass rates by improving what happens in the classroom.
Why faculty? Creativity and innovation are born from passion and the
happy accidents that happen along the way when these are applied to a
subject of deep interest. We find inspiration and evidence from people
like Charles Leadbeater, a leading authority on innovation and creativity.
In Leadbeater's (2008) book, *We-Think: The Power of Mass Creativity*, he
charts the rise of mass, participative approaches to innovation from science
and open source software, to computer games and political campaigning.

As for the second assumption, that achieving our goals would require a
radical rethinking of research, we feel that our faculty/researchers need

a high-octane environment to fuel their work and scale their learning. They need to be an effective learning community despite their diversity (institutional, geographic, and discipline). The power and potential of social media offered an as yet relatively untested but promising path to building out our prototype.

Social media has caught the popular imagination for a range of uses, from social to analytical to commercial. Businesses, by necessity focusing on the bottom line, have recognized one key asset of this digital forum: its renewed power to capture and disseminate information.

> Business leader interest in Web 2.0 technologies has led software vendors of all stripes to add social layers to their applications. Sixty-five percent of firms have adopted at least one Web 2.0 technology, but businesses are focusing on a subset of tools – wikis, discussion forums, and blogs. How are they using these tools? While there are many internal and external uses, businesses have zeroed in on information capture and dissemination. (Keitt, Burris, & Ashour, 2010, Executive Summary)

A digital forum allows a new chance to capture and synthesize a tremendous amount of data – not to boost sales in our case, but rather to contribute gradually to that elusive overarching pedagogy.

And so, moving from theory to practice, we selected as our lead team a group of 26 high-performing basic skills faculty from community college programs in developmental English (writing) and developmental mathematics across the country. The extensive vetting process resulted in a faculty cohort that: (a) are among the top 10% of faculty pass rates for students in basic skills classes for their campus (determined locally); (b) are personally motivated and engaged with improving pedagogy; and (c) have shown the capacity to be creative and scholarly thinkers. Along with the GSCC team, this faculty cohort participates in the research and action program, codifying their practice and participating in detecting and defining themes that will form the basis of the algorithms of success.

DESIGNING THE GUIDED DIGITAL ENVIRONMENT

To build our prototype we looked to arenas where creative and fast innovation is a survival imperative and where social media[3] in particular has had a significant impact (i.e., in health, publishing, music, and the military). Regardless of sector or purpose, when technology is effectively combined with social interaction, value is created.

The Secret is in the Sauce

Our task then was to combine technology and social interaction to facilitate the identification of a GSCC pedagogy framework: to develop a system that would allow us to identify a reliable, adaptable pattern set that consistently results in improved student outcomes. We determined that the GSCC combination, our unique formula (what one person on our team calls "the special sauce") was:

Online community + Faculty ePortfolios + Digital library.

Each element in the formula would take shape around actual and real-time faculty practice. And each would incorporate what we inferred from our research to be necessary to a community of practitioners leading innovation, namely narrative, dialogue, community, analysis, and evidence.

Diana Laurillard, Chair of Learning with Digital Technologies in the Faculty of Culture and Pedagogy at the University of London offers a "communitarian" model to suggest how faculty can take cues from open source technology and their own research to adapt to education's new challenges. She calls this model "open teaching."

> Teaching must become problematized, innovative, and professional, taking research as its model. If lecturers were to conduct the process of teaching as rigorously as they conduct their research, then they would expect: 1. support for some personal development in how to teach; 2. the means to build on the work of others to design their approach; 3. the means to experiment and reflect on what the results imply for their design and their understanding; and 4. the means to articulate and disseminate their contribution. Those four characteristics together define the essentials of what we might call "open teaching" – what James Dalziel has called "open source teaching" – such as an environment in which "educators can freely and openly share best practice teaching. (Laurillard, 2008b, p. 328)

Our own version of "open teaching" took shape between September and December 2009 as we elaborated the Guided Digital Environment curriculum – the activities, schedule and faculty requirements for the ePortfolio and online community.

The Recipe: So What's in Here?

Faculty ePortfolios
Student ePortfolios – an online collection of work in diverse formats organized to meet a particular objective, such as integrating knowledge across

multiple classes or demonstrating expertise – are gaining traction as social media moves to center stage in higher education. As conceptualized by Dr. Paul Arcario and brought to scale by Dr. Bret Eynon, LaGuardia Community College in metropolitan New York City considers the use of ePortfolios for student learning and assessment to be a part of the College's signature pedagogy and has actively developed and promoted portfolio use for colleges and colleagues across the country. Simply put, student ePortfolios can serve as an "education passport" allowing for a portable representation of learning in a fluid and fast-moving society (Clark & Enyon, 2009).

The use of faculty ePortfolios is much less prevalent, but it is also gaining traction. One study title reflects the two opposing potentials of the exercise of documenting a day-to-day teaching experience: "The teaching portfolio: institutional imperative or teacher's personal journey" (FitzPatrick & Spiller, 2010). In GSCC we use faculty ePortfolios for both personal and communal reflection. The GSCC team established three goals for the faculty ePortfolios:

1. to support regular documentation of faculty practice,
2. to enhance faculty reflection on their own practice in order to deepen insight, and
3. to support practice-focused exchange among faculty.

Together with the online community work, which we describe below, the faculty ePortfolios provide the data to populate and conduct our research. By looking across portfolios (and community activity) we can see themes and patterns critical to the project's goals. And we can also see at a granular level what faculty are doing. The portfolios are structured and analyzed to detect and codify insights and findings. Currently, the faculty ePortfolios are open to all members of the GSCC team (faculty and researchers), but as the project develops they can become sites for sharing more widely.

The faculty ePortfolios are structured to capture faculty work in vivo – as it is occurring. Based on the LaGuardia Community College mantra of "collect, select, connect, and reflect," the GSCC faculty use their individual ePortfolios each week to describe what is occurring in one class, to document student work, to connect the goals of their class to the student outcomes, and to reflect on what happened with their students that week. These critical elements are gathered in four separate sections of the faculty ePortfolios entitled Classroom Practice, Student Artifacts and Outcomes, Video and Reflection.

Within a qualitative and quantitative formative evaluation process, faculty have begun to collect evidence of student work linked to classroom practices to determine what is working in their class, share with other faculty their own perceptions, and gain real-time evaluative feedback every two weeks that informs their ability to recalibrate directions and improve practice. Eventually, we believe that the ePortfolios will be the basis for faculty to stage the development of scholarly presentations and related research, and to support the development of tools and resources for the dissemination phase.

The power of the data in the ePortfolio cannot be underestimated. Because it is all digital, the ability to continually mine the data for new ideas, to review patterns that emerge over semesters or years, and to compare the data among faculty is powerful. Use of this new tool has not been without its challenges, however. Faculty, especially college faculty, are not in the habit of being articulate about daily class-level goals, nor about thinking about how to capture daily class-level student work that would provide evidence of the effectiveness of individual classroom activities. Faculty as researcher in their own discipline is common – but faculty as a scholar of their own teaching practice is a new concept, and one that is not yet consistently applied in the GSCC project. And inevitably, there are the technical issues – how to get a class videoed, how a recording technician in the class changes class dynamics, etc. Yet the potency of the data – an in-depth look at what is really happening in the basic skills classrooms of master teachers – is worth the challenge.

Online Community

Where the faculty ePortfolios are the locus of individual reflection on teaching practice, the online community – which Knowledge in the Public Interest has dubbed Polilogue – is the locus of group deliberation. In the GSCC online community, faculty participate through highly structured, biweekly online interactions. More than a sharing of best practices, the online work provides the ability to synthesize the collective knowledge of the entire faculty cohort through an analysis of the digital documentation and a clear feedback mechanism. This online "curriculum" was designed by Brenda Kaulback and the knowledge architecture of the GSCC Polilogue is organized and maintained by Lisa Levinson, both of KPI.

Specifically we have created three types of activities:

1. Pedagogical Circles

    Each faculty member has been assigned to a Circle. These are small disciplinary groups – two for writing and two for math. During each 2-week period one designated faculty posts an example of their practice using any digital medium they choose (Jing, video, document, Power-Point, etc.), explains the context and objective of the work and invites feedback. Over the ensuing 2 weeks, the posting faculty and a designated moderator lead the Circle in an online discussion. The goal of this method of work is to both secure a detailed description of a practice or set of practices that one faculty considers important, and to record the probing and commentary that the group provides. The online data then allows GSCC to observe those practices or ideas that Circle members are subsequently stimulated to adopt or adapt in their own classroom.

2. Choice Events

    Each faculty also presents once each semester to the full community on a subject of their choosing. They might post a video of a part of one of their classes, or describe a particular support program at their college that they feel is beneficial for basic skills students. The Choice event is similarly "live" for a 2-week period of discussion, analysis and debate among the faculty.

3. In addition to these structured interactions, the Polilogue contains an open community space called the *Coffee Klatch*. There is no prescribed participation requirement here, rather it is the virtual water cooler around which ideas and questions are traded. The Coffee Klatch is as much a check on the GSCC work process as it is on pedagogical practice but as such it contributes importantly to our understanding of the work.

Thanks to these structured modes of data capture and online interaction, GSCC – not yet 6 months old – already has an extensive record of practice. As of this writing the ongoing transcript of the Coffee Klatch numbers over 150 pages. Overall we have been averaging about 670 posts to the online community of practice per 2 week period from the 26 faculty. In just 4 months, faculty have made more than 15,000 posts. The dialogue is rich, deep, and challenging.

We also have substantial evidence of practice adaptation because faculty give clear attribution. Beyond practice, however, we observe technological adaptation, where one person uses a particular technology and others then begin to use it as well. Thus the online community supports the work and generates evidence of the work all at the same time.

The platform for the online community is a highly customized version of Moodle, an open source web-based course management system. Developed by Knowledge in the Public Interest, the Moodle-based platform, *Polilogue*, is home to the GSCC virtual office as well. Everything we do, write, and think can be found on Polilogue, which enables a high level of transparency – a guiding principle of the project.

By taking so readily to its new online platform, this academic community created a wide and effective community of practice. The faculty may not have self-identified as such, but they became pioneers for a new type of pedagogical research. Beginning with this 26-member lead team, the digital environment can accommodate ever widening circles of talent and know-how, building on the lead team's captured experience. The digital environment will continue to track evolving practices and revelations, supporting individual faculty achievement while keeping the community focused on innovating basic skills pedagogy. Key to staying on focus is project leadership. Dr. Marisa Klages is the GSCC Project Director. This process need not stop until student basic skills pass rates are consistently at 80% across the United States.

Online Communities in Education: More Theory Than Practice

The chapter "Education Leadership for a Networked World," recognizes a place for these communities in education:

> Virtual Communities of Practice (vCoP) draw their shape from the work on CoP's most identified with Wenger (1998). However, several writers have variously defined and discussed them (Brown, & Duguid, 1991; Lave & Wenger, 1991; Smith, 2003; Wenger, 1998; Wick, 2000). There is ample evidence in the literature of their value to organizations generally for improving practice, driving innovation, increasing value, managing knowledge, and creating knowledge networks (Allee, 2003; Hildreth & Kimble, 2004; Swan, Scarbrough, & Robetson, 2002). While still in its infancy, there is also a respectable body of work on virtual or online communities (Barab, Kling, & Gray, 2004; Dube, Bourhis, & Jacob, 2006; Ellis & Vasconcelos, 2004; Johnson, 2001; Kimble, Hildreth, & Wright, 2001; Dubé, Bouris, & Jacob, 2006; Siemens, 2005). (Woolis, Restler, & Thayer, 2008, p. 48)

Additionally, according to Koch and Fusco (2008) and Schlager and Fusco (2004), researchers at the K-20 level have been exploring social media and online communities for innovating professional development for some time.

Despite this wealth of recent scholarship, social media and online communities had not found their way into large-scale education innovation as of the launch of GSCC in 2009. Nor had education innovators and researchers found their way to social media and online communities as a way to re-conceptualize their efforts.

> Creating a robust set of opportunities for faculty inquiry in community colleges will not be an easy task. For starters there are no easy answers for how to organize the effort. (Huber, 2008, p. 24)

The GSCC model holds out the possibility that online communities "a dispersed group of people who work together in a virtual environment (primarily but not exclusively) to achieve a specific objective within a defined time frame ... which are consciously planned, intelligently introduced, and actively supported" (Restler & Woolis, 2007, p. 89) will provide a highly effective method of inquiry.

Clearly, the "dispersed group of people who work together" part is working for our group. They inform, inspire and improve one another's daily teaching practice. But how to capture it all as the conversation moves on and the records accrue?

Digital Library

> So where does one go in such a wobbly, elusive, dynamic, confusing age? Wherever the librarians ... are. They're sorting it out for us all. (Johnson, 2010, p. 12)

By its nature, we expected GSCC to generate a substantial collection of work on and related to developmental education. As Weinberger (2008) describes it, "We are building an ever-growing pile of smart leaves that we can organize as we need to at any moment" (p. 230). We imagined a microlibrary which would be a well organized digital collection of resources, focused specifically on our project, and employing both traditional library cataloging and organization, and the folksonomy[4] made possible by user-generated tagging.[5] In addition to its collection, our microlibrary would serve faculty in a traditional way with librarians offering reference services. A product of the 21st century and Web 2.0 technologies, cloud computing enables our library to be available to its participants – and to the wider world – anytime and from anywhere.

We are building our library collection in two spaces. First, we have a public-facing collection of reference materials and resources that the librarians, acting as content curators, collect on an on-going basis. These are stored in the social bookmarking tool Diigo as a "group library," in alignment with the model of the GSCC Guided Digital Environment.

Borrowing from a more traditional library model, librarians provide annotation and some standardized, authoritative tagging for each book-marked resource. Members of the GSCC group library can add their own bookmarks, and can tag and annotate other bookmarks in the library, thus promising a "conversation" among participants. We expect that, as the project grows and takes on speed, this social aspect of the public library will grow as well. This public-facing component provides an opportunity for the GSCC project to share proven best practices and the research that helped to develop and support those practices.

The second collection is not fully public, since GSCC is a working project and there are faculty-developed materials that are effectively "working documents," not yet vetted for public consumption. These materials are catalogued and indexed in a database that acts as a pathfinder, which is housed in the same environment as GSCC's online community. Faculty can readily access the materials of their peers in the pathfinder as well as link to the online community where the material was originally posted. Through the life of the project, we expect that some of these documents will contribute to public-facing resources, which can be included in our Diigo library, and upon project completion, these documents can be reviewed and made public as appropriate.

In addition to the librarians cataloguing both public- and private-facing materials, they act in a more traditional (albeit 21st century) reference role; all of this work, too, is done in the cloud.

The library is central to dissemination and "scaling." It is a very public offering. After all, "It's not what you know, and it's not even who you know. It's how much knowledge you give away" (Weinberger, 2008, p. 230).

IN A FIRE HOSE OF DATA, CONTINUOUS ANALYSIS, AND EVALUATION IS SINE QUA NON

We have written elsewhere that analysis of online data is the most significant value-add of social media. Great content and a robust work community are necessary but not sufficient to deliver on the potential of the medium. We knew this and anticipated that GSCC would produce more data, of higher quality, more quickly than traditional research. Several of us have been working in this digital context for some time and planned, we thought, accordingly. In our wildest imaginings we could not have predicted what 26 faculty would do in just the first 4 months.

Collectively they teach approximately 500 students per semester in 14 different states. They maintain an ePortfolio that requires weekly postings of their classroom practice, student artifacts and their reflections, plus all of their course material, including pre-tests of student abilities and final examinations and/or student scores on exit examinations. In the online community they present their work to one other and comment generously. Even our rigorous schedule of check-ins and activities was not sufficient to give voice to their creativity or their desire for connection and dialogue. This led to our creation of the unstructured Coffee Klatch. The topics range from the technical (How do I post a Jing video in my ePortfolio?), to the pedagogically practical (Has anyone used MyMathLab as their solo course online process? <or> What do you think about teaching grammar in a developmental reading class?), to the theoretical (how do we make the discourse communities of poor students respected at the same time as we require them to learn the rhetoric of the academic world?).

It is too early in the project to look at student outcomes. We planned to use the first semester of work to build the GSCC prototype and the subsequent semesters examining the relationship between the prototype and student outcomes. Yet, we have already learned a good deal.

Wading In

The deep and careful analysis of this sea of data is ahead of us. Nonetheless, we have begun to wade in as the information is both compelling and dramatically evident as one looks across different faculty activities and conversations. Every 2 weeks, the GSCC team reviews the online faculty work – reading ePortfolios, Choice Event, Pedagogy circles, and the dialogue that ensues. To frame our review, we have kept logs that ask

1. What themes can you uncover in the data?
2. What in the data led you to identify the theme (with digital data easily allowing a link to a specific data point)?
3. What do the other faculty pick up on?
4. What evidence connects the pedagogy described with student learning outcomes?

This article is then posted on a team ePortfolio, so that the emergent themes become evident. This preliminary analysis has been relatively consistent across multiple reviewers, and was also echoed in the student Jam which was conducted with over 100 students late in the first semester of the project. As aforementioned, the area that awaits more complete data is the linking of the faculty work with specific student artifacts and then to student learning outcomes – indicating to us that it is a challenge even for the best faculty to focus on evaluation of outcomes during a class.

Basic skills faculty respond every day to highly unpredictable and variable situations, tremendous diversity in their student population in every class, and unimaginable constraints of time and other key resources. We hypothesize that successful basic skills facility are so because they are passionate about their students and their teaching, are motivated by the work (certainly not by money, status, or institutional rewards!) and are highly adaptive – they will do and try anything and everything ALL the time to reach their students. These faculty have a robust tool box they can and do employ – usually assembled on their own and based on what they have found (or at least appears to them) to be effective. They excel at intuitively understanding pedagogy as a complex adaptive system.[6]

Envisioning the Lifeboat – A Plan for Knowledge Stewardship

To have a well-organized and efficiently run Guided Digital Environment is an important starting point, but it is not enough. For optimal performance and a chance at reaching our target – advancing the teaching of basic skills to the point of 80% developmental education pass rates – there is a need for knowledge stewardship (Restler & Woolis, 2007). Therefore, a key element of the GSCC online-community is the explicit focus on knowledge cultivation and co-creation, whereby the dialogue among practitioners is mined for emergent knowledge that can then be immediately relayed to practitioners and tested, adapted or modified. The online component creates a deeper practice of engagement and the kind of double-loop learning so important for breakthrough analysis.

In Restler and Woolis (2007), to foster optimal knowledge creation, we are in the process of designing a highly customized and contextualized knowledge stewardship plan. Its three main goals can be considered sequentially, although they can also occur simultaneously:

- *Knowledge Creation*: Organizing a work plan, implementing it, caring for the community and organizing its knowledge objects.
- *Knowledge for Action*: Managing the information that emerges as the community works and capitalizing on it – analyzing, synthesizing, refining, sharing – to help the community achieve its goals. This resource is the single most important contribution that virtual communities make to accelerating the pace of organizational work.
- *Knowledge Sustainability*: Making information easily and permanently available to the online community, individual organizations and ultimately the field as a whole (Lichtenstein & Swatman, 2003). Resources, records of discussions, process descriptions and evolving summaries and syntheses, which accumulate in the course of a virtual community doing its work, can all be searched, retrieved, reapplied and repurposed, even by new community members and visitors focused on similar or emerging issues.

Were GSCC a traditional research project these data, artifacts and interactions would be recorded and catalogued. Perhaps a think tank or research enterprise would mine them and/or conduct interviews and focus groups. But the digital and dynamic nature of the work makes possible not just the analysis described above but an annotatable and social digital library that can by used by anyone anywhere. Such a library can outlive its original project and be expanded by those engaged in any knowledge-based work – such as the project of doubling the number of Americans who gradate from college. Just as GSCC's online community can scale exponentially, its digital library scales the project's growing knowledge base in ways unimaginable without social media.

GETTING TO SCALE WITH THE NEW
SOCIAL OF SCIENCE

GSCC takes small steps in the direction of creating a natural – digital – pathway between doing the work, improving the work, growing the relevant data, scaling the work, advancing the field, and ultimately innovating education as a whole – through the Guided Digital Environment.

Scaling Innovation

There is a good deal of work on scaling innovation[7] including Dede (2005) on innovation in education. Dede proposes five elements of scaling:

1. *Depth*: Changing classroom practice, teachers' beliefs, norms of social interaction, and pedagogical principles as enacted in the curriculum.
2. *Sustainability*: Maintaining those changes over time.
3. *Spread*: Diffusion of the innovation to large numbers of classrooms and schools.
4. *Shift*: Districts, schools, and teachers assuming ownership of the innovation and spreading its impact.
5. *Evolution*: Ongoing revision of the innovation by those adapting it.

We think these are appropriate measures for testing the adoption of both the GSCC Pedagogy Framework and the GSCC Guided Digital Environment. Yet we still need the mechanisms to accomplish these ends. We suggest that that social media and cloud computing can be applied to great benefit, particularly when deployed in the context of developmental education teacher certification.

Faculty who teach developmental education classes do some of the hardest work in education. They should be rewarded more appropriately and they should be certified to teach in this highly challenging and complex environment. But certification in a digital world is a very different thing than what we are accustomed to. Certification is an integrated process that takes place in context and community, is self-reflective and faculty driven, is ongoing, contributes to a larger body of knowledge, and is based on actual outcomes of student learning. In short, participation in a Guided Digital Environment as described in this chapter lays the foundation for what faculty could be required to do to be certified to teach developmental education.

If, as we posit above, the innovation process will increasingly be one of the interactivity and dialogue, the platform for faculty engagement will be permanently altered. Currently, research on the scholarship of teaching, assessment of student learning outcomes, and professional development activities occur in separate spheres. Each sphere is established by an individual faculty member or by a department at one college, creating new activities in their own classroom or their own department, evaluating the innovations themselves, and, if the innovation appears to be successful, writing in journals or presenting the information at professional conferences. This industrial model of creation and dissemination of effective processes is slow, uneven, and discontinuous.

Social media allows for a rich combination of these three elements. What we have begun to see in the process of GSCC is that faculty who are themselves engaged not only in innovation and assessment of their own classes but in dialogue with other faculty, and able to create evaluative criteria (tags, identification of themes, and linkage of student success to these strategies or combinations of these strategies) put the creation and dissemination of innovation on steroids. Moreover, with social media, the adoption and adaptation of innovations by faculty *outside* of the original innovators can not only add student data but an ongoing meta-analysis of the growing collection of individual faculty member's own practice provides unprecedented insight into basic skills pedagogy. As faculty not only learn via social media but also through reflection on their own performance, the practice of professional development moves from static to a dynamic process that is anchored by evidence of effectiveness.

Going for the "Epic Win": Linking Scientists, Practitioners,
Students and Data

Laurillard's learning theory (2002, 2008a, 2008c) posits that effective teaching and learning are fundamentally about "conversation," specifically conversation catalyzed by technology. The process of conversation is amplified in her theory as cycles of iteration, reflection, and practice that incorporate personalization, flexibility, inclusion, and productivity. We believe that this is where we must situate the larger conversation on college completion work. That conversation, by necessity, must be of the 21st century kind – a combination of people to people, human to computer (HCI), and data to data interactions. To achieve the ambitious goal of doubling the number of college graduates, we must lock arms with scientists and practitioners far afield from education and seek their expertise in pursuit of addressing this critical national interest.

> [we]must engage in more direct partnerships among schools, the academy and commercial firms to advance a more effective educational R&D enterprise. (Bryk, 2007, p. 11)

An entirely new class of databases related to college completion is now possible – "large archives of naturalistically created behavioral data" (Albanese, 2010). For example, we can imagine a database that results from a simple thumbs up thumbs down count on student success as indicated by grades. We can think of clickers in the hands of every basic skills student and faculty capturing critical data in real time, or a hand held device or an application for their mobiles phones to provide a steady stream of data. This *is* within our grasp.

In his essay, "Applying Technology To Make A Difference," Jonathan Fanton (n.d.), then President of the MacArthur Foundation suggested "how a range of technologies – both simple and complex – might amplify or enhance the work of grantees in all our fields of work"(p. 4).

- They improve the quality of information and analysis by combining new techniques for gathering, processing, and storing data.
- They make good information widely available to the public, often from or in remote places.
- They facilitate citizen engagement by improving the ability to communicate.

When the conversation on doubling the numbers occurs at the scale of massively multiplayer games we will have what is known as an "epic win."[8]

In tangible terms, this means bringing together an aggressive agenda of social media utilization and sophisticated applications of computational social science for the breakthrough on college completion we so desperately need.[9] The goal is not as far-off as it seems. Indeed, it is underway, online, today, at GSCC. And the faculty have not even been at it for an entire semester.

NOTE

1. *Recommender systems* – A driving principle behind recommender systems is: instead of the user seeking for information, the appropriate information is "finding" the user. The power of recommender systems is based on the effective utilization of the voluminous data, in order to "fill in the blanks" (Labbi, n.d.).

2. Gartner, Inc. is an information technology research and advisory company.

3. Social Media "a group of Internet-based applications that build on the ideological and technological foundations of Web 2.0, and that allow the creation and exchange of user-generated content" (Social media, n.d.).

4. "Folksonomy is the result of personal free tagging of information and objects (anything with a URL) for one's own retrieval" (Vander Wal, 2007).

5. Tagging is a nonhierarchical keyword or term, usually user-defined, assigned to information such as a bookmark, digital image, or computer file (Tag (metadata), n.d.).

6. Complex Adaptive System – fluidly changing collections of distributed interacting components that react to both their environments and to one another. Examples of complex adaptive systems include the electric power grid, telecommunications networks, the Internet, biological systems, ecological systems, social groups, and even human society itself. Many of the multidisciplinary and interdisciplinary problems found within these systems are of such great complexity

that traditional modeling methodologies are often considered inadequate (Macal & Hummel, n.d.).

7. For instance: Dede, Honan, and Peters (2005), Dede (2009), Roschelle, Tatar, Shechtman, and Knudsen (2008), Schaffhauser (2009), and Schneider and McDonald (2006).

8. An "epic win" is an outcome so positive that, before it was achieved, you could not imagine was even possible (McGonigal, 2010).

9. "Computational social science" represents a turn toward the use of large archives of naturalistically created behavioral data. These data come from a variety of places, including popular social web services like Facebook and Twitter, consumer services like Amazon or Netflix, weblog and email archives, mobile telephone networks, or even custom-built sensor networks. What these data have in common is that they grow as byproducts of people's everyday lives. People email, shop, and talk for their own reasons, without thinking about how the *digital traces* of their activity provide naturalistic data for social scientists (Albanese, 2010).

REFERENCES

AERA. (2010). 2010 AERA annual meeting theme: Understanding complex ecologies in a changing world. Available at http://www.aera.net/Default.aspx?id = 7588. Retrieved on June 22.

Albanese, E. (2010), Scaling social science with Hadoop [Web log post]. Available at http://www.cloudera.com/blog/2010/04/scaling-social-science-with-hadoop/. Retrieved on June 22.

Bryk, A. (2007). *Ruminations on reinventing an R & D capacity for educational improvement* [PDF document]. Prepared for the American Enterprise Institute Conference on October 25, 2007. Available at http://www.nekia.org/files/20071024_Bryk.pdf. Retrieved on June 22, 2010.

Clark, J. E., & Enyon, B. (2009). EPortfolios at 2.0 – surveying the field. *Peer Review, 11*(1), 18–23.

Dede, C. (2005). Scaling up: Evolving innovations beyond ideal settings to challenging contexts of practice. In: R. K. Sawyer (Ed.), *The Cambridge handbook of learning sciences* (pp. 551–556). New York: Cambridge University Press.

Dede, C. (2009). Using technology to scale up innovations. *T.H.E. Journal*. Available at http://thejournal.com/articles/2009/05/06/using-technology-to-scale-up-innovations.aspx. Retrieved on June 22, 2010.

Dede, C., Honan, J. P., & Peters, L. C. (Eds). (2005). *Scaling up success: Lessons learned from technology-based educational improvement*. Indianapolis: Jossey-Bass.

Fanton, J. (n.d.) *Applying technology to make a difference*. In *President's Essay*. Available at http://www.macfound.org/site/c.jjJYJcMNIqE/b.2000011/k.F477/Applying_Technology_To_Make_A_Difference.htm. Retrieved on June 22, 2010.

FitzPatrick, M. A., & Spiller, D. (2010). The teaching portfolio: institutional imperative or teacher's personal journey? *Higher Education Research & Development, 29*(2), 167–178.

Gartner (n.d). Special report: Pattern-based strategy. Available at http://www.gartner.com/technology/research/reports/pattern-based-strategy.jsp. Retrieved on June 22, 2010.

Huber, M. T. (2008). The promise of faculty inquiry for teaching and learning basic skills. Available at http://www.carnegiefoundation.org/publications/promise-faculty-inquiry-teaching-and-learning-basic-skills. Retrieved on June 22, 2010.

Johnson, M. (2010). *This book is overdue: How librarians and Cybrarians can save us all.* New York: HarperCollins.

Keitt, T. J., Burris, P., & Ashour, M. (2010). Business web 2.0 buyer profile 2010: Web 2.0 technologies find internal and external roles in firms. Available at http://www.forrester.com/rb/Research/business_web_20_buyer_profile_2010/q/id/56764/t/2?cm_mmc = Forrester-_-RSS-_-Document-_-19&src = RSS_2. Retrieved on June 22.

Koch, M., & Fusco, J. (2008). Designing for growth: Enabling communities of practice to develop and extend their work online. In: C. Kimble & P. Hildreth (Eds), *Communities of practice: Creating learning environments for educators* (Vol. 2, pp. 1–23). Charlotte, NC: Information Age Publishing.

Labbi, A. (n.d.). Recommender systems for sales & marketing. Available at http://www.zurich.ibm.com/mcs/infoanalytics/marketing_sales.html. Retrieved on June 22, 2010.

Laurillard, D. (2002). *Rethinking university teaching: A conversational framework for the effective use of learning technologies.* London: Routledge/Falmer.

Laurillard, D. (2008a). *Digital Technologies and their role in achieving our ambitions for education.* London: Institute of Education, University of London.

Laurillard, D. (Ed.) (2008b). Open teaching: The key to sustainable and effective open education. In: *Opening up education: The collective advancement of education through open technology, open content, and open knowledge.* Cambridge, MA: MIT Press.

Laurillard, D. (2008c). The teacher as action researcher: Using technology to capture pedagogic form. *Studies in Higher Education, 33*(2), 139–154.

Leadbeater, C. (2008). *We-Think: Mass innovation, not mass production.* London: Profile Books.

Lichtenstein, S. & Swatman, P. (2003). *Sustainable knowledge management systems: Integration, personalisation and contextualisation.* Available at http://is2.lse.ac.uk/asp/aspecis/20030083.pdf. Retrieved on June 22, 2010.

Macal, C. M. & Hummel, J. (n.d.). Complex adaptive systems. Available at http://www.dis.anl.gov/exp/cas/index.html. Retrieved on June 22, 2010.

McGonigal, J. (2010). Gaming can make a better world. *TED Talks.* Podcast Available at http://www.ted.com/talks/jane_mcgonigal_gaming_can_make_a_better_world.html. Retrieved on June 30.

Restler, S. G., & Woolis, D. D. (2007). Actors and factors: Virtual communities for social innovation. *The Electronic Journal of Knowledge Management, 5*(1), 89–96.

Roschelle, J., Tatar, D., Shechtman, N., & Knudsen, J. (2008). The role of scaling up research in designing for and evaluating robustness. *Educational Studies in Mathematics, 68*(2), 149–170.

Schaffhauser, D. (2009). Scale. *T.H.E. Journal, 36*(6), 30–36.

Schlager, M., & Fusco, J. (2004). Teacher professional development, technology, and communities of practice: Are we putting the cart before the horse? In: S. Barab, R. Kling & J. Gray (Eds), *Designing for virtual communities in the service of learning* (pp. 120–153). Cambridge, UK: Cambridge University Press.

Schneider, B., & McDonald, S.-K. (Eds). (2006). *Scale up in education; Volume 1: Ideas in Principle, and Volume 2: Issues in Practice.* Blue Ridge Summit, PA: Rowman & Littlefield Publishers, Inc.

Social media (n.d.). In Wikipedia, the free encyclopedia. Available at http://en.wikipedia.org/ wiki/Social_media. Retrieved June 22, 2010.

Tag (metadata) (n.d.). In Wikipedia, the free encyclopedia. Available at http://en.wikipedia.org/ wiki/Tag_(metadata). Retrieved on June 22, 2010.

Vander Wal, T. (2007). Folksonomy. Available at http://vanderwal.net/folksonomy.html. Retrieved on June 22, 2010.

Weinberger, D. (2008). *Everything is miscellaneous.* New York: Holt.

Woolis, D., Restler, S., & Thayer, Y. (2008). Education leadership for a networked world. In: P. Hildreth & C. Kimble (Eds), *Communities of practice: Creating learning environments for educators* (Vol. 2, pp. 45–65). Charlotte, NC: Information Age Publishing.

ENHANCING IN-CLASS PARTICIPATION IN A WEB 2.0 WORLD

Steve Rhine and Mark Bailey

ABSTRACT

Previous research has demonstrated that students' participation in class is an important factor in their learning; yet, significant barriers exist to all students' participation during whole group discussions. These barriers include dynamics related to class size and available time as well as personal dimensions such as gender, age, and learning preferences. The emergence of new forms of social media can help break down those barriers by enabling collaborative construction of understanding. The present study examined whether the concurrent use of a shared learning document during class might provide a means of enhancing participation and learning. Because of the natural tendency of students' attention to wander over time, the study examined whether providing a parallel learning and sharing space might serve to "focus distraction" in productive ways. During graduate and undergraduate courses in two different universities, the authors used a single Google document, open to every class member. Analysis of these collaborative documents and their use are described, along with student self-reports and videotapes. Data indicate that this approach created the type of participatory space we intended. Its use often broadened the numbers of students involved and

Educating Educators with Social Media
Cutting-edge Technologies in Higher Education, Volume 1, 303–325
Copyright © 2011 by Emerald Group Publishing Limited
All rights of reproduction in any form reserved
ISSN: 2044-9968/doi:10.1108/S2044-9968(2011)0000001018

increased the quality of spoken and virtual conversations as students negotiated meaning. When attention began to drift, the shared document created new opportunities for students to stay focused and explore course content through its use as an alternative back-channel. This approach also facilitated self-differentiation, as students determined which mix of available media best met their needs.

The opportunity to articulate one's thinking, formulate questions, and negotiate meaning with other students and the professor are essential features of the learning process. Some professors have gone to great lengths to get students involved, including awarding points for participation and bribing them with extra credit (Boniecki & Moore, 2003; Foster et al., 2009; Sommer & Sommer, 2007). Yet, given the time constraints of a class, a limited number of people can usually participate in whole group discussions. Furthermore, not every student is comfortable interjecting their thoughts into conversations nor creating coherent, reasoned, and well-evidenced arguments instantaneously. The dawn of Web 2.0, in which the Internet has become a medium for anyone to not only acquire information but also to contribute content, has transformed the Internet into a space for social engagement. One type of Web 2.0 social media tool, collaborative software such as Google Docs (http://docs.google.com), capitalizes on this environment by allowing all students to write simultaneously on a single, collective document. This tool has the power to transform the nature of class participation in higher education.

The authors represent two different universities at which they have used Google Docs in graduate and undergraduate classrooms for the past four years. In this chapter, we describe our experience of students participating and negotiating meaning in a virtual parallel space simultaneously with whole-class lecture and discussion. We also introduce the concept of "focused distraction," discuss multitasking in the classroom, self-differentiated learning, explain the potential that collaborative software has for maximizing participation in higher education classes, and provide qualitative research data on our students' experience. We begin with a discussion of the participation dynamic in the classroom.

OBSTACLES TO PARTICIPATION

As long as there have been students in classrooms, teachers have concerned themselves with getting those students to participate. Instructors have many reasons for encouraging participation including stimulating thinking and as a way of holding students accountable for information (Jones, 2008). When students are actively involved in their learning, they develop stronger critical thinking skills (Ewens, 2000; Garside, 1996; McKeachie, 1990), increase their retention of information (Bransford, 1979), develop appreciation for diverse perspectives (Brookfield & Preskill, 1999), and develop different levels of thinking (Brookfield, 1995; Steen, Bader, & Kubrin, 1999). Research also finds that increasing students' willingness to ask questions or offer comments in class is likely to enhance their intellectual development (Fassinger, 1995). Overall, "substantial evidence suggests that students learn more when they are actively engaged with the material, their instructor, and their classmates" (Howard, James, & Taylor, 2002, p. 214).

However, studies also indicate that a number of barriers to participation exist. First, classes are social constructions. Even though they have a short duration, they have qualities such as beliefs, leaders, and norms that can influence students' participation in class (Fassinger, 1997). Norms of discourse determine who participates and who does not (Sykes, 1990), whether students feel comfortable disagreeing with the instructor or other students, and establishing what kinds of questions are acceptable (Hirschy & Wilson, 2002). One such norm in a typical college classroom is the "consolidation of responsibility" (Howard et al., 2002; Karp & Yoels, 1976), or the phenomenon in which a few students take on the responsibility for most of the participation in class. Typically, only 6–12% of a class accounts for the majority of interactions in a class session (Crombie, Pyke, Silverthorn, Jones, & Piccinin, 2003; Weaver & Qi, 2005). Other students are often content to allow that consolidation to take place to relieve them of the social dynamics of participation or intellectual engagement.

Besides the domination of class conversation by a few, there are other significant barriers to participation in class. For instance, researchers have engaged in considerable discussion regarding the potential role that gender may play in limiting class participation. Some studies suggest that there can be a "chilly climate" in classrooms in which women are discouraged from participating because of gender bias in pedagogy or the socialization of girls and women (Hall & Sandler, 1982; Sandler, Silverberg, & Hall, 1996). Although some researchers assert there is little evidence this type of atmosphere exists extensively in higher education (Howard & Henney, 1998; Drew & Work, 1998; Howard et al., 2002), others report that characteristics of a "chilly climate" do exist in college classrooms (Janz & Pyke, 2000; Sands, 1998; Stalker & Prentice, 1998; Whitt, Edison, Pascarella, Nora, & Terenzini, 1999). For example, there are findings that females may participate in greater percentages but that males speak more frequently in class, interrupt more often, and have longer interactions with instructors (Crombie et al., 2003). Factors that may affect female participation include class size, male/female mix in the classroom, and class subject matter (Seifried, 2000). Aleman (1998) contends that women can be particularly concerned with how others in the class view them. Therefore, instead of participating in class, they may engage in thoughtful discussion and critique outside of class with friends, outside the purview of their teachers. Aleman suggests that breaking women's classroom silence requires faculty to create "a safe space in a climate of challenges, critique, and reflection" (p. 7).

Research also suggests that the age of students and size of class can be significant factors in participation. Specifically, in mixed-age classrooms, twice as many nontraditional students (age 25 or over) participate than traditional students and they contribute up to three times as much to a discussion (Fritschner, 2000; Howard & Baird, 2000; Howard et al., 2002). When students are in smaller classes, they are almost twice as likely to talk than in larger classes (52–29%) and five times as likely to make two or more comments (Fassinger, 1995; Howard, Short, & Clark, 1996). Fassinger (1996) found that smaller classes "increase the likelihood that all students may become verbally involved" (p. 31).

Howard et al. (2002) researched students' perspectives and propose that the only thing that really counts in regard to participation is who talks and who does not. Talkers believed that students were responsible for taking an active role in their own learning. They had a greater awareness of how they personally benefitted from participating: "I learn more when I participate" (p. 224). On the contrary, nontalkers gave some of the following as their reasons for nonparticipation (p. 226):

- "[because] of the chance I would appear unintelligent to the instructor/ other students."
- "My ideas are not well enough formulated."
- "I didn't do the readings."
- "I am shy."
- "The class is too large."
- "I don't like to talk in front of a bunch of people."

Whereas talkers were more likely to believe instructors gave them enough time and opportunity to ask questions or make comments, nontalkers said they needed more time to think to put their thoughts, ideas, or questions together before they participated in discussion. Although there is not a clear cause and effect, talkers regarded their professors more positively and had a more favorable view of their classroom experience than nontalkers (Crombie et al., 2003).

In summary, research has established that students' participation in class is an important factor in their learning, but there are significant barriers to all students participating in a class session. These barriers may include dynamics related to gender, age, class size, and orientation to the class. However, most of the research tends to focus upon the composition of the actively participating group or why students with particular characteristics are not part of that group. It is implied that the true issue is who gets to be in that 6–12% of talkers. However, this focus seems to ignore the most significant constraint, which is time. Perhaps there is really no time in a class to include more than 6–12% of students in a discussion. If a class is to progress, everyone cannot have their chance to contribute their thinking to a class discussion, unless there was an innovative means of expanding the temporal and participatory constraints that limit discussion.

THE COLLABORATIVE SOFTWARE TOOL

Technology is becoming ubiquitous in college classrooms as a greater number of students bring their laptops to class. Some professors are fighting this trend (McWilliams, 2005) and some are embracing it and looking for opportunities. Social media creates one of those opportunities for the classroom. In the Web 2.0 world, users can create and control content on the Internet. "Read/write" tools are now available to support the collaborative construction of ideas and they have significant implications for learning.

Since the 1980s, wikis, such as Wikipedia, have allowed anyone to manipulate the content of a webpage. However, much like a class discussion, wikis allow only one person at a time to actively engage in the conversation; a wiki is only changed asynchronously. That is, only one person can write in a document at a time. Only after they write and save can the next person contribute. Professors have been creative in using wikis for teaching, such as using a wiki as the textbook for a course (Havenstein, 2007), creating learning communities, and developing writing (Cummings & Barton, 2008). A blog also takes advantage of the capability of users to create content. It is growing in popularity as an instructional tool for the college course (Downes, 2004; Higdon & Topaz, 2009) as well as for scholarly musings (Glenn, 2003). A blog is often used for students to reflect on class content or course readings individually or as a discussion space. These tools help promote a new "architecture of participation" that centers on student-created content (Doolan, 2010; O'Reilly, 2004; Wheeler, Yeomans, & Wheeler, 2008).

Relatively new to the social media scene are collaborative document editing tools such as Google Docs. Unlike blogs and wikis, collaborative software has not been previously considered as a potential tool for the classroom as a dynamic, synchronous location for student contributions. The potential of this tool for simultaneous conversation was demonstrated initially at an Emerging Technologies Conference in 2003 during a speaker's presentation. Tim O'Reilly organized the conference and observed,

The potential of this tool for simultaneous conversation was demonstrated initially at an Emerging Technologies Conference in 2003 during a speaker's presentation. Tim O'Reilly organized the conference and observed that the electronic back-channel is changing our culture. The ability to comment and bring in new information like that enriches the experience, making it more immersive. The blending of physical and electronic world experiences is going to be a salient change. (Rhine & Bailey, 2008)

In a Google Doc (http://docs.google.com), people can work synchronously in the same classroom or across the world to create and edit a document. Users easily make use of the typical word processing format and functionality such as manipulating text, adding images, and creating weblinks. As it is web-based, it operates seamlessly across Macs, PCs, and portable devices that allow Web access (such as Blackberries and iPhones). This type of collaborative tool makes unique approaches to instruction possible and has the potential to influence the participation dynamic in the classroom (Bailey & Rhine, 2008).

Before exploring our experience with how Google Docs influence the participation dynamic in our classroom, we examine the literature base that informs our thoughts and goals for participation. Three frames of reference guide our thinking on the use of collaborative software in the classroom: social construction of knowledge, the power of student explanation, and the role of multitasking in learning.

PARTICIPATION AS SOCIAL CONSTRUCTION OF KNOWLEDGE

Students do not simply make carbon copies in their minds of information presented to them. The context, culture, and form of activity in which students' engage influence their learning (Lave & Wenger, 1991). Social construction of knowledge assumes that every concept or "reality" is dynamic because we each use our own subjective frame of reference to interpret information gathered from interaction directly with others or indirectly with media (Vygotsky, 1978). However, meaning making in a classroom is not a solitary act, regardless of a student's level of participation. Students test ideas with others and reflect on information they encounter, trying to resolve the disorder and incongruity between their prior knowledge and what is new. Every resulting construction of ideas is therefore unique because of the way it is framed by past and present interactions with media and other individuals. Therefore, the way students participate in class, engaging with content and others' perspectives, impacts the meaning they construct.

Participation in a classroom is not sought simply to hear other voices talking. In the classroom, the professor seeks students' construction of meaning or "intersubjectivity" – a sense of common understanding with students. A student's prior knowledge, understanding, and experience meet with the professor's knowledge and goals for the student's understanding somewhere in the space between the two. Ogden (1999) describes this space as the "analytic third," which is the jointly created, unconscious life of an idea that is negotiated between the analytic pair. In the process of negotiating meaning, the professor must recognize the "differences that the individuals, as unique 'collections' of subjectivities and positionings, bring to the situation" (p. 137). The greater the diversity of perspectives students encounter in the process of negotiating that meaning, the richer and more comprehensive that meaning becomes.

Furthermore, one of the goals of participation is to have students explain their thinking. Research supports that objective. Students who explain their reasoning must evaluate their comprehension of an idea, organize their thinking, and then clarify it in their minds before trying to make it understandable to others (Bargh & Schul, 1980; Mayer, 1984; Wittrock, 1990). Through this process, students typically identify gaps in their thinking, seek to fill those gaps, and make more coherent connections between their prior learning and the new information they encounter. Students can be more effective than a teacher in communicating a concept in class to their peers (Noddings, 1985). They may use vocabulary of a shared language that facilitates other students' understanding. However, explanations must have certain characteristics to increase learning. They must be "(a) relevant to the target student's need for help, (b) timely, (c) correct, and (d) sufficiently elaborated to enable the target student to correct his or her misconception or lack of understanding (i.e., detailed explanations, not just the answer)" (Webb, Farivar, & Mastergeorge, 2002, p. 14).

Collaborative software can create that participatory space for explaining and constructing meaning in the classroom. In a whole classroom discussion, the professor typically engages with one individual at a time with questions and thoughts in the hope the whole class benefits from each conversation and discussion of meaning. It is unclear whether that hope is realized in the classroom when so few have the opportunity to participate. How much does a student benefit when they are not the one explaining their thinking and negotiating meaning? In contrast, a Google Doc establishes a "back channel" or parallel discussion space during class that allows every student to "talk" and negotiate the language being used and how closely it represents the concept. The collaborative software environment is dynamic, in that one student can write something and another student can change that sentence. As students socially construct meaning, they often explain their rationale to alter a communally constructed sentence or paragraph. This may include explanations of their confusion and posing of new questions because students may feel less vulnerable in an anonymous, collaborative, working space. Professors can also enter that space to clarify and assess how close the negotiated meaning is to his or her intended meaning.

As noted earlier, research suggests that two primary barriers to negotiating meaning in class are time and class size. A collaborative document can mitigate the constraints of both time and space by allowing all to "talk" simultaneously. Furthermore, in the typical class structure, once a topic has been discussed, the moment is gone for a student to participate. A Google Doc provides the opportunity for students who need more time to think about what they want to say to take as long as they need – in minutes or days – before contributing to the conversation. The barrier to participation identified earlier, "My ideas are not well enough formulated," is addressed because there are no temporal limits to engaging in the social construction of knowledge and meaning. We also know from research the powerful effects that wait time has on participation in the classroom (Rowe, 1987; Van Zee, Iwasyk, Kurose, Simpson, & Wild, 2001). When students have at least three seconds to think, they provide longer responses, give more supportive evidence for their arguments, more students participate, and students raise more questions. Use of collaborative software has the potential to maximize the effect of wait time.

In using a Google Doc, the instructor has the choice of whether to allow students to be anonymous in the discussion. Although there are dangers when students do not have ownership of their words, such as discriminatory comments, there also can be benefits. Contributions lose the power of the person and magnify the power of the idea. A number of barriers to participation identified earlier relate to complications based on who is talking: "I don't like to talk in front of a bunch of people," "[because] of the chance I would appear unintelligent," "I am shy," and issues of gender and age. In a sense, the conversation on a Google Doc can be "purer" – potentially erasing a "chilly climate" for women to contribute, broadening rather than consolidating responsibility for participation, and allowing students to contribute without having to overcome social dynamics in the classroom. Of course, use of Google Docs does not imply a professor can neglect creating a trusting environment for conversation in the class. As with all classroom or online communities, trust is a critical dimension that contributes to the sense of safety. That sense helps members "expose gaps in their learning and feel that other members of the community will respond in supportive ways" (Rovai, 2002, p. 5). Professors will want to be as thoughtful in establishing principles for safe conversation online as they do for face-to-face.

MULTITASKING THAT CONTRIBUTES TO LEARNING

When we began this use of collaborative software, we had initial concerns about our students' comfort and capability to multitask during class. Would they be able to manage the online environment while simultaneously engaging face-to-face with the professor and peers and would this detract or contribute to their learning? Recent research on multitasking indicates that it can result in superficial learning (Foerde, Knowlton, & Poldrack, 2006; Gorlick, 2009; Wolpert, 2006). The cognitive demands of a task may overload the processing capacity of a student's brain (Clark, 1999; Sweller, 1999). However, there is also research that finds individuals have different tolerances for multitasking, that they respond differently to the cognitive demands, and that people can learn to multitask more effectively (De la Casa, Gordillo, Mejias, Rangel, & Romero, 1998; Ishizaka, Marshall, & Conte, 2001; Richards, Bennett, & Sekuler, 2006; Riding, Grimley, Dahraei, & Banner, 2003). For instance, type A individuals are comfortable with and capable of focusing their attention on one element of their environment to remember details in a task, while ignoring information that interferes with their performance. In contrast, type B individuals are less capable and comfortable ignoring competing information and struggle to focus on either stimulus. In other words, if you look at individuals by type, some individuals have the skills to multitask by focusing their primary attention on one task while simultaneously thinking about another task with lower quality. Others cannot multitask effectively and can only focus on one task at a time. Although it is the case that the learners in our classrooms bring differing constellations of preferences and abilities, the digital generation appears to manifest an increasing comfort with multitasking in many aspects of their lives (Montgomery, 2009). Furthermore, much of the multitasking research requires people to engage in cognitively divergent tasks such as counting beeps while simultaneously learning to sort cards. However, we were curious about what might happen if the tasks were related to each other. If students engage in multiple cognitive activities that are focused on related material, could it actually enhance learning?

Although there are individual differences in the perceptual preferences and comfort levels associated with varied modes of acquiring information, we know that after a period of time spent focusing on material in class, students' attention will begin to drift as the brain seeks alternative stimulation. Research suggests that students may need these "drift times" as coping mechanisms that serve as "mini-rejuvenating respites" (Simplicio, 2001, p. 199). The brain can become cognitively overloaded. We have a limited ability to process material and each person has a different overload point (Mayer & Moreno, 2003).

Therefore, one of our premises is that "focusing students' distraction" on the Google Doc might provide that respite from auditory input (lecture or class discussion) while productively engaging them in content in a different form (visual or text-based). That multitasking on a relevant theme might help students maximize their learning capacity rather than detracting from it by continually allowing them to seek the modality of input that is preferred and is most beneficial. Tomlinson describes differentiation as efforts to "respond to variance among learners in the classroom" (2000). We view focused distraction as the opportunity for students to continually differentiate their own instruction. The approach is also in line with a principle of universal design for learning; to "provide multiple, flexible methods of presentation" (Hall, Strangman, & Meyer, 2009). Students in our classes are free to choose whether or not to multitask with the collaborative software. They have the power to monitor their cognitive load and self-differentiate instruction by attending to whole class or online interactions, or to both – whichever medium or combination of media is the most useful in helping them construct an understanding.

USING COLLABORATIVE SOFTWARE
IN THE CLASSROOM

Our goal is to maximize students' engagement in the content of our classes as a means of fostering learning. Accordingly, we often use small group work, project-based learning, and other means of capturing students' interest and challenging them to develop sophisticated and rich understanding of concepts. While collaborative software can certainly be a useful tool in those contexts, we focus here upon the times in which whole class instruction is appropriate and necessary to help students construct meaning. In our experience, whole class instruction can often lead to a confining Question–Answer–Evaluation cycle (Freebody, Ludwig, & Gunn, 1995), with a single student participating with an answer. Research indicates that this type of interaction tends to support learning at lower levels of Bloom's taxonomy (1956). In using collaborative software, our intent is to achieve continual, high levels of engagement and thinking by the entire class.

Students have varying access to technology at our institutions, so, depending on the situation, we can rely on students bringing laptops or we bring in a mobile laptop cart when we want to use Google Docs in class. As Google Docs is web-based, we do not need to worry about platform issues or additional software. The professor has the option to start a document by "inviting" students by e-mail or simply provide a class e-mail and password that all students can use to access the document. When students are invited individually, their contributions to the document will not be anonymous, as the document is automatically saved every 15 seconds with an indication of who has contributed. The professor and students can therefore view the history and responsible party for revisions to the document. If a professor chooses to use a single e-mail, he or she has the option of whether to have students identify themselves in the document or keep it anonymous. One of the frustrations of using Google Docs is that words can get lost if two or more students type in the same place and one saves before the other. However, once students understand the behavior of the document, they are typically patient or else they choose not to contribute.

Data for this study were gathered across two academic years. A range of students participated including part-time and full-time, graduate and undergraduate, with ages from 21 to 57 at two liberal arts universities in the northwest United States. Classes typically consisted of between 15 and 25 students. To triangulate our results, we analyzed the collaborative software documents students created in class, a Collaborative Software Implementation Survey, and videotape of classroom instruction. Surveys were distributed to students on the last day of class, and we used class time to encourage them to provide us with feedback. Thirty-three students responded to the survey that asked 14 questions about their experience of using the Google Doc in the classroom. On two occasions, we positioned a video camera in the rear of the classroom. This allowed us to observe students interacting on their computers as a means of learning more about how they were participating on the Google Doc.

RESULTS OF OUR STUDY

Use of the collaborative software varied significantly across the broad range of our students. Similar to the participation research on "consolidation of responsibility," video analysis revealed that we generally had a group of about four to eight students who consistently contributed to the Google Doc. However, about half of the students contributed something during a course, including those who did not have a laptop but told a partner what to type in the document. Furthermore, another third of the class read the document occasionally. Typically, about half of the students who normally took on the "consolidation of responsibility" in whole class discussions also contributed significantly to the Google Doc, thereby straddling both worlds. Given the range of ages in our classes, it was apparent that younger students tended to be the ones participating most with the document. The extent to which students used the Google Doc also varied across courses. Some classes developed a culture in which they actively used it throughout a course while others used it sporadically. Upon examination of the Google Documents created in our classes (e.g., Fig. 1), we noted two categories of implementation that emerged: collaborative construction of class notes and focused distraction.

Collaborative Note Construction

Students used collaborative software first and foremost as a place for notes during class. As intended, they negotiated the completeness and accuracy of the information by arguing for ways of phrasing information as well as extending the discussion into new areas of thought such as the potential male bias of Kohlberg (Fig. 1). Images such as that of Piaget, continuums, hierarchies, and graphical representations were cut and pasted from the Internet to enrich the notes. In the survey, one student noted,

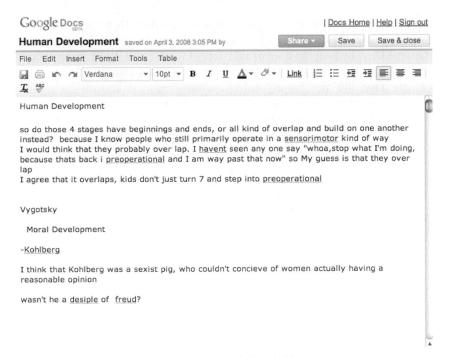

Fig. 1. Example of Google Doc.

"The positive attribute of this collaborative note taking is that it helps in ensuring that you won't miss a key point. It helps make sure that the notes taken are the whole jist (sic) of the lecture without gaps that one person may have in their own personal notes." An additional benefit of the Google Doc was the ability of students to participate synchronously or asynchronously from home if they were not physically able to attend class. Another student commented, "I was absent one day and I was able to get on our class document and read what was going on in class from the comfort of my home. This was really helpful. I was able to keep up with class information."

In the surveys, a few students pointed out a disadvantage of using collaborative software, that is, some students could disengage and simply rely on the class-constructed notes. However, many students maintained their own set of notes while using the class notes to ensure they captured everything of importance. One student said, "This helps me in case I missed something, I can look at the document and see what others got and what I missed or even help out people who missed something as well. I use this (Google Doc) by keeping a set of side notes I work on in Word and just copy and paste as I get more." Analysis of the class notes also revealed that the Google Doc did not merely capture class-generated content, but often included much more of students' life experiences. Students felt free to embellish the notes with commentary of how the current class information related to their lives or perspectives. For example, when discussing how to create a positive classroom community, a side conversation began with a student posting the question, "Has anyone worked in a public kindergarten yet? How realistic is the model [we are discussing]? In a half day kindergarten class of twice as many students, with state standards to meet, how would one foster community and allow as much freedom among the students?"

Further examination of the collaborative documents and survey results demonstrated that it did create the type of participatory space we intended. Instead of fleeting moments of opportunity for individual students to contribute to a whole class discussion, students were able to use the Google Doc to hear multiple voices simultaneously, and the chance to contribute to the conversation never passed them by. Individuals used the collaborative document to ask questions, interpretations, or implications of the content without interrupting the flow of the verbal exchange in class. One student noted, "Nice to get feedback, that's why I post a question. It works because of the participation from classmates."

Initially, we did have concerns of losing the richness of a whole class conversation as a virtual back channel to class conversations might overtake the nonvirtual, decreasing face-to-face interaction, and increasing silence in the classroom while students communicated on the computers. However, with reasonable attention to both processes, this fear was not realized. Creating an opportunity for more students to participate and get their ideas out through the Google Doc often increased the quality of both conversations. A student explained that "being able to see what other people take for notes is helpful because it stimulates my thinking process and helps me think about things I wouldn't normally." Most students demonstrated the capability of moving between both worlds easily. Often, the two conversational spaces converged by students or the professor bringing a comment from one to the other. We monitor the Google Doc at different points during class, and therefore, we can raise points or questions established in the Google Doc. Students perform the same function. For instance, a student in a whole class discussion commented, "Someone wrote on the Google Doc that Piaget began as a biologist and that influenced his perspective on development. How do you think his theories were affected by a biologist's way of thinking?"

Focused Distraction

We define "focused distraction" as an opportunity for our students, who have a natural tendency to be distracted over time, to allow their minds to wander into class productive areas rather than unproductive areas. As discussed earlier, researchers know that our brains crave stimulation and our attention spans are considerably less than the length of a typical class. When students can participate in a parallel space, then they can be "on task" and learning about current class topics while having respite from the whole class focus. With students having laptops in class, they have the world's knowledge at their fingertips. Therefore, instead of seeing the Internet as a nemesis during class, we encouraged students to explore the present topic on the Web while we discussed it in class to enhance their learning and potentially enrich the learning of others. One of the nice features of class-created collaborative notes was that it was relatively easy for students who strayed from whole class discussion to explore relevant tangents and then return to the mainstream class topic in progress.

In analysis of the student-created collaborative documents, it was clear students took this encouragement to heart, as they included images, visual representations of theories, elaboration of ideas, and connections to other similar or contrasting topics in the notes. One student explained, "I search for more information on topics if it is unclear. I try and find a summary." Another commented, "every person we studied about I look their theories up on the net for supplemental information." In the document, students added notes such as "You can find a good explanation of Adler's theory at this website". This form of participation often created an atmosphere of a community working together to support each other's construction of meaning.

When we first began using Google Docs in class, there were times in which we felt we had lost the class to the other world. Apparently, more interesting things were being discussed and explored online than in class. In those instances, we either asked them to refocus their attention to the class or stopped trying to compete, took a moment to read the Google Doc, and then talked about those ideas in the larger forum. When we merged the virtual with the nonvirtual, students were interested to see how those ideas took shape in a different context. This crossover also tended to encourage students who may have only felt comfortable in the text discussion to contribute an already tested idea in the face-to-face discussion. Overall, we believe that the web of ideas and thoughts generated in the two worlds ultimately resulted in a broader range of thinking with a greater amount of student collaboration and participation.

Students' Experience

As part of our research into the effects of using collaborative documents during our classes, we surveyed students to determine whether they felt the Google Doc enhanced their learning experience. We initiated our survey with a question for students to self-report on their personality, given De la Casa et al.'s (1998) findings that there are differences in multitasking capabilities between type A and type B personalities. We asked students if they preferred multitasking, focusing on one thing at a time, or whether it depended on the situation. Our hypothesis was that students who preferred multitasking would be more comfortable with these tools. However, we found no correlation between this self-report and how students used these tools. For most students (63.6%), multitasking comfort depends on the nature of the task (Table 1). Therefore, use of collaborative software did not appear to favor individuals who expressed a particular modality preference.

Question no. 11 explored whether students felt that the Google Docs helped or hindered their learning. Overwhelmingly, students replied that the tool helped their learning (81.8%). However, a significant number of students also responded (question no. 4) that the Google Docs distracted them (54.5%). Most students (69.7%) did feel that reading the collaborative document was useful to their learning while participating by posting their thoughts to the class document (question no. 7) was "somewhat" or "very helpful" (48.5%). Finally, we asked students how they felt about our efforts to focus their distraction (question no. 9): "How engaging has it been for you to be encouraged to focus your distractions on course content?" Most students (69.7%) felt that the Google Doc did focus their distraction in an engaging way, and approximately 70% of students said they accessed relevant Internet content (question no. 8).

We also asked students to explain the thinking behind their responses. The following comments were from students who found the use of Google Docs helpful:

- It contributes to my learning and understanding because I am able to see points of view that add value. My classmates are able to make connections that I don't.

Table 1. Collaborative Software Implementation Survey.

1. Self-description	Prefer multi-tasking 18.2%	It depends 63.6%	Prefer one task 18.2%		
4. Class pages during class	Distracting 54.5%	Useful 30.3%	Did not respond 15.1%		
6. Reading posts of others	Not at all useful 0%	Not very useful 18.2%	Neutral 12.1%	Somewhat useful 43.9%	Very useful 25.8%
7. Posting comments	Not at all helpful 15.1%	Not very helpful 6.1%	Neutral 33.3%	Somewhat helpful 30.3%	Very helpful 18.2%
8. Explored relevant Internet content	Yes 69.7%	No 30.3%			
9. Focusing distraction	Not at all engaging 6.1%	Not very engaging 9.1%	Neutral 15.2%	Somewhat engaging 63.6%	Very engaging 6.1%
11. General response	Helps 81.8%	Hinders 3.0%	Did not respond 15.2%		

- It gives me something to do when I lose focus.
- It is nice because I am still on topic, but I can focus on something else for a little bit.
- It helps because if someone is unsure of something they (sic) can ask with no pressure. Also, examples can be given and we can bounce ideas off one another.
- It makes our notes so much better when everyone can contribute.
- I cannot always catch everything that is said and with the doc I can use what others know and heard.
- As there is so much content, having these relevant sites to look at on our own time gave me other perspectives to consider and things I had not considered to think about.
- It is really a cool tool because people can post things/info and other people can read it and edit something if it is not accurate.
- It also helps when I misunderstand something. It is normally written in a different way by someone.

The following comments are typical of those from students who did not find the use of Google Docs in class as helpful:

- Too many things coming into my brain at one time does not work for me.
- I get lost easily. If I drift or am distracted, I feel like I have missed something.
- I get a lot more from class if I am physically writing. Because we are typing, I did not feel I got everything out of each lesson as I could have if I were writing in a notebook.
- It is distracting because I start to do other things on the Internet.
- It is hard for me to listen and take in what the instructor or students are saying while typing or looking at the pages.
- I do not know if I trust all of the information that is put up there.
- I would rather take my own notes and have a verbal discussion. I hate computers.

Students also gave mixed feedback:

- I would say it is a bit of a distraction as there is Internet available and to be honest there are times when I completely zone out and surf online. However, I do think that the ability to exchange notes, communicate quickly, and without distractions is a wonderful tool to have. Using this, I have better notes, better reflections. Also, notes from other people's point of view.

In summary, some students did not like using the tool, but appreciated having the option to not participate in that way. Most students felt that using Google Docs in class was distracting at times, but helped them learn in class and supported their learning after class. In the surveys, students who chose to participate in the Google Doc confirmed our hypothesis that this tool helped them be more engaged in class, gave them access to ideas and conversations beyond class time constraints, and facilitated their construction of meaning.

CONCLUSION

Although collaborative software was not an effective tool for every student in our classes, it did broaden the type of participation and the numbers of students involved and encouraged students to extend and negotiate the meaning of course content. Our hope was that this back-channel would break down barriers to participation, particularly for those students who feel constrained from contributing in a whole class environment. The documents and surveys lead us to believe that we were partially successful on that front. However, providing an alternative participatory space did not necessarily help us achieve equitable distribution of student power in our classes. "Consolidation of responsibility" occurred as much with the Google Doc as it did with whole class interaction. In some ways, that was a positive feature, as there were students who took responsibility for organizing the notes in the Google Doc so that all the entries had some structure. However, it still raises concerns about who participates and wields power and influence over how ideas get negotiated. There were students who tended to dominate participation in whole class discussions that were also capable of working in both worlds simultaneously, thereby lessening the broadening of participation we intended. As in our whole class discussions, we occasionally needed to intervene in the collaborative document to encourage broader participation.

Yet, we do consider ourselves successful at creating new opportunities for participation with social media. Some individuals found this new participatory space more accessible to them than whole class discussions. "It helps with understanding by being able to ask questions anonymously without having to be ashamed of asking something dumb." Some students took advantage of the opportunity to use more time to develop their thoughts and added their ideas to the Google Doc a few minutes after a discussion had finished. In particular, many students found relevant and interesting connections and extensions on the Internet that enriched the collaborative notes. There were even students who typically dominate the discussion that expressed appreciation that they could hear the voices of students who do not normally contribute to class conversations. "It definitely helps my learning by providing a source to hear other's thoughts who may not feel comfortable sharing orally. It gives people the opportunity to voice their opinion or thoughts about subject matter anonymously without pressure of orally speaking in class."

As professors of higher education, our most important task is engaging students in learning. We look to social media not as the latest fad but as a potential vehicle to help us achieve our goals in the classroom. We are especially intrigued by the concept of focused distraction and negotiation of meaning in a parallel space during teaching and have come to believe that collaborative software moves us closer to maximizing student participation and engagement in learning.

REFERENCES

Aleman, A. M. (1998). Girlfriends talking. *About Campus, 2*(6), 4–8.
Bailey, M., & Rhine, S. (2008). Social collaboration and focused distraction: Sharing notes in our classroom. *Leading and Learning With Technology, 36*(4), 30–31.
Bargh, J., & Schul, Y. (1980). On the cognitive benefits of teaching. *Journal of Educational Psychology, 72*(5), 593–604.
Bloom, B. S. (1956). *Taxonomy of educational objectives, handbook I: The cognitive domain.* New York: David McKay Co Inc.
Boniecki, K. A., & Moore, S. (2003). Breaking the silence: Using a token economy to reinforce participation in a college classroom. *Teaching of Psychology, 30*, 224–227.
Bransford, J. D. (1979). *Human cognition: Learning, understanding and remembering.* Belmont, CA: Wadsworth.
Brookfield, S. D. (1995). *Becoming a critically reflective teacher.* San Francisco, CA: Jossey-Bass.
Brookfield, S. D., & Preskill, S. (1999). *Discussion as a way of teaching: Tools and techniques for democratic classrooms.* San Francisco: Jossey-Bass.
Clark, R. C. (1999). *Developing technical training.* Washington, DC: International Society for Performance Improvement.
Crombie, G., Pyke, S., Silverthorn, N., Jones, A., & Piccinin, S. (2003). Students' perceptions of their classroom participation and instructor as a function of gender and context. *The Journal of Higher Education, 74*(1), 51–76.
Cummings, R., & Barton, M. (2008). *Wiki writing: Collaborative learning in the college classroom.* Ann Arbor: University of Michigan Press and University of Michigan Library.
De la Casa, L. G., Gordillo, J. L., Mejias, L. J., Rangel, F., & Romero, M. F. (1998). Attentional strategies in Type A individuals. *Personality and Individual Differences, 24*, 59–69.

Doolan, M. A. (2010). Developing a Web 2.0 pedagogy to engage the net generation learner in a community for learning in higher education. *Proceedings of the 5th international blended learning conference 2010 (June)*. Hatfield, University of Hertfordshire, UK.

Downes, S. (2004). Educational blogging. *EDUCAUSE Review, 39*(5), 14–26.

Drew, T. L., & Work, G. G. (1998). Gender-based differences in perception of experiences in higher education: Gaining a broader perspective. *The Journal of Higher Education, 69*(5), 542–555.

Ewens, W. (2000). Teaching using discussion. In: R. Neff & M. Weimer (Eds), *Classroom communication: Collected readings for effective discussion and questioning* (pp. 21–26). Madison, WI: Atwood Publishing.

Fassinger, P. A. (1995). Understanding classroom interaction: Students' and professors' contributions to students' silence. *The Journal of Higher Education, 66*(1), 82–96.

Fassinger, P. A. (1996). Professors' and students' perceptions of why students participate in class. *Teaching Sociology, 24*(1), 25–33.

Fassinger, P. A. (1997). Classes are groups: Thinking sociologically about teaching. *College Teaching, 45*, 22–25.

Foerde, K., Knowlton, B., & Poldrack, R. (2006). Modulation of competing memory systems by distraction. *Proceedings of the National Academy of Science of the USA, 103*(3), 11778–11783.

Foster, L., Krohn, K., McCleary, D., Aspiranti, K., Nalls, M., Quillivan, C., Taylor, C., & Williams, R. (2009). Increasing low-responding students' participation in class discussion. *Journal of Behavioral Education, 18*(2), 173–188.

Freebody, P., Ludwig, C., & Gunn, S. (1995). *Everyday literacy practices in and out of schools in low socio-economic urban communities: A summary of a descriptive and interpretive research program*. Canberra: Commonwealth Department of Employment, Education, and Training.

Fritschner, L. M. (2000). Inside the undergraduate college classroom: Faculty and students differ on the meaning of student participation. *Journal of Higher Education, 71*, 342–362.

Garside, C. (1996). Look who's talking: A comparison of lecture and group discussion teaching strategies in developing critical thinking skills. *Communication Education, 45*, 212–227.

Glenn, D. (2003). Scholars who blog. *Chronicle of Higher Education, 49*(13), A14–A16.

Gorlick, A. (2009). Media multi-taskers pay mental price, Stanford study shows, August 24. *Stanford Report*. Available at http://news.stanford.edu/news/2009/august24/multitask-research-study-082409.html

Hall, R., & Sandler, B. (1982). *The classroom climate: A chilly one for women?* Washington, DC: Association of American Colleges.

Hall, T., Strangman, N., & Meyer, A. (2009). *Differentiated instruction and implications for UDL implementation* (Available at http://www.cast.org/publications/ncac/ncac_diffinstructudl.html. Retrieved on December 4, 2010). Wakefield, MA: National Center on Accessing the General Curriculum.

Havenstein, H. (2007). Wiki becomes textbook in Boston College classroom. *Computer World* (August 15). Available at http://www.computerworld.com/s/article/9030802/Wiki_becomes_textbook_in_Boston_College_classroom

Higdon, J., & Topaz, C. (2009). Blogs and wikis as instructional tools: A social software adaptation of just-in-time teaching. *College Teaching, 57*(2), 105–110.

Hirschy, A. S., & Wilson, M. E. (2002). The sociology of the classroom and its influence on student learning. *Peabody Journal of Education, 77*(3), 85–100.

Howard, J. R., & Baird, R. (2000). The consolidation of responsibility and students' definitions of the college classroom. *The Journal of Higher Education*, 71, 700–721.

Howard, J. R., & Henney, A. L. (1998). Student participation and instructor gender in the mixed age college classroom. *The Journal of Higher Education*, 69, 384–405.

Howard, J. R., James, G. H., & Taylor, D. R. (2002). The consolidation of responsibility in the mixed-age college classroom. *Teaching Sociology*, 30, 214–234.

Howard, J. R., Short, L. B., & Clark, S. M. (1996). Student participation in the mixed-age college classroom. *Teaching Sociology*, 24, 8–24.

Ishizaka, K., Marshall, S., & Conte, J. (2001). Individual differences in attentional strategies in multi-tasking situations. *Human Performance*, 14(4), 339–358.

Janz, T. A., & Pyke, S. W. (2000). A scale to assess student perceptions of academic climates. *Canadian Journal of Higher Education*, 30(1), 89–122.

Jones, R. C. (2008). The "why" of class participation. *College Teaching*, 56, 59–62.

Karp, D. A., & Yoels, W. C. (1976). The college classroom: Some observations on the meaning of student participation. *Sociology and Social Research*, 60, 421–439.

Lave, J., & Wenger, E. (1991). *Situated learning: Legitimate peripheral participation.* New York: Cambridge University Press.

Mayer, R., & Moreno, R. (2003). Nine ways to reduce cognitive load in multimedia learning. *Educational Psychology*, 38(1), 43–52.

Mayer, R. E. (1984). Aids to prose comprehension. *Educational Psychologist*, 19, 30–42.

McKeachie, W. (1990). Research on college teaching: The historical background. *The Journal of Educational Psychology*, 82, 189–200.

McWilliams, G. (2005). The laptop backlash. *Wall Street Journal*, B1(October 14), 81.

Montgomery, K. C. (2009). *Generation digital: Politics, commerce and childhood in the age of the internet.* Cambridge, MA: MIT Press.

Noddings, N. (1985). Small groups as a setting for research on mathematical problem solving. In: E. A. Silver (Ed.), *Teaching and learning mathematical problem solving* (pp. 345–360). Hillsdale, NJ: Lawrence Erlbaum Associates.

Ogden, T. H. (1999). The analytic third: Working with intersubjective clinical facts. In: S. Mitchell & L. Aron (Eds), *Relational psychoanalysis: The emergence of a tradition* (pp. 459–492). Hillsdale, NJ: Analytic Press.

O'Reilly, T. (2004). Open source paradigm shift. Available at http://tim.oreilly.com/articles/paradigmshift_0504.html

Rhine, S., & Bailey, M. (2008). Collaborative software and a parallel universe: Technology facilitated changes in teacher–student dynamics in classrooms. In: J. Luca & E. Weippl (Eds), *Proceedings of world conference on educational multimedia, hypermedia and telecommunications 2008* (pp. 4375–4381). Chesapeake, VA: AACE. Available at http://www.editlib.org/p/28992.

Richards, E., Bennett, P., & Sekuler, A. (2006). Age related differences in learning with the useful field of view. *Vision Research*, 46(25), 4217–4231.

Riding, R., Grimley, M., Dahraei, H., & Banner, G. (2003). Cognitive style, working memory and learning behaviour and attainment in school subjects. *British Journal of Educational Psychology*, 73, 149–169.

Rovai, A. P. (2002). Building sense of community at a distance. *The International Review of Research in Open Distance*, 3(1), 1–16.

Rowe, M. B. (1987). Wait time: Slowing down may be a way of speeding up. *American Educator*, 11(1), 38–43.

Sandler, B., Silverberg, L., & Hall, R. (1996). *The chilly classroom climate: A guide to improve the education of women.* Washington, DC: The National Association for Women in Education.

Sands, R. G. (1998). Gender and the perception of diversity and intimidation among university students. *Sex Roles, 39,* 801–815.

Seifried, T. (2000). The chilly classroom climate revisited: What have we learned, are male faculty the culprits? *PAACE Journal of Lifelong Learning, 9,* 25–37.

Simplicio, J. (2001). How to recognize and counteract student inattentiveness in the classroom. *Journal of Instructional Psychology, 28*(3), 199–201.

Sommer, R., & Sommer, B. A. (2007). Credit for comments, comments for credit. *Teaching of Psychology, 34,* 104–106.

Stalker, J., & Prentice, S. (Eds). (1998). *The illusion of inclusion: Women in post-secondary education.* Halifax, NS: Fernwood.

Steen, S., Bader, C., & Kubrin, C. (1999). Rethinking the graduate seminar. *Teaching Sociology, 27,* 167–173.

Sweller, J. (1999). *Instructional design in technical areas.* Camberwell, Australia: ACER Press.

Sykes, G. (1990). Learning to teach with cases. *Journal of Policy Analysis and Management, 9*(2), 297–302.

Tomlinson, C. A. (2000). Differentiation of instruction in the elementary grades. ERIC Document Reproduction Service No. ED443572.

Van Zee, E., Iwasyk, M., Kurose, A., Simpson, D., & Wild, J. (2001). Student and teacher questioning during conversations about science. *Journal of Research in Science Teaching, 38*(2), 159–190.

Vygotsky, L. S. (1978). *Mind in society.* Cambridge, MA: Harvard University Press.

Weaver, R. R., & Qi, J. (2005). Classroom organization and participation: College students' perceptions. *The Journal of Higher Education, 76,* 570–601.

Webb, N., Farivar, S., & Mastergeorge, A. (2002). Productive helping in cooperative groups. *Theory Into Practice, 41*(1), 13–21.

Wheeler, S., Yeomans, P., & Wheeler, D. (2008). The good, the bad and the wiki: Evaluating student-generated content for collaborative learning. *British Journal of Educational Technology, 39*(6), 987–995.

Whitt, E. J., Edison, M. I., Pascarella, E. T., Nora, A., & Terenzini, R. T. (1999). Women's perceptions of a "chilly climate" and cognitive outcomes in college: Additional evidence. *Journal of College Student Development, 40,* 163–177.

Wittrock, M. (1990). Generative processes of comprehension. *Educational Psychologist, 24,* 345–376.

Wolpert, S. (2006). Multi-tasking adversely affects brain's learning, UCLA psychologists report, July 26. *Eureka Alert.* Available at http://www.eurekalert.org/pub_releases/2006-07/uoc-maa072506.php

PART V
EVALUATING INSTRUCTION THAT USES SOCIAL MEDIA SKILLS

(SOCIAL) MEDIA LITERACY: CHALLENGES AND OPPORTUNITIES FOR HIGHER EDUCATION

Mark A. Gammon and Joanne White

ABSTRACT

Today's students are powerful consumers and producers of media. Yet for all their access and use of media, many students need assistance from educators to develop critical media skills. These skills are necessary for participation in a culture increasingly characterized by the prevalence of the Internet and social web. However, despite significant changes in contemporary culture, the focus of media literacy remains much the same – meeting the challenge of accessing, analyzing, evaluating, and creating various media forms. Educators and students need to recognize that each has significant roles to play in developing a rigorous approach to media literacy. In embracing all forms of media as well as roles that extend beyond passive consumption, both educators and students are able to discover newly empowering skills that will provide best practice opportunities for better civic and educational engagement.

Educating Educators with Social Media
Cutting-edge Technologies in Higher Education, Volume 1, 329–345
ISSN: 2044-9968/doi:10.1108/S2044-9968(2011)0000001019

INTRODUCTION

Contemporary students are intensive consumers and producers of media. Thanks to the Internet and social web including Facebook, Twitter, blogs, smart phones, and text messaging, most students increasingly live in a world where information and access to communication technologies is both pervasive and persistent. For example, a 2010 Pew Internet and American Life study reports that 93% of young adults age 18–29 use the Internet, 73% of American teens use social networking sites, and 75% have a cell phone (Lenhart, Purcell, Smith, & Zickuhr, 2010). This media climate is distinguished by collaborative and networked technologies that are reconfiguring how we interact with the world around us. The deepening integration of media and culture is further blurring the boundaries between these two concepts (Carey, 1989; Jenkins, 2001, 2006b). However, despite their access and massive use of media, students are not always equipped with media literacy skills that can help them to effectively analyze, understand, and evaluate new forms of information and make smart decisions about its quality and uses (Rowlands et al., 2008). As the influence of the Internet and social web continues to expand, attending to this gap in literacy skills is becoming increasingly important. Educators and students need to recognize both responsibilities and opportunities for working together to develop a more robust media literacy infrastructure. Indeed, despite substantial changes in the media environment, the core concept of being media literate has not changed significantly. Rather the challenge lies in adapting the fundamental ideas of media literacy for contemporary contexts.

If we accept the definition of media literacy as "the ability to access, analyze, evaluate and create messages in a variety of forms" (Livingstone, 2004, p. 5), then we can see that educators must be prepared to provide students with the tools to embrace each of these demands across all media formats. From unilateral forms of message dissemination made by mass media, to the immediacy afforded through messages posted by individuals on Twitter and Facebook, students must be able to filter, mine, collaborate, and create credible information. While some educators have been attentive to these skills, particularly in relation to mass media, the rapid growth of the Internet and social web is demanding more sustained and comprehensive engagement.

To date, media literacy education in the United States has typically involved a somewhat simple process of sorting the content of the major mass media enterprises into their appropriate boxes. Even the skills of filtering or contextualization have been minimized, amounting to little more than looking for the masthead of a piece of media content to understand its potential bias and the story the content is not telling. It is arguable that for some mainstream media, the masthead itself tells the story without having to decode any of its actual content. However, the landscape has changed, and we have never before encountered so many combinations of media formats, content, and reach. The level of access to original and aggregated content from myriad international sources means students (and educators) have opportunities to be better informed than ever before.

These opportunities also carry with them significant challenges. The ready availability of information in simple, accessible forms combined with a decoupling of content production from traditional media institutions places new responsibilities on both educators and students. Students must recognize their role in critically assessing the content they are using. And educators, often frustrated by students who treat all resources as equally credible, must address these concerns more directly and in ways that acknowledge the complexity of contemporary media production and distribution. Educators must recognize the fact that students now also create much of the content they are evaluating. As content producers, students must be equipped by educators to apply media literacy in ways that acknowledge this changed landscape in which everyone is both a producer and a receiver of media. Being media literate today calls on students and educators to understand best practices in both consuming and creating media. While this is a big task, it is not necessarily new.

This chapter emphasizes the changing dynamics of contemporary culture and echoes previous calls (see Giroux, 2006; Jenkins, 2006a; Mioduser, Nachmias, & Forkosh-Baruch, 2008; Lasica, 2009) for a greater emphasis on media literacy skills. Specifically, we identify the need for educators and students to work collaboratively in addressing the critical competencies necessary for accessing, analyzing, evaluating, and creating media content. The chapter includes discussions of the emergence and history of media literacy, new contexts for media literacy, contemporary learning paths, students and educators, creating and engaging with quality content, and teaching media literacy.

EMERGENCE AND HISTORY OF MEDIA LITERACY

Media literacy has historically dealt with the concept of mass media, and it is important to understand the treatment of mass media when considering how we educate students to be media literate. The definition of "mass media" can be traced from three historical roots. According to Lowery and De Fleur (1983), these are *industrialization* in Europe where the individual became one of many in a process of production; *urbanization*, particularly in the USA where immigration saw people form cultural groups in society that helped bond themselves to each other, but did not connect those cultural groups well; and finally *modernization* that included the massive rise of consumption and the middle class – another way of creating delineations between groups of people and de-emphasizing the importance of the individual. Rather than individuals, people became identifiable as part of their membership in a group.

As a result of these changes in the framework of society, "mass media" can be understood as mediated communication which is broadcast to the non-individualized masses. Media literacy, therefore, is tightly woven with the need to address the effect media have on society, whether treated from a structural, behavioral or cultural approach. Inherent in the study of media effect is the ability to assess the content and the content creator as well as the nature of the media formats themselves. Historically, media literacy education has come from a position that separates the receivers of content from its production, even while recognizing that attitudes and opinions that impact our reception of content are primarily formed through these same producers. Today, however, we cannot distance ourselves from the production of media. Instead, we both produce and consume it.

In the words of Manuel Castells (2009), the realm of media is where power is decided. Educating students in media literacy has been largely focused on passive reception, screens, and paper. It takes different skills to be literate in each form of media. Decoding a news story in a mainstream newspaper calls on different skills than the same story on television and then again for radio. All of them call on students to be able to analyze messages through filtering content. Ideally students will use multiple ways to determine the credibility of a piece of information they have gathered. Evidence such as the publisher, the date the content was produced, the editor, location, etc. as well as a wider frame of considering what social, political and economic forces may have influenced the production of the content are all weighed and compared with other media content on the same topic. No single piece of media exists on its own. Students can engage and evaluate different treatments of a story and synthesize the results.

This evaluation has been made easier in more established mass media formats because the proprietors of large media conglomerates number less than 10 and continue to decline (Arsenault & Castells, 2008). The reality of this global cross-media ownership means that students are called on less to make as many distinctions of operation when evaluating content. Mass media forms have been classified and stereotyped (see Li & Izard, 2003; DellaVigna & Kaplan, 2007), and students are rarely asked to evaluate media from an unfamiliar frame – however the need for educators to equip students to be media literate in different contexts and environments has always been the case.

NEW CONTEXTS OF MEDIA LITERACY

Significant changes in the media landscape, driven by the ubiquity of the Internet and social web, are placing increased attention on the skills that individuals require in order to effectively engage and participate in the contemporary environment. This new context is distinguished by the emergence of interactive technologies that are reshaping opportunities for engaging with each other and the larger world. Computers used to be business machines that sat on a desk in the office. Now they are woven into the cultural fabric and are increasingly central to our social connections with others. Similarly, while media have historically been produced by a small set of organizations and consumed by large audiences (at the movie theater or in their living rooms), the social web has enabled the masses to become both media producers and consumers, creating content on the fly and uploading it for others to use and reuse. While access to technology remains unequal and divided (Castells, 2001), the hybridization of media and culture (see Carey, 1989; Jenkins, 2006a) is resulting in a context that provides both new demands and new opportunities to its citizens.

Several prominent media scholars have turned their attention to the evolving climate of literacy and are helping to define the contours and skill areas necessary for an effective and meaningful citizenry. Professor Henry Jenkins suggests that many contemporary teens are engaged in what he terms *participatory culture*. Participatory culture is characterized by "relatively low barriers to artistic expression and civic engagement, strong support for creating and sharing one's creations, and some type of informal mentorship whereby what is known by the most experienced is passed along to novices" (Jenkins, 2006a, p. 3). He suggests that the potential benefits of this culture include peer learning opportunities, differing perceptions of intellectual property, expanded cultural expression, workplace skill development, and an empowered notion of citizenship. Noting that participatory culture can help shape which youth will succeed and which may be left out, Jenkins argues for both "policy and pedagogical interventions" to ensure access and opportunity (p. 3). However, these interventions focus not only on access, but also on fostering new media literacies, which are defined as "a set of cultural competencies and social skills that young people need in the new media landscape" (p. 4). Built on traditional forms of literacy, the 11 new media skills identified by Jenkins include: play, performance simulation, appropriation, multitasking, distributed cognition, collective intelligence, judgment, transmedia navigation, networking, and negotiation.

Internet scholar Howard Rheingold also highlights what he sees as a growing need for media literacy in this technologically saturated environment. Emphasizing the intensifying influence of the Internet and social-mobile technologies in everyday life, Rheingold points to the need for media education and skills to help individuals successfully navigate contemporary culture. In a recent video interview (Lasica, 2009) Rheingold suggested four key areas of new media literacy: attention, participation, collaboration, and critical consumption.

These scholars' recommendations suggest a diverse set of social skills and competencies that are increasingly necessary for successful participation in modern life. Both Jenkins' and Rheingold's contributions highlight broad ideas such as participation, experimentation, adaptation, collective engagement, negotiation, interpretation, and evaluation (for further discussion of specific skills, see Jenkins, 2006a and Lasica, 2009). These skill areas are deeply interconnected and help to define a larger picture of media literacy. The focus of this chapter particularly relates to the overlapping ideas of judgment, transmedia navigation, and critical consumption. According to Jenkins (2006a), judgment refers to the "ability to evaluate the reliability and credibility of different information sources" while transmedia navigation is the "ability to follow the flow of stories and information across multiple modalities" (p. 4). In discussing the concept of critical consumption, Rheingold (Lasica, 2009) notes that we live in an age where "you can get the answer to anything out of the air, but how do you know what to trust?" Taken together, these ideas help to surface and illuminate a key area in media literacy, the identification and creation of credible information and information producers in modern contexts. Although this area of literacy is not new, contemporary culture presents fresh challenges for both students and educators.

The Internet as an "always-on" window of nearly endless information acts both as a source of opportunity and as a site of tremendous challenge, particularly when it comes to determining the quality and validity of that information. As previously noted, the quality and reliability of media content has historically resided within institutions such as schools, libraries, publishers, and media production companies. Thus, despite ongoing efforts at media literacy, this model has meant that most content consumers have not always been actively engaged in evaluating the validity and reliability of the information they take in. Instead, most consumers (including students and educators) have defaulted to allowing various institutional gatekeepers to do the evaluative work for them. For example, when checking out a geography book at the library, an individual is likely to assume that the content (e.g., a map) is accurate and reliable because the author has been vetted by a publisher, the content viewed by an editor, and the book selected by a librarian or library committee. By virtue of its affiliation with institutions such as publishers and libraries, most readers are likely to assume that the information is generally reliable (though not necessarily perfect or agreed upon). However, within a contemporary context of the Internet where information and content is easily created (and recreated), widely available, and vastly distributed, this default practice is no longer sufficient (if it ever was).

Although the diminishing role of institutional gatekeeping is often hailed as a key feature in the move to a more democratic and "flattened" information economy where everyone is able to contribute, this flattened structure also brings with it new challenges. Obviously not all information or all sources of information are equivalent. When information and content is produced and easily shared by potentially any individual, how do consumers of that content determine and evaluate its validity and credibility? What responsibilities do content creators have in the production of their materials? While there are no simple answers to these questions, it is important to acknowledge that the rise in decentralized opportunities for creation and sharing must be met with a concomitant recognition of the distributed responsibility for critical analysis and evaluation. To date, this equation remains out of balance with much attention focused on the new possibilities of content creation and sharing without sufficient recognition of the resulting need for additional literacy skills. The remainder of this chapter seeks to further elaborate this challenge by exploring the new learning patterns and paths of contemporary students and how educators can, and should, contribute to media literacy.

CONTEMPORARY LEARNING PATHS

There is little doubt that students are coming to their educational experiences with different challenges and expectations as a result of their immersion in modern culture. Availability, interactivity, engagement, peer learning, content creation, and collaboration are just a few of the areas where student expectations about education are changing. For example, in its report *Higher Education in a Web 2.0 World*, the Committee of Inquiry into the Changing Learner Experience (2009) notes that web savvy students are often quick to share and participate, but can also be impatient and show a penchant for "quick answers." The report underscores ensuring access to technology and the skills to search, authenticate, evaluate, and attribute material from a range of sources as two critical areas regarding the use of social media tools in higher education. The researchers also suggest that present-day students are effectively acting as a bridge group by helping to manage the "disjuncture" between old and new but warn that the next generation is likely to be less accommodating and that higher education must change if it hopes to continue to provide relevant and effective learning experiences (see p. 9).

These recommendations are echoed by a recent MacArthur Foundation study, *Living and Learning with New Media*, which examined young people's participation in the new media climate. In their assessment of the changing conceptions of education and learning, the authors emphasize the increasing role of self-directed and peer-based learning whereby young people "create and navigate new forms of expression and rules for social behavior" (MacArthur Foundation, 2008, p. 1). For these youth, learning is accomplished through exploration and play with various forms of emerging media. Utilizing tools such as search engines, chat rooms, online forums, and social networks, young people actively direct their own learning paths and in the process they develop important technology and media skills. The report notes that teens also actively create and share content with others online, obtaining feedback and gaining reputations. Within these online paths, activities are typically self-directed and result in learning that is more exploratory and emergent than that attained in traditional education settings. Emphasizing how emerging media forms are altering both socializing and learning, the study suggests several implications for educators including increased openness to online experimentation and exploration, recognition of both friendship- and interest-driven activities, support for peer-based learning, and a broad re-examination of education, with the authors asking "what would it mean to really exploit the potential of the learning opportunities available through online resources and networks?" (pp. 2–3) Thus rather than seeing online activities as distraction and a waste of time, how might educators rethink the role of new media forms for contemporary learning?

One step in this process is listening to students, particularly when they talk about their learning. Rather than remaining stuck in more traditional educational delivery and direction, it is vital that educators undertake a more collaborative approach with students and media literacy. This strategy appreciates student initiative and self-direction in "going deeper" with media content and the verification skills required to be successful in creating learning paths and critically interrogating what they find along the way.

One example of a student thinking about their learning is the following blog post from a Canadian college student produced as part of her work for an education course. The post offers the student's personal reflection about the learning paths she created based on a piece of information provided in class:

> My ECMP355 professor, Alec, included a quote in one of his presentations which was written by some guy named Tagore. I had never heard of 'Tagore' before, but I liked his quote so I decided to Google him. I found out that his full name was Rabindranath Tagore. Further curiosity took me to a Wikipedia page and I learned that Tagore was from India and lived about a century ago. He was a poet, novelist, musician, and a play write and he also won a Nobel prize in literature in 1913. I didn't know how to pronounce his name, so I found a website which pronounces it for me, another one with more quotes by him, a YouTube video about him, and even a Facebook fan page. I learned just about everything I could possibly want to know about Rabindranath Tagore in a matter of about 10 minutes and it could not have been easier.
>
> Now that I have informed myself (and you) about the once mysterious Tagore, I'll get to the quote that Alec had in his presentation. The quote was "don't limit a child to your own learning, for he was born in another time". Without the internet, social networking sites, and other sites that can be found on the web, I would still be clueless as to who Tagore was and why he was included in Alec's presentation. I wouldn't have known that Tagore was a brilliant man of the early 1900's. I wouldn't have got to read more of his quotes, and I would be on my way to becoming the teacher who teaches from the past rather than in the present and for the future.
>
> Teachers (and schools) need to be aware that in the 21st century, one should not limit herself to the boundaries of her own classroom. In the 21st century: networking, sharing information, and sharing ideas with people across the world is an asset. Preparing students for the technologies that are to come should be among the priorities within the classroom. Today's children are tomorrow's future. So if we deny the children of today the right to learn about their world, where will we leave them when tomorrow comes? My hopes are that we do not find out. (Bashforth, 2010)

This blog post raises many important aspects of contemporary students' learning paths and highlights opportunities for engagement by educators. Despite her lack of knowledge about Rabindranth Tagore during class, this student chose not to ask for more information in class, but instead opted for a more self-directed learning process using various Internet tools. Rather than following an information path directed by her teacher, this student designed her own way of gathering information based upon a dynamic and unfolding understanding of the topic. In doing so, she applied aspects of transmedia navigation (Jenkins, 2006a) along with qualifying information through finding additional and varying sources and evaluating the content to determine where to dig deeper. Her learning path utilized multiple tools and media forms including a search engine (Google), Wiki, text-to-speech (pronunciation), video, and social networks (Facebook). This varied sourcing is one way that students can "triangulate" and corroborate the information they gather. While emphasizing the ease and speed with which she was able to educate herself about the subject matter, the student also notes that this activity was used to supplement her in-class learning. This hybrid approach is one strategy that educators can apply to address student frustrations with the artificial boundaries of the classroom and which can also incorporate opportunities for creating, sharing, and networking.

As the Internet and social web reroute the learning paths of young people, increased attention must be paid by educators to the underlying media literacy skills that students will need to help them make smart and effective decisions along the way. The decoupling of content production from traditional forms of institutional gatekeeping means that students have tremendous opportunities both in determining their own learning and in the ways of sharing that learning. However, these new opportunities also require that students make informed decisions and ask critical questions as they engage with new media. Educators need to work with students to recognize and develop literacy skills for determining the value of content and content production. For example, students can be invited to (a) dig deeper, checking a source's source, (b) investigate widely, looking for similar topical information by other authors and/or other information by the same author, and (c) utilize their networks to verify information and authors with trusted resources. Educators have a vital role to play in helping students to identify both the questions and strategies that will shape the experiences and outcomes of their media use.

STUDENTS AND EDUCATORS

One of the most widely circulated terms for helping to conceptualize the new generation of students is "digital natives." Popularized by Marc Prensky in his 2001 essay *Digital Natives, Digital Immigrants*, the idiom describes the first generations of young people to come of age in the world of the Internet, mobile, and web technologies. As a result of their immersion in these media and technologies, digital natives are fundamentally different from previous generations. According to Prenzky, these natives think and process information in ways that differentiate them from those who were not born into the digital world, people he terms "digital immigrants." While adaptable to new contexts, immigrants are distinguished by their legacy socalization in the pre-digital world, what Prenzky calls their "accent" (p. 2). While immigrants can learn and adapt, they will never be native speakers, never quite fully comprehending the perspective of digital natives. Using this distinction, Prensky argues that the most significant problem in education is the disjuncture of "language" between natives and immigrants. To overcome this dilemma, he suggests that immigrant educators must reevaluate both *how* and *what* they teach. Although Prensky's work provides a useful framework for conceptualizing significant changes in our educational environment, the rapid adoption and pervasive use of the term digital native as a descriptor for all young people is problematic. First, this ubiquity implies both a simplicity and uniformity about young people's relationship to technology that is not always born out. For example, Hargittai (2010) argues that knowledge about the Internet is typically associated with factors like gender, parental education, and socioeconomic status. A second pitfall is the widely held, though often misplaced, belief that high levels of exposure necessarily results in critical, interpretive, and applied understandings of media. Finally, while conceptual groupings can be useful, it is easy to view these distinctions as dichotomous rather than reflecting a wider spectrum of traits among and across people.

There is clear support for arguments that contemporary students who have come of age in an era of the Internet and social web are bringing with them new expectations and new challenges for education professionals. Given the contemporary context in which separating media from culture (and indeed everyday life) is no longer relevant, educators must make concerted efforts to further understand and engage with emerging media. A key aspect of the contemporary media literacy challenge is that its responsibility is widely distributed. Literacy is not only about asking students to do the work but also about educators stepping up to better develop their own skills. Educators must recognize that they continue to play a central role in helping students to understand and effectively engage with the world around them. Despite their seeming omniscience about media and technology, many young people are in need of assistance from educators to develop and apply critical media literacy skills in this new culture. Many of these literacy skills are not altogether new or unique, but instead are core social and cultural proficiencies that need to be understood within contemporary contexts. In this regard, it is vital that educators not make the simple assumption that their students already "know it all" when it comes to the Internet and social web. Educators must resist the easy allure of labels like "digital native" that can sometimes serve to distance them from the important part they play in aiding students in this new cultural environment.

In addition, educators ought not assume that they are inherently deficient in the skills and competencies for working effectively with students. Rather, it is imperative that educators (and students) engage directly and collaboratively on issues of media literacy. Indeed when it comes to concepts like judgment, credibility, critical evaluation, and information sourcing, educators are highly suited to the task.

CREATING AND ENGAGING WITH QUALITY CONTENT

The creation of lesson plans designed to help students become good receivers of information is just one aspect of teaching media literacy; however, the call to aid students in creating quality content has gone largely unheeded. Speaking to this concern in his work on critical pedagogy, Giroux (2006) notes, "the technologies and content of this culture must be available to students in schools not only so they can read these cultures critically, but also so they can become cultural producers within these new communicative domains" (p. 6) It is one thing to get students to produce their own stories, posts and comments, and entirely another to invite them to understand the complexities and impact their content may have. Students need to be attentive, accountable, and responsible for what they create and share. Until recently, responsible media creation simply has not been at issue because the ability to produce content has been limited to sources that are filtered prior to publication. The contemporary media environment no longer has those gatekeepers ensuring that content is credible and valuable; and today content is spread so quickly and easily, the potential reach and effect of one person's content is greater than ever before – rivaling even that of long-established media conglomerates.

While it has been suggested that young people "understand the conventions and merits of professionally produced material if they have experience making it themselves" (Livingstone, 2004, p. 7), to date there have been very limited opportunities for educators to evaluate media literacy skills when students create their own content. Quite often the errors of judgment in online publication are common to both young and old. In some ways, both educators and students suffer the disadvantage of limited access to experience in this cultural environment. Having access to the Internet and web is not the same as having access to real education on responsible use of these technologies. We can teach the functional aspects quite easily with standardized books and rote learning; however, media literacy in modern culture also requires more complex and nuanced social and cultural skills.

There is a very real need for maturity in engaging with content created by others. This maturity is the task of media literacy that calls on students to determine appropriate responses to material they may decide is questionable, reliable, and authentic or inauthentic. The maturity of engagement also informs students' responses to others who engage with the content they themselves have produced. Areas such as appropriate ways of discussing content in an online forum, locating and linking to evaluated sources, making a clear point, expressing an opinion and even simply thanking a content producer for the material they have created and suggesting additional content they may want to discover are all examples of skills students must have to be media literate today.

TEACHING MEDIA LITERACY

Teaching media literacy involves walking a fine line between being cognizant and critical about media and their messages without becoming incapacitated by suspicion and skepticism. Media literacy is not about withholding media that may be uncomfortable or untrustworthy for whatever reason from students. Nobody is served if students are taught to avoid or be inherently distrustful of media in any form. Educators need to realize that limiting the media channels they are prepared to engage with does not mean that students will also limit their own engagement, only that they will be less well prepared for those media. The goal of media literacy is to equip students with the tools to dig, verify, and evaluate content. If educators ban Wikipedia, students will not stop using the site, they will simply have missed an opportunity to learn how to use it effectively and to demonstrate that they can discern valuable information. Treating media in this way is likely to result in students engaging with less content because they do not know what they can believe. They may also publish and comment even less of their own views and creative work. This is certainly not the goal for educators of media literacy.

Teachers should be encouraging students to critically engage with media on multiple levels, in every way. Consuming, creating, and commenting are all ways of participating with media that can help students to focus and hone their skills. In order to achieve this, educators need to give up some of the step-by-step direction they are used to providing. Students do not need to be given check boxes of approved media sources. Rather, they need support in building competencies for understanding and identifying what quality sources are for themselves. Instead of building the road for students and asking them to follow it, we must give students the goals and equipment to build the road themselves. Furthermore, we should assist them in determining and understanding the "rules of the road" by inviting them to create and drive it with their own vehicles. Instead of giving students a book list of acceptable authors, we should be instilling in them a desire to find the best sources and the accompanying critical skills necessary to qualify them as such. Only then will their skills be constantly and dynamically relevant. Educators also need to be curious and ready to perform engaged inquiry alongside their students.

We must be aware of the need for students to develop skills that they can use to evaluate media from different countries, cultures, and perspectives (see iEarn.org, MyGLife.org, newlitcollaborative.ning.com, and mediated-cultures.net as examples for further discussion). Educators must reach beyond local and national media to embrace and recognize the global nature of contemporary media.

Key elements of discussion and reflection are involved in effectively teaching media literacy. As noted in the previous discussion of the student blog post, students can complement their in-class learning by being asked to dig deeply across a range of additional sources and then reflect on that process and the decisions made. Asking students in all fields to identify the processes they use to find and create content, developing a discussion around those processes, and finishing with reflection on their effectiveness and impact are strategies that might be implemented by educators. Assessable components of curricula should include these factors. For example, Renee Hobbs (2001) has created a valuable outline for investigating and interrogating information that looks at issues of media literacy and is primarily focused on discussion and reflection. While Hobbs' work focuses on a K-12 education environment, the strategies and goals are also relevant for higher education. The extensive research being undertaken by

The Good Work Project's Developing Minds and Digital Media (DM2) Project (goodworkproject.org) seeks to understand how adolescents understand, navigate and engage with digital platforms. This Project's work is another useful resource for educators that can help determine questions to ask students in developing discussion and reflections.

CONCLUSIONS

Most contemporary students live in an information rich world where access to media and communication technologies is ever-present. This cultural climate is increasingly defined by the collaborative and networked technologies of the Internet and social web. This new context demands increased recognition from educators about the skills and strategies that students need in order to become responsible and engaged citizens. However, despite significant changes in the contemporary climate, the core focus of media literacy remains much the same – meeting the challenges of accessing, analyzing, evaluating, and creating various media forms.

Educators and students need to recognize that each have significant roles to play in developing a rigorous approach to media literacy. The pervasive character of the Internet and social web means that responsibility for media literacy must be shared and achieved collaboratively. Educators – including teachers, counselors, librarians, and administrators – have an important responsibility to play in helping students ask critical questions and apply appropriate strategies as they engage with media. To meet these expectations, it is vital that educators assess their own knowledge of media literacy and be willing to further increase and expand their understanding in ways that will help them in working with students. Educators must also challenge and push back on simplistic depictions, both by themselves and others, of students as uniformly savvy and astute users of media/technology. Even experienced and confident users can benefit from regular augmentation of their understanding and application of critical media skills. Finally, rather than relying only on their own conceptions and assumptions about education and learning, educators need to continue to listen to their students and embrace the opportunities of collaborative engagement and reciprocal learning.

As members of an increasingly participatory culture (Jenkins, 2006a), students must appreciate that they are accountable to engage, create, and contribute. They must also consider their responsibility for critically evaluating the content they both consume and create. As participants of interactive contexts, students need to recognize that they have obligations to both peers and wider communities. The networked character of contemporary culture provides opportunities but also significant responsibilities for each member to contribute to the overall experience. Students need to understand how they are a part of this process and also determine how they can make positive additions.

The landscape of media has broadened from the one-to-many mass media model to one where every individual is not only a consumer of media, but also a producer. In endeavoring to prepare students to become truly media literate, educators must become more willing to demonstrate the core values of responsible media literacy and offer students the opportunity to explore all forms of media themselves. It is only through working collaboratively with students and embracing the full spectrum of media in all its forms that both students and educators will be able to discover best practice media literacy skills.

REFERENCES

Arsenault, A., & Castells, M. (2008). The structure and dynamics of global multi-media business networks. *International Journal of Communication, 2,* 707–748.

Bashforth, A. (2010, January 30). Tech task #3: Tagore. Available at http://allybii.wordpress.com/2010/01/30/tech-task-3-tagore/

Carey, J. (1989). *Communication as culture.* New York: Routledge.

Castells, M. (2001). *The internet galaxy: Reflections on the internet, business, and society.* Oxford; New York: Oxford University Press.

Castells, M. (2009). *Communication power.* Oxford; New York: Oxford University Press.

Committee of Inquiry into the Changing Learner Experience. (2009). *Higher education in a Web 2.0 World.* Available at http://www.clex.org.uk/ourfindings.php

DellaVigna, S., & Kaplan, E. (2007). The fox news effect: Media bias and voting. *Quarterly Journal of Economics, 122*(3), 1187–1234. doi:10.1162/qjec.122.3.1187.

Giroux, H. (2006). *America on the edge: Henry Giroux on politics, culture, and education.* New York: Palgrave Macmillan.

Hargittai, E. (2010). Digital na(t)ives? Variation in internet skills and uses among members of the "Net Generation". *Sociological Inquiry, 80*(1), 92–113. doi:10.1111/j.1475-682X.2009.00317x.

Hobbs, R. (2001). Classroom strategies for exploring realism and authenticity in media messages. *Reading Online, 4*(9). Available at http://www.readingonline.org/newliteracies/lit_index.asp?HREF = /newliteracies/hobbs/index.html

Jenkins, H. (2001, June). Convergence? I diverge. *Technology Review, 93.* Available at http://web.mit.edu/cms/People/henry3/converge.pdf

Jenkins, H. (2006a). Confronting the challenges of participatory culture: Media education for the 21st century. Available at http://newmedialiteracies.org/

Jenkins, H. (2006b). *Convergence culture: Where old and new media collide.* New York: New York University Press.

Lasica, J. D. (Producer). (2009, June 18). 21st century media literacies. Available at http://vimeo.com/5659525

Lenhart, A., Purcell, K., Smith, A., & Zickuhr, K. (2010, February 3). *Social media and young adults.* Available at http://www.pewinternet.org/Reports/2010/Social-Media-and-Young-Adults.aspx

Li, X., & Izard, R. (2003). 9/11 attack coverage reveals similarities differences. *Newspaper Research Journal, 4*(9), 204–219.

Livingstone, S. (2004). Media literacy and the challenge of new information and communication technologies. *The Communication Review, 7,* 3–14.

Lowery, S. A., & De Fleur, M. (Eds). (1983). *Milestones in mass communications research.* New York: Longman.

MacArthur Foundation. (2008). Living and learning with new media: Summary of findings from the digital youth project. Available at http://digitalyouth.ischool.berkeley.edu/report

Mioduser, D., Nachmias, R., & Forkosh-Baruch, A. (2008). New literacies for the knowledge society. In: J. Voogt & G. Knezek (Eds), *International handbook of information technology in primary and secondary education* (pp. 23–42). Berlin; Heidelberg; New York: Springer.

Prensky, M. (2001). Digital natives, digital immigrants. *On the Horizon, 9*(5), 1–6.

Rowlands, I., Nicholas, D., Williams, P., Huntington, P., Fieldhouse, M., Gunter, B., Withey, R., Jamali, H. R., Dobrowolski, T., & Tenopir, C. (2008). The Google generation: The information behaviour of the researcher of the future. *Aslib Proceedings, 60*(4), 290–310. doi:10.1108/00012530810887953.

SOCIAL MEDIA KILLED THE LMS: RE-IMAGINING THE TRADITIONAL LEARNING MANAGEMENT SYSTEM IN THE AGE OF BLOGS AND ONLINE SOCIAL NETWORKS

Danielle M. Stern and Michael D. D. Willits

ABSTRACT

The advent of Web 2.0 technologies invites educators to fundamentally rethink the systems we choose to manage our courses. Although many scholars have examined the democratizing functions of online and hybrid learning (Hall, 1999; Kibby, 2006; McCormick, 2006) and offered case studies of successful social media integration (Dunlap & Lowenthal, 2009), a need exists to theorize about how faculty and students actually envision the changing role of learning technologies, particularly the LMS and now social media, in their everyday education. Grounded in critical pedagogy and building from a brief history of the learning management system and new media learning technologies, we examine which features have been most beneficial to the shared learning experience between faculty and students. Through this discussion we provide a working model

Educating Educators with Social Media
Cutting-edge Technologies in Higher Education, Volume 1, 347–373
ISSN: 2044-9968/doi:10.1108/S2044-9968(2011)0000001020

of a re-imagined learning technology platform that integrates the best tools of the LMS with the more shared, democratizing features of social media in common use among today's students and faculty. We envision a shift from that of a management system to a dynamic platform built from the ground-up to integrate traditional course technologies such as grade books and testing, with the open, collaborative nature of social media. Toward this end, the chapter includes examples of combining Wordpress, Buddypress, and Twitter into a tri-fold approach that reaches beyond the physical classroom walls to build a community of learning where students are the educators via content creation and critical analysis of cultural institutions.

During the debut of the learning management system (LMS) in the late 1990s, the LMS, including commercial products (e.g., Blackboard, WebCT, Desire2Learn, and Angel) and open source projects (e.g., Moodle and Sakai) has promised to revolutionize teaching and learning. However, the reality of the LMS concept has been far from revolutionary. Even with the patchwork addition of features such as discussion boards, testing, integrated gradebooks, and email communications, and recently elements of social media tools like wikis and blogs, the concept of the LMS has not evolved sufficiently to keep pace with the changing landscape of academic technology, especially with modes of interaction and collaboration fostered by popular online social networks like Facebook and Twitter.

The advent of Web 2.0 technologies such as blogs and online social networks invites educators to fundamentally rethink the systems we choose to manage our courses. Although many scholars have examined the democratizing functions of online and hybrid learning (Hall, 1999; Kibby, 2006; McCormick, 2006) and offered case studies of successful social media integration (Dunlap & Lowenthal, 2009), a need exists to theorize about how faculty and students actually envision the changing role of learning technologies, particularly the LMS and now social media, in their everyday education. Grounded in critical pedagogy and building from a brief history of the LMS and learning technologies, from more traditional means such as Blackboard and Moodle, to social media such as wikis, blogs, and Twitter, in this chapter we examine which features have been most beneficial to the shared learning experience between faculty and students.

Through this discussion we provide a working model of a re-imagined learning technology platform that integrates the best tools of the LMS with the more shared, democratizing features of social media in common use among today's students and faculty. We envision a shift from that of a management system to a dynamic platform built from the ground-up to integrate traditional course technologies such as gradebooks and testing, with the open, collaborative nature of social media. We believe a modern, adaptable platform such as this offers an environment better-suited than a traditional LMS to fostering the types of community interactions that are conducive to learning in today's academic environment, whether in the traditional classroom, or in a hybrid or online learning environment. Although social media may not appear to fit all pedagogical design, we provide a case study from one of the author's courses in popular culture as one example of how to incrementally build a dynamic course platform that fits individual disciplinary needs. By moving beyond the closed walls of the institutional, proprietary LMS, a learning platform built on a foundation of socially mediated knowledge communities helps fulfill the goals of critical pedagogy to disrupt formal power imbalances between student and faculty while also tearing down the walls of the ivory tower.

For the purposes of this chapter, we choose to use the term learning management system (LMS) specifically because our emphasis is not so much on the technology of these systems, but in the pedagogical sense of interogating the structures and uses of such systems. Both commercial products and open source projects typically fall under the course management system (CMS) moniker. However, we are careful to delineate our inquiry from others examinations that place emphasis on the use of these systems for the management of *courses* and *content* (e.g., course materials, assignment submissions, and grade information). Although we found LMS and CMS concepts used interchangeably, we are interested in how these systems – and those who use these systems – manage (and mis-manage) *learning*.

COMMUNITY, TECHNOLOGY, CRITICAL PEDAGOGY, AND STUDENT NEEDS

Teachers and scholars across disciplines have been arguing for the importance of community in the classroom for many years (Ellsworth, 1989; Jenkins, 2009; Kellner, 2000). In the digital era, a movement emerged to embrace the potentials of community in online environments (Rheingold, 2000), which so often occupy much of our modern learning spaces. Some public academics have been more critical of the role of technology in our everyday lives. For example, 25 years ago Postman (1985) explained how television would foster generations of a passive citizenry interested only in entertainment and detached from political life. Later Postman (1992) extended his criticism to technology beyond entertainment media. He warned that society was becoming a "technopoly" full of techno-citizens disconnected from social communion. In a sense, his arguments blamed technology for dehumanizing the population.

Recently other scholars have defended technology and popular cultural forms and argued that television and other electronic and digital media actually help make us more connected and intelligent. For example, Jenkins (2006) explained that the satire of comedy news programs like *The Daily Show* and *The Colbert Report* actually demand an engaged audience to discern fact from fiction. Similarly, Johnson (2005) argued that complex, character-driven prime-time dramas such as *24* and *Lost*, attract an intelligent audience to keep up with intricate, long-term story arcs. No longer are viewers happy to sit back and be entertained for an hour. A community of fandom and popular culture participation has emerged where viewers blog and tweet about their understandings of the screen and page.

This emergence of the engaged citizen of popular culture coincided with the development of interactive media forms such as the digital video recorder, text messaging and Facebook. Ott (2007) has explained how new information technologies can help us achieve community. He identified our emerging entertainment era as the "Conceptual Age," a major paradigm shift in the medium of television characterized by three major trends: convergence, interactivity, and mobility. Through our social connectivity – and despite our ideological attachments or political affiliations (Jenkins, 2006) – we ignite collective action that builds diverse knowledge communities. Popular culture, especially via socially mediated forms, builds bridges to conversations that might not otherwise occur in traditional face-to-face interactions. Our differences, including not only in our entertainment wants and needs, but also our learning styles, unite us in the 21st century. This current state of entertainment and political engagement becomes important for educators because this is the diverse, techno-mediated, participatory culture (Jenkins, 2006) that populates our student bodies. And increasingly, as faculty become more immersed in as well as raised on technology ourselves, we are at a crucial moment to capitalize on using this collective intelligence and desire to be connected to improve our pedagogies and enhance student learning.

Just as the turn toward more participatory media forms has increased the current generation's desire for community with and about their favorite pop culture forms, scholars of computer mediated communication and critical pedagogy have argued that students today desire less rigid displays of teachers as givers of knowledge (Giroux, 1985; Rhode, 2009). This banking metaphor of education (Freire, 1988), where teachers are the sole providers of information – and students the recipients – does not work for most disciplines in an era when students demand more involvement in their learning. Alexander (2005) has embraced a need for "geographies of learning," which recognize that even though the critical pedagogy faithful seek to disrupt these power structures, teachers inherently possess specific types of power (grading, authority, and classroom climate) that our course designs must address and strive to move beyond. As educators, we must embrace this challenge and seek a LMS that inspires students despite our grading power and authority. Moreover, it is our duty to work toward an inclusive, imaginative classroom environment – both offline and online, especially since students now expect a more social approach to learning that extends outside the physical space of the classroom (Brooks, 2009).

According to Lockard and Pegrum (2006), since online learning forms are still in their infancy, educators can make a significant impact on the direction of how we build and use e-learning. Although the authors of this chapter are not advocating a turn toward an entirely e-based pedagogy, we do see the benefits of using a LMS to enhance more traditional approaches to teaching. Scholars have already argued for the benefits of a hybrid pedagogy that blends face-to-face classroom learning with whatever online means are available, whether email, blogs, Blackboard, or others (Kibby, 2006; Precel, Eshet-Alkalai, & Alberton, 2009). However, we also realize that a LMS, when designed properly, can stand on its own merits and replace the classroom walls as needed in some cases. However, the intent of this essay is not to weigh the merits of online versus offline learning. Faculty should not have to choose, though we realize slim university budgets may already be shifting pressure on administrators and faculty alike to offer streamlined, affordable online courses (Ess, 2006). That said, if the LMS is built around sound, community-oriented pedagogy and theory, then the actual geography of where classes meet should not matter. As educators informed by critical pedagogy, the goal is to operate in a learning space of collaboration and respect unbound from knowledge hierarchies.

The modern social institution of higher education has by its very design encouraged and simultaneously been bound by the very knowledge hierarchies we eschew in this chapter. These knowledge hierarchies act as a double-edged sword, at once being partly responsible for structuring academe in the United Sates as we know it today, and at the same time preventing higher education from capitalizing on rapid innovations, namely in technology. In fact, higher education throughout its history has maintained a precarious balance between tradition and new technology (Morgan, 2003). Mott and Wiley (2009) assert that the introduction of new technologies, rather than ushering in a new future, simply continue the cycle of reinventing and repackaging the past. If anything, the implementation of technology in higher education, rather than ushering reformation in teaching and learning, so often succeeds merely in bringing greater efficiency to the status quo, while doing little to encourage institutions to challenge their existing practices. Although this chapter is not the appropriate forum for a targeted exploration of the history of technology in higher education, it is useful to the present discussion on challenging knowledge hierarchies (and by extension, the LMS structure) that in the following section we take a brief diversion into the evolution of the American higher education system, which coincidentally, will highlight why the LMS exists in its current form.

RE-INVENTING THE PAST

Germane to the scope of this chapter, the history of American higher education is arguably about standardization and the mass consumption of knowledge within a democratic society in need of practical knowledge combined with the wisdom to become productive citizens of an emerging nation, unto itself struggling to find structure amid the chaos of revolution and rapid expansion. As Morgan (2003) contends, the university operates as a social institution whose key role is to prepare a student population for a rapidly growing post-industrial nation. The promise of a liberal education is that of enlightenment, the deep exploration of thousands of years of accumulated wisdom and preparation for thoughtful, considerate future citizens. However, in order to achieve this ideal on a mass scale, as has been the goal of education in the United States, the art of the professoriate necessarily yielded to such modern (at the time) efficiencies as the lecture hall, which standardized the forum of delivery and effectively ensured the transmission from experts of as much knowledge to as many assembled students as possible in a time-limited system (Morgan). Thanks in part to the printing press, further standardization emerged in the form of the textbook, which as Morgan remarks, was "the course management software of its day" (p. 82).

For as old as they are, the lecture hall and the textbook continue to exemplify the standardization and commodification of higher education's main product – knowledge. That Frederick Taylor would find comfort in the efficiencies of such innovations should come as no surprise; that the lecture hall and the textbook today continue to be the de facto tools employed by institutions, however, points to the huge gap that exists between the world in which our students live and the industrial, one-size-fits-all model of education they still experience during their tenure in college. This gap is nowhere more apparent than in the transformational impact of technologies in every other aspect of culture, society, the economy (Mott & Wiley, 2009), and in the productivity of industry.

As modern universities grew in abundance across the United States, they increasingly isolated themselves intellectually from the outside world, erecting gleaming ivory towers and building vast walled gardens, eventually becoming in the 20th century, as Clark Kerr (2001) terms, "Cities of Intellect," with which Kerr associates to the modern research university's aggregation of largely unrelated disciplines within the walled gardens, as in contrast to his closely knit "village" characterized by the liberal arts college "community of scholars" atmosphere. Much can be said of the criticisms levied on higher education for its disconnectedness from the needs of modern society. Indeed, scholars, business leaders, government officials, and for that matter, students collectively decry the failing of higher education to prepare adequately a future citizenry, but to do so falls short of recognizing that higher education is itself a product shaped by society. Given higher education's tenacious grasp on tradition, our analogy serves to bridge the space between our targeted exploration of the structural history of higher education and the introduction of the LMS.

We begin with Morgan's (2003) assertion that "introducing course management systems into a community of scholars with more than a millennium of tradition is a radical and disquieting act" (p. 86). As with most technologies introduced in academe, we suggest that the original LMS technologies, while initially both innovative applications of the day's available technologies and audacious expressions of what their progenitors envisioned teaching and learning could be, nevertheless fell victim to the same oft-maligned fate as the lecture hall and textbooks: as much a part of higher education as Coca Cola is to Americana, yet with the unsatisfying taste of the 1985 introduction of New Coke.

In our review of the literature on faculty and student perceptions and use of the LMS, we noted a clear love–hate relationship, especially with the LMS structures. From its humble beginnings in the 1970s, the LMS is today an integral part of almost every institution's enterprise technology infrastructure (Delta Initiative, 2009; Morgan, 2003; Mott & Wiley, 2009). The challenges faced by administrators harkens to Clark Kerr's (1991, 2001) lament that, since the 1950s, few issues have been as perennial to higher education as student promiscuity, athletics for alumni, and the grievances held by faculty over campus parking. Surely if Kerr were alive today, he might be tempted to add the CMS to his list. As with parking, the LMS is both a panacea and a bane for institutions (Caruso, 2006) that exists in some form or another at nearly all higher education institutions (Caruso, 2006; Mott & Wiley, 2009). Even with all the problems associated with parking, one is hard-pressed to imagine a campus without it. Still, even as more land is leveled, paved, marked with spaces, and regulated by meters and parking passes, the frustrations with parking continue to grow. And, although the parking issue itself has not changed much since the 1950s, little has changed in how the issue is addressed.

If the only business that institutions of higher education operated was parking (and surely many administrators may feel as much), there would be little incentive to change, as the parking lot is hardly a space one would deem as a site ripe for innovation. Indeed, that a parking space from 1950 looks the same as a space in 2010 is hardly remarkable. That a classroom or textbook – and to this point, teaching practices – from 2010 look much the same as they did in the 1950s is disconcerting. So what of the innovations promised by educational technologies, particularly the CMS, for the last several decades? As evidenced by a 2009 Delta Initiative, even with over 90% of institutions studied having some sort of standardized LMS, and amidst a 500% increase in average licensing costs per campus between 2000 and 2008, since 2004, innovation in the LMS had all but stalled. If we are to learn anything from the campus parking situation, it is that the education–industrial complex performs well at standardizing and commodifying available resources *en mass*; it *does not*, however, adapt well to opportunities for innovation. In fact, the considerable investments in technology infrastructures, despite promises of revolutionizing teaching and learning, have largely underwhelmed in terms of innovating existing teaching and learning practices (Cuban, 2001). Parking lots are expensive. So are investments in the LMS. Looking at a modern campus, however, one wonders if the institution is in the parking industry (especially anyone who has received a parking ticket). Taking a similar glance at the current adoption of CMS technologies, might higher education be, as Herrington, Reeves, and Oliver (2005) contend, merely in the *information industry*?

Despite the omnipresence of the LMS, the professoriate's traditional prerogative within the walls of the classroom to determine pedagogy as they see fit remains as vital as ever. From their infancy in the mid-1990s (Morgan, 2003) to the monolithic infrastructures of today, the creators of the LMS could not have envisioned the extent to which the structures they created would eventually shape pedagogy or threaten faculty hegemony. Nonetheless, in practice, the LMS structure, as the textbook and lecture halls already accomplished, has done both at remarkable cost.

Scholars remark on the hypocrisy of LMS structures that, while lauded as convenient and empowering technologies for faculty and students to usher them into the online world (Campbell, 2009), nevertheless tend to force them into pre-determined, one-size-fits-all teaching toolboxes (Mott & Wiley, 2009). What we find in the typical LMS are tools and a design focused on maximizing *administrative efficiencies*, rather than improving *teaching and learning effectiveness*. According to Lane (2008):

> Creating an online class is a task of construction. A course management system (CMS) provides faculty with a set of tools, a kit to use as we build our classes. We want to construct classes according to our own pedagogy – what we know works with our learners and our teaching style. ... it would be silly to let the tools in our toolbox determine what we construct and how we construct it. I wouldn't set out to build a Victorian dollhouse and switch to a modernist garden bench because I couldn't find the scroll saw. And yet this type of shift often happens when faculty encounter a CMS. (p. 4)

As Fig. 1 illustrates, these tools tend to situate within five administrative areas identified by Morgan (2003).

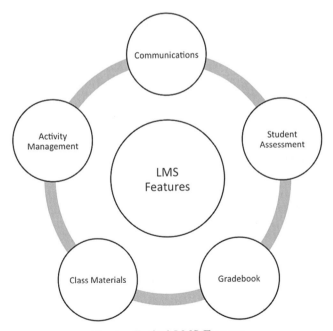

Fig. 1. Typical LMS Features.

DECONSTRUCTING THE IVORY LMS TOWER

The first step to move past the rigid structures described in the previous section is to redefine our concept of the LMS, which is a system to manage learning. The LMS concept implies a manager, which in-turn indicates a hierarchy of control in the production and distribution of both learning and course content. The LMS simply relocates the confines of the classroom and its four walls to an online environment, administered in this case not by faculty, but by the IT department. The IT department becomes the de facto arbiter of learning by prescribing what tools are made available and how precisely these tools are to be distributed and used. Instead of faculty and students feeling empowered to craft a shared learning experience, the complexities inherent in current LMS design force a sense of learned helplessness, not the least of which is by requiring lengthy training (provided by IT) to manage even simple tasks, let alone to take advantage of any of the advanced features offered.

In recent years with the advent of social media, LMS providers have struggled to keep pace, tacking onto already cumbersome systems a variety of Web 2.0 and social media-like tools. Such efforts have been half-hearted at best with little more than a cursory nod to the spirit of real Web 2.0 and social media technologies readily available to faculty and students outside the protective walled garden of their LMS. Arguably, the inclusion of Web 2.0 and social media tools by LMS providers only serves to bring a stale air of social capital to their LMS products accompanied, of course, by additional fees levied upon institutions wishing to avail themselves of these new tools, lest they be at risk of falling behind the technological curve. Unfortunately, the reality of current LMS Web 2.0 tools is disappointing and indicative of how antiquated the LMS is today, as if eight-track tape player manufacturers were to trumpet wireless networking as the latest and greatest upgrade option, when the rest of the world has already moved on to digital content via the iPod.

In Morgan's (2003) exploration of the LMS, she positions teaching and learning as fundamentally social endeavors. These endeavors necessitate a social contract of sorts between instructor and student, one that ideally empowers both to be active contributors and participants in the learning process. However, this relationship is made difficult given the top-down hierarchy assumed by the typical LMS structure. How then do we as educators who hope to operate in a more egalitarian, organic space of learning do so within the existing domain of the LMS? In short, we do not. Instead, educators need to seek out innovative, yet simple, course technologies inspired by those online spaces our students already occupy and live by daily. In no way do we advocate co-opting students' private spaces for the public realm of the classroom. Rather, we turn to these sites as building blocks for a more dynamic learning experience in which students – and faculty – want to be involved. As such, we argue for a shift to an understanding of a Dynamic Course Platform (DCP) that accounts for the ways educators have embraced learning technologies beyond the proprietary spaces of the LMS.

The development of a DCP is informed by the needs of educators to create a dynamic, effective platform that aids our teaching and students' learning. Rather than conforming pedagogy to the capabilities and limitations of the LMS, educators can shape a DCP to fit their instructional needs, and students are empowered to integrate a DCP into the technologies and routines to which they are accustomed. Instead of being a destination in-and-of itself as is the LMS, a DCP (Fig. 2) works seemlessly behind the scenes and in conjunction with other technologies selected à la carte as appropriate to the desired learning experience.

To be sure, our idea of a DCP is hardly revolutionary, and this is a good thing. Other scholars, similarly frustrated with the status quo of stagnant, inflexible LMS offerings, have suggested alternative approaches that, during the course of our research into the literature, closely support our initial perspective. Like us, other scholars envision creating a flexible platform that integrates with vital elements of the existing university infrastructure, whereas providing faculty and students with an intuitive social space that fosters good pedagogy, rather than merely a cumbersome administrative portal. Whether in the form of an Open Learning Network (OLN) (Mott, 2010; Mott & Wiley, 2009), a Personal Cyberinfrastructure (Campbell, 2009), a Personal Learning Network (PLN) (Mott, 2010), or a custom-built mini-CMS (Lane, 2008), the future course platform eschews the education-industrial LMS that situates the instructor of producer and distributor for a structure that encourages – even demands – participation, collaboration, and most importantly, the production of knowledge by students to equally share, critique, and build upon.

An important element of a DCP is the integration with the existing university infrastructure. Critical to the success of predominant commerical LMS products like Blackboard and Desire2Learn, as Moodle and other opens source projects, is their tight integration with the institution's student information system (SIS), which provides the LMS with information on courses, student registrations, and related data necessary to construct and populate courses each semester (Mott, 2010; Mott & Wiley, 2009;

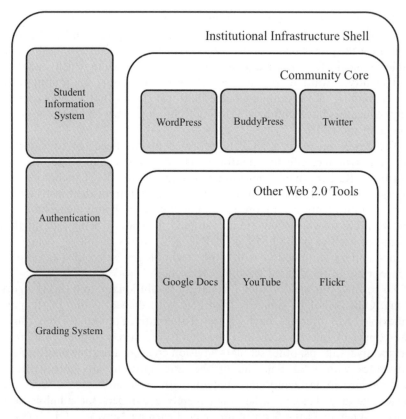

Fig. 2. Dynamic Course Platform Structure.

Sclater, 2008). The risk faculty take of stepping outside the walled garden of their institutions' LMS is having to build and populate a new mini-LMS for each course every semester. To do so, as both authors experienced, is a daunting task indeed, and something from which less adventurous and technically savvy faculty shy away. Thus, in our proposal for building a DCP, we continue with the importance of co-habitation of contemporary Web 2.0 and social media tools with aspects crucial to administering courses and student registrations, such as the SIS.

Although we are aware of and agree with many principles of work that calls for a complete dismissal of all aspects of the institutionalized LMS (see, e.g., Kamenetz, 2010; Young, 2008) we are also sensitive to the fact that IT departments and university administrations are for the most part, still entrenched in maintaining control and standardization to the greatest extent possible across the enterprise. Nevertheless, for institutional leadership to continue ignoring or even imposing restrictions on the growing exodus of faculty and students choosing to use tools outside the bounds of institutional control only reinforces the education–industrial complex that is higher education. For academe to truly evolve, there must be an embracing of these tools that are intuitive, easy-to-use, and dare we say, fun? The opportunity for IT in particular is to situate itself as a guide for faculty and students to navigate the Web 2.0 and social media world. IT support staff should help educators choose appropriate and effective instructional tools, and *then* do the technical work of integrating these tools into existing IT infrastructure toward an essentially common institutional shell, in which a DCP functions to connect seamlessly the types of Web 2.0 and social media tools we discuss in the following section with the core services necessary to operate a university.

CROSSING OVER FROM TRADITIONAL LMS

If the previous sections served as a brief summary of where LMS has *been*, then the rest of this chapter expands on what LMS can achieve as a pragmatic platform outside only traditional proprietary means. Here we summarize goals and outcomes of individual courses in the communication studies discipline where we worked together to try out a combination of social media and Web 2.0 tools in combination with traditional LMS. In the summer of 2009, with Michael's assistance, Danielle began prepping a 300-level communication studies elective for the following fall titled, Critical Theory and the Study of Popular Culture. Although the course was not listed as a hybrid, Danielle's experiences using Wordpress blogs for an online gender communication summer class proved successful enough to extend into the offline classroom.

The previous summer, in 2008, Danielle taught an online course for the first time, a beginning news writing class, using only a proprietary LMS, which at that institution was Desire2Learn. She and her students barely survived that three-week period of uploading and downloading assignments into folders at the mercy of the university's servers. When Danielle took on an online course the following summer at her new institution, which contracts with Blackboard for course management, she knew she did not want to limit the summer online experience to the proprietary system. Danielle sought an open-source, social media platform that might provide a more inviting space than the controlled environment of Blackboard to discuss the more sensitive and political realm of gender topics. Social media invite a return to Kerr's (2001) village conceptualization of higher education, reflecting a do-it-yourself attitude such as that explored by the recent Edupunk movement championed by daring educational technologists like Jim Groom from the University of Mary Washington on his blog (see Groom, 2008) and explored by scholars such as Anya Kamenetz in her 2010 work, *DIY U*.

Having been familiar with Blackboard since her time as a graduate student teaching media studies, Danielle knew that students liked it for keeping tabs on grades and sometimes as a communications tool for tasks such as email and group file sharing but little else, an observation supported by our review of the literature (see Caruso, 2006). Only one of Danielle's professors at her undergraduate institution used the designated LMS, WebCT, for discussion boards and quizzes, but her graduate level instruction, despite being in the media studies field, was decidedly low-tech and offline. As Lane (2008) notes, faculty teaching courses using some form of LMS often experience considerable pressure to demonstrate a level of savviness when it comes to using available technologies, especially for promotion and tenure reasons; however, these otherwise enterprising faculty are not often "webheads," as Lane describes, and are pressed into using technology with little or outdated experience in using web-based tools effectively.

More often, these faculty, while talented instructors in traditional settings, experience considerable difficulty translating classroom-based instructional methods into techno-mediated environments. So, while Danielle received a thorough education in critical theory and media criticism, as well as seminars on successful pedagogy, she never experienced instruction in how to successfully "manage" course content online. To this point, we could not agree more with Caruso's (2006) emphasis on the importance of institutions not only doing more to provide existing faculty with incentives to attend training sessions on both LMS and alternative technologies, but to provide developmental guidance to soon-to-be educators, such as in preparing future faculty programs at the graduate school level.

To compensate for her lack of training in LMS, Danielle turned to her personal use of blogs and online social networks to inform a professional course design, which is where Michael became an integral figure, introducing Danielle to Wordpress as a blogging site and eventual course platform. The instructional technology resources of her own institution at the time did offer an unofficial institutional blogging platform built on Wordpress; however, visibility of the system was happenstance (one had to know someone who knew whom to contact), access was far from convenient (requiring hand completion and time-consuming approval of forms and all blogs had to be created by a system admin) nor were the capabilities of the system sufficient to support the needs of her course (students were prohibited from creating blogs and features were kept to a minimum). In full disclosure, Danielle's institution now has a contract with Google for email, document management and simple website building platform called Sites (though it is still a closed system available only within the university's domain by registered students, faculty, and staff). After a few very simple lessons with Michael about Wordpress basics, Danielle had a theme, pages, tags, and customized discussion settings, demonstrating the ease with which faculty can jump into social media course platforms.

The conversations generated on that summer course Wordpress blog were more complex, respectful and heuristic than most either author had experienced in the physical classroom. Student comments on the daily posts were multiple paragraphs long rather than the few meager sentences we had come to expect in the existing LMS discussion boards. At the close of the semester Danielle asked students to share their likes and dislikes of the blog course design and was delighted to learn that most of the 25 students preferred it to the LMS experience. A few of them did explain that although the technological learning curve of Wordpress was difficult without face-to-face instructions (we had supplied detailed instructions online but not all students were able to attend the optional lab day where Danielle walked them through the Wordpress system) once they learned to navigate the online space of choosing a theme and blog settings they appreciated the personalization features.

Until the gender class, the students' online course experiences were limited to Blackboard discussions and assignment dropbox tools, which the students shared were uninviting and also technologically "screwy" at times in that if the university server was down then they could not reach their course content. Not only did students like being able to tailor their online learning environments to their individual aesthetic desires, then, they also enjoyed the openness and availability of a nonproprietary system. In effect, Danielle created what Mott and Wiley (2009) explain as a figurative "campfire," around which people choose to gather. Based on her experience, Danielle's students not only gathered around her campfire for as Mott and Wiley suggest as the fire's tangible benefits of heat and light (in this case,

course assignments, rubrics, and other administrative content) but also –
and more importantly – because it afforded them a comfortable, inviting
space to draw together and interact socially *about knowledge*.

Although these disclosures justified the use of Wordpress over Blackboard for the online course, these results did not approach to the revelation
by many students that the course blog made them want to revisit posts many
times daily to see how classmates responded. Some students commented
multiple times daily to a single blog prompt. To be sure, as with the physical
classroom, some students communicated more than others. However, a
number of students who normally would not have felt comfortable
disagreeing with their classmates – or their professor – in the traditional
classroom shared that they felt a sense of safeness and equality on the course
blog. In all, the students in the summer online gender course admitted being
excited by the learning process in ways not experienced before. These
students had quite literally created a community of knowledge about gender
topics in societal institutions as varied as education, media, politics, and the
workplace. We knew that we wanted to recreate that sense of community in
the popular culture course.

Building the Dynamic Course Platform

What began with slowly working outside the proprietary means of LMS
had evolved into a desire to mashup the learning tools even more. Our
personal use of blogs had previously encouraged us to incorporate them into
limited exercises in the traditional gender communication classroom, which
then led to designing the same course using only Wordpress blogs. We
should mention here that at the time we were using Wordpress.com, where
students visited the home site of Wordpress.com to register a blog. After
the success of that course, and with Michael's encouragement, Danielle
decided to pursue the next step in DIY pedagogy, a multiuser blog platform
from Wordpress.org. We registered a domain (through Go Daddy) and
affordable hosting site (Just Host in this case) toward what became
popacademy.org. We were, after all, embarking on a new course for the
major that was listed as an upper level elective critically engaging popular
culture.

Shifting from the dot-com to dot-org side of Wordpress provides
much greater personalization and community building within a blog
learning platform. Although both are free and generally look and operate
the same for the students, customizable features such as themes, widgets

(small extensions) and Buddypress provide a more organic, connected experience. For example, whether a student registers a blog on Wordpress. com or popacademy.org, the dashboard of selecting a theme and privacy settings looks relatively similar. However, through the multiuser Wordpress.org account, faculty and/or instructional technology support staff can embed more diverse themes and options that assist in students' blogs being decidedly individualized spaces over which students can claim and be proud of ownership. Since Danielle also planned to use Twitter in the pop culture course (which we will expand on later in this section), it was important to select themes that supported a Twitter widget. Through a simple widget called Twitter Tools, students could choose to have their course blog posts update to their Twitter feed, have their tweets publish as blog posts, update their Twitter status from a blog sidebar, as well as see a running scroll of recent tweets on their blogs. The blog post announcement via Twitter proved especially helpful when students wanted to keep tabs on which blog posts were ready to read for their weekly assignments.

Beyond weekly blog assignments, the students also had to work toward a final group project, which is where Buddypress, a Facebook-like group feature, proved tremendously helpful. Once students registered a blog with popacademy.org, they could create a profile complete with a picture, brief bio and contact info (all optional) and were automatically linked as "friends" of other registered users, which at the time included only the instructor and the other students. However, students could choose to cancel a friendship, though no one has used this feature thus far. In addition to building an instant community to get to know classmates and the instructor, students can create groups via Buddypress. The groups feature seems mostly designed to facilitate easier group communication through a centralized site that allows for the creation of forum topics and RSS feeds. Once Danielle assigned students into their respective project groups, most students voluntarily created their groups in Buddypress, while one group ended up using Facebook (which is more than okay considering the point is for students to use the tools that will most help toward their group experience). One group began with Ning but after some technical issues came back to Buddypress. Half of the groups kept their team pages private but invited Danielle to become a member so that she could follow their progress, whereas the other half created public groups open to viewing and commenting by everyone registered within the site.

Another key reason for the switch to the multiuser platform was the linking together of individual student blogs, as well as group blogs for their team projects, via Buddypress. From the main popacademy.org site, visitors can link to other blogs either by browsing a tab for members or blogs, as well as click on the running scroll of recent sitewide blog updates in a sidebar. Again, the point of these options is to encourage community and connectedness in the online space of the hybrid classroom. Blogging is a crucial component of the pop culture course design in that so much of what we experience in popular culture today is re-received via blogs and online news sites. Students can link to headlines of celebrity gossip, political scandals, media criticism, and other popular news directly from individual posts. What we found in the pop culture class is that these online references, to which other students and Danielle, as the instructor, replied to in the form of comments, carried over into informed, enthusiastic discussions in the physical classroom.

Moreover, customizable Wordpress blogs become dynamic multimedia environments impossible to create in the current structure of the LMS. Have you tried embedding video from YouTube or Vimeo into a Blackboard discussion forum? You can attach images and audio and video files, but linking to a URL is not an option. The last thing the authors want to do is come off as bashing Blackboard. However, since Blackboard is the contracted LMS option available to the university – and it does not fulfill our interactive course needs – then we must use other means to facilitate a community of popular culture discourse. We do realize that Blackboard and other LMS frameworks can link to web pages and online video. However, if students cannot do so themselves, on their own learning spaces with the ease and spontenaity of doing similarly on social network sites, then what purpose does the LMS serve? For now, grades and long-form assignment uploads, since students post blog entries and short essays on their individual Pop Academy sites for others to read and comment. Although Danielle still uses her university's proprietary LMS options for these administrative reasons, we know that in the DIY-learning era, faculty are just a few mouse clicks away from disrupting those structures as well. Before we conclude this section and explain more about how DCP fulfills important faculty and student needs in the digital age, we want to explain one more crucial component of DCP in the popular culture course: Twitter.

#community

Of the 30 students enrolled in the pop culture course, only 3 had been actively using Twitter before the start of the fall 2009 semester. Another three had only recently created profiles but had yet to cultivate a Twitter network. Danielle joined Twitter in January 2009, well behind Michael (ever the early adopter) and soon discovered its pedagogical uses, especially for popular culture topics. The summer she began prepping the critical theory course coincided with a number of celebrities and organizations battling it out for the most Twitter followers. Additionally, Danielle had been following a number of academic blogs, where posts abounded about Twitter "experiments" in the classroom. She read plenty of cross-references to other academics' use of Twitter, including YouTube clips and lists of sample projects. However, as with the rest of Danielle's social media pedagogy growth, she wanted to challenge herself to integrate a semester-length Twitter project into the syllabus. Since this course was designed to get students thinking critically about popular culture, we could not think of a better approach then to encourage students to embrace their active agency as consumers *and* producers of the popular (Jenkins, 2006). In combination with the Pop Academy blogs based on Wordpress and Buddypress, as well as Blackboard for administrative course tasks and organization, Twitter completed our tri-fold dynamic course platform (Table 1).

To begin, Danielle created a professional Twitter profile @popacademy in addition to her personal @daniellestern account. She asked students to create their own Twitter accounts and follow her professional @popacademy account. Danielle used @popacademy to tweet topics specific to assignments and discussion topics in the pop culture class. This separate account also served as a guide for students to know which other students to follow, for the only people Danielle follows via @popacademy are students enrolled in the pop culture course. Student Twitterers could see the @popacademy following list and then follow each other. She also created a list specific to course users so that students could choose to follow that list. The next step was to use the #comm326 hashtag (a folksonomic means by which to organize and make searchable users' tweets) as another way of identifying course tweets. It took a few weeks for most students to get the hang of the new language and dynamics, including the functionality of hashtags and other Twitter conventions such as retweets and @ replies, but the course hit a good rhythm about a month in, right around the time a major pop culture event took over the Twittersphere and the classroom, which we expand on a bit later in this section.

Because the use of Twitter was meant to extend conversations about popular culture beyond the physical classroom and course blog, Danielle did not want students to just tweet occasionally during assigned times. Building from the literature we have already cited here on increasing community in

Table 1.   Use of Tools in Tri-fold Dynamic Course Platform.

Wordpress
- Easy facilitation for group projects
- Group blogs
- Group pages similar to Facebook
- Individual blogs
- Sitewide aggregation for finding peer blogs
- Blogs not limited by university access
- Elicit participation from otherwise nontalkers
- Customizable blog settings, including design, functionality, *and* privacy
- Can link to other online social networks
- Mobile access, including smartphones, with a simple, open source WP application
- Course instructions and assignment rubrics (either via blog pages or PDF uploads)
- Builds excitement over commenting to peer blogs and course blog

Twitter
- Instant group communication for course reminders
- Ability to direct message individual students privately when necessary
- Ability to create lists of classmates (and other noncourse communities depending on course topic) for easy accessibility
- Searchable record of conversations
- Creation of hashtags to mark types of course announcements
- Industry-specific networking beyond classroom (for potential jobs and/or graduate school)
- Elicit participation from otherwise nontalkers
- Builds community based on many types of interests (educational, social, political, and cultural)
- Establishes public credibility for institution and department

Blackboard (or other LMS)
- Gradebook
- Access to copyrighted supplemental course readings under fair use law
- Quiz and exam facilitation
- Coursewide email

---

the classroom and similar to the use of Twitter by nursing educators to facilitate a connection between students, patients and the health care community (Billings, Kowalsk, & Bristol, 2010) and cultivating active engagement with cultural forms (Jenkins, 2009) as well as literature examining the importance of fostering social presence in the online sphere using social media (Dunlap & Lowenthal, 2009) and enhancing opportunities for student "ownership" of learning (Fiedler & Valjataga, 2010), we wanted to see if semester-long use of Twitter would help accomplish these goals. As such, we provided a detailed description of their expected Twitter tasks. The four areas of assessment included: (1) cohesiveness of a student's theme as a Twitterer; (2) thoroughness of students' engagement with the technology and fellow "tweeps" (other Twitter users); (3) thoughtful inclusion of course material in students' use of Twitter; and (4) evolution of a student's Twittersphere as a whole as the course progressed.

As outlined in Table 2, Danielle included the following details of Twitter assignment expectations for when she would check in on students' Twitter use, which occurred four times throughout the semester.

Because Danielle had encouraged students to go beyond simply tweeting their status, location and links without comments, most of her new student Twitterers did not know how best to engage the platform. Then Kanye West stole the microphone from Taylor Swift during her acceptance speech for an award at the MTV Video Music Awards in September 2009. Up to that point students had barely begun cultivating their following and followers and increasing their use of hashtags, @ replies, RTs, and including commentary with forwarded links. However, before West could say, "I'mma let you finish," he was a trending topic, solidifying a sense of purpose for the course in a way Danielle's own words, actions, and online guide books could not articulate. Students were tweeting unprompted questions of whether it was inappropriate for Kanye to have stolen the moment, if race played any role, how the music genres of hip hop and country were constructed differently by MTV. We could continue, but the point is that the students' use of Twitter as a tool for cultural critique and analysis had officially taken shape.

Table 2. Twitter Assignment Expectations.

Grading Criterion	Sample Feedback to Student
For cohesiveness	You follow a good blend of different types of Twitterers. Your following, @ replies and hashtags make sense within a wider framework. You have found a natural place in the Twitterzsphere
For engagement	You actively used the tools of Twitter technologies (hashtags, @ replies, retweets, and others) to make sense of and contribute to popular culture and social discourse
For inclusion of course material	You thoughtfully incorporated your interpretations from readings and course discussion (in the classroom and on the blogs) rather than simply link to stories and headlines. You contributed to the dialogue via critical theory (instead of simply sending tweets without context)
For evolution of use	You clearly enhanced your social and technological use of Twitter over the course of the semester. Your end product looks significantly better than your first couple of weeks of using Twitter

Not surprisingly, the Swift-West incident took over Danielle's planned lecture on Marxism the next day. Danielle and her students watched the clip online, as well as Beyoncé Knowles' turn at the microphone when she took it upon herself to afford Swift time to give the speech that West cut off. These viewings then led to discussions of what students read on blogs and online news, as well as the Twittersphere, regarding construction of race and gender in popular media. They discussed expectations of femininity, masculinity, as well as blackness and whiteness, for top-selling performers. The co-opted Marxism lecture reshaped into a critique on the pressures of the recording industry to mold artists into particular images. Students noted the rigid identity roles constructed by West, Swift, and Knowles, comparing the "bad boy" image of the black rapper West to that of the pure white country songstress Swift, with Knowles' morphology from cookie-cutter girl group member to mainstream diva coinciding with a struggle between a decidedly "whitewashing" of her image and moments of "ghetto."

That class period marked a turning point when students, and Danielle, all seemed, finally, to *get* what Twitter could provide for the learning process. To be sure, we could have easily covered these topics via a series of structured question prompts in a discussion forum within the LMS then referred to the comments in our physical classroom. However, because so many students were already signed into their blogs and Twitter applications as the VMAs were happening live, students pulled *themselves* into a broader conversation not confined to classmates and professors. Moreover, Danielle did not assign students to view the VMAs then write a blog post about the program, nor did she ask them to live Tweet the experience. This was all their doing, resulting in what we as practitioners of critical pedagogy strive to achieve in our learning environments. The students, *not* the professor, were teaching the course.

Students continued to build their portfolios with diverse blends of the types of celebrities, politicians, academics, organizations, news outlets, and other students they followed. They posed thoughtful questions specific to assigned course material. Although most students seemed delighted when people beyond the #comm326 list responded, some were still wary of "strangers" communicating with them. However, most students understood the importance of not closing off discourse to just those enrolled in the course (Campbell, 2009; Mott & Wiley, 2009). Popular culture is a topic that demands engagement outside the classroom walls. Before long, students began creating and using hashtags for other courses, swapping research ideas, sharing helpful links for course material and planning study sessions all via Twitter. They also asked the professor quick, easily answerable questions as tweets instead of email messages.

The instant, interactive nature of Twitter, which Dunlap and Lowenthal (2009) characterize as "freeflowing just-in-time interactions," proved helpful in winning over those students initially resistant to the medium. For example, questions one student asked were often helpful to other students, which reduced Danielle's need for sending mass emails or posting announcements via Blackboard. The Twitter bug also infected students in other courses in the department, beginning with students enrolled in Danielle's required senior-level theory course, as some were co-enrolled in the pop culture course. By the end of the term, students and faculty had opted for the #commnerd hashtag for tweets nonspecific to course material but related to research interests and potential seminar topics. Twitter, as an integral part of the DCP, had succeeded in increasing community not only in the classroom but beyond its former confining walls.

EXPANDING THE SOCIAL MEDIA DCP OUTSIDE THE CLASSROOM

In the months that followed the fall 2009 pop culture course, a number of moments emerged to reaffirm the use of social media as a dynamic course platform. First, as aforementioned briefly, the students kept using Twitter and encouraged other majors to do so, which resulted in more conversations between faculty and students – but especially among students – that might not otherwise have happened face-to-face or via email, firmly establishing a community of #commnerds. Similar to Dunlap and Lowenthal (2009), who suggest that technologies such as Twitter help foster the development of meaningful interpersonal relationships that benefit learning, we stress the immediate, shared nature of Twitter as an inviting approach to not only build community but also, dare we say it, make research fun. The #commnerd hashtag eventually became a t-shirt and a term of endearment in the department.

The second occurrence confirming the success of social media pedagogy extended to its impact on original student research after the semester was long over. Of the #commnerd undergraduates whose research was accepted for presentation at a major regional conference in spring 2010, the majority of them were active Twitterers and/or bloggers who had swapped ideas and planned research as tweets and blog posts. Moreover, many of these students became so involved in social media that they ended up building components of their senior research projects around the impact of social media in popular culture, relationships, politics, sport, and other communication topics. Some even explored the research and collaborative potential of Google Wave just as Google released the beta version. These research ideas were not isolated incidents but semester-long projects over which students collaboratively lived, breathed, created, and *critiqued* social media.

A third telling result of the positive impact of this sample learning platform was the realization that majors were getting jobs because of their social media expertise. Because of his professional practice of Twitter as a public relations tool to build a brand community, one student's part-time job turned into a full-time position in social media for an international airport after graduation. Other students made connections for interviews and job leads based on their Twitter networks. Additionally, the social media research that students presented at the spring conference discussed above led to inquiries from graduate school recruiters, building the social media academy of the future. Social media had grown from course assignment to knowledge community to post-grad staple.

Although the experiences of Danielle's students with social media in and outside the classroom are surely not unique, it is nonetheless important to link these moments of pedagogical empowerment with the continued task of educators seeking innovative course design. According to a 2010 Pew Study, 93% of teens and young adults spend time online, with a marked increase in social network participation (Lenhart, Purcell, Smith, & Zickuhr, 2010) from previous years, numbers likely to rise as Facebook, Google, and other online environments continue to command our time. Arguing that the "walled garden of the CMS has been breached," Mott and Wiley (2009) contend that faculty and students, when given the opportunity and incentive, readily discover new modes of dialogue and collaboration, which results in producing rich, engaging content such that the standard LMS model has achieved irrelevance. New models of interaction that embrace social media such as our suggestion of the DCP, as well as the Open Learning Networks and Personal Learning Networks described by other scholars, are the new models for educational technologies. Although online social networks admittedly contribute to the institutionalization and consumerism inherent in American culture today (Zollers, 2009), these networks' potential to infuse community and disrupt power structures in our current education–industrial complex must compel educators to tap these creative resources toward the design and integration of a dynamic course platform grounded in the community principles of social media.

REFERENCES

Alexander, B. K. (2005). Critically analyzing pedagogical interactions as performance. In: B. K. Alexander, G. L. Anderson & B. P. Gallegos (Eds), *Performance theories in education: Power, pedagogy, and the politics of identity* (pp. 41–62). Mahwah, NJ: Lawrence Erlbaum.

Billings, D. M., Kowalsk, K., & Bristol, T. J. (2010). Twitter: Consider the possibilities for continuing nursing education. *Journal of Continuing Education in Nursing, 41*(5), 199–200.

Brooks, L. (2009, May/June). Social media by design: The role of social media. *Knowledge Quest, 37*(5), 58–60.

Campbell, G. (2009, Sept./Oct.). A personal cyberinfrastructure. *Educause Review, 44*(5), 58–59. Retrieved from http://www.educause.edu/EDUCAUSE + Review/EDUCAUSE-ReviewMagazineVolume44/APersonalCyberinfrastructure/178431

Caruso, J. B. (2006). Measuring student experiences with course management systems. *Educause Center for Applied Research Research Bulletin, 2006*(19). n.p. Available at http://www.educause.edu/ECAR/MeasuringStudentExperienceswit/157577

Cuban, L. (2001). *Oversold and underused: Computers in the classroom.* Cambridge, MA: Harvard University Press.

Delta Initiative. (2009). *The state of learning management in higher education systems.* Report for the California State University System. Available at http://www.deltainitiative.com/picts/pdf/deltainitiativelmswebinar09-2.pdf

Dunlap, J. C., & Lowenthal, P. R. (2009). Tweeting the night away: Using Twitter to enhance social presence. *Journal of Information Systems Education, 20*(2). n.p. Available at http://www.patricklowenthal.com/publications/Using_Twitter_to_Enhance_Social_Presence.pdf

Ellsworth, E. (1989). Why doesn't this feel empowering? Working through the repressive myths of critical pedagogy. In: C. Luke & J. Gore (Eds), *Feminisms and critical pedagogy* (pp. 90–119). New York: Routledge.

Ess, C. (2006). Liberal arts and distance education: Can Socratic Virtue and Confucius' exemplary person be taught online? In: J. Lockard & M. Pegrum (Eds), *Brave new worlds: Democratic education and the internet* (pp. 189–212). New York: Peter Lang.

Fiedler, S., & Valjataga, T. (2010). Interventions for second-order change in higher education: Challenges and barriers. *Electronic Journal of e-Learning, 8*(2), 85–92.

Freire, P. (1988). *Pedagogy of the oppressed* (M. B. Ramos, Trans.). New York: Continuum.

Giroux, H. (1985). Critical pedagogy, cultural politics & the discourse of experience. *Journal of Education, 167*(2), 22–41.

Groom, J. (2008). The glass bees. [Web log]. Available at http://bavatuesdays.com/the-glass-bees

Hall, M. (1999). Virtual colonization. *Journal of Material Culture, 4*(1), 39–55.

Herrington, J., Reeves, T., & Oliver, R. (2005). Online learning as information delivery: Digital myopia. *Journal of Interactive Learning Research, 16*(4), 353–367. Available at http://ro.uow.edu.au/cgi/viewcontent.cgi?article = 1032&context = edupapers

Jenkins, H. (2006). *Convergence culture: Where old and new media collide.* New York: New York University Press.

Jenkins, H. (2009). *Confronting the challenges of participatory culture: Media education for the 21st century.* Cambridge, MA: MIT Press.

Johnson, S. (2005). *Everything bad is good for you.* New York: Riverhead.

Kamenetz, A. (2010). *DIY U: Edupunks, edupreneurs, and the coming transformation of higher education.* White River Junction, VT: Chelsea Green Publishing.

Kellner, D. (2000). Multiple literacies and critical pedagogies: New paradigms. In: P. P. Trifonas (Ed.), *Revolutionary pedagogies: Cultural politics, instituting education, and the discourse of theory* (pp. 196–221). New York: Routledge.

Kerr, C. (1991). *The great transformation in higher education 1960–1980.* Available at http://books.google.com/books?id = DjrTK9v-o2YC&lpg = PA235&ots = LGbduuKxVV&dq = kerr%20%22parking%20for%20the%20faculty%22&pg = PA235#v = onepage&q&f = false. Retrieved from Google Books.

Kerr, C. (2001). *The uses of the university* (5th ed.). Cambridge, MA: Harvard University Press.

Kibby, M. D. (2006). Hybrid teaching and learning: Pedagogy versus pragmatism. In: J. Lockard & M. Pegrum (Eds), *Brave new classrooms: Democratic education & the internet* (pp. 87–104). Lang: New York.

Lane, L. M. (2008). Toolbox or trap? Course management systems and pedagogy. *Educause Quarterly, 31*(2), 4–6. Available at http://www.educause.edu/EDUCAUSE + Quarterly/EDUCAUSEQuarterlyMagazineVolum/ToolboxorTrapCourseManagementS/162865

Lenhart, A., Purcell, K., Smith, A., & Zickuhr, K. (2010). Social media and mobile internet use among teens and young adults. Available at http://pewresearch.org/millennials/. Retrieved from Pew Research Center website.

Lockard, J., & Pegrum, M. (2006). *Brave new worlds: Democratic education and the internet.* New York: Peter Lang.

McCormick, M. H. (2006). Webmastered: Postcolonialism and the internet. In: J. Lockard & M. Pegrum (Eds), *Brave new classrooms: Democratic education & the internet* (pp. 75–86). Lang: New York.

Morgan, G. (2003). Faculty use of course management systems. *Key Findings.* Available at http://www.educause.edu/ECAR/FacultyUseofCourseManagementSy/158560. Retrieved from Educause Center for Applied Research website.

Mott, J. (2010). Envisioning the post-LMS Era: The open learning network. *Educause Quarterly, 33*(1). n.p. Available at http://www.educause.edu/EDUCAUSE + Quarterly/EDUCAUSEQuarterlyMagazineVolum/EnvisioningthePostLMSEraTheOpe/199389

Mott, J., & Wiley, D. (2009). Open for learning: The CMS and the open learning network. *Education, 15*(2). n.p. Available at http://www.ineducation.ca/article/open-learning-cms-and-open-learning-network. Retrieved on March 28, 2010.

Ott, B. L. (2007). *The small screen: How television equips us to live in the information age.* Malden, MA: Blackwell.

Postman, N. (1985). *Amusing ourselves to death: Public discourse in the age of show business.* New York: Penguin.

Postman, N. (1992). *Technopoly: The surrender of culture to technology.* New York: Vintage.

Precel, K., Eshet-Alkalai, Y., & Alberton, Y. (2009). Pedagogical and design aspects of a blended learning course. *International Review of Research in Open and Distance Learning, 10*(2). n.p. Retrieved on February 2, 2010 from EBSCOhost database (AN 39342362).

Rheingold, H. (2000). *The virtual community: Homesteading on the electronic frontier* (Revised edition). Cambridge, MA: MIT Press.

Rhode, J. F. (2009). Interaction equivalency in self-paced online learning environments: An exploration of learner preferences. *International Review of Research in Open and Distance Learning, 10*(1). n.p. Retrieved on February 2, 2010 from EBSCOhost database (AN 36875661).

Sclater, N. (2008). Web 2.0, personal learning environments, and the future of learning management systems. *Educause Center for Applied Research Bulletin, 2008*(13). Available at http://www.educause.edu/ECAR/Web20PersonalLearningEnvironme/163047

Young, J. (2008). Frustrated with corporate course-management systems, some professors go 'Edupunk.' Available at http://chronicle.com/blogPost/Frustrated-With-Corporate/3977. Retrieved from *The Chronicle of Higher Education* website.

Zollers, A. (2009). Critical perspectives on social network sites. In: R. Hammer & D. Kellner (Eds), *Media/cultural studies: Critical approaches* (pp. 602–614). New York: Peter Lang.

TWITTER IN HIGHER EDUCATION

Lisa Chamberlin and Kay Lehmann

ABSTRACT

Twitter is a simple tool allowing users to send 140 character messages to their followers. Although the tool itself is relatively simple, the benefits of using Twitter can be immense. Using Twitter educators and their students can tap into a global network of others interested in educational topics. Twitter is powerful in both range and immediacy. Students, faculty, and other university personnel including librarians are using Twitter to communicate both inside the classroom and beyond. This chapter includes how-to information for those who are new to Twitter, ways to use Twitter, tips on getting the most out of this tool, and a list of additional resources and tools which will magnify the positive effects of using Twitter.

CONFESSIONS OF THE CONVERTED

Admittedly, the authors of this chapter came late to the Twitter party. Despite being pioneers in online/distance learning and educational technology, we failed to see the value of Twitter as a professional learning and educational communications tool. Now we lament how much we missed during the year we thought Twitter was a teenage fad notifying friends of minor nonevents.

The authors were not the only ones who failed to *get* the power of Twitter right away. Jim Groom, known as @jimgroom on Twitter, is famous in the

Educating Educators with Social Media
Cutting-edge Technologies in Higher Education, Volume 1, 375–391
Copyright © 2011 by Emerald Group Publishing Limited
ISSN: 2044-9968/doi:10.1108/S2044-9968(2011)0000001021

educational technology circles as the chief edupunk (loosely defined as "student-centered, resourceful, teacher- or community-created rather than corporate-sourced, and underwritten by a progressive political stance" – Downes, 2008). Groom (J. Groom, personal communication, May 4, 2010) stated his reluctance with Twitter this way:

> At first I thought it was the stupidest thing ever ... I mocked it for a month or two, all the while still dabbling, but I really couldn't see its value ... for a while. (I credit folks like [Cole] Campelese, [D'Arcy] Norman, and [Alan] Levine with seeing its potential rather early in this regard, and I slowly came over to their camp – at least to some degree.) I was pretty much a blogging snob (in fact, I remain so) and saw Twitter as a rather unappealing, stripped-down version of the Facebook status update (FB being my least favorite service in the world). Not at all exciting, but at the same time, oddly compelling given I could follow real time updates from friends and colleagues around the globe. But I was more or less waiting for the trend to peter out, and ridiculing it along the way.

For Groom, an Instructional Technology Specialist and adjunct professor at the University of Mary Washington, realizing Twitter's potential was about realizing its real time relationship building potential in the virtual space.

> I follow Twitter to feel closer to a group of colleagues that are distributed around the globe, and for that it is unparalleled. It brings the everyday banter around which relationships are both made and maintained to the online space, and that, for me, is its true value. It took me a while to realize this, but what gets sucked out of online learning in the traditional sense is the space for play, banter, and chit chat, and twitter, unlike any other tool I have seen, reintroduces this to the mix. And while it may seem trivial, I would argue it is downright revolutionary in this regard. Bringing play into online learning maybe one of the most important advancements in this arena. (J. Groom, personal communication, May 4, 2010)

HOW POWERFUL AND IMMEDIATE IS YOUR NETWORK

How many responses to a question can you get from your colleagues via personal conversation, email, or by phone in under two hours? On April 29, 2010, Eric Sheninger of New Milford High School in New Jersey, who tweets as @NMHS_Principal, posted this request on Twitter: "PLN: Why should kids be allowed to use social media? What results from banning it? use #WINS Pls help me ROCK this interview!" (NMHS_Principal, 2010). Between 9:44 am when his message was posted and 11:30 am he received 102 responses from his personal learning network (PLN). This is just one example showcasing Twitter's power as a networking and personal learning tool.

HISTORY OF TWITTER

Twitter was created in 2006 by Jack Dorsey. According to Wikipedia (2010), the creators originally named it *twttr* based on five character codes in use at the time for short messaging services, known as SMS. The idea was to send SMS-style messages but be able to send them to a group, rather than to individuals. Twitter took hold in 2007 at a South by Southwest (SXSW) conference. Its usage tripled in just a few days as conference goers tweeted to each other about conference events. That was then. There are now more than 10 million registered Twitter users, only 17% of which are under 18 (Miller, 2009). In March 2010 Twitter's growth reached a whopping 131% making it the fastest growing Internet property for that time period (comScore, 2009).

Some of that growth is occurring among educators. In the February 2010 issue of Educational Leadership William Ferriter (2010) explains why teachers should try Twitter:

> Although many Twitter users post personal messages that might be described as "digital noise" (such as "Having Chinese takeout for dinner"), teaching professionals have found ways to use Twitter to share resources and lend quick support to peers with similar interests. For educators who use this tool to build a network of people whose Twitter messages connect to their work, Twitter becomes a constant source of new ideas to explore. (p. 73)

THE SURVEY SAYS

Midyear of 2009, Faculty Focus – a thrice weekly e-newsletter with 25,000 subscribers – surveyed approximately 2000 higher education professionals about their Twitter knowledge and use. The results showed that, while Twitter had been successful at getting its brand name recognized, it had not been as successful at getting its relevancy and value understood within higher education circles.

According to the survey, "Twitter in Higher Education: Usage, Habits, and Trends of Today's College Faculty," 30% of higher education professionals are actively using Twitter, and just under 13% have quit using it after a trial period. That leaves roughly 56% of faculty, administration, and support staff reporting they have had no experience whatsoever with Twitter. Many in this group, however, "say they plan to test the waters for the first time when the new school year begins this fall, and a few more say they are willing to give it a try, but aren't sure where to start or are taking a 'wait and see' before adding Twitter to their growing arsenal of teaching tools" (Faculty Focus survey, 2009, p. 4). One anonymous survey respondent summarized this attitude with his commentary, "Until I understand the relevance of Twitter, I don't see the need to jump on the bandwagon" (p. 8). Another summed it up a little less delicately, "I believe Twitter is and should remain a tool for social networking, not education" (p. 8). Twitter advocates and social networking evangelists would argue those two concepts, social networking, and education, are not mutually exclusive. "To realize the benefits of Twitter you need to build a strong network of at least 30–50 people to follow, and that takes time ... Twitter allows you to expand your network beyond those you see and talk to every day so you're exposed to new ideas and fresh perspectives" (Faculty Focus survey, 2009, p. 18).

Make no mistake, despite the oft reported average age of a Twitter user being 35 or older, Twitter use is growing on college campuses (Martin, 2009). Tweeting higher education professionals make up 30% of the surveyed population, yet Twitter, currently, is utilized by only 10% of all active Internet users (Martin, 2009). This suggests that higher education is out pacing the general Internet-user population in Twitter adoption at a roughly 3 to 1 pace.

Statistically speaking, Twitter has not been a dominant social media force for long enough to make big predictions about where it will go from here. But, anecdotal feedback from the 30% group of users (and the recently converted) helps to tell the story. "Twitter is the ultimate personal networking tool. I have been in touch with so many more thought leaders in educational technologies since I started using it. It keeps me up to date in my field of expertise" (Anonymous respondent, Faculty Focus survey, 2009, p. 14).

Gina Minks, (@gminks), an online graduate student living in Boston but attending Florida State University, uses Twitter as a means of feeling connected with her classmates and instructors.

> The biggest way I have used Twitter is as an extension of my PLE. I live outside Boston, MA but I am a graduate student at Florida State University. My entire program is online. So I can't drop into an instructor's office, or go have coffee with my fellow students. But I can send out a tweet when I'm confused or conflicted about something I'm reading for a class. (G. Minks, personal communication, April 25, 2010)

She goes on to describe how she has been able to add major thought leaders of her field to her personal learning network by being part of a weekly virtual tweet up called #lrnchat.

My degree will be in Instructional Systems. So my questions have centered around learning theory and instructional design methods. If I ask something, people like Marcia Conner, Jay Cross, Stephen Downes, George Siemens, Harold Jarche, or Clark Quinn (to name a few) answer me. They answer with links to relevant research and blog posts. (G. Minks, personal communication, April 25, 2010)

Finally, she summarizes just what Twitter has come to mean for her.

Twitter has helped me with the topics that I learned during my classes, but it has also embedded me into the learning community. It totally changed my grad school experience, and presented me with opportunities I wouldn't have had if I stayed within the normal brick and mortar experience. (G. Minks, personal communication, April 25, 2010)

David Parry, an assistant professor of Emerging Media and Communication at the University of Texas-Dallas, relayed his experiences with Twitter in a "Chronicle of Higher Education" article. By the time Parry's initial experimenting ended, he was referring to Twitter as "the single thing that changed the classroom dynamics more than anything else I've ever done in teaching" (Young, 2009).

For the uninitiated, Twitter may come across as so much fluff in an ever-increasing stream of Internet noise. The press coverage of celebrity Tweeters only adds to this reputation. But for those who have spent the time to learn and build a PLN using it and other forms of social media, Twitter is radically altering how they do the business of teaching and learning. Understanding Twitter – the what and the how of it – is the first step in putting this dynamic tool to productive use. The best part is Twitter is easy to use.

I've said it 1,000 times, if Web 2.0 is worth anything, it's because the technology requires no instruction whatsoever. It should be as easy as talking or making a wisecrack. Unlike many of the Web 2.0 programs, Twitter (largely) does exactly what it's supposed to do without any learning curve. (Stager, comments on Weblogg-ed, April 27, 2010)

THE WHAT – WHAT IS TWITTER EXACTLY

How can educators stay up-to-date about current events, articles, and research, often within seconds of its release? Twitter is the answer! Educators who have developed a strong personal learning network on Twitter have access to the most recent information on any topic imaginable. It is an immediate and powerful Web2.0 communication tool. It presents information or comments in short messages and is accessible on a smartphone or computer. Used effectively, Twitter can be a community building tool, as well. In addition to being a part of a personal learning network, there are micro and macro uses of Twitter for the classroom.

The Basics

Twitter, in a nutshell, is a communication tool. The publication of these ultrashort messages like this is referred to as microblogging and is very much like text messaging. Although on a smart phone, the sender has to select which person of his/her contacts will receive the text message. On Twitter, however, all followers (self-subscribed contacts) receive the message. This is akin to sending a text message to everyone of your contacts file every time you text. These 140 character messages (called tweets) can be broadcast to all of the sender's followers or directed to certain individuals depending on how the tweet is formatted. The process of sending and receiving Twitter messages is called tweeting. Twitter is not difficult to use, but its usefulness is not always readily apparent to the beginning user. Understanding does develop with time and a little perseverance.

As aforementioned, Twitter users tweet messages to their followers and receive messages by following others. To follow someone simply means to subscribe to that person's tweetstream so his or her messages will appear in the user's own tweetstream. Tweetstreams (or message feeds) are the posted and received messages, displayed list-style in chronological order. These appear on the user's home page. As a new user follows more individuals, more tweets arrive and provide a wider array of opinions and resources on the topics of interest. Although asynchronous conversations of a sort do develop, thinking of tweeting as a discussion forum may lead to confusion for some users. Tweets are, essentially, independent bursts of commentary, news, or the sharing of a resource – in the same way that one blog post is, more or less, independent from the rest of the posts in the writer's archive.

How would a new Twitter user find people to follow? And how do Twitter users develop a following? The Twitter "Find People" search tool is a place to start. Other ways include mining relevant tweeters from the tweetstreams of a user's current followers. By lurking in others' tweetstreams, which means reading their tweetstream but not adding to it, a new user can discover other experts in his/her field and start following them as well. Lurking can also provide a feel for the type of messages that are appropriate and less appropriate as tweets.

Following strong Twitter users, who are recognized experts in a field, is an enlightening experience. With the right group of people to follow, it quickly becomes clear that Twitter can be so much more than tweets about the brand of toothpaste someone uses or what she ate for lunch. It is, instead, a very rich stream of ideas, resources, and knowledge. As New York Times technology columnist David Pogue concluded, "Twitter is whatever you make of it" (Faculty Focus, 2009, p. 11).

Using Twitter's search tool, a user can find colleagues, other experts, or other users with similar interests. There is no limit to the number of people who can be followed (except for a few spamming safeguards) or the number of different areas of interest which can be explored. When the new user begins to contribute to the information stream, his or her own following naturally develops. New users who have observed good tweeting during their lurking phase, generally begin by retweeting messages of interest (like forwarding email) to those in their field. From there, new users find their comfort level with Twitter and begin tweeting their own knowledge-base. This is the give and take of social networking at its richest and most dynamic.

How to Tweet

The basics outlined above become clearer with a little more exploration and practice with the Twitter interface. To get started, a new user must go to the Twitter home page (http://www.twitter.com) and register for an account. Registering involves entering your email address, adding a password of your choice, and choosing a user name. User names can be all or part of a real name, or can be completely anonymous such as otl99 (this is an unused Twitter name at the time this chapter was written). Twitter usernames are written with the @ symbol directly in front of the name such as @otl99.

Real or fake name? There are pros and cons of using a real name on Twitter and other social media sites. Many people are still leery of the security of publicly accessed online sites and the ease with which others on the Internet can find personal information about complete strangers. Since this chapter is about using Twitter in higher education, however, it is assumed students would already know the name of their professor. Therefore, using a real name makes it easier for students to locate an instructor. In addition, a real name makes it easier not only for Twitter-using students but also professional colleagues to find and follow a new Twitter user. As Patricia Ransom, a Twitter-using higher education student stated

Social Media is a conversation. And conversations are about sharing. At first I didn't want people to be able to find me or know who I was. But I realized that goes against this entire concept of social media. I needed to have faith and put myself out there so others could find me. (P. Ransom, personal interview, March 20, 2010)

Using a real name is a part of developing a professional brand, so to speak. Branding is a new term, borrowed from business marketing strategists, for building a professional reputation. To build a following and grow a personal learning network, a social media user should be willing to publicly associate his identity with his brand. Publications, presentations, and other high-profile activities identify a professor's contribution to the field and build that instructor's professional reputation (or brand). In higher education, professional reputations have always been associated with personal names. Tweeting under a real name is just an electronic extension of this idea. Dean Shareski, a prolific Twitter user and professor at the University of Regina, sums it up best when he says, "I don't use any pseudonyms in any of my online spaces. I want people to know who I am" (D. Shareski, personal communication, March 14, 2010).

Once the user name is selected, the new user completes the registration process and the main Twitter webpage opens. This is where the fun really begins. The next step is to take a moment to set up the profile. The profile should showcase areas of expertise. Those using Twitter for professional purposes, who are comfortable using their real names, may also want to post a standard headshot – similar to what one would use for a conference brochure. Students and colleagues are then able to visually verify that they have found the correct person for whom they were searching. As the process of finding people to follow is explained the usefulness of profiles becomes more evident.

How to find quality people to follow? Use the Find People link in the top right portion of the main Twitter page to open the search page. Searches can be conducted using a full name, an email address, or keywords. Keywords from a field of expertise, or the names of experts in that field, are good choices with which to begin. The search results provide a list of possible Twitter followees and their most recent tweet. Clicking on the user name (pretend the first name on the list is our fake user @otl99) displays @otl99's profile. Looking at the profile is a good way to see if the user has similar interests. Other information available there includes how many people @otl99 follows, how many followers @otl99 has, and how many tweets @otl99 has posted.

Why would this information be important? Ransom (P. Ransom, personal interview, March 20, 2010) explains "Regardless of how I find people, I never ever follow them without reviewing my criteria. If I answer no to any of these, I usually don't follow." Ransom's criteria includes:

- Do they have a profile? If no (or it's just a sentence) I do not follow.
- Is that profile more than a URL? If no, I do not follow.
- Do I find their profile relevant in some way, shape or form?
- Is their ratio of followers to following relatively less than 4:1? If it's completely off (10,000 following and only 30 followers) then I consider them spammers.
- Finally I look at how often they tweet – if it's more than once an hour, I do not follow them cause they will clog up my tweetstream.

In the Classroom

How to tweet should be clearer now, but the usefulness of tweeting may still be a mystery. As noted earlier, there are micro and macro uses of Twitter. Micro uses of Twitter occur within a small defined group. On the other hand, when tweets go out to a broad or unlimited audience, often with searchable markings called hashtags, macro usage of Twitter occurs. Tweeting questions and insight during live classes or in a lecture hall is a micro use. This tweetstream occurring during a presentation (known as the 'backchannel' or backchanneling) helps shape the content to a degree. Tweeted questions and comments from face-to-face listeners are aggregated and responded to during the presentation, perhaps changing the direction of the lecture, further developing a point, or speeding the presentation up if tweeters remark they have heard this all before.

Getting information via tweets during a lecture allows the professor to "hear" questions from the silent majority who never raise their hand or who are drowned out by the vocal few. Or, in the case of 700 seat lecture halls, it allows the professor a chance to interact on a more personal level than the overwhelming number normally would allow. If a number of very similar questions are asked via tweet, the lecturer knows there is a widespread need for clarification. During a conference event, a presenter who is using the backchannel will know if she is delivering the information her target audience desires, and she can adjust accordingly.

Using a backchannel effectively during a lecture or presentation requires the help of at least one additional person. After all, a professor who is speaking may lose his train of thought if he tries to read tweets mid-lecture. Having an assistant filter and collate the tweets, and then relay a summary of the pertinent messages to the presenter is the best way to have a microlevel backchannel.

One way backchannel tweets can be organized is through a twibe which is a defined group of Twitter users. Once a Twibe is created, others from the backchanneling group can join. More information on Twibes can be found at http://www.twibes.com/.

Another way to gather the backchannel messages from a defined audience is to use hashtags. Hashtags are acronyms or keywords used by search engines to filter for tweets about a certain topic or event. Preceded by a # symbol, hashtags are easily recognizable in tweets. There might be a hashtag for a conference such as #NCCE10 or an abbreviated key phrase #edtech, a product name #iPad, or a concept #hcr (health care reform). In the case of a lecturer who is filtering backchannel messages, student tweets can be labeled with a specific hashtag such as #Bio101Apr10. The assistant then filters for all the messages about the Biology 101 lecture occurring on April 10 as the lecture is delivered. Having a short, but very specific hashtag helps to ensure all the comments and questions from the audience are seen by the presenter.

Although hashtags can be used in defined groups as noted above they are also very useful for broadcasting the backchannel to a wider, global, audience. When a presentation involves concepts of interest to others who are not in face-to-face attendance, the hashtag helps to disseminate the knowledge and insights beyond the geography of the four walls of the lecture hall. This purposeful broadcast to a wider audience is a macro use of Twitter.

Backchannel messages from conference presentations are quite common in professional circles today. By following the conference hashtag, a nonattendee can read every major point made by presenter – all courtesy of a tweeting face-to-face audience. A global audience is able to follow, and comment on, every word a presenter utters. Chris Lehmann's School 2.0 speech April 20, 2010, at the 140 Characters Conference was a great example of this phenomenon. Lehmann's macro-Twitter use was done both in real time, and after the event ended (Sass, 2010). All that listeners needed was the hashtag associated with the presentation and an entire transcript of comments became available world-wide. One caveat if new Twitter uses would like to try a macro backchannel themselves – currently, Twitter stores tweets for only a few days in their searchable archives. It is important to use a 3rd party archiving tool like Archivist or Twapperkeeper if a user wants to keep the tweetstream indefinitely.

Dunlap and Lowenthal (2009), faculty and technology coordinator respectively, at the University of Colorado, explain how to effectively integrate Twitter into the higher education experience. "With Twitter, as with all social-networking tools, the value of the experience hinges on three things: (1) who you are connected to and with; (2) how frequently you participate; and (3) how conscientious you are about contributing value to the community" (Dunlap & Lowenthal, 2009).

Dunlap and Lowenthal (2009b) offer guidelines for improving the relevancy and effectiveness of Twitter for both instructor and student alike:

- Establish relevance for students
- Recommend people for students to follow
- Model effective Twitter use
- Encourage students' active and ongoing participation
- Build Twitter-derived results into assessments
- Continue to actively participate in Twitter (Dunlap & Lowenthal, 2009).

REACHING BEYOND THE CAMPUS

Twitter involves higher learning beyond just standard teacher/student interaction. Faculty can reach out to other faculty (both within their own institution and around the globe) for brainstorming. Athletic departments tweet sports' scores, schedules, and build fan bases. Inclement weather and associated cancellations are tweeted as needed. And some faculty have earned virtual rock star status within the global learning community. They earned this reputation because of their generosity with the sharing of resources, ideas, and challenging the status quo with their followers. Faculty new to Twitter might start with following these leaders as a place to start. Michael Wesch (@mwesch), George Siemens (@gsiemens), Alex Courosa (@courosa), Jim Groom (@jimgroom), and Dean Shareski (@shareski).

As a macro tool, disseminating messages to others outside their own institution's brick and mortar encourages a community of learning to continue beyond the scope of the content. It is personal professional development. Twitter can be an asynchronous, virtual hallway conversation, allowing learners to stay involved in the concepts and share additional resources with one another.

REAL-TIME RELEVANCY

Twitter is quietly changing the landscape of higher education. Some professors are tweeting extra resources to their students while others are sharing their courses' backchannels with the entire world. This real-time discourse and feedback via Twitter is growing.

As campuses expand their reach, introductory courses can run in the 500–700 student range. It would be impossible for a professor to feel they have the pulse of the student body of these classes that are larger than some rural towns. Through the use of Twitter's hashtags, however, both the professor and students can feel more bonded to the topic of discussion, and by default, more connected to the course and its instructor. "A hashtag that catches on forms an instant community around it" (Fitton, Gruen, & Poston, 2009, p. 127).

Higher education is utilizing Twitter in a variety of ways. One might tweet assignments to student followers, while the students may be asking their professors follow up questions or asking each other for help or advice. One such student of a course organized around the hashtag #ed422 recently tweeted for help from her fellow classmates. "What is the web address for the classroom 2.0 assignment in #ed422? thanks: (RosalindaLove, 2010). Students and professors alike find the organization around hashtags to be especially handy for reviewing the discourse occurring during backchannels as an instructor lectures. Imagine a law professor lecturing to 300 students on the legalities of Mirandizing a suspect. Although the professor speaks and, perhaps, shares a set of PowerPoint slides, the students are tweeting their questions, insights, comments, and links all organized around a pre-chosen hashtag. Later that day, while preparing for the next class, the professor is able to search for #prelaw101 and review the entire tweet stream. Particularly insightful comments and questions can be discussed the following day. The students also can search the tweet stream and review those same insights and questions as part of their notetaking and studying for the course. This kind of Twitter use is a reality in universities across the country. One tweeting law school professor, @lessig (Lawrence Lessig – Harvard Law), uses Twitter to inform students of resources recently posted, "Just posted the 4 lectures given in the last week at http://lessig.blip.tv" (lessig, 2010).

As stated earlier, higher education also makes use of hashtags to share thoughts about various conferences attended. Attendees use the hashtag for tweetups (face-to-face meetings organized via Twitter), for sharing points made by keynote speakers with followers, and even for conference quality feedback.

One growing use of Twitter falls under the category of personally driven professional development. Higher education professionals are joining virtual tweetups (online, real-time discussions, with a dedicated hashtag, usually using a real-time Twitter-feed program like Tweetchat). These live "chats" generally have an individual or small group of moderators who pose open-ended questions relating to the interests of the self-created community. Twitter-based live chats are arranged for specific times and dates, and participants bond through their shared learning in these communities. Some examples are #edchat on Tuesdays where educators debate and evaluate solutions to the topics of the day, #lrnchat (dedicated to the topic of learning and collaboration), and #artsed (about the importance of the arts in education) on Thursdays.

In one recent live #lrnchat chat, community members were asked what publications they were reading to get their professional development after the demise of a certain trade print magazine – answers made it clear that Twitter provided for the participants needs and they would be hard-pressed to replace it.

> @joe_deegan: Are there still training publications? I'm all about Twitter and blogs. (joe_deegan, 2010)

> @ simbeckhampson: Twitter is my publication source. (simbeckhampson, 2010)

> @LizPreedy: I have learnt more from Twitter + follow up in last 18 months than any pub in last 18 yrs. (LizPreedy, 2010)

> @mrch0mp3rs: Can't say that I ever relied much on publications (periodicals) but if Twitter shut down, I'd need something to replace it. (mrch0mp3rs, 2010)

> @JudithELS: Actually I was thinking today what I would do without Twitter – a horrendous thought so I thought about something else. (JudithELS, 2010)

> @mrch0mp3rs: I'd seriously freak out with gaping hole in my cognitive development left in Twitter's wake. (mrch0mp3rs, 2010a, 2010b)

WEB 2.0 AND TWITTER

As Web2.0 tools grow into mainstream use, Twitter has become incorporated into them. For example, Facebook and Twitter can be connected so that a tweet on one (or status update on the other) will automatically post the same message to the other site. All the major blogging sites can be configured to tweet the title and a link to the most recent post. Other tools will allow the user to immediately tweet about a website they are viewing also with a link. It is with these tools that Twitter users are able to share resources, thoughts, and questions to their followers.

Twitter Compared to Other Web 2.0 Tools

	Twitter	Skype	Blog	Wiki	Facebook	Online Meeting Space
Connect:						
* students w/students in same class	X	X		X	X	X
* w/ people around the world	X	X		X	X	X
* students w/instructor	X	X	X	X	Depends	X
* students or instructor w/experts	X	X	X	X	X	X
Real-time or synchronous uses	X	X		X	X	X
Asynchronous uses	X	X	X	X	X	
One author	X		X		X	
Multiple authors collaborating	X	X		X		X
Unlimited message size	140 char	X	X	X	X	X
Taggable	X		X	X		X
Searchable	X	X				
Messages open to public	X		X	Depends		Depends
Permanent URL	X		X	X		If archived
Allows for public reply	X		X	Depends		

Fig. 1. Twitter Compared to Other Web 2.0.

A simple search for "Twitter apps" will bring up an ever-growing list of applications a user can incorporate into his or her experience.

How does Twitter compare to other Web 2.0 tools, including other tools discussed in this book? Fig. 1 shows how Twitter can be utilized for communications throughout higher education.

TWITTERBITS, TIPS, AND RESOURCES

The following Twitterbits, tips, and resources are meant to be a quick summation of Twitter functionality and helpful websites for the new Twitter user. It is by no mean all-inclusive, as add-on tools and directories continue to be built.

- Twitter messages, called tweets, are short messages similar to text messages. Tweets are 140 characters or less, which includes spaces and punctuation.
- Tweets go out to a whole list of followers while phone text messages are sent to only the people selected from the Contacts list.
- New users of Twitter can find people to follow using the Search tool in Twitter. Searches can be conducted in a variety of ways including searching for a specific person, searching for a topic or field of expertise, or searching for keywords. There are 3rd party websites dedicated to helping new users find interesting people to follow including *Tweepz* (http://www.tweepz.com/), *Twello* (http://www.twellow.com/), and *WeFollow* (http://wefollow.com/).

- There is no limit to the number of people who can be followed, or who can follow the new user.
- Lurking, reading tweets but not contributing any messages, is a good way to begin understanding the usefulness of Twitter.
- New users often begin tweeting by forwarding messages posted by others, this is known as retweeting.

There are a variety of applications, both downloadable to your own PC and out on the Internet, which make Twitter more efficient to use.

- *Tweetdeck* (http://tweetdeck.com/beta/) has both a desktop application and an iPhone one. It allows users to organize tweets, searches, hashtags, etc., into handy columns, and can run without a browser window needing to be open.
- *Tweetie for Mac* (http://www.atebits.com/tweetie-mac/) is another desktop tool for helping the user to see/understand the flow of discussion on Twitter.
- *Tweetchat* (http://www.tweetchat.com) allows users to follow specific hashtag tweets in real time. This site is particularly useful for virtual tweet ups.
- *Bit.ly* (http://bit.ly/) is a URL shortener. This becomes important when sharing links and resources in Twitter's limited 140 character environment.
- *Twitpic* (http://twitpic.com/) is a photo-hosting site which will allow users to link between their tweetstream and images uploaded via computer or cell phone to share with their followers.
- An *RSS feed* link provided with all Twitter accounts (look for the RSS feed symbol on the right hand border of the home page) allows users to read tweets from a feedreader rather than logging into Twitter.
- *The Twitter Tim.es* (http://www.twittertim.es/) is an application the works with your own Twitter account to create a newspaper-like interface of the trending topics, links, and images of your stream. For those users who wish to mine Twitter for resources more than they wish to join in with the conversation, this may be an ideal way of looking at tweets.

CONCLUSION

Although the authors advocate for trying Twitter for professional and classroom learning, like any tool, Twitter may not always work as the

professor intends. Meghan Dougherty (M. Dougherty, personal communication, April 19, 2010), Assistant Professor at Loyola University Chicago
School of Communication, eloquently stated this and also self-reflected
about why Twitter use may sometimes fail.

> For each class, I announce a hashtag (the course number). I encourage students to follow
> the hashtag (easier to do in 3rd party clients like TweetDeck than on twitter.com).
> Occasionally I tweet articles, news, links, etc that I think are relevant to the class topic.
> Students usually follow my example (this was an utter FAIL this semester ... not a single
> tweet in any class, but has been very successful in other classes past. Reason for the
> FAIL? I think it was because I didn't participate as much. Students want to imitate
> someone's lead ... when I do not actively lead, they do not take up the work on their
> own).

Other users question the depth of conversation which can occur in a
series of messages of 140 characters or less. Featured educational speaker
and blogger, Will Richardson (2007) started an in-depth discussion on his
blog when he expressed this concern, "My question then is do they go
beyond the easy Twitter interactions into more complex participation? In
other words, is Twitter a gateway to participation, or is it the end
game?"

Every tool has benefits and challenges, capabilities, and limitations. As
was noted earlier, New York Times columnist David Pogue says "Twitter is
whatever you make of it" (Faculty Focus, 2009, p. 11). To make something
of it, you have to give it a try. Quite literally, give it the old college try! Here
is how Associate Professor Scott McLeod (S. McLeod, personal communication, April 19, 2010) described his personal journal in getting started
with Twitter.

> I tried Twitter four different times before I finally "got it." My early Twitter usage is
> marked by a week or two of Tweets, followed by a month of two of nothing,
> then another week or two of Tweets, followed by several months of nothing. And
> so on ... It finally 'clicked' for me when I made the commitment to Tweet several times
> a day for several months. Then the snowball started gathering and I haven't looked
> back since.

REFERENCES

comScore (2009). Twitter traffic more than doubles. Available at http://www.comscore.com/
    Press_Events/Press_Releases/2009/4/Twitter_Traffic_More_than_Doubles
Downes, S. (2008). Introducing edupunk. Available at http://www.downes.ca/cgi-bin/
    page.cgi?post = 44760

Dunlap, J. C., & Lowenthal, P. R. (2009). Horton hears a tweet. *Educause Quarterly Magazine*, *32*(4).

Faculty Focus. (2009). *Special report: Twitter in higher education usage habits and trends of today's college faculty*. Madison, WI: Magna Publications.

Ferriter, W. M. (2010). Why teachers should try Twitter. *Educational Leadership*, *67*(5), 73–74.

Fitton, L., Gruen, M. E., & Poston, L. (2009). *Twitter for dummies*. Hoboken, NJ: Wiley Publishing.

joe_deegan (2010). Are there still training publications? I'm all about Twitter and blogs [Twitter update].

JudithELS. (2010). Actually I was thinking today what I would do without Twitter – a horrendous thought so I thought about something else [Twitter update].

lessig. (2010). Just posted...at http://lessig.blip.tv [Twitter update].

LizPreedy. (2010). I have learnt more from Twitter + follow up in last 18 months than any pub in last 18 yrs [Twitter update].

Martin, D. (2009). Teens don't tweet, Twitter's growth not fueled by youth. *NielsenWire*. Available at http://blog.nielsen.com/nielsenwire/online_mobile/teens-dont-tweet-twitters-growth-not-fueled-by-youth/

Miller, C. C. (2009). Who's driving Twitter's popularity? Not teens. *The New York Times*. Available at http://www.nytimes.com/2009/08/26/technology/internet/26twitter.html

mrch0mp3rs. (2010a). I'd seriously freak out with gaping hole in my cognitive development left in Twitter's wake [Twitter update].

mrch0mp3rs. (2010b). Can't say that I ever relied much on publications (periodicals) but if Twitter shut down, I'd need something to replace it [Twitter update].

NMHS_Principal. (2010). PLN: Why should kids be allowed to use social media? What results from banning it? Use #WINS Pls help me ROCK this interview! [Twitter update].

Richardson, W. (2007). Re: Step away from the twee [Web log message]. Retrived from http://weblogg-ed.com/2010/step-away-from-the-tweet/

RosalindaLove. (2010). What is the web address for the classroom 2.0 assignment in #ed422? thanks:) [Twitter update].

Sass, J. (2010). An education on education: Chris Lehmann talks "school 2.0" at #140Conf. Available at http://dadomatic.com/an-education-on-education-chris-lehmann-talks-school-2-0-at-140conf/

simbeckhampson (2010). Twitter is my publication source [Twitter update].

Stager, G. (2010). Comments in reply to Weblogg-ed: Step away from the tweet [Web log message]. Retrieved from http://weblogg-ed.com/2010/step-away-from-the-tweet/

Wikipedia. (2010). Twitter. Retrieved from http://en.wikipedia.org/wiki/Twitter

Young, J. R. (2009). Teaching with Twitter: Not for the faint of heart. *Chronicle of Higher Education*. Retrieved from http://chronicle.com/article/Teaching-With-Twitter-Not-for/49230/

ABOUT THE AUTHORS

Malik Aleem Ahmed is a Ph.D. candidate in the Values and Technology Department (Section of Philosophy) and Infrastructure Systems & Services Department (Section of Information and Communication) at Faculty of Technology, Policy, and Management at the Delft University of Technology in the Netherlands. He has earned a masters degree in Business Administration with specialization in Information Technology Management from Pakistan. His areas of research interests are ICT and Ethics, ICT for Governance in developing countries. His Ph.D. research concerns the usage of ICT for better Governance in developing countries. The main emphasis of the research is on the public sector institutional strengthening with the help of ICT in the developing countries and the effect of intercultural variations of values. He has worked in different capacities in the field of Information and Communication Technology for seven years in Pakistan. His last job was in the capacity of "IT Advisor" for a USAID sponsored project (Pakistan Legislative Strengthening Project) in Pakistan. He has also been involved in the field of teaching at University level. He is also serving as the webmaster of this 3TU.Centre for Ethics and Technology website.

Mark Bailey is a professor of Education in the College of Education at Pacific University in Forest Grove, Oregon. Mark became fascinated with the process of learning, particularly in young children, while teaching as an undergraduate at the Grinnell College Laboratory preschool. He continued to be intrigued by the role of engagement and attention during his years as a classroom teacher, and earned his Ph.D. in educational psychology from the University of Wisconsin Madison. For the past 25 years Mark has been exploring the use of pedagogically powerful technological tools to support learning. As a cofounder of the Oregon Technology in Education Network, he has collaborated on writing and administering two funded Federal grants: Preparing Tomorrow's Teachers to Use Technology (PT3) and a Technology Quality Enhancement Partnership (TQEP) grant. His work has included explorations of collaborative and project-based learning tools and he has written and presented about the manner in which technology could be used with young children. As a strong advocate for the appropriate use of

393

technology to support early learning, Mark has presented extensively through the National Association for the Education of Young Children. After receiving a large grant from the Bill and Melinda Gates Foundation, he founded an early childhood learning center at Pacific University serving children aged 3–6 years. The center he designed utilizes a blend of pedagogical models that include play and active learning at their core, and incorporates innovative applications of technology to support the explorations of its digital age students. He currently serves as Director of the Pacific University Child Learning and Development Center, as well as the ECE specialist for graduate and undergraduate students.

Lisa Blaschke is a doctoral student at Oldenburg University in Oldenburg, Germany and an assistant professor (adjunct faculty) within the Master of Distance Education (MDE) program in the Graduate School of Management and Technology (GSMT) at the University of Maryland University College (UMUC). Her research interests are primarily within the areas of online collaborative learning, pedagogical application of web 2.0 technology, and user interface design. Lisa is also head of a communications consulting firm, Kreative Kommunikation, which specializes in a wide range of distance education services, from e-learning design and development to project management.

Lisa Chamberlin is a Freelance Instructional Designer and Adjunct Online Instructor for various institutions of higher learning including University of Wisconsin-Stout, University of San Diego, and Walla Walla Community College. She has designed many online courses and was author of *Making the Move to eLearning: Putting Your Course Online* (2009) and "Copyright For Teachers In The Digital Age" (Teaching Today, 2007). She was Gates Foundation/Teacher Leadership Project Recipient/Trainer (2000) and US WEST/NEA Learning Space Recipient (1994).

Joseph Rene Corbeil is an associate professor at The University of Texas at Brownsville/Texas Southmost College. He earned his doctoral degree in Education-Curriculum and Instruction with an emphasis on Instructional Technology from the University of Houston, and a Master of Education in Educational Technology from the University of Texas at Brownsville. Currently, he teaches fully web-based undergraduate and graduate courses in Educational Technology. Research interests include best practices in synchronous and asynchronous communication and enhancing social presence and teacher immediacy in e-learning environments through the use of Web 2.0 and social networking tools like blogs, wikis, and podcasts. He is also interested in exploring the potential of portable communication/computing technologies for mobile learning (m-learning) in adult education programs.

Maria Elena Corbeil is an assistant professor at The University of Texas at Brownsville/Texas Southmost College. She currently develops and teaches fully online technology education and corporate training courses offered for two applied technology bachelor degrees. She earned her doctoral degree in Education with an emphasis in Curriculum and Instruction from the University of Houston; a postgraduate certificate in Online Teaching and Learning from the University of Florida; a master degree in Education from The University of Texas at Brownsville; and a Bachelors degree in English from Florida International University. She began her career at UTB/TSC as an English as a Second Language instructor, after which she became a Learning Instructional Specialist, and later, director, of the student learning center. Her experience in adult learning and training, combined with her interest in distance education has served as a foundation for her research and publications in innovations in distance and adult learning.

Campbell Dalglish graduated from the Yale School of Drama and is currently a tenured professor in the film program at City College of New York where he teaches screenwriting and directing. Campbell is also founding director of D'Arc Productions and an award winning playwright, screenwriter, and director. He is also a Film Commissioner for Suffolk County on Long Island. His short narrative film *Dance of the Quantum Cats* won over a dozen international awards and was selected by CINE to represent USA at the 12th International Film Festival of Peace in Hiroshima, Japan. Dalglish has also been a script consultant for The Shooting Gallery and the Independent Film Project (IFP) as well as a frequent panelist on screenwriting for the Institute of International Film Financing. Recently he moderated a panel at the Native American Finance Conference in Las Vegas titled "Hollywood: American Indian Film." Together with Executive Ron Pate, Chickasaw, Campbell co-founded the native owned Red Warrior Films and Entertainment and is currently producing a Historical Listening Tour across America recording stories from American Indian elders and developing a slate of feature screenplays for production in the next five years. He lives in Patchogue, New York, where he and his wife, Catherine Oberg, co-founded the Plaza Media Arts Center.

Martina A. Doolan is a principal lecturer in the School of Computer Science at the University of Hertfordshire (UH). Martina is a fellow of the Higher

Education Academy, (HEA) in the UK and a member of the British Computer Society. Martina was awarded a fellowship of the National Teaching Fellowship Scheme from the minister of Higher Education (THE, 2007). Martina was nominated by the University of Hertfordshire for internal, national, and international recognition of her work in innovative practice using technologies such as blogs, wiki, podcasts, discussion fori, video, and audio among others. Martina acted as an external evaluator for their institutional wide initiatives of staff innovative use of Blackboard social media functions included wiki, blogs, and discussion forum. In addition, Martina worked with Technology Enhanced Learning (TEL) team to share practice of technology use including social media in Higher Education. Martina is also a member of various JISC, Higher Education Academy (HEA) and other groups and committees, the majority by invitation. Martina is Blended Learning Fellow and a University Teaching Fellow working with the Centre of Excellence in Learning and Teaching (CETL) and across the institution, in addition to, the Higher Education sector. Martina plays a key role in the development of the CETL and has done so since its inception in 2005. The Wiki functionality of the in-house built Managed Learning Environment was based on Martina's work with Web 2.0 technologies, in particular the use of a wiki application in learning, and teaching practice over 5 years.

Gloria Edwards is an associate professor of Education at Georgian Court University, Lakewood, New Jersey where she teaches graduate and undergraduate courses in technology integration and instructional design. Her research interests focus on digital and web-based tools and how the ability or inability to use such tools impacts the attitudes and productivity of diverse groups of learners in classrooms (traditional and non-traditional) and the workplace.

Mark A. Gammon is a sociologist and educator working at the intersection of people and technology. Mark completed his Ph.D. in sociology at the University of Massachusetts in 2009. His dissertation focused on college students and better understanding of the meanings and implications of new technologies on social relationships. He is co-founder and director of the consulting and strategic engagement company, Connect.Us Labs, where he focuses on supporting clients as they navigate social, Web, and emerging media.

Oliver Grundmann is a clinical assistant professor in the Department of Medicinal Chemistry at the University of Florida. He teaches and develops graduate classes for the Pharmaceutical Chemistry and Forensic Sciences Distance Education programs. He earned his Ph.D. in Pharmaceutical Sciences and M.S. in Forensic Toxicology from the University of Florida after graduating from the University of Münster, Germany, with a B.S. in Pharmacy. His research interests focus on development and implementation of instructional policies for graduate science classes in distance education. He is also involved in collaborative clinical studies in various areas of pharmaceutical sciences.

Hope J. Hartman is a professor of Education at City College of New York and professor of Educational Psychology at City University of New York Graduate Center. She is the former director of the City College of New York Center for Excellence in Teaching and Learning. She is the author of five books, the most recent of which is *A Guide to Reflective Practice for New and Experienced Teachers* (McGraw-Hill: 2009).

Nina Heinze received her B.Sc. (Honors) from the University of Colorado at Boulder (2002) and her M.A. in Mediapedagogics from the University of Augsburg, Germany. She started working on her Ph.D. in November 2007 as part of a project to foster key competencies with new technologies funded by the German Research Foundation (DFG). She worked as a research associate at the Institute for Media and Educational Technology (imb) at the University of Augsburg before coming to the Knowledge Media Research Center in Tübingen in 2009. Here she is a member of the STELLAR Network of Excellence. She is interested in research and design of digital learning environments in formal settings and web-based informal learning as well as socio-technical communities.

Gila Kurtz is an assistant professor (adjunct faculty) within the Master of Distance Education (MDE) program in the Graduate School of Management and Technology (GSMT) at the University of Maryland University College (UMUC). Currently, Dr. Kurtz is a professor in-charge of an M.A. Program at the School of Education titled "Online Learning and Technology" at the Center for Academic Studies in Israel. Her research interests include pedagogical application of online technology especially Web 2.0 technologies. Gila has a background in Distance Education for more than 15 years.

David G. Lebow is president/CEO of HyLighter, Inc. and inventor of HyLighter, a new product for social highlighting and annotation and hypermedia authoring that supports collaborative study of online documents and document-centered group work. He holds a Ph.D. and is currently engaged in research, development, and dissemination.

Kay Lehmann is Adjunct Online Instructor for several universities including University of Wisconsin-Stout, California State University-East Bay, and the University of San Diego. She received her Ed.D. in Educational Leadership from Walden University and is author of *Making the Move to eLearning: Putting Your Course Online* (2009), *Creating Cooperative Learning Groups That Work: The Role of Type A/B Personality* (2008), *How to Be a Great Online Teacher* (2004), *Surviving Inclusion* (2004), and dozens of online courses. She has been awarded the Milken National Educator 1999 and recipient of Don E. Ackerman Research Fellowship (2007).

Dale W. Lick is president and Professor Emeritus of Florida State University. He is also co-developer of HyLighter, an advanced social media/collaboration tool. His present research efforts focus on transformational leadership, learning communities, school improvement, and new learning systems. He is the author or co-author of 7 books and over 90 professional articles, book chapters, and proceedings.

Beth Martin is a doctoral student in Adult Education at North Carolina State University and a Clinical Assistant Professor in the School of Education Library and Information Studies Program at the University of North Carolina at Greensboro. She has a master in Technical Writing/ Rhetoric and also in Library and Information Science. Before academia Beth spent 15 years as a network engineer at companies such as Lucent Technologies and eMusic.com

Gail O. Mellow is president of LaGuardia Community College in Long Island City, Queens. Since Dr. Mellow joined LaGuardia in 2000, the College has won numerous awards, among them the prestigious 2006 MetLife Foundation Community College Excellence Award for Service to Underserved Students, and was named one of the Top Three Large Community Colleges by the Community College Survey of Student Engagement in 2003. As the co-author of her most recent publication, *Minding the Dream: The Process and Practice of the American Community College* (Rowman & Littlefield, 2008), Dr. Mellow is nationally recognized expert on the history, development, and future of the American community college. She is in demand as a speaker both here and abroad, and has shared her expertise with educators and public officials in several countries, including Chile, Greece, France, and China. On a national level, Dr. Mellow has received numerous awards, sits on the boards of the Carnegie Foundation for Teaching and Learning, Jobs for the Future, Excelencia, and the Center for an Urban Future. She has presented to audiences throughout the country on the vital role that community colleges play in educating students for a global economy and spurring job creation.

Lina Morgado is a professor at the Department of Education at Universidade Aberta, Portugal (the Portuguese Open University). Her interests and expertise are focused on the development of an e-learning pedagogy in higher education. She designed and taught online courses on distance education, online pedagogy, virtual learning environments and educational psychology, and she is course coordinator of a master degree in e-learning pedagogy. She is co-author of the distance education pedagogical model for Universidade Aberta. She is a member of the Distance Education Lab where she conducts research on teaching and learning with social media and Web 2.0 tools, and the implications of emerging technologies in communication and relationships.

Barbra F. Mosley is an assistant professor of Instructional Technology in the Department of Curriculum and Instruction at North Carolina A&T State University. Her research interests focus on identifying what emerging technologies are being used, how they are used, what the implications for usage are, and identifying ways these technologies can be integrated to maximize learning in any educational setting.

Caroline Lego Muñoz is an associate professor of Marketing at Fairleigh Dickinson University in Madison, New Jersey. Dr. Munoz's specialization is consumer behavior. Specifically her research interests include themed environments, marketing pedagogies, social network sites, and cross-cultural consumer issues. Her marketing pedagogy work has been published in *Marketing Education Review*, *Journal of Advertising Education*, and *Journal of Business Education*.

Larysa Nadolny received her BS in Animal Science from Virginia Tech, her MAT from Boston University, and after several years teaching in K-12 education, her Ed.D. from the University of Delaware. She is currently assistant professor at West Chester University of Pennsylvania. She teaches educational technology courses to students in the College of Education and works with local teachers on technology integration. She uses social media tools throughout her courses, including student blogs, Second Life, and YouTube. Her research includes new and emerging technologies for the classroom, including immersive education. She was recently awarded a National Science Foundation grant to develop ethics simulations in Second Life, as well as the E. Riley Holman Award for Creativity. She also recently published "Implementation and Outcomes of a Laptop Initiative in Career and Technical Education" in the *Journal of Educational Computing Research* (Mouza, Cavalier, & Nadolny, 2008).

Stella C. S. Porto is a professor and the director of the Master of Distance Education (MDE) program in the Graduate School of Management & Technology (GSMT) at the University of Maryland University College. Her research interests include the management of distance learning and emerging technologies for online education. Stella has a background in Computer Science and has worked in higher education for more than 20 years.

Wolfgang Reinhardt received his B.Sc. (2005) and Diploma in Computer Science (2006) from the University of Paderborn, Germany. He now works as a research assistant at the Computer Science Education Group at the University of Paderborn where his tasks include Computer Science Tutor training. His Ph.D. deals with the enhancement of group awareness in online learning communities. Therefore he developed the model of Artifact-Actor-Networks, which is applied to the before mentioned seminar setting. His main interests include the social semantic web and learning in online informal learning settings.

Kyle F. Reinson is an assistant professor of Communication/Journalism at St. John Fisher College in Rochester, New York. He earned his B.A. in Journalism (Public Relations) from the Donald W. Reynolds School at the University of Nevada, and his M.A. in Communication (Multimedia Journalism Studies) from Florida Atlantic University in Boca Raton. He is completing his Ph.D. in Urban and Regional Geography at the University at Buffalo (SUNY). Before his career in higher education he was a corporate and agency public relations executive, counseling senior executives and directing external consulting relationships for two of America's largest publicly traded real estate developers. Reinson's teaching and research engage emerging media technologies and their connections to the exchange of information in individual, group and institutional communication settings as well as technology's influence on higher education and public memory. His book chapter, "Quasars: Silent Celebrities, Ethical Implications," appeared in Ethics and Entertainment (2010) edited by Howard Good and Sandra L. Borden. In 2009, Reinson's book review essay concerning his own teaching and the tenth anniversary publication of The Cluetrain Manifesto appeared in the Association for Education in Journalism and Mass Communication's (AEJMC) Educator and he has also published invited book review essays in peer-reviewed publications such as the Journal of Communication Inquiry, American Journalism and the Democratic Communiqué, the Journal of the Union for Democratic Communications. Reinson has served as research co-chair for the Cultural and Critical Studies Division of AEJMC and was invited to attend the 2009 and 2010 Edelman New Media Academic Summit, an international forum where educators and professionals discuss emerging trends in public relations practice, technology, and higher education. He has trained professional accountants and auditors in business writing and was an invited presenter on the topic of social media at 2008's Sales and Marketing Institute Summit in Jacksonville, Florida. Reinson was named a 2008 Indiana University Teaching Fellow.

Steve Rhine is a professor of Education in the Graduate School of Education at Willamette University in Salem, Oregon. Dr. Rhine completed his Ed.D. at UCLA in 1994 and began a career in teacher education that now spans 16 years. He has been passionately and actively involved in examining and experiencing the role of technology in education since 1993 when he was part of the team that developed a Technology Leadership Academy in Los Angeles. Since that time he has been awarded numerous federal and other grants focusing on uses of educational technology. In particular, he co-wrote a $1.3 million grant for the Preparing Tomorrow's Teachers to Use Technology (PT3) program that funded the Oregon Technology in Education Network (OTEN), which he directed from 2001 to 2004. He also co-wrote and participated in the $1.5 million Teacher Quality Enhancement Partnership grant that funded OTEN 2004–09. In 2000, he participated on the writing team for the International Society for Technology Education's National Educational Technology Standards (NETS) for Teachers. He has presented at and reviewed proposals for multiple educational technology conferences. Dr. Rhine has taught courses in Educational Technology, Educational Psychology, Action Research, Multicultural Education, and Mathematics Education. His current research includes work on conducting online dialogue with student teachers based on digital video clips of their teaching, the role of Web 2.0 in classrooms, and the transition of Mexican and Ukrainian im/migrant students into Oregon schools.

Jeremy Sarachan is an assistant professor of Communication/Journalism at St. John Fisher College in Rochester, New York, where he teaches courses in digital media, cyberculture, web design, and documentary film. His research interests focus on understanding how diverse groups use social networking to form online communities and how digital technologies can improve pedagogical practices in higher education. He has a BA in film studies and psychology from the University of Rochester and an MS in Information Technology from the Rochester Institute of Technology. He authored two book chapters: "Self-Representation and the Profile Picture" in Facebook and Philosophy from Open Court Publishing Company and "Doctor Who Fan Videos, YouTube and the Public Sphere" in Ruminations, Peregrinations, and Regenerations: A Critical Approach to Doctor Who from Cambridge Scholars Publishing. He is currently working on projects involving the use of virtual worlds in communication departments and the thematic content of "daddy blogs."

Danielle M. Stern is an assistant professor of Media Studies in the Department of Communication Studies at Christopher Newport University in Newport News, Virginia. Her research interests include the tenuous interrelationship of popular culture production and consumption, especially television, and social media. Danielle teaches courses in media and cultural studies, as well as communication and critical theory. As a social media enthusiast, she incorporates collaborative tools such as blogs and Twitter into her research and pedagogy when appropriate.

Marlyn Tadros teaches computer science at The New England Institute of Art in Brookline, MA. She was a Visiting Scholar at the Women's Department at Northeastern University and occasionally teaches human rights and Middle East Studies in the Political Science Department. She was also a Visiting Fellow at the Human Rights Program at Harvard University. Dr. Tadros is also Executive Director of Virtual Activism, a nonprofit organization based in Rhode Island that deals with the intersection between technology and human rights. Dr. Tadros served on several boards of directors for nonprofit organizations including Grassroots International, Boston, and has been appointed to the International Fellowships Panel of the American Association of University Women. She is author of numerous papers on the Middle East as well as on the uses of technology and has several publications in both English and Arabic.

Terri L. Towner is an assistant professor of Political Science at Oakland University, where she teaches American politics, public opinion, and quantitative methods. Her specific research lines include investigating the role of race in politics, attitudes toward war, the influence of new media on political attitudes, and the pedagogical value of social networks. Dr. Towner is currently the webmaster for the *American Democracy Now* (McGraw-Hill College Publishers) Facebook group, which shows instructors how to use Facebook as a classroom tool and innovative learning opportunity.

Charles Wankel is associate professor of Management at St. John's University, New York. He holds a doctorate from New York University. He serves at Erasmus University, Rotterdam School of Management, on the Dissertation Committee and as Honorary Vice Rector at the Poznań University of Business. He has received numerous awards from the Academy of Management, including the 2010 Service Award of its Organizations and the Natural Environment Division. His recent books include *Teaching Arts and Science with the New Social Media* (March 2011), *Higher Education Administration with Social Media: Including Applications in Student Affairs, Enrollment Management, Alumni Relations, and Career Centers* (2011), *Cutting-Edge Social Media Approaches to Business Education* (2010), *Being and Becoming a Management Education Scholar* (2010), *Emerging Ethical Issues of Life in Virtual Worlds* (2010), and *Global Sustainability as a Business Imperative* (2010). He is the leading founder and director of scholarly virtual communities for management professors, currently directing eight with thousands of participants in more than 70 nations. Charles has taught in Lithuania at the Kaunas University of Technology (Fulbright Fellowship) and the University of Vilnius (United Nations Development Program and Soros Foundation funding). Invited lectures include Distinguished Speaker at the Education without Border Conference, Abu Dhabi and Keynote speaker at the Nippon Academy of Management Conference. Corporate clients include McDonald's Corporation's Hamburger University and IBM Learning Services. Pro bono consulting assignments include total quality management programs for the Lithuanian National Postal Service.

Joanne White is an academic, educator, and startup founder who has taught at colleges in both the USA and Australia. Her master's thesis, completed at the University of Colorado at Boulder, focused on the strength of connections made in social media communities. She is currently a Ph.D. student at ATLAS at CU, where she performs research in the ConnectivITy Lab. She is co-founder and director of the consulting and strategic engagement company Connect.Us Labs, and is also co-founder of Tribevibe, a social media analytics company which seeks to find equitable methods of measuring quality content in digital media.

Michael D. D. Willits is an Online Course Development Instructional Designer in the Hampton Roads Virtual Learning Center at WHRO in Norfolk, Virginia. He is responsible for planning, designing, and developing interactive Web applications and technologies for online courses developed by WHRO on behalf of and in cooperation with the public schools in southeastern Virginia. His scholarly interests include exploring the benefits of emerging technologies in teaching and learning practices, as well as the intersection of youth culture and the evolution of social interaction within technology-mediated communities such as online social networks. Michael regularly consults with faculty and staff on integrating technologies effectively in their teaching, including the use of learning management systems, Web 2.0 applications, and social media. Recent projects have focused on integrating Wordpress-based blog publishing platforms with Twitter and Facebook to create active, engaged learning communities.

Diana D. Woolis is the co-founder of Knowledge in the Public Interest (KPI) a company focused on transforming education through web-based collaboration. Founded in 2001, KPI leverages web-based collaborative strategies to tap groups large and small and build robust knowledge networks and resource bases for their clients. Most recently, she is co-author of Education Leadership for a Networked World in Communities of Practice: Creating Learning Environments for Educators. She received her doctorate and master degrees in education from Teachers College, Columbia University.

SUBJECT INDEX